The Third Reich in the Ivory Tower
Complicity and Conflict on American Campuses

This is the first systematic exploration of the nature and extent of sympathy for Nazi Germany at American universities during the 1930s. Universities were highly influential in shaping public opinion, and many of the nation's most prominent university administrators refused to take a principled stand against the Hitler regime. Universities welcomed Nazi officials to campus and participated enthusiastically in student exchange programs with Nazified universities in Germany. American educators helped Nazi Germany improve its image in the West as it intensified its persecution of the Jews and strengthened its armed forces. The study contrasts the significant American grassroots protest against Nazism that emerged as soon as Hitler assumed power with campus quiescence, and with administrators' frequently harsh treatment of those students and professors who challenged their determination to maintain friendly relations with Nazi Germany.

Stephen H. Norwood, who holds a Ph.D. from Columbia University, is Professor of History at the University of Oklahoma. His two-volume *Encyclopedia of American Jewish History*, co-edited with Eunice G. Pollack (2008), received the Booklist Editor's Choice Award. He is also the author of three other books in American history and the winner of the Herbert G. Gutman Award in American Social History and co-winner of the Macmillan/SABR Award in Baseball History. His articles have appeared in anthologies and numerous journals, including *American Jewish History*, *Modern Judaism*, and the *Journal of Social History*.

To Eunice G. Pollack

The Third Reich in the Ivory Tower

Complicity and Conflict on American Campuses

STEPHEN H. NORWOOD
University of Oklahoma

CAMBRIDGE UNIVERSITY PRESS
Cambridge, New York, Melbourne, Madrid, Cape Town, Singapore, São Paulo, Delhi

Cambridge University Press
32 Avenue of the Americas, New York, NY 10013-2473, USA

www.cambridge.org
Information on this title: www.cambridge.org/9780521762434

First published 2009

Printed in the United States of America

A catalog record for this publication is available from the British Library.

Library of Congress Cataloging in Publication data

Norwood, Stephen H. (Stephen Harlan), 1951–
The Third Reich in the ivory tower : complicity and conflict on American
campuses / Stephen H. Norwood.
p.   cm.
Includes bibliographical references and index.
ISBN 978-0-521-76243-4 (hardback)
1. Education, Higher – United States – History – 20th century.   2. National socialism
and education – United States – History.   I. Title.
LA227.1.N67   2009
378.73'09043–dc22   2008046266

ISBN   978-0-521-76243-4 hardback

Contents

List of Figures

Abbreviations

AAUP	American Association of University Professors
ACLU	American Civil Liberties Union
ACUA	American Catholic History Research Center and University Archives
ADL	Anti-Defamation League
AFL	American Federation of Labor
AJC	American Jewish Committee
AJCongress	American Jewish Congress
AL	Alexander Library
ALDJR	American League for the Defense of Jewish Rights
ASU	American Student Union
AUA	American University Archives
BL	Butler Library
BMCA	Bryn Mawr College Archives
BTCI	Board of Trustees Committee, Investigation of the Charges of Lienhard Bergel
CCNY	City College of New York
CF	Central Files
CU	Columbia University
CUACL	Columbia University Archives – Columbiana Library, Low Library
CURBML	Columbia University Rare Book and Manuscript Library
EC	Emergency Committee in Aid of Displaced German Scholars

ECADFS Papers	Emergency Committee in Aid of Displaced Foreign Scholars Papers
FBI	Federal Bureau of Investigation
FC	Foreign Counterintelligence
FS	Foreign Study
FSPDS	Records of Foreign Service Posts of the Department of State
FSR	Foreign Study Records
FUA	Fordham University Archives
GLLD	German Language and Literature Department
HAA	Harvard Athletic Association
HLSP	Herbert Lehman Suite and Papers
HUA	Harvard University Archives
ICASR	Intercollegiate Committee to Aid Student Refugees
IPA	Institute of Public Affairs
JBCPP	James B. Conant Presidential Papers
JGMP	James G. McDonald Papers
JHU	Johns Hopkins University
JRAPP	James R. Angell Presidential Papers
JSS	Jewish Students Society
JTA	Jewish Telegraphic Agency
JWV	Jewish War Veterans of the United States of America
LC	Library of Congress
MAD	Manuscripts and Archives Division
MHCA	Mount Holyoke College Archives
MIT	Massachusetts Institute of Technology
MSEL	Milton S. Eisenhower Library
NA	National Archives
NCCJ	National Conference of Christians and Jews
NCWC	National Catholic Welfare Conference
NJC	New Jersey College for Women
NSANL	Non-Sectarian Anti-Nazi League to Champion Human Rights
NSL	National Student League
NYPL	New York Public Library
NYU	New York University
OAF	Office Administrative Files
QCA	Queens College Archives
RBML	Rare Book and Manuscript Library
RG	Record Group

RL	Regenstein Library
ROP	Records of the Office of the President
RU	Rutgers University
RUBTME	Rutgers University Board of Trustees, Minutes and Enclosures 1935
SA	*Sturmabteilung*
SC	Special Collections
SCA	Smith College Archives
SCRC	Special Collections Research Center
SCUA	Special Collections and University Archives
SL	Sterling Library
UC	University of Chicago
UCLA	University of California at Los Angeles
UDA	University of Delaware Archives
UFA	Universum-Film Aktiengesellschaft
UN	United Nations
UVA	University of Virginia
VCA	Vassar College Archives
VFW	Veterans of Foreign Wars
WYC	World Youth Congress
YU	Yale University
YWCA	Young Women's Christian Association

Germany Reverts to the Dark Ages

Nazi Clarity and Grassroots American Protest,
1933–1934

As soon as Hitler came to power on January 30, 1933, the American Jewish press compared him to Haman, and the plight of Germany's Jews to those of ancient Persia, whom Haman had threatened with extermination. Boston's *Jewish Advocate* declared on March 7 that Germany's entire Jewish population of 600,000 "is under the shadow of a campaign of murder which may be initiated soon." It drew its readers' attention to an article published a few days before in the London *Daily Herald* that predicted that the Nazis would initiate a pogrom "on a scale as terrible as any instance of Jewish persecution in 2,000 years."[1] At Purim in mid-March 1933, the festival celebrating the Jews' deliverance from Haman, many rabbis devoted their sermons to condemning the rise of Nazi anti-semitism in Germany. Rabbi Mordecai Kaplan indicated that Hitler was even more threatening than Haman in that he was attempting to make the whole world unsafe for Jews. Kaplan predicted that Nazi Germany could ultimately destroy modern civilization and thrust all of humanity "back to the days of ancient barbarism."[2]

On March 20, 1933, shortly after the Nazis assumed power in Germany, the *New York Times* declared that testimony from Americans returning home from visits to Germany left no doubt that to be Jewish there "now constitutes a crime." It reported the declaration of Prussian high commissioner Hermann Goering and minister of propaganda Josef Goebbels that the "Jewish vampire" was responsible for "all the troubles from which the Reich is suffering." The Nazi leaders proclaimed that it was "the duty of all Germans to persecute and harass" the Jews.[3] No Jew was exempt from such treatment. The Nazis physically attacked

Jews; forcibly shut down Jewish businesses; drove Jewish professors from their lecture halls; barred Jews from practicing law, medicine, and other professions; and embarked on a campaign to prevent them from finding gainful employment in nearly any field. The Manchester *Guardian* noted that by shutting down Jewish-owned stores and savagely beating Jews in the streets, the Nazis had graphically demonstrated that they were immediately putting into effect a sweeping antisemitic doctrine.[4]

That same month German Jewish refugee Lion Feuchtwanger, whose home had been ransacked by Nazis while he was abroad and his manuscripts destroyed, told the *New York Times* that the Nazis had initiated "pogroms such as Germany has not seen since the Jewish persecutions of the fourteenth century," which were precipitated by the ludicrous accusation that Jews had caused the Black Death that destroyed one-third of Europe's population. Feuchtwanger had spoken with Jewish refugees in Paris, who told him of acts of antisemitic violence they had experienced or witnessed in Germany compared to which "the atrocities during the war paled." These refugees had insisted to Feuchtwanger that "[e]very Jew in Germany must expect to be assaulted in the street or to be dragged out of bed and arrested, to have his goods and property destroyed." Jews were dragged from automobiles and beaten, just because they were Jews. "Day after day," the corpses of Jews slain in antisemitic attacks were found "mutilated beyond identification."[5]

An American just returned from Berlin told the *New York Times* that he had cut short his trip there after witnessing a platoon of Nazi storm troopers brutally beat Jewish businessmen at a restaurant who had refused to purchase Goebbels's newspaper *Der Angriff*. Seizing the Jews, the storm troopers formed a double line and forced them to pass through a gauntlet to exit the restaurant. As each of the Jews attempted to make his way to the door, every storm trooper, "first on one side and then on the other, smashed him in the face," with brass knuckles and "kicked him with heavy boots," turning his face into "beef steak."[6]

A British visitor to the German capital described a similar anti-Jewish atrocity to the London *Daily Herald* not long afterward. As he sat in a café, five Nazis entered and without any provocation repeatedly beat the Jewish proprietor with rubber truncheons. They left the premises shouting, "Get out, you cursed Jew!" As the proprietor lay unconscious on the floor in a pool of blood, his wife rushed to his side and cradled his battered head in her lap. When the British visitor asked her to call for an ambulance, she replied, "What good is that? There are only Nazi doctors . . . and they will not attend to anyone attacked by the Nazis."[7]

The American and British press provided extensive coverage of such incidents of antisemitic violence, which occurred with great frequency during the early months of Nazi rule. On March 25, 1933, the Manchester *Guardian* emphasized that the Nazi terror "did not consist of sporadic excesses [and] was not a series of disorders" but was "systematic and integral" to the Nazi system of government.[8]

The Nazis delighted not only in beating defenseless Jews, including the elderly and women, but in publicly degrading them. On April 4, 1933, the Manchester *Guardian* published a photograph, taken at Chemnitz in Saxony, that a Social Democratic refugee had smuggled out of Germany, showing grinning Nazis parading a Jew through the streets in a refuse cart. At Worms in late March 1933, the Nazis arrested three Jews, took them to a *Sturmabteilung* (SA) headquarters, and subjected them to a terrible beating. The storm troopers then entertained themselves by forcing the Jews to strike each other with cudgels.[9] Several days later in the same city, the Nazis confined arrested Jews in a pigsty.[10]

On April 1, 1933, the Hitler government staged a nationwide boycott of Jewish businesses and professional establishments, signaling the Nazi intention of making it impossible for Jews to earn a living. Fully half a million Nazi storm troopers enforced the boycott, forming squads in front of Jewish stores and offices that warned customers not to enter them. H. R. Knickerbocker, Pulitzer–prize winning Berlin correspondent of the New York *Evening Post*, reported that storm troopers had forcibly prevented his *Evening Post* colleague Albion Ross from entering a Jewish-owned department store in the Rosenthalerstrasse, and beat him after they ejected him from the doorway, shouting, "Damn dog!" while a policeman looked on indifferently.[11]

After reading Knickerbocker's dispatches from Berlin in the *Evening Post*, John Haynes Holmes, minister of New York City's Community Church, wrote to him that Germany had reverted to the Dark Ages.[12] Particularly frightening was the symbol that the storm troopers pasted over the entrance to every Jewish-owned store and physician's and lawyer's office as a "badge of shame": a yellow circle on a black background. This was the mark Christians had required Jewish businessmen, lawyers, and physicians to use during the Middle Ages to identify themselves, and it indicated a reversion to the vicious antisemitism of that era.[13]

James G. McDonald, League of Nations high commissioner for refugees from 1933 to 1935, stated that the boycott, which he observed in Berlin, was effective because it demonstrated "that Jewish trade could be completely stifled." McDonald noted that although the Nazis had scheduled the boycott to last only a day, "an equally destructive discrimination against all Jews in law, medicine, school, civil service, shops, and industry . . . continue[d] unabated."[14]

The day after the boycott, the National Socialist Women's Federation in Berlin called on German women to never again patronize a Jewish store, physician, or attorney, and to ensure that their families did not "until Jewry has been destroyed." It reminded German women that they were "fighting a holy war."[15]

On April 7, 1933, the Hitler government enacted a law discharging Jews from the civil service. Professors were included because universities in Germany were administered by the state. Jews were defined as persons with at least one Jewish grandparent, and non-Jews married to Jews were included in the decree. Only those who were war veterans or had been appointed to their posts prior to 1914 were exempted, because of pressure from President Paul von Hindenburg. As a result, many of Germany's leading academics and intellectuals were forced into exile.[16]

As succeeding chapters will show, Germany's institutions of higher learning quickly deteriorated to the point that they could not properly be called universities. Martha Dodd, daughter of William E. Dodd, U.S. ambassador to Germany from 1933 to 1938, who had served as president of the American Historical Association, stated that when she lived with her father in the Third Reich, Germany's universities were just "elevated institutions of Nazi propaganda." She recalled that Ambassador Dodd, a longtime professor who had studied in Germany at the University of Leipzig around the turn of the century, "was so shocked and sickened" by the damage the Nazis inflicted on higher education that "he dreaded even passing through a university town." He refused to accept any honorary degree from a German university.[17]

On April 24, 1933, Frederick T. Birchall, *New York Times* correspondent in Berlin, wrote that the Jews in Germany were facing an impending catastrophe. The Nazis had relegated them to a position even lower than second-class citizens – they were "to be like toads under the harrow."[18] Thousands of them had been deprived of homes and driven from employment but lacked the funds necessary to leave. American reporter Dorothy Thompson wrote in Berlin in May 1933 that Germany's Jews were "truly in a hopeless state," because they were no longer permitted to earn a living.[19] Those Jews with the means to escape Germany were required by the Hitler government to leave behind nearly everything they had. The *New York Times* reported in early May that Jewish refugees were arriving in Paris at a rate of 200 a day, and that nearly all were "reduced to a state of poverty."[20]

During the spring and summer of 1933, American and British journalists continued to publish alarming reports about Nazi persecution, drawn from their own observations and investigations, and from refugees able to flee to France, the Saar, the Netherlands, Poland, and Spain. By April 1933, the Nazis had confined an estimated 45,000 political opponents and Jews in newly established concentration camps and in SA headquarters, known as Brown Houses, that the Manchester *Guardian* called "nothing less than torture chambers."[21] (SA members were known as Brown Shirts, and brown was the Nazi color.)

A Manchester *Guardian* correspondent, reporting from Germany, declared that "[t]he inquirers by digging only an inch below the surface, will in city after city, village after village, discover such an abundance of barbarism committed by the Brown Shirts that modern analogies fail." He considered the storm troopers far more dangerous and sadistic than American gangsters, professional killers whom they somewhat resembled. The American gangster at least led a life of danger, confronting far more powerful armed government forces. By contrast, the German government's armed police and military forces were allied with the storm troopers. The Brown Shirts, carrying revolvers and pistols, and in some places armed with carbines and steel helmets, confronted as adversaries "helpless Jewish shopkeepers" and "defeated and unarmed Republicans."[22]

American newspaper reporters posted in Berlin emphasized to James G. McDonald on his visit there in the spring of 1933 the horror of Nazi brutality and antisemitism. Charles Elliot of the New York *Herald Tribune* told McDonald that "the degree of violence and intolerance was unprecedented in Western Europe." McDonald found Pulitzer Prize–winning reporter Edgar Ansel Mowrer, Berlin correspondent for the Chicago *Daily News*, "highly overwrought" when he met with him on March 30, 1933. Mowrer "could talk of little but terror and atrocities" and described the Nazi leaders as "brutes [and] sadists," McDonald noted in his diary.[23]

McDonald also found very ominous Adolf Hitler's remarks to him about what he planned to do to Germany's Jews in a personal conference with the Fuehrer in Berlin on April 8, 1933. When McDonald returned to the United States later in the month, he reported that Hitler had told him: "I will do the thing that the rest of the world would like to do. It doesn't know how to get rid of the Jews. I will show them." McDonald told James Warburg, son of prominent Jewish banker Paul Warburg, that Hitler had said at their meeting, "I've got my heel on the necks of the Jews and will soon have them so they can't move." In his conversation with Warburg, McDonald "predicted that German Jews would retrogress to medieval ghetto status."[24]

Because no country allowed any significant number of Jewish refugees to enter, Germany became, as Lord Melchett stated in May 1933, "an absolute death trap" for its 600,000 Jews. Lord Melchett emphasized that "there was no escape of any kind" for them.[25] *New York Times* correspondent Otto Tolischus wrote from Berlin in September 1933 that, if other countries including the United States lowered their immigration barriers, there was no doubt that "the vast majority" of Jews would leave Germany immediately. But unfortunately, "few of those seeking to emigrate entertain any hope of finding room in the other western countries."[26]

Tolischus stated that the majority of Jews in Germany were doomed. Because under the Hitler regime "Jews are in practice barred from all higher schooling and all the 'academic' professions," they had no prospects other than manual laborer. He noted that German Jews already referred to the older members of their community as "the lost generation," fated to struggle for a short time living on handouts "and then die out."[27]

Michael Williams, editor of the Catholic magazine *The Commonweal*, returning in June 1933 from a trip to Germany to investigate Nazi persecution, also considered the plight of Jews in Germany so desperate that they could not survive there. Williams stated that the Nazis' intention was to "absolutely eliminate the Jewish portion of the German nation." Williams asserted in the *New York Times* that the Nazi oppression of Jews "probably surpasses any recorded instance of persecution in Jewish history." He called the situation of Jews in Germany "deplorable beyond words." Williams appealed to the League of Nations to "come quickly and strongly to the rescue!" to prevent "the worst crime of our age" from proceeding: "the deliberate extinction of nearly 1,000,000 men, women, and children."[28]

That same month, the American Jewish Committee (AJC) published the 112-page *White Book*, designed to provide the American public with as complete an account as possible of the Hitler government's antisemitic laws and regulations, and of Nazi brutality and threats against Jews, from 1923 until May 1933. The AJC *White Book*, whose publication was announced in the *New York Times*, presented translations of the complete text from the official German law gazette, of "the numerous decrees promulgated under Chancellor Hitler prohibiting the employment of Jews in the professions, State services, [and] the schools." This was followed by eyewitnesses' reports of "the acts [of] oppression and violence" against Germany's Jews.[29]

American Jewish leaders observing developments in Germany during the summer and fall of 1933 concluded that Jews had no future there. Rabbi Stephen S. Wise, honorary president of the AJCongress, who spent time in Europe that summer speaking with refugees from Germany, wrote that "the Jews of Germany are finished." Judge Julian Mack stated that the Jews in Nazi Germany faced a fate worse than they had in Inquisitorial Spain.[30] Alexander Brin, editor of Boston's *Jewish Advocate*, one of America's leading English-language Jewish weeklies, on his return to the United States in October 1933 after a trip to Germany, called the Hitler government "the most barbaric and savage movement since the Dark Ages."[31]

In September 1933, Germany's most eminent novelist, Thomas Mann, winner of the Nobel Prize for Literature, expressed the deepest pessimism about the impact of Hitler's rule. Mann had chosen to go into exile in France because of his anti-Nazi convictions. Emphasizing that Nazi rule was not an ephemeral phenomenon but would have long-term impact, he declared that Nazi policies would transform Germany into a place "intellectually so barren" that it would take "centuries before she can regain something of her former intellectual and cultural prestige."[32]

Albert Einstein, the most renowned exile from Nazi Germany, publicly condemned the Hitler regime from the beginning. Outside the country when the Nazis assumed power, Einstein declared that he would never return to Germany, and stated: "I do not desire to live in a country or belong to a country where the rights of all citizens are not respected and where freedom of speech among teachers is not accorded."[33] He appealed for world protest against Nazism. Shortly after the Nazis came to power they ransacked Einstein's weekend home at Caputh, outside Berlin, and confiscated his belongings. They also seized his bank account and securities.[34] In March 1933, Einstein resigned from the Prussian Academy of Sciences, to which he had belonged since 1913, in protest against Nazi policies. He expressed disgust with German scientists who had "failed in their duty to defend intellectual values."[35] Einstein sailed permanently for the United States in October 1933 and never went back to Germany. He became a faculty member at the Institute for Advanced Study in Princeton, New Jersey, a center for research and postgraduate training organized by Jewish educator Abraham Flexner on an endowment by Jewish department store magnate Louis Bamberger and his sister, Caroline Bamberger Fuld.[36]

Because of Einstein's stature as one of the most eminent scientists of modern times, the American press gave particular attention to his denunciations of Nazi persecution of Jews and political opponents. The Hitler government's abusive and insulting treatment of such a highly respected man of learning was further confirmation to many in the West that Germany had lapsed into barbarism.

When the Hitler government arrested British journalist Noel Panter of the London *Daily Telegraph* in late October 1933 on charges of transmitting "atrocity reports" abroad and espionage, the American press speculated that the Nazis were attempting to extend to the foreign press the censorship it enforced on German newspapers. Panter was charged with espionage because, in reporting on a speech Hitler made in Kelheim, Bavaria, he had noted the military character of the massive storm troopers' demonstration that accompanied it. Panter described 20,000 uniformed storm troopers goose-stepping past SA chief of staff Ernst Roehm, "with rifles at the slope and with steel bayonets," and noted participation by the Reichswehr (German army) in the demonstration. Germany had recently withdrawn from a League of Nations disarmament conference, and the SA's display of military equipment raised fears in the West that the Hitler government was preparing for a significant military buildup.[37]

The American press, like the British, voiced grave concern about Panter's arrest and the Nazis' refusal to allow him counsel or any contact with British consular officials, although academia remained silent. The *New York Times* reported that British public opinion was "thoroughly aroused" over Panter's imprisonment. The Nazis held Panter incommunicado for three days, denying him even a toothbrush or razor, while the British cabinet met to discuss its options and the British press expressed "the strongest editorial indignation." Panter faced at least two years in prison under the charges. British emissaries managed to gain access to Panter after three days, and six days later the Hitler government expelled the British journalist from Germany. Arriving in Britain, Panter declared in a radio address that liberty had completely vanished from Germany.[38]

Summing up eleven months of Nazi rule in late December 1933, the *New York Times* concluded that the calendar year was ending with Germany's Jews in a dismal situation. They had been degraded to "pariahs." The Hitler regime had shut down a large proportion of Jewish-owned businesses and forced a great many others to "replace Jewish directors, managers, and other important employees with Nazis." The minister of finance had decreed that tax and customs officials refuse contact with "non-Aryan" representatives of businesses, even if they were war veterans. The *New York Times* noted that many marketplaces and fairs prohibited Jews from engaging in any business, and that some of Germany's towns now forbade Jews from entering them.[39] Jews were virtually barred from the professions and from higher education.

The *New York Times* also reported that the Nazis had made life miserable for Jewish children in the common and intermediate schools. They were ostracized and harassed by their fellow pupils and teachers. The *Times* cited the account of the twelve-year-old daughter of an American diplomat in Germany, who described how the teacher on a class excursion had separated the Jewish pupils from the rest of the class and ordered them to keep their distance from the "Aryans" on their walk. School curricula gave significant emphasis to the propagation of Nazi antisemitic doctrines.[40] Alexander Brin wrote in October 1933 that Germany's public schools had promulgated so much antisemitism in the classrooms that were the Hitler regime to be "overthrown tomorrow," it would probably take generations to repair "the damage that has been done by the poison instilled into the minds of the children."[41]

During late 1933 and early 1934, some of the journalists in the West best informed about German affairs, who had visited Nazi Germany for extended periods during the early phases of Hitler's rule, astutely warned about the very real possibility of a large-scale genocide of Germany's Jews. Writing in November 1933 in the Jewish magazine *Opinion*, edited by Stephen S. Wise, Belgian journalist Pierre van Paassen, drawing on interviews with Jews that he had recently conducted in three widely separated cities in Germany, stated that "the position of the German Jews is getting worse every day" and called for international action to save the German Jewish community "from physical extinction." He endorsed Rabbi Wise's call for the settling of 150,000 German Jews in Palestine. But van Paassen warned that unless such a plan were carried out at once, "there will be no 150,000 German Jews left to be settled in Palestine."[42]

Dorothy Thompson wrote in *Opinion* in March 1934 that the Nazis' aim was "to *eliminate* the Jews." Thompson, wife of novelist Sinclair Lewis and a non-Jew, had served as Berlin correspondent for the New York *Evening Post* and had published a series of articles in May 1933 on Nazi atrocities against Jews in the *Jewish Daily Bulletin* and for the Jewish Telegraphic Agency. In her *Opinion* article, entitled "Germany Is a Prison," Thompson stated that because the Nazis were unable "to assassinate half a million Jews in cold blood," they had launched a "cold pogrom," forcing the Jews to leave Germany "by closing down one by one opportunities to earn a living or educate their children beyond the elementary grades, and by social ostracism." This "campaign of persecution" had caused a large number of Jews in one year of Nazi rule to leave Germany, despite the enormous difficulties of stiff immigration barriers everywhere in the world. Those Jews remaining in Germany, driven by the Nazis from their businesses, jobs, and schools, faced economic catastrophe.[43]

By the spring of 1934, the American reading public had access to books in which prominent journalists, politicians, and Jewish leaders described Nazi Germany as barbaric and detailed Nazi atrocities. In March a symposium entitled *Nazism: An Assault on Civilization* was published that included passionate denunciations of the Hitler regime by former New York governor and presidential candidate Al Smith, Unitarian minister John Haynes Holmes, Rabbi Stephen S. Wise, and writer Ludwig Lewisohn. AFL president William Green and reformer Alice Hamilton analyzed and forcefully condemned Nazi labor and women's policies, respectively. Dorothy Thompson described the "wanton cruelties" inflicted by the Nazis. In the concluding article, Governor Smith wrote that if Nazism prevailed, those who had fought "for spiritual and political freedom have fought in vain."[44] *Germany Unmasked* by Robert Dell, veteran Manchester *Guardian* correspondent, appeared at the same time. It opened with a statement by a diplomat stationed in Berlin: "The conditions here are not those of a normal civilized country and the German Government is not a normal civilized Government and cannot be dealt with as if it were one."[45]

That spring, the American and British press reported yet another ominous development in Germany: the Nazis' revival of the medieval blood libel accusation, which they aggressively disseminated throughout the Reich using official party newspapers. The blood libel, which had no basis in fact, charged the Jews with kidnapping Christian children, torturing and murdering them to mock Jesus, and draining their blood to mix with matzoh at Passover (*Pesach*) and with Purim pastries. On May 1, 1934, Julius Streicher, Nazi *gauleiter* of Franconia and political commissar of the Bavarian state government, published a special May Day edition of the Nazi newspaper *Der Stürmer* of 130,000 copies, devoted to documenting 131 alleged Jewish ritual murders from 169 B.C.E. to 1929 C.E. The May Day ritual murder issue contained two heavily underscored red banner headlines declaring "Jewish murder plot against non-Jewish humanity exposed." The cover depicted two Jews, one holding a blood-stained knife and the other collecting in a dish streams of blood gushing from the slashed throats of "Aryan" women. Other illustrations showed "children being done to death in the most revolting circumstances by Jews."[46]

The London *Times* called *Der Stürmer*'s ritual murder issue "a crudely horrible production" that was "designed to excite racial fanaticism to a bloodthirsty pitch."[47] Besides the "obvious incitements to violence" against Jews, the *Times* editorialized that reviving the ludicrous and long-discredited blood libel accusation "did grave damage to the intellectual reputation of the new Germany."[48]

Western journalists believed that the publication of *Der Stürmer*'s special ritual murder issue placed all of Germany's Jews in immediate physical danger because, as the London *Times* noted, the person responsible was no less than Julius Streicher, "one of the most prominent members of the Nazi 'inner circle.'" The *New York Times* reported that succeeding issues of *Der Stürmer* were "as full of anti-Jewish hatred as their predecessors" and that they published "the usual caricatures and epithets."[49]

Indeed, belief in the blood libel accusation against the Jews was sufficiently widespread in Germany that it had inspired a pogrom shortly before the appearance of *Der Stürmer*'s May Day issue. During the night of March 25–26, 1934, residents of the town of Ellwangen, Mittelfranken (Central Franconia), in Bavaria smashed the windows of Jewish homes, while onlookers shouted in chorus: "In this Pesach there flows no Christian but Jewish blood."[50]

The publication of the ritual murder issue of *Der Stürmer* coincided with the Hitler regime's opening of a series of special performances of the intensely antisemitic Oberammergau Passion Play, discussed in Chapter 4, which was highly popular among American exchange students studying in Germany and visiting American academics. The Nazis believed that exposing Americans to the passion play's images of the Jews as a race forever cursed for their crime of deicide would help them spread antisemitism abroad. In May 1934, they decided to exploit *Der Stürmer*'s ritual murder issue in the same manner. The *New York Times* reported that Julius Streicher, in a storm trooper's uniform, had in Nuremberg personally presented a copy of the issue to each of the nineteen members of a delegation of British journalists on their way to attend the passion play at Oberammergau.[51]

In the latter part of the month the Berlin periodical *Fridericus* and *Der Deutsche*, organ of the German Labor Front, also put forward the blood libel accusation. *Fridericus* warned that "[t]hrough the Jews, peoples and their culture die" and predicted that there no longer would be any more room for Jews in Germany. How the Jews' removal was to be accomplished, by expulsion or by extermination, it did not say.[52]

Anti-Nazi Protest in the United States During the Early Months of the Third Reich

From the very beginning of Nazi rule in Germany, there was an outpouring of protest in the United States, largely initiated by Jews, but joined by some concerned non-Jews. The leaders of America's universities, however, remained largely silent. On March 19, 1933, 1,500 representatives of Jewish organizations met at New York City's Hotel Astor to plan nationwide protests against Nazi antisemitism. Bernard Deutsch, president of the AJCongress, stated that his organization's offices were "being flooded with messages from all over the country demanding protest action." The assembled representatives passed a resolution to stage mass protest meetings "in every Jewish community" in the United States.[53] Two days later, on March 21, the AJCongress announced that the mass meetings would be staged in at least eleven U.S. cities, including New York, Boston, Chicago, Philadelphia, Baltimore, Cleveland, Miami, and Pittsburgh.[54]

The three orthodox rabbinical associations in New York City announced that these meetings would be marked by a day of fasting to protest the Nazi persecution of Jews. They issued a proclamation in Hebrew calling on rabbis in New York City to devote their upcoming Sabbath sermons to the plight of Germany's Jews, and to urge their congregations to participate in the mass protest rally at Madison Square Garden.[55]

On March 23, several days before the nationwide protests, the Jewish War Veterans of the United States (JWV) staged a disciplined anti-Nazi protest march in New York City, in which 4,000 participated. Mayor John P. O'Brien reviewed the march and received its demands for a boycott of German goods and for the U.S. government to issue a diplomatic protest against Nazi antisemitism to Germany. Mayor O'Brien expressed his solidarity with the march, declaring that Nazi Germany was "bound to meet the moral opposition of the entire world."[56]

Three days later in Boston, 8,000 Jews turned out for a mass rally at Temple Mishkan Tefila in the heavily Jewish district of Roxbury, "resolved to stand shoulder to shoulder with their persecuted brethren in Germany." To accommodate all those wishing to participate, it was

FIGURE 1.1. Every available seat in New York City's Madison Square Garden is filled at a mass rally against antisemitism in Nazi Germany, March 27, 1933. Courtesy of AP Images.

necessary to hold two overflow meetings, at the Temple's school and at a nearby synagogue.[57]

So many people turned out to protest against Nazi antisemitism in the nationwide protests of March 27 that the streets surrounding the auditoriums were jammed with huge throngs of people unable to gain entry, who listened to the speeches over amplifiers. The *Christian Science Monitor* estimated that 1 million Jews joined in the protest. In New York City, 35,000 people, standing shoulder to shoulder, filled the blocks around Madison Square Garden, where former New York governor Al Smith, Senator Robert Wagner, and Rabbi Stephen S. Wise delivered speeches denouncing Nazi persecution of Jews to a packed house. It was the largest protest meeting in the city's history until that time. Chicago's huge Auditorium Theater was similarly filled to capacity, with thousands more gathered outside.[58]

Numerous well-attended protest gatherings held throughout New Jersey and on Long Island, New York, to coincide with Madison Square

FIGURE 1.2. Mass demonstration against Nazi antisemitism in the heavily Jewish neighborhood of Brownsville in Brooklyn, New York, Stone and Pitkin Avenues, March 27, 1933. Courtesy of AP Images.

Garden's revealed significant grassroots determination to combat Nazism outside the larger cities. Such meetings were held in Newark, Jersey City, Hackensack, Trenton, and Atlantic City in New Jersey, and in Mineola, Port Chester, and Nassau County on Long Island. The New Jersey state legislature unanimously passed a resolution denouncing the persecution of Jews in Germany.[59]

The next day the New York *Evening Post* reported that, in the wake of the nationwide mass rallies against Nazi antisemitism, there was a definite movement among many New York City merchants and consumers toward a boycott of German goods and services, which the JWV had already proposed. AJCongress president Bernard Deutsch stated that because of the last reports from Germany of anti-Jewish persecution, a boycott was "almost unavoidable."[60] An anti-Nazi meeting attended by 3,000 Jews in Williamsburg, Brooklyn, revealed considerable grassroots support for the boycott in the Jewish community. The meeting, in the name of 100,000 Jewish residents of Williamsburg, adopted a resolution strongly endorsing a boycott to protest Nazi atrocities against Jews in Germany. Those present pledged themselves to persuade their friends to join the boycott. The meeting voted to send copies of the resolution to President Roosevelt, New York's senators Robert Wagner and Royal Copeland, and the American embassy in Berlin. The *New York Times* on March 30 reported that famed Yiddish theater actor Ludwig Satz had announced he would not travel on any German ship so long as Germany persecuted the Jews.[61]

At a mass protest rally in Baltimore on March 30, three U.S. senators forcefully denounced the Hitler regime's antisemitic policies. Senator William H. King of Utah urged the U.S. government to sever diplomatic relations with Germany if Nazi persecution of the Jews continued. Senator Millard Tydings of Maryland strongly encouraged further mass anti-Nazi protest, informing the crowd that previous demonstrations and rallies had made the German government aware that "a wave of indignation" against its antisemitic policies was sweeping across the United States. Maryland's other senator, Phillips Lee Goldsborough, delivered an "impassioned speech" in which he predicted that Jews would still be living in Germany in a thousand years, long after Hitler was gone, implying that the Nazi objective was their expulsion or annihilation.[62]

College and university presidents and administrators did not convene protest meetings against Nazi antisemitism on the campuses, nor did they urge their students and faculty members to attend the nationwide mass rallies held on March 27, 1933. With very few exceptions, they did not encourage them to attend subsequent protests, or to speak at them, at least until after the Kristallnacht in November 1938. To be sure, there were students and professors at some universities sufficiently concerned about the plight of Germany's Jews to organize protests or forums about it on campus, but these rarely attracted significant participation or press coverage.

President James Rowland Angell of Yale University refused the request of Rabbi Edgar E. Siskin to speak on March 27, 1933, at a community-wide mass meeting in New Haven called to voice "dismay and indignation at the anti-Semitic excesses now being carried out in Germany." President Angell told Rabbi Siskin: "I greatly fear the unfavorable effect of public demonstrations." Rabbi Siskin was deeply disappointed that President Angell declined his invitation and told him, "Your presence with us would have added greatly to the effect of our protest locally."[63]

At the Massachusetts Institute of Technology (MIT), a meeting held on March 30, 1933, to protest "the violation of rights of German Jews by the Hitler government" failed to achieve its objective when President Karl Compton personally intervened. The MIT chapters of the Menorah Society (a Jewish students' organization), the Liberal Club, the radical National Student League (NSL), and the Socialist Club sponsored the meeting. These groups had obtained about thirty student and faculty signatures on a petition that condemned the Nazis' "unprincipled terrorism on unarmed and defenseless" political opponents and Jews. It was the intention of these groups in convening the campus meeting to gain endorsement for sending the petition, in the form of a telegram, to Adolf Hitler. The meeting was attended by about 100 MIT students and faculty members.

When the petition was put forward for discussion, President Compton, "an unexpected visitor at the meeting," was the first to object to sending it. He argued that the petition represented the views of only "a meager number" of MIT students and faculty.

President Compton was supported by MIT mathematics professor Norbert Wiener, who, "while decrying [Nazi] violence," declared that public protest against Nazi persecution "would exert no influence." When Elihu Stone, attorney and president of the New England Zionist Region, "pleaded the Jewish cause," MIT mechanical engineering professor Wilhelm Spannhake "sprang indignantly to Hitler's defense." His son, MIT senior Ernst Spannhake, declared that the Nazis had committed no atrocities and justified the April 1 boycott of Jewish businesses in Germany. The meeting accepted President Compton's argument that the telegram should not be sent to Hitler because it "might easily be misconstrued" as expressing the position of the MIT student body and therefore "misused," and they voted overwhelmingly not to do so, by a margin of eighty-four to twelve.[64]

A very different mood prevailed at a meeting in early April attended by 7,000 people at Boston's Faneuil Hall, at which Jewish leaders and sympathetic non-Jews, including Mayor James Michael Curley and reformer Alice Stone Blackwell, excoriated Nazi persecution of Jews. This meeting adopted resolutions expressing to the U.S. State Department "profound concern" and indignation over official discrimination against Jews in Germany, "the removal of Jewish judges from the bench, exclusion of Jewish lawyers and physicians from the bar and hospitals, the closing of universities to Jewish professors and students," and the April 1 boycott of Jewish businesses. The Boston *Herald* reported that "the great gathering" had "with a tremendous display of emotion...jeered the name of Hitler each time it was mentioned." Alice Stone Blackwell declared that for the Hitler regime "to deprive the Jews of Germany of the right to a livelihood" was an atrocity. Mayor Curley praised American Jews for their patriotism and their tremendous contributions to the United States. He noted that George Washington had held the Jews in high esteem, and that the completion of Boston's Bunker Hill monument had been made possible by a Jewish philanthropist. Among the speakers was President Daniel Marsh of Boston University, one of the very few university presidents or administrators to speak publicly against Nazism at protest rallies or forums.[65]

A few days later, Jewish college organizations in the Boston area held an anti-Nazi protest rally at Boston University's School of Education. They enlisted as speakers Jewish leaders and rabbis and a few liberal professors and journalists, but no college or university administrators.[66] Professor Thomas Chalmers of Boston University's History Department, in an address to students the previous day, took strong issue with anti-Nazi protest, urging instead a "hands off" policy toward Hitler. He argued that Germany must be allowed to solve its own problems, and that American intervention could "do no good."[67]

On April 15, representatives of Jewish organizations assembled at the Hotel Pennsylvania in New York City to formulate a program of "rigorous resistance" to the Hitler government's antisemitic policies. The call for the conference, issued by the AJCongress, stated that immediate action was needed to combat the "dry pogrom" that the Nazis were carrying out "with shocking vigor." The Nazis were driving from their positions "Jewish lawyers, physicians, teachers, nurses...students, and even Jewish school children." Germany's Jews were "being cut off from every source and avenue of economic activity."[68]

The next day delegates affiliated with the Hebrew Sheltering and Immigrant Aid Society met in New York City to plan a campaign to raise funds to make it possible for Jewish refugees to leave Germany and to assist them in other ways. The New York *Evening Post* noted that the Society's branches in Chicago, Philadelphia, Boston, Baltimore, and San Francisco were initiating similar fund-raising campaigns for the Jewish refugees from Germany.[69]

The Nazis' announcement that they would conduct public burnings of Jewish and other "un-German" books at universities across Germany on the night of May 10, 1933 (discussed in Chapter 3), led American Jewish organizations to schedule mass street demonstrations against Nazism in major American cities on that date. Surprisingly, university presidents and administrators did not organize any campus protests against the Nazi book burnings, a blatant display of anti-intellectualism and antisemitism. Nor did they publicly express support for the mass protest marches.

On May 14, the boycott movement against Nazi Germany, in which the JWV and many Jews at the grass roots were already engaged, received a significant boost when the newly founded American League for the Defense of Jewish Rights (ALDJR) held a conference to promote it at the Hotel Astor in New York City. The ALDJR's Samuel Untermyer, a very wealthy New York attorney and the most prominent Jewish boycott leader, had given a highly publicized address on May 7, entitled "Germany's Medieval Challenge to World Jewry and Civilization," asking Americans not to purchase goods manufactured in Germany, and not to sail in German ships or to visit Germany. The ALDJR proceeded to form district councils to organize the boycott at the neighborhood level throughout New York City. The persons participating invested considerable effort in investigating stores to determine whether they were selling German goods, and in identifying sources where substitute products could be obtained. The day after the Hotel Astor conference, the *New York Times* reported that the boycott call had assumed nationwide proportions, as the ALDJR was being "swamped with telegrams pledging support of the movement."[70]

Because it wanted to emphasize that it had a significant non-Jewish membership, the ALDJR changed its name later in the year to the Non-Sectarian Anti-Nazi League to Champion Human Rights (NSANL), with Untermyer as president. It vigorously championed the boycott during the next several years, urging all Americans to "REMEMBER That every cent you spend on German steamers and in Germany is aiding Germany's war preparations and the spread of Nazism the world over."[71]

In New York City and its environs particularly, the boycott movement's impact was significant. By the end of March 1934, many of the nation's leading department stores, a majority of them Jewish-owned, had stopped importing German goods, including Macy's, Gimbel's, Saks, Bloomingdale's, Hearn, Best, Constable, Lord & Taylor, and Sears, Roebuck. That month the New York store of Wanamaker's, which was not Jewish owned, notified the NSANL that it had not imported any German goods since November 1933 and maintained no offices in Germany. In April 1934, Kresge's department store in Newark, New Jersey, announced that it had terminated purchases from Germany when the Nazis assumed power. In July 1934, Bamberger's department store in Newark issued a statement proclaiming that "[t]he consumer boycott of German merchandise has been so effective that the store has not purchased a dollar's worth of German goods in many months. The old and broken stocks of German goods are probably as small as in any department store in the metropolitan area."[72]

From the beginning, the NSANL appealed to universities and to their students, urging them to participate in the boycott. In 1933, the NSANL sent out a circular letter to students asking them to notify it if their university was selling goods manufactured in Nazi Germany. The NSANL asked students to particularly check the source of goods in the following categories: stationery, pencils, art supplies, scientific and calculating instruments, chemicals and laboratory supplies, medical and dental supplies, musical supplies, sporting goods, and clothing.[73]

University administrations showed no interest in the boycott against Nazi Germany but did provide Untermyer with an immediate specific opportunity to bring the boycott to wider public attention. Untermyer announced the day after the Hotel Astor conference that he and others were engaged in efforts to change the scheduled sailing of a group of nineteen Columbia University students, booked on a German ocean liner "in connection with their work in the university." The group included eight Jewish students, whom the university administration required to sail on the German ship with the rest of the party. Untermyer attempted to persuade the Columbia administration to transfer the students to an American liner. The *New York Times* reported that he had offered to pay the difference in cost himself for the entire group, to spare the Jewish students the indignity and humiliation of having to travel on a vessel flying the swastika flag and manned by a Nazi crew, as well as to deprive the Hitler government of much-needed foreign currency.[74]

University presidents themselves frequently traveled across the Atlantic on German liners flying the swastika flag, choosing to publicly violate the boycott. Newspapers such as the *New York Times* regularly published lists of prominent passengers making Atlantic Ocean voyages, on German and other ships. Those who traveled on Nazi Germany's vessels felt no shame about the public knowing what they were doing. President Nicholas Murray Butler, head of the Carnegie Foundation for International Peace, who attended numerous European conferences, often sailed on German vessels, as mentioned in Chapter 3. Harvard's newly inducted president James Bryant Conant traveled to Europe on Nazi Germany's North German Lloyd liner *Europa* in May 1933. When Robert Maynard Hutchins, president of the University of Chicago, sailed across the Atlantic on the *Europa* in August 1933, it "provoked much adverse comment." President Hutchins told Chicago attorney Leo F. Wormser upon his return to the United States that "the propriety or impropriety of the selection of a German ship under existing conditions had not occurred to him."[75] He continued to sail on the *Europa*, however, making trans-Atlantic trips on the German liner in July 1934 and in August 1937.[76]

College students regularly crossed the Atlantic on German vessels, most notably on their way to study at German universities, often as participants in Junior Year Abroad programs, as described in Chapter 4. Nazi Germany's North German Lloyd and Hamburg-American lines often placed advertisements in college newspapers. In May 1935, the *Harvard Crimson* reported that the Harvard student band, the Serenaders, was booked to perform on the Hamburg-American vessel *S.S. Albert Ballin* from June 27 through the end of the summer. Bands from six other American colleges signed agreements with the Hamburg-American line to play on its ships that summer.[77] In March 1936, the University of Chicago *Daily Maroon* ran an advertisement for Hamburg-American and North German Lloyd voyages to Europe on the *Bremen, Europa,* and *St. Louis* that proclaimed: "Your brothers and sisters are already booked, many with their cars, on the special student sailings – college orchestras aboard." The advertisement specifically appealed to students interested in taking summer courses at German universities, enrolling in Junior Year Abroad programs or pursuing graduate studies "at leading [German] universities," vacationing in the Third Reich, or attending that summer's Olympic games in Berlin.[78]

On May 10, 1933, massive numbers of people in New York City, Chicago, Philadelphia, Cleveland, Pittsburgh, and other cities answered the call of the AJCongress to join a second wave of nationally coordinated street demonstrations against Nazi persecution of Jews in Germany. In New York, 100,000 marched for six hours, as thousands more lined the streets to show their support. In the history of the city until that time, the demonstration was equaled in size only by the victory parades that followed the Armistice. Mayor O'Brien reviewed the parade from the steps of City Hall. Jewish stores, offices, and other businesses shut down early in the afternoon to permit their employees to participate. The marchers included uniformed veterans of the World War, members of Zionist organizations, students at high schools, colleges, and Jewish religious institutions, "a labor contingent of many thousands, scores of rabbis in long black robes, bearded denizens of the East Side, dapper young men and women, professional men, and representatives of the literary, artistic, and

FIGURE 1.3. Anti-Nazi protesters march through New York City's Washington Square Park on their way to a mass rally in Battery Park against antisemitism in Germany, May 10, 1933. Courtesy of AP Images.

theatrical worlds." Many carried placards that read "Hitler – This is Not the Period of the Dark Ages," and "Hitler – Remember What Happened to Spain." The undertakers' union marched with a sign that said "We Want Hitler." A large group of city officials and judges, led by the Manhattan borough president, also joined the procession. Major general John F. O'Ryan declared that he had accepted the AJCongress's invitation to lead the parade because "of the conviction that non-Jewish Americans owe it to our Jewish citizenry...to indicate where we stand in relation to the insult by the Hitler Government to their race and before the world." There was no mention in the press of any college or university president or administrator participating.[79]

The demonstrations in other cities were equally enthusiastic and socially diverse. In Chicago, 25,000 marched to protest not only Nazi antisemitism and the burning of books but Hitler's sending of an emissary to Chicago's Century of Progress exposition. The Chicago *Tribune* reported that "children and gray-bearded men with skullcaps marched side by side . . . [and] all professions were represented." In Philadelphia, "patriarchal Jews with long, flowing beards, smooth-shaven shopkeepers and business men and hundreds of earnest housewives" marched together against Nazism.[80]

In early June 1933, the Anti-Defamation League (ADL), established in 1913 to combat antisemitism, began a sweeping investigation of "Nazi activities in American universities." Alarmed by numerous reports that exchange students from Nazi Germany were "making addresses justifying the anti-semitic methods of Hitler" on American campuses, the ADL sent a circular letter to its supporters in academia asking them to document such activity. It also requested information about efforts by German exchange students to organize pro-Nazi student groups at American colleges and universities. The ADL emphasized that the German exchange students were engaged in "extremely destructive" political activities on the American campus. Fearing that Nazi propaganda was already seriously impacting the campus, the ADL asked its contacts to transmit the information they gathered by airmail, so that it could immediately respond to it.[81]

That same month, Arturo Toscanini, conductor of the New York Philharmonic Orchestra, canceled his contract to direct the program of Wagnerian music at the annual Bayreuth festival in Bavaria to protest the Hitler government's antisemitic policies and, specifically, its persecution of Jewish musicians. Toscanini, an Italian, had been the only non-German ever asked to conduct at Bayreuth. The *New York Times* reported that the Hitler regime was worried about the impact on its image abroad of the refusal of one of the world's preeminent symphony conductors to perform at its most important music festival.[82]

The American Jewish press highlighted Toscanini's bold defiance of the Nazis, contrasting it with American universities' academic exchanges with the Third Reich, which they carried on until nearly the onset of World War II. Arthur Bodansky, former director of the Metropolitan Opera, had asked Toscanini shortly after the April 1, 1933, Nazi boycott of Jewish stores to join eleven other musicians in a cable of protest to Chancellor Hitler against Nazi antisemitism. The *American Hebrew* reported that "Toscanini not only gave his instant assent, but put his own name at the head of the list." Toscanini later refused to conduct at the Salzburg Festival in Austria because the performance would be broadcast into Germany. In 1936, he traveled to Palestine to conduct an orchestra of Jewish refugee musicians from Germany.[83]

On June 10, 1933, two of the most prominent members of the U.S. Senate, majority leader Joseph Robinson of Arkansas and Senator Robert Wagner of New York, forcefully condemned Nazi persecution of the Jews on the Senate floor. In a prepared speech, Robinson called Nazi antisemitism "sickening and terrifying" and warned that it would lead the United States to curtail its trade with Germany. He noted that the Nazis had barred Jews from nearly "every profession and vocation" in Germany, and from universities. Making the Jews' plight even more desperate were the Hitler regime's decrees prohibiting them from leaving the Reich. Senator Wagner declared that he was horrified by the reports of "intolerance, discrimination, and . . . violence" against Jews in Germany. Four other senators rose to express support for Senator Robinson's remarks.[84]

America's higher education leaders' lack of insight into, or indifference to, Nazism's core tenets and objectives was strikingly revealed in early July 1933 in their first joint public protest about events in Germany, when many of them signed a deeply flawed statement circulated by the National Conference of Christians and Jews (NCCJ). The document, composed by a group of prominent social scientists, received the backing of 142 presidents of American colleges and universities, the vast majority of them minor institutions. Addressed to the heads of German universities, it asked them to recognize and respect the rights of Jews and all minorities "as essential to culture and civilization." But the document was undermined by its trivialization of the Nazis' antisemitic campaign.

Everett R. Clinchy, director of the NCCJ, who solicited signatures on the document from college and university presidents, identified it as a statement about "the hostility between Christian and Jewish groups in Germany" and emphasized that it was "in no sense a 'protest.'" Astonishingly, he declared that "the time for protest is past." The document did not provide any sense of the savagery of the Nazis' antisemitic violence or the extent of the damage they had already inflicted on Germany's Jews, and it was vague about who was responsible for the turmoil in Germany. It began by explaining that the signers were "fully aware that the recent happenings" in the Third Reich, which were not specified, were "in large part the result of the lack of fair play to Germany" on the part of the Western democracies, and their "slighting of German rights and needs."

Refusing to characterize Nazi persecution as unique, or even highly unusual, the document emphasized "that minorities are suppressed and discriminated against to some degree in every land." The most prominent college and university presidents signing the document were James Rowland Angell of Yale, Ernest M. Hopkins of Dartmouth, Clarence A. Barbour of Brown, Ray Lyman Wilbur of Stanford, Robert G. Sproul of California, Frank P. Graham of North Carolina, Mary E. Woolley of Mount Holyoke, Henry N. MacCracken of Vassar, Ellen F. Pendleton of Wellesley, and Frank Aydelotte of Swarthmore.[85]

Opening at Chicago's Century of Progress exposition on July 2, 1933, the "mighty pageant" titled *The Romance of a People* rivaled the mass demonstrations of March and May as a spectacular display of grassroots opposition to Nazism. With a cast of 6,200 actors, singers, and dancers, the largest ever assembled in the United States, *The Romance of a People* depicted forty centuries of Jewish history, largely in pantomime. The pageant, performed in Chicago's enormous Soldiers Field stadium, included scenes about the Jews' enslavement in Egypt and their liberation under Moses, their exile in Babylon, and the Roman wars against Judaea. When Titus's legions attacked Jerusalem, "Judah's sons fight like lions; they die, but do not surrender." Then "2,000 years of wandering and exile are thrown upon the stage in a tapestry of motion," until Jews were once again able "to turn thoughts" to restoring their "ancient civilization in Palestine." The pageant was designed to stimulate an intense pride in Jewishness, and to instill respect for the Jews' vitally important contributions to world civilization and empathy for their centuries-long suffering. Proceeds from the pageant were earmarked for the settlement of German Jewish refugees in Palestine.[86]

More than 125,000 people were seated at the opening performance, a larger turnout than the Dempsey-Tunney heavyweight title fight in Chicago had attracted to Soldiers Field in 1927, one of the most heavily attended sports events in history. Because the stadium was filled to capacity and had to turn away thousands of people, a second performance was held a few days later, which attracted 55,000 more. The *New York Times* noted that the two-day attendance was enough "to give any Broadway [play] performance a lengthy run."[87]

In September, *The Romance of a People* opened in New York City, with Samuel Untermyer and New York governor Herbert Lehman as honorary chairs of the sponsoring committee and Senator Robert Wagner as honorary vice-chair. The *New York Times* strongly endorsed the pageant, editorializing that "[g]iven Hitler's efforts to stigmatize a great people as an aggregation of pariahs and public enemies, perhaps the best thing is to let the historic record speak for itself." Originally scheduled for the Polo Grounds, the production was shifted after several days of rain indoors to the nation's largest armory, in the Bronx. A series of about a dozen performances there attracted 400,000 people, including former governor Al Smith and his wife and Albert Einstein, who attended in October, the night after his ship arrived in the United States, as the personal guest of Mayor O'Brien.[88]

In February 1934, *The Romance of a People* moved to Philadelphia, where the Philadelphia *Public Ledger* called it "unquestionably...the greatest spectacle ever presented" there. On opening night, Mayor Moore of Philadelphia declared to the audience at the Convention Hall before the performance that he was greatly pleased to be present to lend official recognition to the pageant. The *Public Ledger* reported that a packed house that included Albert Einstein sat "enthralled" for two hours by "the splendor and beauty of the pageant." When the "swelling rhythm of traditional Hebrew music filled the auditorium," many in the audience wept "openly and unashamed." The *Public Ledger* stated that "[t]hroughout the prologue and the seven breath-taking episodes ran the single, unifying thread of Jewish courage and aspiration, which has been the dominant trait of the race for the forty centuries of its existence."[89] About 70,000 people attended the eleven Philadelphia performances of *The Romance of a People*.[90]

In September 1934, *The Romance of a People* was revived at New York City's Roxy Theatre in abridged form, with a reduced cast. Sponsors of the new version included both of New York's U.S. senators, Mayor La Guardia, and former governor Smith.[91]

Although *The Romance of a People* drew very large audiences in three of the nation's leading metropolises, none of America's higher education leaders were mentioned in the press as sponsors of the pageant, as speaking favorably about it, or even as having been in attendance. Nor is there any evidence that university presidents or administrators made any effort to promote it on their campuses.

On July 21, 1933, the *New York Times* directed attention to the international dimension of Jewish grassroots protest against the Hitler regime when it reported that 20,000 Jews had staged a massive parade and rally in London against Nazi antisemitism. The *Times* called it the largest demonstration in the history of British Jewry. Most of the participants came from the East End Jewish quarter, which was deserted for the "day of mourning." Shops were shut down everywhere in the district and no business was conducted. In the famous Petticoat Lane pushcart section, guards were posted to ensure that outsiders did not attempt to operate there. The *Times* noted that the East End shopkeepers had been "carrying on an effective boycott of German goods for many weeks." Upon reaching Hyde Park, the marchers joined an immense crowd that had gathered to receive them, and resolutions calling for a "boycott of everything German" were "carried with roars of acclamation." The London *Times* stated that "a substantial part of the Jewish population of London" participated in the demonstration.[92]

Former suffragist leader Carrie Chapman Catt's announcement in August 1933 that 9,000 women across the United States had signed a petition to the League of Nations against Nazi antisemitism, and the refusal of permission for the display of the swastika flag in Chicago and San Francisco, provided further evidence of the breadth and intensity of protest in the United States against Germany's oppression of the Jews. Catt's petition stated that "the German pogrom against the Jews" was the most shocking event since the Great War. It denounced the Nazis' removal of Jews from university faculties, the bench and bar, medical practice, and many other occupations.[93] In Chicago that month, threats by Jewish women's organizations to boycott the Women's Day celebration at the Century of Progress Exposition resulted in assurances that the swastika flag would not be flown at the German-American building.[94] San Francisco's acting mayor, J. Emmet Hayden, would not allow the flying of the swastika flag at that city's German Day celebration in September 1933. As a result, the United German Societies, the sponsoring organization, which had planned to display it as a mark of respect for the German consul-general, the main speaker, had to celebrate German Day privately, without city sponsorship. In denying permission, Hayden noted that San Francisco's Board of City Supervisors had adopted a resolution denouncing Nazi policy toward Jews.[95]

At its annual convention in October 1933, the American Federation of Labor (AFL) announced it was joining the boycott of German goods and services, including shipping lines. AFL president William Green's "impassioned speech" against the Nazis' destruction of the German labor movement and persecution of Jews "brought the delegates to their feet in a spontaneous outburst of approval." Green declared that the AFL was determined to use the boycott "to strike a real blow" against Nazism. Selma M. Borchardt of the American Federation of Teachers, recently returned from a trip to Germany, told the delegates that she had seen a fifteen-year-old girl in Berlin forced to wear a placard stating "my father has sinned" because he, a Christian, had married a Jew, her mother. Senator James J. Davis of Pennsylvania, formerly U.S. Secretary of Labor, called Nazi Germany "an insult to civilization."[96]

Two months later, the boycott received strong endorsement from important professional associations representing physicians, dentists, and pharmacists at a meeting arranged by the Allied Dental Council in New York City. Its representatives, along with those of twenty-two other organizations representing those engaged in these occupations, whose combined membership totaled 15,000, declared their determination to combat Nazi intolerance with the boycott.[97]

The fiercest and most dramatic confrontation over Nazism in the United States during the first year of Hitler's rule occurred in Boston on November 26, 1933, as thousands protested the appearance at the Ford Hall Forum of one of Hitler's leading propagandists, Dr. Friedrich Schoenemann. The Forum had invited Schoenemann to speak on "Why I Believe in the Hitler Government." Professor of American literature at the University of Berlin, Schoenemann had been a German instructor at Harvard from 1913 to 1920. The Nazis considered him one of their top authorities on American affairs and culture. During the fall of 1933, Hitler sent Schoenemann on a speaking tour of the United States to promote the Nazi cause.[98]

Invited to deliver an address at Drew University in Madison, New Jersey, in late October 1933 by its treasurer, Noel Bensinger, Professor Schoenemann praised Hitler for achieving for Germany "a new dignity" and "a sense of social justice that it ha[d] lacked since the World War." Schoenemann told the campus audience that when he visited a German concentration camp, he found 1,800 men "living in cleanliness and order, almost as though they were in college."[99]

Boston's Ford Hall Forum, a public lecture hall, proved a far less inviting environment for Schoenemann than the campus. Frank W. Buxton, editor of the Boston *Herald*, one of the Hub's leading newspapers, had informed U.S. ambassador William E. Dodd in Berlin in July 1933 of an "anti-Hitler rage" in Boston. He noted that Boston's Jewish population "reads every word that comes from Berlin." Buxton was horrified by Nazism, which he believed denied "the fundamental truths of civilization." He considered Hitler's tactics "far more cruel than those of the Middle Ages." Hitler's objective was to make the Jews "a degraded race, condemned from birth to obscurity, inferiority, and contumely." Buxton told Dodd that an effective "quiet boycott" against German goods prevailed in Boston.[100]

Schoenemann's presentation at the Ford Hall Forum on Beacon Hill resulted in the most disorderly meeting in its twenty-five-year history, as those in attendance repeatedly challenged his statements from the floor, and thousands of anti-Nazi protestors clashed with the police outside. The Boston press emphasized the intensity of the anti-Nazi sentiment both inside and outside the hall. The Boston *Globe* considered the confrontations, which turned Beacon Hill "into an embattled area," the most violent to have occurred since the Sacco-Vanzetti case. The Boston *Post* stated that the demonstrations surpassed "the wildest of Boston's May Day riots."[101]

The highly engaged audience made clear it detested everything Schoenemann said and stood for from the moment Nazi Germany's consul-general in Boston, Baron Kurt von Tippelskirch, introduced him. It responded to Schoenemann's opening remark, that he was not at the Forum to dispense propaganda, "with laughter, hisses, and shouts of 'liar.'" More hisses and boos greeted his claim that the Nazi revolution was "among the most unbloody in history," and someone shouted, "Let's have some facts." Schoenemann's statement that he had noticed nothing "dirty, abnormal, or mean" during visits to concentration camps was greeted with derisive laughter. When he declared that the 1918 revolution in Germany was "started by a Jew named [Karl] Liebknecht," there were "a dozen cries of 'He was not a Jew. You're a liar.'" After Schoenemann claimed that the Nazis did not believe in confiscation, "'What about Einstein?' came from a dozen throats." A tremendous uproar broke out when Schoenemann asserted that the "genesis of the Jewish question" was Jewish involvement in corruption. The Boston *Post* reported that "liar" was the least of the epithets shouted at the speaker. Schoenemann concluded his speech "amid hisses and catcalls."[102]

As Schoenemann spoke, squads of police, many of them mounted, battled a crowd of demonstrators estimated at between 3,000 and 5,000 in the shadow of the State House. The police finally managed to drive the protestors, many of whom carried banners proclaiming "Down With Hitler" and "Down With the Nazi Butcher," down the steep slopes of Beacon Hill, chasing them a half-mile through the streets and "smashing heads right and left." The demonstrators, "fighting every inch of the way," pulled some policemen off their horses and pummeled them. Police reinforcements finally "lifted the siege of Beacon Hill."[103]

Prominent American opponents of Nazism formed the American Inquiry Commission to expand awareness of the Nazi terror by providing a platform for refugees from the Third Reich and others qualified to provide information about it by means of well-publicized hearings. On July 2 and 3, 1934, the Commission, chaired by Clarence Darrow and composed of seven notable Americans, including civil liberties attorney Arthur Garfield Hays and U.S. senator Edward P. Costigan of Colorado, heard testimony from nearly thirty individuals. Dr. Kurt Rosenfeld, former Prussian Minister of Justice and a Social Democrat, told the Commission that 165,000 persons were currently confined in Nazi concentration camps. He stated that the People's Courts, newly established to try political opponents of the regime and composed entirely of Nazis, offered the innocent "absolutely no chance of defense or acquittal." Rosenfeld told the Commission that the Nazis would take anyone into custody "if they don't like the shape of his nose... and keep him indefinitely." Martin Plettl, formerly president of the German Federation of Clothing Workers, who had been a concentration camp inmate, described how the Nazis had destroyed Germany's trade unions. During a visit to New York City's mayor Fiorello La Guardia while the Commission was in recess, Clarence Darrow described Hitler as "very dangerous" and expressed the hope that he would be killed.[104]

Refugee Scholars: The Limits of University Assistance

In the spring of 1933, Americans alarmed by Nazi persecution of Germany's Jews created programs to find academic positions in the United States for professors whom German universities had discharged because they were Jews or political opponents of the Nazis. Their efforts were impeded by a longstanding tradition in American colleges and universities of excluding Jews from their faculties and by administrators' unwillingness to appoint refugees to anything but very short-term positions. American institutions of higher learning employed few Jews as professors through the 1930s.[105] Universities were also reluctant to recruit refugee scholars because of budgetary reductions during the Depression and concern about the impact of competition on the career prospects of younger American faculty members.

Some wealthy Jews privately communicated to university presidents their fear that granting faculty positions to Jewish refugees from Nazi Germany would provoke an antisemitic backlash in this country. When President Robert Maynard Hutchins of the University of Chicago approached Jewish philanthropist Albert D. Lasker about providing financial support for hiring refugee scholars, Lasker told him that "he was entirely opposed to bringing any Jewish professors to America" because "it might lead to a development of anti-Semitism." Hutchins noted that Lasker was "regarded as the key man" in Chicago for raising funds for Jewish victims of the Nazis and doubted he would be able to "unlock much money without him."[106]

The most significant achievement on behalf of refugee scholars from Nazi Germany was the opening of the University in Exile at the New School for Social Research in New York City in October 1933. In May 1933, Dr. Alvin Johnson announced plans to establish a university in exile that would employ a faculty of about fifteen "Jewish and liberal professors" in the social sciences whom the Nazis had forced out of German universities. They were to offer graduate courses only, in English. Established in 1919, the New School for Social Research in 1933 was a small adult education institution with only four or five full-time faculty members. Before Johnson announced the formation of the University in Exile, a Jewish businessman, Hiram Halle, had pledged to completely fund it.[107]

Alvin Johnson had decided to establish the University in Exile after encountering resistance from university administrators and department heads when he sounded them out about hiring Jewish refugee scholars. He had initially believed that "the appropriate thing to do was to induce every university faculty to extend its hospitality to one or more of the professors who have been dismissed [by German universities]." However, American academics' response to this proposal, which he had voiced in an article published in the *American Scholar*, suggested to him that advocating such a course would only provoke antisemitism inside the universities. As a result, he had decided to focus instead on placing refugee scholars in one small institution, his University in Exile, and to concentrate only on the social sciences. Because there was significant opposition to hiring refugee scholars, particularly Jews, both inside and outside of academia, Johnson was well aware that the University in Exile would only develop "inch by inch, painfully."[108]

Having secured the services of fourteen refugee scholars from Nazi Germany by August, Johnson described the University in Exile as "a most vigorous protest against the restrictions placed on scholarship by the Hitler government." The refugees were offered two-year appointments only, with the possibility that they might be extended. At the same time, Johnson emphasized that the University in Exile was designed "purely as a center of scholarship, instruction, and research." It would combat Nazism by providing an opportunity for talented scholars, mostly Jews, driven from their lecture halls and homes to conduct research and teach graduate seminars.[109] The University in Exile opened officially in October 1933 as the Graduate Faculty of Political and Social Science. Student enrollment was 92 for the fall semester of 1933 and increased to 520 by the fall of 1940.[110]

Perhaps to alleviate the concerns of business and higher education leaders unwilling to associate themselves with a project identified with Jewish rescue, Johnson informed the press that the University in Exile considered only scholarship, not "race," in selecting faculty. He emphasized that "[t]he University in Exile is not a charitable venture." The mostly Jewish faculty was hired strictly on the basis of merit.[111]

The faculty's largely Jewish composition, as well as the New School's marginality in American academia, provided refugee scholars with a far more supportive environment than could be found at any American university. As Dan A. Oren noted in a study of American university antisemitism: "Only on the graduate faculty of . . . [the] New School for Social Research, founded in 1933 as the University in Exile, were refugee scholars truly welcome."[112]

Some university presidents appeared willing to endorse Johnson's plan for the University in Exile, at least privately, as an alternative to having a larger number of refugee scholars distributed among many American universities. President Isaiah Bowman of Johns Hopkins University, for example, while expressing support for the project, warned fellow academicians not "to bob up and down on waves of emotion." He urged them not to "load our university budget with burdens that are assumed because of sympathy." Moreover, he believed that universities' hiring of refugee professors undermined "the just claims of younger [American] men" to faculty positions, and their opportunities for promotion. Because American universities were experiencing financial distress, President Bowman recommended that those attempting to assist refugee scholars from Nazi Germany proceed "slowly and experimentally and on a small scale."[113] Johnson later informed Bowman that President James B. Conant of Harvard University had said the same thing to him. Indeed, Johnson indicated to Bowman that he himself shared the same outlook.[114]

In May 1933, the same month that Alvin Johnson founded the University in Exile, Jewish donors provided funding to establish and support the Emergency Committee in Aid of Displaced German Scholars (EC) to place refugee professors from Nazi Germany on the faculties of American universities. The EC covered half the salary (up to $2,000) of the refugee scholars the universities themselves appointed, for positions lasting up to two years. The EC recruited several gentiles to serve on its executive board, to downplay the uniqueness of the Jewish plight in Germany and to attract non-Jewish support. In part to offset fears that competition from refugees would reduce the job prospects in academia for younger American academics, the EC did not grant funds for displaced German scholars under the age of thirty. Unlike Alvin Johnson, who publicized the University in Exile in the press, the EC avoided newspaper coverage for fear of provoking antisemitism.[115]

The EC also disassociated itself from political protests against Nazism, such as the boycott of German goods and services, out of concern that they would drive away potential donors. Although Johnson believed that Nazism was strongly entrenched in Germany and hoped to establish the University in Exile on a permanent basis, the EC assumed that what it viewed as "Nazi excesses" would last only for a short time. As a result it lacked the sense of urgency shared by many anti-Nazi activists. Indeed, after only two years of Nazi rule, it considered the "emergency" to be "largely over," although it continued to operate until World War II. It refused the American Jewish Congress's invitation to become a sponsoring organization of its Madison Square Garden anti-Nazi mass rally in March 1934.[116]

Antisemitism and financial constraints seriously limited university assistance to refugee scholars, whose appointments were usually for two years or less. In December 1934, University of Chicago trustee James M. Stifler noted that although his institution, because of its large graduate school, was in a better position to hire refugee scholars than most universities, it had made no permanent appointments. It listed all German refugee appointees as visiting professors or lecturers. Most were hired for two years, and sometimes for only one. These positions were funded largely by the EC and the Rockefeller Foundation, which in 1933 established a special fund to provide matching grants to American universities that appointed displaced German scholars to their faculties. Individual Chicago Jews also contributed. Stifler stated that, given the University of Chicago's limited financial resources, "we would be quite unable to do anything else, nor have we any hope of doing more in the future."[117] By January 1938, the University of Chicago had managed to hire only ten displaced German scholars, on appointments ranging from one year to "indefinite tenure."[118]

Neither Harvard nor Yale, America's most prominent universities, displayed much interest in hiring refugee scholars from Nazi Germany. President James Rowland Angell of Yale was only "superficially concerned with the plight of the German refugees" and "reluctant to commit scarce university funds to provide them employment." Yale relied largely on EC grants in hiring six German refugee scholars, several of whom were not Jewish. Only two of the appointments lasted more than three years. The Yale faculty's attitude was "one of indifference."[119] During the 1930s, most of the university's departments were unwilling "to tolerate Jews on even a temporary basis."[120]

Harvard did not respond when the EC in May 1933 invited fifteen of America's leading universities to hire a displaced German scholar and promised to pay half the salary ($2,000), with the Rockefeller Foundation providing the other half. That month, President A. Lawrence Lowell declined the Schurz Memorial Foundation's offer to cover the salary if Harvard employed a refugee scholar as a visiting curator at the University's Germanic Museum. Lowell responded that the proposal "appeared as an attempt to use the College for purposes of propaganda." If Harvard hired a refugee scholar, "it would be trumpeted all over the country by Jewish organizations." At its May 29, 1933, meeting, the Harvard Corporation (equivalent to the board of trustees) decided to take no action on the EC's offer, and did not reply to it.[121] When James G. McDonald in March 1934 asked to talk to the newly retired Lowell about displaced German scholars, his secretary replied that the former president "wasn't interested in German refugees."[122]

Lowell's successor as Harvard's president, James Bryant Conant, who assumed office in September 1933, and the Harvard Corporation, indicated that the university was not interested in cooperating with the EC in hiring refugee scholars on its faculty. In January 1934, the *New York Times* reported that Harvard "adheres to the stand taken last year by Dr. A. Lawrence Lowell when president, that the university would not make a place on its faculty for any man because he was an emigré, or as a protest to the Nazi removal of educators from German universities."[123] The next month, President Conant informed EC secretary Edward R. Murrow that "[n]o appointments have ever been made at the University by means of funds supplied by the Emergency Committee."[124]

Conclusion

During the early months of Nazi rule in Germany, many Americans recognized that the Hitler regime represented an unprecedented relapse into barbarism. James Waterman Wise declared in 1933, in one of the first books to be published about Germany under Nazi rule, that the Third Reich was conducting "[a] bloodless war of extermination" against the

Jews, "which gives no quarter and recognizes no non-combatants." He emphasized that "[f]or what it has done, there is neither example nor parallel in the antiquity of primal brutality, in the Middle Ages of religious persecution, or in the darkest days of Tsarist Russia."[125] In May 1933, Lord Melchett described Germany as a death trap for its entire Jewish population. The Nazis had expelled Jews from the professions and university faculties, shut down their businesses, and brutally beat them in the streets, in torture cellars, and in concentration camps. They delighted in inflicting the most degrading and humiliating forms of punishment on Jews, often in full public view. Respected American and British journalists, reporting directly from Germany or drawing on interviews from refugees from the Third Reich in neighboring countries, regularly provided detailed accounts of Nazi antisemitic atrocities, discrimination, and harassment.

As succeeding chapters demonstrate, the leaders of America's colleges and universities remained for the most part uninvolved as others in this country forcefully protested the Nazis' barbaric treatment of Jews. The Nazis' antisemitic terror in 1933 precipitated demonstrations and boycotts on an unprecedented scale, often initiated at the grassroots level. Several U.S. senators and big-city mayors joined in these protests, which the American press widely publicized. But although academicians were the Americans most conversant with European affairs, few engaged in public anti-Nazi protest. As many working and lower-middle-class Americans marched in the streets and struggled to organize a nationwide boycott of German goods and services, American universities maintained amicable relations with the Third Reich, sending their students to study at Nazified universities while welcoming Nazi exchange students to their own campuses. America's most distinguished university presidents willingly crossed the Atlantic in ships flying the swastika flag, openly defying the anti-Nazi boycott, to the benefit of the Third Reich's economy. By warmly receiving Nazi diplomats and propagandists on campus, they helped Nazi Germany present itself to the American public as a civilized nation, unfairly maligned in the press. Influenced by their administrators' example, and that of many of their professors, college and university students for the most part adopted a similar outlook, although there was significant student protest against Nazism at some schools, such as Columbia, which is analyzed in Chapter 3.

Chapter 2 considers the role of America's most prestigious institution of higher learning, Harvard University, in legitimating the Hitler regime. It focuses particularly on President James Bryant Conant; on the undergraduate newspaper, the *Harvard Crimson*, which reflected the outlook of the most influential segment of student opinion; and on alumni. Chapter 3 examines the role of this nation's most prominent university president, Columbia's Nicholas Murray Butler, in enhancing the image of the Third Reich, and on his highly vocal student opponents, some of whom edited the undergraduate newspaper, the *Columbia Spectator*. The *Columbia Spectator*'s outlook toward Germany and antisemitism differed significantly from that of the *Harvard Crimson*. Chapter 4 focuses on the Seven Sisters, the elite women's colleges, which were centrally involved in promoting student exchanges with Nazi Germany. Chapter 5 examines this nation's most prestigious foreign policy symposia, sponsored by the University of Virginia's Institute of Public Affairs. During the 1930s, these symposia provided an important forum that permitted apologists for Nazi Germany's domestic and foreign policies to reach American audiences. Chapter 6 explores the role of university German departments in the 1930s as disseminators of Nazi propaganda in the United States, and in hosting campus visits by Nazi Germany's diplomats. Chapter 7 analyzes the role of Catholic colleges and universities in promoting appeasement of Nazi Germany and providing a platform for propagandists for Mussolini and Franco. Chapter 8 examines the limits of protest against Nazism within academia during 1938, a year that culminated in the Kristallnacht, when German barbarity finally instilled widespread alarm. The Epilogue explores the role of former Harvard president James Bryant Conant in encouraging the parole of Nazi war criminals during the 1950s, as U.S. high commissioner for Germany and as ambassador to West Germany. It also focuses on the effusive praise and respect prominent American higher education leaders accorded Mircea Eliade during his long postwar career as a professor at the University of Chicago, despite his role as propagandist for Romania's antisemitic Iron Guard, enthusiastic collaborators with the Nazis during the 1930s and the Holocaust.

Legitimating Nazism

Harvard University and the Hitler Regime, 1933–1937

The Harvard University administration during the 1930s, led by President James Bryant Conant, ignored numerous opportunities to take a principled stand against the Hitler regime and its antisemitic outrages and contributed to Nazi Germany's efforts to improve its image in the West. Its lack of concern about Nazi antisemitism was shared by many influential Harvard alumni and student leaders. In warmly welcoming Nazi leaders to the Harvard campus; inviting them to prestigious, high-profile social events; and striving to build friendly relations with thoroughly Nazified universities in Germany, while denouncing those who protested against these actions, Harvard's administration and many of its student leaders offered important encouragement to the Hitler regime as it intensified its persecution of Jews and expanded its military strength.

The few scholars who previously addressed this subject devoted insufficient attention to antisemitism in the Harvard administration and student body and underestimated the university's complicity in the Nazis' persecution of the Jews. William M. Tuttle Jr., to be sure, criticizes Conant's unwillingness to help place German scholars exiled by the Nazis at Harvard, calling this "a failure of compassion." Morton and Phyllis Keller, in their recent history of Harvard, similarly describe its administration as slow to appoint refugees from Nazism to the faculty, particularly Jews. They describe Conant as "shar[ing] the mild antisemitism common to his social group and time" but then go on to state that an alleged commitment to meritocracy "made him more ready to accept able Jews as students and faculty." The Kellers acknowledge that under Conant Harvard restricted the number of Jewish students admitted and hired few Jewish professors, so the trend toward meritocracy was limited. Tuttle, while conceding that Conant publicly criticized the Hitler regime only for suppressing academic freedom and "ignor[ed] other and related Nazi crimes," nonetheless praises him as "one of the more outspoken anti-Nazis in the United States" from 1933 until World War II. This, however, was hardly the case.[1]

From 1933, when he assumed the presidency of America's oldest and most prestigious university, through 1937, Conant failed to speak out against Nazism on many occasions when it really mattered. He was publicly silent during the visit of the Nazi warship *Karlsruhe* to Boston in May 1934, some of whose crew Harvard entertained. He welcomed the high Nazi official Ernst (Putzi) Hanfstaengl to the June 1934 Harvard commencement. In March 1935, the Harvard administration permitted Nazi Germany's consul general in Boston to place a wreath bearing the swastika emblem in the university chapel. Conant sent a delegate from Harvard to the University of Heidelberg's 550th anniversary pageant in June 1936, and he extended warm greetings to the Georg-August University in Goettingen on its 200th anniversary in June 1937. In providing a friendly welcome to Nazi leader Hanfstaengl, President Conant and others prominently affiliated with Harvard communicated to the Hitler government that boycotts intended to destroy Jewish businesses, the dismissal of Jews from the professions, and savage beatings of Jews were not their concern. Conant's biographer, James Hershberg, trivialized Hanfstaengl's 1934 visit to Harvard by calling it "farcical"; it was, in fact, highly dangerous.[2]

President Conant remained publicly indifferent to the persecution of Jews in Europe and failed to speak out against it until after Kristallnacht, in November 1938. He was determined to build friendly ties with the Universities of Heidelberg and Goettingen, even though they had expelled their Jewish faculty members and thoroughly Nazified their curricula, constructing a "scholarly" foundation for vulgar antisemitism, which was taught as "racial science." The anniversary ceremonies in which Harvard participated, by sending a representative or friendly greetings, were simply brown shirt pageants designed to glorify the Nazi regime. James Hershberg admits that Conant "dignified a crudely Nazified spectacle," but he ascribes his eagerness to do so to "fear of igniting controversy," rather than to insensitivity to Jewish suffering.[3] Harvard invited Nazi academics to its September 1936 tercentenary celebration, which it held on Rosh Hashonah. (Conant ignored numerous requests not to schedule it on a Jewish High Holiday.) During this period Harvard engaged in an academic student exchange program with Nazi universities, refusing to heed the call for a boycott. Conant also displayed impatience with, and often contempt for, Jewish and other activists determined to publicly expose Nazi barbarism.

To be sure, Conant did express formal opposition to Nazism and never assumed the role of public apologist for the Hitler regime, as did the chancellor of American University in Washington, D.C., Joseph Gray, who in August 1936 returned from Europe filled with praise for the "New Germany." Chancellor Gray declared that Hitler had restored hope to a troubled nation, preventing it from going the way of strife-torn Spain. "Everybody is working in Germany," he gushed, liberal education was available, and the cities were "amazingly clean," without beggars. But even Gray a year and a half later signed the petition circulated among academic leaders denouncing Poland's 1937 introduction of segregated seating in universities for Jewish students, while Conant did not.[4]

President Conant's behavior was certainly influenced by the anti-Jewish prejudice he harbored. His predecessor as Harvard's president, A. Lawrence Lowell, had voiced his antisemitism publicly, notably during the controversy in 1922 surrounding his proposal that Harvard introduce a formal quota to reduce Jewish enrollment. In justifying a quota, President Lowell, a former vice-president of the Immigration Restriction League, had declared that "a strong race feeling on the part of the Jews" was a significant cause of the "rapidly growing anti-Semitic feeling in this country."[5] Lowell managed thus to blame the Jews for antisemitism. Conant, then a Harvard chemistry professor, had voted in favor of the anti-Jewish quota at a special faculty meeting. Early in his presidency, Conant appointed as chair of Harvard's Committee on Admissions the headmaster of a Philadelphia preparatory school who was known for having tightly restricted Jewish admissions. Harvard deliberately limited Jewish enrollment during Conant's presidency in the 1930s using more subtle methods than a formal quota.[6]

Conant's antisemitism is evident in his correspondence with the chemical director of the Du Pont Corporation, who sought his advice in September 1933 about whether to hire the Jewish chemist Max Bergmann, whom Germany's Kaiser-Wilhelm-Institute for Leather Research had discharged after the Nazis assumed power. Du Pont was impressed with Bergmann's record as a research chemist but worried that he might possess undesirable personality and physical traits that Du Pont executives, and President Conant, associated with Jews. Chemistry was a well-established scientific field from which Jews had for the most part been excluded in the United States.[7] Although President Conant could have exerted his influence against chemistry's highly restrictive approach to Jews, when given the opportunity, he chose not to do so. In fact, he was not just silent in the face of discrimination; he actively collaborated in it.

Du Pont's chemical director knew that Bergmann had "a great reputation" as an organic chemist, Conant's field, but he contacted Harvard's president because the corporation's London representative had alerted him that he was "decidedly of the Jewish type." If this were the case, Du Pont feared it could adversely affect its relations with American universities. Conant responded that Bergmann was "certainly very definitely of the Jewish type – rather heavy," probably dogmatic, with "none of the earmarks of genius," a view he admitted many American chemists did not share. He recommended that Du Pont not hire Bergmann.[8] Thus given the opportunity to stand up against bigotry and exclusion, even behind closed doors, in a way that would cost him nothing, he chose to do the opposite: to shore up anti-Jewish prejudice. When he died a decade later, the *New York Times* identified Bergmann as "one of the leading organic chemists in the world."[9]

Conant reacted differently a few weeks later when Sir William Pope, director of the chemical laboratory at the University of Cambridge in England, wrote to him on behalf of a non-Jewish chemist, Wilhelm Schlenk of Berlin University in Germany. Pope was hoping that Conant might help secure an academic position for Schlenk in the United States. Berlin University had discharged Schlenk because he had attempted to assist Fritz Haber, one of Germany's top chemists and a Christian convert from Judaism, when the Nazis forced him out of his position. Pope assured Conant that Schlenk had "no Jewish blood." He was, in fact, "one of the most charming men" Pope knew. Schlenk had never been associated with "socialist or communistic politics," involvement in which, Pope asserted, was "the cause of the disgrace" of many German Jewish chemists. Conant did not challenge this claim. For an individual who was not "of the Jewish type," unlike Bergmann, Conant indicated a readiness to help.[10]

At the very beginning of Nazi rule in 1933, Boston's Jews mobilized in a massive parade and rally to protest against antisemitic persecution in Germany, but Conant and the other local university presidents did not take part. The November demonstration, sponsored by the New England branch of the American Jewish Congress, was staged in the Dorchester/Mattapan section, where most of Boston's Jews were concentrated, only a few miles from Cambridge. But unlike many of Boston's leaders, Conant did not even send greetings, much less speak.[11] By contrast, the president of Harvard during the next several years sent greetings to German universities when they were staging anniversary commemorations, even though they were clearly intended as Nazi propaganda spectacles, and American newspapers described them as such. Conant did not endorse the boycott of German goods that began in 1933, which was well organized in Boston, or call for Harvard not to buy them.

Nor did President Conant express support for the resolution that Senator Millard Tydings of Maryland introduced in Congress in January 1934 condemning Nazi oppression of Jews in Germany and asking President Roosevelt to inform the Hitler government that this country was profoundly distressed about Germany's antisemitic measures. Senator Tydings noted that the U.S. government had denounced antisemitic persecution in foreign countries at least nine times between 1840 and 1919. Few of America's academic leaders endorsed the resolution, and it remained bottled up in the Senate Foreign Relations Committee.[12]

William M. Tuttle Jr. notes that President Conant was "timid at crucial moments" but minimizes his failure to take a consistent stand against the Nazis by arguing that "he was not alone in his reticence." Tuttle claims that "leaders with constituencies to serve," including university presidents, union leaders, and politicians, "were notoriously silent during the 1930s." Yet there were still some who took a principled stand. President William Green and the leadership of the American Federation of Labor (AFL) vigorously promoted the boycott of German goods almost from its inception in 1933. They specifically denounced "the ruthless persecution of Germany's Jewish population." Pennsylvania governor Gifford Pinchot prominently associated himself with the boycott from the beginning. Senator Tydings pressed vigorously for the U.S. government to confront Nazi Germany about its antisemitic persecution and helped bring it to wider public attention by introducing his resolution. Other leading politicians like New York City's Mayor Fiorello H. La Guardia frequently denounced Nazi antisemitism, and even U.S. representative John McCormack of Irish American South Boston sent greetings to the American Jewish Congress's November 1933 Dorchester/Mattapan rally against Nazi antisemitism.[13]

The university over which Conant presided itself remained largely indifferent to the persecution of Germany's Jews and displayed a shocking lack of awareness of Nazism. This is best revealed in a mock debate Harvard held on Adolf Hitler's conduct in late October 1934. After two teams of Harvard undergraduates presented arguments, a panel consisting largely of Harvard professors acquitted the Fuehrer on two of four charges. The panel "ruled out as irrelevant" the subject of Hitler's "persecution of Jews." By a 4–1 vote, it found Hitler guilty of having General Kurt von Schleicher killed without trial. Von Schleicher had preceded Hitler as chancellor and was murdered by the SS during the "Blood Purge" of June 30, 1934, directed primarily against the *Sturmabteilung* (SA) leadership. The panel also found Hitler guilty, by a 3–2 vote, of sending men to concentration camps without definite charges. But by 3–2 votes, it acquitted Hitler of "invading the sanctity of homes without warrant" and of ordering the murder of seventy-seven Germans in the June 30 purge. The panel accepted Hitler's own figure of seventy-seven slain; it was probably at least twice that, and may have exceeded a thousand.[14]

Harvard's student newspaper, the *Harvard Crimson*, strongly condemned another mock trial of Hitler staged in New York City the previous spring, which had devoted serious attention to his persecution of the Jews and found him guilty of "a crime against civilization." Sponsored by the American Jewish Congress, the AFL, and approximately fifty other Jewish and liberal groups, it was held at Madison Square Garden before 20,000 people. Twenty "witnesses for public opinion" had presented "The Case of Civilization Against Hitlerism." They included former New York governor Al Smith, New York City mayor Fiorello H. La Guardia, Rabbi Stephen S. Wise, the honorary president of the American Jewish Congress, AFL vice-president Matthew Woll, and Senator Millard Tydings. Chancellor Harry Woodburn Chase of New York University explicitly denounced the Nazis for denying Jews the right to study and teach in universities. He declared that it was the duty of all "teachers, scientists, and men of letters" to "resist with all their power" Nazi Germany's higher education policies – a view not shared by Conant or the other presidents of elite universities. The event's organizers had invited Germany's ambassador, Hans Luther, to defend Hitler, but he had declined. The *Harvard Crimson* dismissed the Madison Square Garden mock trial as having "proved nothing" because Hitler had not been provided with a defense. Moreover, it claimed that the audience, containing many Jews, was "rabidly prejudiced."[15]

Almost a year and a half later, in March 1936, one of Harvard's leading history professors, William L. Langer, a renowned authority on the World War, vigorously defended Nazi Germany's recent occupation of the Rhineland and disputed the charge that Hitler was a militarist. Hitler's retaking of the Rhineland removed a critical obstacle blocking a German military invasion in the West. The victorious powers in the World War had demilitarized the Rhineland to prevent just such a scenario. Langer claimed that Hitler's motives were no different from those of the

French and the British. The latter had imposed an "unfair treaty" on Nazi Germany, which had rearmed to protect itself, "like everyone else." He insisted that "Hitler's desire to . . . control" the Rhineland was "perfectly understandable," because "it belongs to Germany, and is populated with Germans." The United States in such a situation would have acted just like Nazi Germany: "If . . . New York or Massachusetts were left unguarded against foreign enemies, our immediate instinct would be to fortify it, and that is just what Hitler has done with the Rhineland."[16] Langer was in a position to strongly influence Harvard students' view of contemporary European affairs.

Prominent Harvard alumni, student leaders, the *Harvard Crimson*, and several Harvard professors assumed a leading role in the ten-day welcome and reception accorded the Nazi warship *Karlsruhe* when it visited Boston in May 1934 on what the Nazi government described as a goodwill mission. President Conant did nothing to discourage this, although Boston's Jewish community was outraged. Boston's Port Authority had arranged the *Karlsruhe*'s visit in 1932, before the Nazis came to power in Germany. By May 1934, it was obvious that the Nazi government was fiercely persecuting the Jews, as well as political opponents of the regime, large numbers of whom had already been seized and confined in concentration camps.[17]

Massachusetts governor Joseph Ely and Boston mayor Frederick Mansfield nonetheless sponsored an official reception for the *Karlsruhe*, a 6,000-ton battle cruiser carrying a 589-man crew, a showpiece of Nazi Germany's navy. The crew included 119 naval cadets, the equivalent of Annapolis midshipmen, who were undergoing training on the vessel. Ely's lieutenant governor and the mayor were on hand to greet the Nazi warship as it sailed into Boston harbor flying the swastika and tied up at a berth next to the War of 1812 frigate *U.S.S. Constitution*, a venerated American patriotic symbol.[18] In the days that followed, leading members of the Harvard University community staged and were major participants in highly publicized social events designed to honor and entertain the warship's crewmen and officers, who loudly praised Adolf Hitler and the Nazi government.

When it was announced on the day of the Nazi warship's arrival that an "elaborate program" of "lavish reception[s]" was planned in Boston and Cambridge for its officers and crew, Boston's Jewish community erupted in protest. About five months before, Boston's Jews had vigorously protested to the U.S. State Department when the German consulate in Boston began openly displaying the swastika flag.[19] Conant had said

FIGURE 2.1. Dr. Hans Luther, Nazi Germany's ambassador to the United States, gives the Nazi salute on board the *Karlsruhe* during its visit to Boston, May 1934. Courtesy of the Boston Public Library, Print Department.

nothing. Rabbi Samuel Abrams declared that "the coming to our shores of the German battleship, flying the swastika, emblem of hate and darkness, should be condemned and protested in no uncertain terms." Jennie Loitman Barron, director of the Women's Division of the American Jewish Congress in Boston, stated that the city's greeting of the *Karlsruhe*, representing a nation that "savagely flouts every American principle," was "an insult to the Jewish people [and] . . . to every American citizen."[20]

These comments were ignored by Boston officials and prominent Harvard alumni, eager to welcome the *Karlsruhe* sailors, whose officers sported swastika pins on their caps. The Boston *Herald* noted that many of the officers' cabins displayed portraits of the "mustached man of destiny." Several Boston churches provided special religious services for the crewmen the day after their arrival. On May 16, a large bodyguard of Harvard students escorted four *Karlsruhe* cadets to the campus, where they were entertained at Lowell House.[21] The next evening, a supper dance to honor the warship's officers and crew was held at the Egyptian

Room of Boston's Brunswick Hotel. The affair's patrons included several prominent Harvard alumni, as well as Professor Francis P. Magoun, who served as chairman of Harvard's Modern Languages Division. Magoun was an ardent Nazi sympathizer who had urged Houghton Mifflin to issue an English edition of Hitler's *Mein Kampf.* According to the *Harvard Crimson*, Magoun was a close friend of Harvard president James B. Conant.[22]

Boston Jews on May 17 joined with an assortment of anti-fascist groups, including most prominently the National Student League (NSL), to mount a massive demonstration against the *Karlsruhe* at the Charlestown navy yard, where it was docked. The protestors confronted what the Boston *Herald* described as "one of the most formidable police forces ever concentrated" in Boston.[23] The several Harvard and Massachusetts Institute of Technology (MIT) students who carried signs marked "No Welcome for Persecutors of the Jews" were outnumbered by classmates who arrived determined to give the anti-Nazis "a good licking."[24] A large contingent from Harvard shouted "Up with Hitler!" and "Hurrah for the Nazi!" Members of the Harvard *Lampoon* staff, intending to mock the demonstrators, arrived in an automobile carrying students dressed as Hitler and Mussolini. The Boston *Post* commented that "[o]f the undergraduates who were in the crowds, less than 2 percent appeared to be in sympathy with the purposes of the demonstration."[25]

Before the protestors could gather for speeches in Charlestown's City Square, the police charged, mounted and on foot, injuring scores with clubs and fists. According to the Boston *Herald*, City Square resembled Red Square in Moscow, as police "singled out and subdued in hand to hand battle" all the march's leaders. However, several witnesses described police arrests as indiscriminate. Of twenty-one people arrested, two were from Harvard and two were MIT students. They were charged with inciting to riot, illegal handbill distribution, and disturbing the peace.[26]

Although Harvard's administration was publicly silent, several liberal professors denounced the police for making arrests without cause and for brutality. They insisted that there was no evidence that the students had incited a riot.[27] By contrast, the *Harvard Crimson*'s editorial justified the methods employed by the police. It also reprinted an editorial from the Dartmouth student newspaper supporting the police's "skull crunching," which remarked, "That supposedly intelligent students of two of the country's leading educational institutions should affiliate themselves with [such] a demonstration . . . seems remarkable to us." The *Crimson* praised Boston's police commissioner for the courtesy he showed to the

Karlsruhe's crew. Two years later, the *Crimson* continued to refer to the demonstration as "discourteous."[28] A judge sentenced seventeen of those arrested to prison terms of six months or more.[29]

MIT's administration, which had entertained a group of *Karlsruhe* cadets on campus, made no comment about the police's violent disruption of the City Square anti-Nazi rally. Dean Harold Lobdell, in fact, personally tore down posters in an MIT building advertising the demonstration. He also attempted to persuade Boston's newspapers not to report that MIT students were among the arrested protestors.[30]

The protest by Jews and other anti-fascists was overshadowed by a series of social events staged by Boston society leaders, many of them associated with Harvard, whose purpose was to convey appreciation for the Nazi warship's officers and men. As the police were breaking up the demonstration at the navy yard, many *Karlsruhe* cadets, escorted by Boston debutantes, were headed into Boston for a round of dinners and dances. Some rode in limousines driven by liveried chauffeurs. A sizeable number of *Karlsruhe* officers and cadets also attended Harvard's Military and Naval Ball, making it a "distinguished event," according to the *Harvard Crimson*.[31]

A few hours after the demonstration was suppressed, more than a thousand Bostonians, including Harvard faculty, assembled at the luxurious Copley Plaza Hotel to honor the officers and men of the *Karlsruhe*. The swastika flag hung over the stage alongside the Stars and Stripes. The *Jewish Advocate*, Boston's English-language Jewish newspaper, called this the "basest kind of blasphemy." The *Karlsruhe*'s commander gave what the Boston *Post* called "a stirring defense of the Nazi government," and other speakers denounced the Jewish-led boycott of German goods. Those in attendance gave the Nazi salute when the *Karlsruhe* band played both the "Star-Spangled Banner" and the Nazis' "Horst Wessel Song." Harvard German professor John Walz, later president of the Modern Language Association, was one of the speakers.[32] Several Harvard faculty members also attended the reception for the *Karlsruhe*'s officers and Nazi Germany's ambassador to the United States, Hans Luther, at the Newton estate of German consul Baron Kurt von Tippelskirch.[33]

Ambassador Luther visited Harvard a few days later as guest of the administration, touring the Germanic Museum and Widener Library. Concerned that Luther be insulated from anything critical of Nazism, his Harvard hosts "carefully protected" him from "the influence of an exhibition by [artist] Marta Adams, who [had] recently moved from Germany" because she found the Hitler regime distasteful.[34]

FIGURE 2.2. Officers and diplomats from Nazi Germany at Baron von Tippelskirch's estate in Newton, Massachusetts, May 1934. Left to right: (front row)
Baron Kurt von Tippelskirch, Nazi Germany's consul general in Boston; Captain
von Enderndorf of the *Karlsruhe*; Dr. Hans Luther, Nazi Germany's ambassador
to the United States; and Baroness von Tippelskirch and (back row) General Boetticher; Captain Witthoeft; and Lt. Commanders Gadow and Krabbe. Courtesy of
the Boston Public Library, Print Department.

When the *Karlsruhe* returned home to Germany the next month after
its eight-month world tour, Nazi defense minister General Werner von
Blomberg declared that the warship "had made friends for the Third
Reich in all places where she dropped anchor."[35] The crew considered
their reception in Boston the friendliest of any port in a trip that had taken
them three-quarters of the way around the world. Undoubtedly influenced
by the warm welcome Harvard and others in Boston had accorded the
Karlsruhe, German seamen were soon "carrying anti-Semitic... propaganda to 'ridiculous lengths'" in every American port in which they
docked.[36]

The *Karlsruhe* later patrolled the coast of Spain during that country's
Civil War and helped spearhead the German invasion of Norway in
April 1940. It effectively protected Nazi landing parties at Kristiansand

FIGURE 2.3. Diplomats from Nazi Germany at Harvard's Germanic Museum, May 1934. Left to right: Baron Kurt von Tippelskirch, Nazi Germany's consul general in Boston; Dr. Hans Luther, Nazi Germany's ambassador to the United States; and Gerrit von Haeften, attaché at the German embassy in Washington. Courtesy of the Boston Public Library, Print Department.

in southern Norway, before a British submarine torpedoed and badly damaged it, requiring the German navy to sink it.[37]

Harvard's administration in many ways helped legitimate the Nazi regime during the next several years. It did not hesitate to publicly defend the Class of 1909's invitation to Ernst (Putzi) Hanfstaengl, a Nazi leader and close friend of Adolf Hitler, to attend the class's twenty-fifth reunion at the Harvard commencement on June 21–22, 1934. Hanfstaengl served as the Nazi party's foreign press chief. The Harvard administration joined with prominent alumni and the *Harvard Crimson* in extending Hanfstaengl a warm welcome. It made every effort to stifle protests against Hanfstaengl's participation in the commencement ceremonies. As they had with the *Karlsruhe*, Boston's Jewish leaders strongly denounced Hanfstaengl's visit, but to no avail. The appearance at Harvard of one of Hitler's inner circle again illustrated that Boston socialites, in these years very influential in Harvard's affairs, were favorably disposed toward Nazism.[38]

Scion of a wealthy Munich family, Hanfstaengl had been one of Hitler's earliest backers, joining his Nazi movement in 1922 largely because he shared Hitler's virulent antisemitism.[39] After the abortive Beer Hall Putsch in 1923, Hitler had taken refuge at Hanfstaengl's country villa outside Munich, where he was arrested. Hanfstaengl provided important financial assistance to the Nazi party when it was first establishing itself in the early 1920s. He also later claimed to have introduced the stiff-armed Nazi salute and *Sieg Heil* chant, modeled on a gesture and a shout he had used as a Harvard football cheerleader.[40]

Hitler considered Hanfstaengl valuable because his wealth, air of sophistication, and fluency in English helped legitimate the Nazi party in conservative, upper-class circles, both in Germany and abroad. Hanfstaengl was descended on his mother's side from a prominent Back Bay family, the Sedgwicks, which facilitated his entry into influential Boston Brahmin circles.[41]

Hanfstaengl was determined to use his office to aggressively spread Nazi antisemitism outside Germany. On April 3, 1933, he informed American diplomat James G. McDonald that "the Jews must be crushed." Hanfstaengl called the Jews "the vampire sucking German blood." McDonald noted in his diary that after defending "unqualifiedly" the Nazis' April 1 boycott of Jewish stores, Hanfstaengl "launched into a terrifying account of Nazi plans." April 1 was "only a beginning." Hanfstaengl declared to McDonald that "[o]ur plans go much further." Noting that Germany during the World War had taken 1.5 million prisoners, Hanfstaengl stated that "600,000 Jews would be simple." The Nazis would assign a storm trooper to each Jew, and "in a single night it could be finished." McDonald was not certain whether this meant that the Nazi plan was for the imprisonment of Germany's Jewish population, or its "wholesale slaughter."[42]

Hanfstaengl did not hesitate to express his virulent antisemitism in the Harvard College twenty-fifth anniversary report of the Class of 1909. He accused the U.S. government of forcing the sale of the New York branch of his family's Munich-based art reproduction business, considered "alien property" during World War I, to a Jewish firm for far less than its market value. Advancing the Nazi slur that Jews were war profiteers and parasites, he declared, "This may serve as a hint... as to who in reality won the war." Hanfstaengl also informed his classmates that, in 1922, "I ran into the man who has saved Germany and civilization – Adolf Hitler."[43]

Hanfstaengl also supervised the production of, and composed the music for, the fiercely antisemitic *Hans Westmar*, one of the earliest Nazi propaganda films. It was based on Hans Heinz Ewer's 1932 book romanticizing storm trooper Horst Wessel, the most prominent Nazi martyr, killed by anti-fascist workers in 1930. "Hans Westmar," a phonetic substitute for Horst Wessel, opened in New York City in December 1933. It portrayed Jews as villains spreading the viruses of Communism and "internationalism," and as cowards afraid of street fighting. During the filming, uniformed Nazis forced bearded Jews to act the part of Communists and cry "Red Front!" and "Hail Moscow!" from rooftops as a Nazi procession passed. In another scene, an "overfed Jew" greedily devoured a fat goose, while at a nearby table "a faint and hungry 'Aryan'" shared a meager herring with his wife. While the film was in production the *New York Times* noted that in Germany "there is much misgiving among the Jews about the effect of its exhibition on the public, especially in country districts where a few Jewish families live in virtual isolation." Hanfstaengl indicated that he was considering taking the film, which he had already screened for Benito Mussolini, to show at the Harvard reunion.[44]

In late March 1934, American newspapers reported that the chief marshal of the Harvard twenty-fifth reunion Class of 1909, Dr. Elliott Carr Cutler, Harvard Medical School professor and a leading heart surgeon, had invited Hanfstaengl to come to the June commencement ceremony as one of his aides, a position of honor. Cutler was a close friend of Hanfstaengl's and during medical school had spent a summer with him in the Bavarian Alps and in Munich. This sparked outrage from Jewish and other alumni, and from Boston's major Jewish newspaper, the *Advocate*.[45] The first to publicly protest against the Nazi leader's visit was Benjamin Halpern, Harvard Class of 1932, a Jew who was then a Harvard graduate student, and later a distinguished historian of Zionism.[46] He was immediately joined by Dr. William Leland Holt, Harvard Class of 1900, who charged in a letter to President Conant that the invitation implied Harvard administration approval of the Nazi regime.[47] Conant could have easily denounced the visit, but did not.

The administration refused to debate the issue, claiming it was entirely an alumni matter. As the commencement approached, it emphasized that "Ernst Hanfstaengl is a Harvard man" who would "be warmly welcomed."[48] The *Harvard Crimson* editorialized that Hanfstaengl, "as a man of ability and distinction," deserved consideration as a chief marshal's aide. It called the protests "extremely childish." The editors did not believe politics should "enter into this question."[49] Shortly before his arrival in the United States, the *Crimson* called for Harvard to bestow on the Nazi official an honorary degree, as a mark "of honor appropriate to his high position in the government of a friendly country."[50]

Hanfstaengl's visit to Harvard quickly became a national issue. The Baltimore *Sun*, which condemned Hanfstaengl's visit as insulting to "racial groups" whose relatives the Nazis had "tortured and harassed," called the *Crimson*'s suggestion "puerile" and "absurd."[51]

Fearing an embarrassing demonstration at the commencement, Cutler and Hanfstaengl decided it would be better for the Nazi official to come just as a regular member of his class. Nonetheless, a large crowd shouting anti-Nazi slogans greeted Hanfstaengl's ship when it arrived in New York, presaging trouble in Cambridge. Well-known New York *World-Telegram* columnist Heywood Broun noted that there were "hundreds of thousands of people [in New York] who have relatives and friends . . . suffering at this very moment under the heavy hand of Hitler."[52]

By contrast, Harvard administrators and distinguished alumni extended a friendly greeting to the Nazi official when he arrived in Cambridge. Elliott Carr Cutler entertained Hanfstaengl at his Brookline home, where he discussed German politics and history with Harvard's former president, A. Lawrence Lowell. The Boston *Globe* reported that "Hanfstaengl's voice was of worship every time he mentioned the name of Hitler." Hanfstaengl was also received by classmate Louis Agassiz Shaw, distinguished professor at Harvard Medical School, at his Beverly Farms estate, where he was an overnight guest.[53]

The next day, a "fashionable and sporty" party gave the Nazi official a "cordial welcome" at the home of George Saltonstall West, Harvard Class of 1910. After luncheon, Hanfstaengl accompanied the group to the country club horse races, where he shared a box with West, Dr. Shaw, and their wives. Hanfstaengl placed only one bet, choosing the horse, he told reporters, because its jockey wore a brown shirt like the Nazis. After the races, he attended a tea at the house of President Conant, who shook his hand. In his autobiography, published in 1970, long after the Holocaust, Conant continued to insist that Hanfstaengl "had every right" to participate in the reunion.[54]

Boston newspapers repeatedly emphasized how fond his Harvard classmates were of Hanfstaengl. Several of them were delighted to pose with

FIGURE 2.4. Ernst Hanfstaengl (right) with Frank J. Reynolds at the Harvard Class of 1909 reunion, June 1934. Courtesy of the Boston Public Library, Print Department.

him for newspaper photographers. These men included many of the nation's leading financiers, industrialists, educators, corporate attorneys, scientists, and physicians. The Boston *Globe* reported that Hanfstaengl was the most popular attendee at the Class of 1909 party held at the Harvard Union on the evening of June 18, where he was "surrounded constantly by his classmates." According to the Boston *Post*, "all through dinner . . . he was besieged by the[ir] sons and daughters . . . who sought his autograph."[55] Hanfstaengl recalled for his classmates the "many long nights" he and Hitler had spent at his villa near Munich, "talking of 'the day,'" and he exclaimed excitedly to his rapt listeners, "Now the day is here."[56] The following day the Boston *Herald*, a newspaper with a large circulation in the business community, described the Nazi official as the "Life of the Party" when his class gathered for a field day on the 5,000-acre estate of railroad tycoon Frederick H. Prince, whose fortune during the Depression was estimated at $250 million.[57]

FIGURE 2.5. Rabbi Joseph Solomon Shubow (center), who confronted Ernst Hanfstaengl in Harvard Yard in June 1934 and demanded to know whether the Nazi
plan for the Jews was extermination. Courtesy of the Boston Public Library, Print
Department.

As the Nazi official partied with his classmates, campus and municipal police carefully prepared to suppress any protests against Hanfstaengl's visit. Following instructions from the Harvard administration,
campus police tore down scores of anti-Nazi stickers that protestors had
attached to the fence around Harvard Yard during the night. These signs
proclaimed, "Drive the Nazi Butcher Out," and suggested that Harvard
award Hanfstaengl the degree of "Doctor of Pogroms."[58] Each day during
the week prior to commencement, Boston police arrested Jews and other
anti-fascists picketing the German consulate, charging them with illegally
displaying signs. The Municipal Court judge denounced the defendants
as "troublemakers," fined them, and declared, "I cannot understand why
you fight European battles in Boston."[59]

The joyous festivities were briefly interrupted when Rabbi Joseph
Solomon Shubow confronted Hanfstaengl as he was talking to reporters

FIGURE 2.6. Ernst Hanfstaengl speaking with newspaper reporters at Harvard, June 1934. Courtesy of the Boston Public Library, Print Department.

in Harvard Yard. Rabbi Shubow demanded to know the meaning of a remark Hanfstaengl had made to the press on June 17, that "everything would soon be settled for the Jews in Germany." "Tremb[ling] violently," Rabbi Shubow cried out, "My people want to know...does it mean extermination?" The Nazi official replied that he did not care to discuss political matters, and the Harvard police immediately ushered Hanfstaengl away to President Conant's house.[60]

The "traditional formality" that the Harvard administration so prized at commencement exercises was "momentarily shattered" when two young women chained themselves to a railing near the speakers' platform and interrupted President Conant's remarks by chanting, "Down with Hitler!" The Boston *Post* noted that "a record of three centuries of peaceful and orderly exercises centering around commencement at Harvard was broken." Policemen immediately arrested the two women. The disturbance shocked and angered the Harvard administration and an alumni audience that included "some of the wealthiest and most distinguished men in the country."[61] By contrast, Dr. Samuel Margoshes,

FIGURE 2.7. Ernst Hanfstaengl (center, with raised arm) in the Harvard Class of 1909 parade, June 1934. Courtesy of the Boston Public Library, Print Department.

Zionist leader and editor of the New York Yiddish newspaper *The Day*, spoke with awe of the young women, extolling their "magnificent and undying courage."[62] Shortly after the disturbance in Harvard Yard, other demonstrators began a protest against the university's welcoming of Hanfstaengl in Harvard Square, but police squelched it by immediately arresting those who attempted to speak, seven in all.[63]

Although President Conant privately persuaded a judge to have the charges dropped against the two women arrested in the Yard, he declared that he had "very little sympathy" when the seven arrested in the Square received very harsh sentences. The demonstrators, six men and a woman, were charged with disturbing the peace and speaking without a permit. They were initially sentenced to thirty days in jail, but when they appealed, the Superior Court ordered each confined in the Middlesex House of Correction for six months at hard labor and fined $20. In arguing for stiff punishment, the district attorney declared that the defendants had "on a day ... sacred in the eyes of educated people ... staged a demonstration against one of the most respected of institutions." The Superior Court judge agreed, handing down sentences of six months at hard labor "as a deterrent to those who hold views similar to yours."[64]

President Conant refused to intervene after the Superior Court sentencing, claiming that Harvard was not concerned with actions that occurred outside university grounds. He declared that the protest in Harvard Square "seemed to me very ridiculous." President Conant rejected a professor's private request that the university "register its disapproval of the severe sentence imposed," although in his reply he expressed doubt that it would serve society's best interests. He warned the professor, however, not to quote him on that.[65]

Conant was unsympathetic when Mrs. Joseph Dauber, the wife of one of the convicted demonstrators, a recent MIT graduate, appealed to him to "disclaim any support" for the "cruelly repressive measures" the Superior Court had imposed after ordering her husband imprisoned for six months. She informed Conant that the prison permitted her to visit her husband only one half hour a week, and only allowed him to write a letter to her every two weeks. On Mrs. Dauber's letter, Conant or his secretary scrawled "write regrets," indicating he would do nothing.[66]

Upon Hanfstaengl's triumphant return to Germany, Hitler bestowed on him the honor of opening the sixth convention of the Nazi party at Nuremberg in September 1934. As the Fuehrer made his entrance amid the throngs that cheered him as the "Savior of Germany," Hanfstaengl praised the adoption by the Third Reich of the doctrine of the "purity of the race."[67]

President Conant later that fall refused the Nazi official's offer to the university of a $1,000 scholarship to permit a Harvard student to study in Germany for a year, including six months in Munich. Conant explained that the Harvard Corporation was "unwilling to accept a gift from one who has been so closely associated with the leadership of a political party which has inflicted damage on the universities of Germany."[68] The Harvard Club of Berlin, whose secretary, a General Electric executive, was president of the American Chamber of Commerce in the German capital, passed a resolution protesting the rejection of Hanfstaengl's scholarship. The club fully endorsed Nazi higher education policy, which it claimed was part of a necessary "program of national sanitation."[69]

In Germany, the Nazi press noted that the *Harvard Crimson* had denounced the Corporation's decision, claiming it deprived students of

FIGURE 2.8. Dr. Hans Luther (right), Nazi Germany's ambassador to the United States, presents Roscoe Pound, dean of Harvard Law School, with an honorary degree from the University of Berlin, September 1934. Courtesy of the Boston Public Library, Print Department.

the opportunity to study in "one of the greatest cultural centers of the world." The Nazis declared that the *Crimson*'s dissent exposed a wide gulf between a promising postwar American student generation that resembled Hitler's young followers and a decadent faculty "still clinging to old-fashioned Wilsonism."[70]

Columnist Paul Mallon reported that feeling was widespread at Harvard that the university had turned down Hanfstaengl's offer because of the adverse public reaction to Harvard Law School dean Roscoe Pound's recent acceptance, in a public ceremony on campus, of an honorary degree from the University of Berlin, personally presented by Nazi Germany's ambassador Hans Luther. Luther and Nazi Germany's consul, Kurt von Tippelskirch, had hosted a luncheon for Dean Pound and members of the Law School faculty after the ceremony.[71]

Dean Pound was known to be sympathetic to Hitler, which President Conant acknowledged in a personal conversation with Felix Frankfurter, the lone Jew on the Harvard Law School faculty.[72] Pound spent part of his vacation in Nazi Germany during the summers of 1934, 1936, and 1937. In July 1934, he attended a full-day performance of the virulently antisemitic passion play at Oberammergau in Bavaria (described in Chapter 4), and pronounced it "wonderful."[73] Describing his impressions of Bavaria to the Paris *Herald* on August 4, 1934, Pound declared, "I never saw any indication of tension or fear of the future." He claimed that freedom of speech prevailed in the Third Reich: "People discussed Hitler and everything else openly, just as we talk of Roosevelt in the United States."[74] On his return to the United States, Pound expressed his admiration for Hitler in the New York *Herald Tribune* and claimed that in Nazi Germany "there was no persecution of Jewish scholars or of Jews ... who had lived in [Germany] for any length of time."[75]

When Felix Frankfurter learned that Ambassador Luther was to present Dean Pound with his degree at the Law School, he protested to President Conant that Harvard was tying "a tail to the Nazi kite" – that is, lending its prestige to the Hitler regime. He did not ask Conant to forbid Pound from accepting the degree, but he did not want the ceremony held at Harvard. Conant replied that there was nothing he could do, and that, moreover, he "could not stay away" from the ceremony himself "without insulting a friendly government." Deeply disappointed, Frankfurter terminated the meeting after fifteen minutes and left. He noted in a personal memorandum about the encounter: "I abstained from pointing out to Conant that to exercise a veto power on Pound's personal right to accept the degree from Germany is one thing; to allow Langdell Hall [the Law School building] to be turned into a Nazi holiday quite another."[76]

Unlike Conant, Frankfurter refused invitations from both Dean Pound and Ambassador Luther to attend the ceremony. He wrote to Pound: "I cannot attend any function in honor of a representative of a government which Mr. Justice Holmes has accurately characterized as 'a challenge to civilization.'" Frankfurter declared that he could not "suppress my sense of humiliation that ... my beloved Law School, the centre of Anglo-American law, should ... confer special distinction upon an official representative of enthroned lawlessness."[77]

The Harvard administration's friendly reception of Hanfstaengl at the June commencement provided a rationale for Yale University president James Rowland Angell's decision to welcome a delegation of Italian Fascist students to his campus in October 1934. The *Yale Daily News* rushed to President Angell's support, justifying his decision by "cit[ing] President Conant's hospitality to Ernst F. S. Hanfstaengl last June." The *Harvard Crimson* ran a news story entitled "Yale Follows Harvard's Lead Greeting Italians."[78]

President Conant officially welcomed the Italian Fascist student delegation to Harvard several days before it visited Yale. The 350-student delegation, including about forty athletes, was touring American campuses on behalf of the Mussolini government to promote friendship between Italy and the United States. Conant greeted 160 of the Italian Fascist students at Harvard's University Hall, the administration building, on October 5, 1934, and in a brief address reviewed the history of Harvard. Harvard's president then shook the hand of each Italian Fascist student. The president of Harvard's Student Council, E. Francis Bowditch, and a group of Harvard undergraduates then led Mussolini's emissaries on a tour of the campus. The remaining members of the Italian student delegation, who spent the morning sightseeing in Boston, joined the 160 for lunch at seven of Harvard's undergraduate houses.[79]

During the afternoon, the Italian Fascist student athletes participated in a track meet at Harvard Stadium, competing against representatives of New England colleges, including Harvard, MIT, Brown, Holy Cross, Boston College, and Boston University. It was one of the largest track meets that had ever been held in the East. The track meet began with a parade of the entire Italian Fascist student delegation into the stadium, preceded by Italian trumpeters and accompanied by the Harvard band. When the delegation reached the center of the field, it sang the Fascist song. The *Harvard Crimson* praised Conant for welcoming the Italian Fascist students to the university and asserted that "[t]heir reception, tour of the buildings, and the track meet . . . will be a step towards establishment of a close bond of friendship and understanding between the two nations."[80]

A few months later, in March 1935, the Harvard administration permitted Nazi Germany's consul in Boston, Baron von Tippelskirch, to place a wreath bearing the swastika emblem in the university's Memorial Church (Appleton Chapel). It was laid below a tablet Harvard had attached to the chapel wall "recognizing the heroism" and honoring the memory of four Harvard men killed in action fighting for Germany during the World War. The Boston *Post* declared that "for the first time since she received Ernst F. S. Hanfstaengl, Chancellor Hitler's right-hand man, at his class reunion last June did Harvard, by allowing the swastika to be displayed in her chapel, recognize and accept the new German Nazi state." It noted that the ceremony, which occurred on the day Germany annually commemorated its war dead, was attended by "a small group of prominent Harvard faculty members" and visiting professors from Nazi Germany. Some Harvard students protested against the placement of the "swastika wreath" on campus by an official representing a nation that "conducts hysterical racial massacres." But the *Harvard Crimson* supported the administration's commitment to what it called "Harvard's breadth of mind."[81]

On April 30, 1935, President Conant personally received Mussolini's ambassador to the United States, Augusto Rosso, and his consul general in Boston, Ermanne Armao, at his office at Harvard. President Conant's secretary, Harper Woodward, then escorted the Fascist diplomats on a tour of Widener Library, the Memorial Chapel, the Indoor Athletic Building, and Lowell House.[82]

Although Conant turned down the Hanfstaengl scholarship, Harvard chose not to follow the example of Williams College, whose president, Tyler Dennett, terminated student exchanges with German universities in April 1936. About sixty students from Nazi Germany attended American colleges and universities each year, solicited by schools in this country, while many Americans studied in Nazi Germany. Hanfstaengl, in fact, noted in October 1935 that the enrollment of Harvard students at the University of Munich had greatly increased since Conant had turned down his scholarship offer.[83]

Harvard continued the student exchanges, even though the German official in charge of them publicly announced in April 1936 that his government sent its students abroad to serve as "political soldiers of the Reich." German youths studying at foreign universities were required to first receive special training in "the principles of National Socialism." They also had to present to the Reich Ministry of Education a certificate from a Nazi party functionary attesting to their enthusiasm for Nazism. The Hitler government regarded exchange students as "an important element in Germany's foreign propaganda."[84]

Stephen Duggan, director of the Institute of International Education, which encouraged American student exchanges with foreign universities, in late 1937 correctly predicted that "Harvard, Yale, Columbia, Princeton," and other American universities that provided fellowships for students from Nazi Germany would remain impervious to mounting calls to terminate them. Nor, he added, would "any of the fine women's colleges – Barnard, Vassar, Bryn Mawr, Holyoke, Smith, Wellesley, and Radcliffe – which have had German exchange students practically every year," agree to join a proposed boycott. Duggan noted that many of America's "ablest" students were anxious to study in Nazi Germany in order "to see a modern French Revolution in actual operation."[85]

Harvard contributed significantly to the Hitler regime's effort in 1936 to gain international respectability by accepting the University of Heidelberg's invitation to send a representative to the 550th anniversary ceremonies of Germany's oldest institution of higher learning. More than twenty other American colleges and universities participated in the Heidelberg ceremonies. By contrast, no British university was willing to send a representative.

The Nazis wanted to favorably influence foreign perceptions of Germany as they embarked on a major rearmament program and stepped up persecution of the Jews. Germany reinstituted military conscription in March 1935. Shortly before Berlin was swept by savage antisemitic rioting in July, the *New York Times* quoted Propaganda Minister Josef Goebbels declaring, "We do not want the Jew.... Certain classes of intellectuals have interposed that, after all, the Jew is also a human being. Well... the flea is an animal, but it is not a very pleasant animal." In September, the Nazis implemented the Nuremberg race laws, which deprived Jews of citizenship. Hitler sent his troops into the demilitarized Rhineland in March 1936, undermining the postwar security arrangement that prevented a German invasion of the West.[86] The Nazis believed that by hosting scores of distinguished academic guests from the United States and other Western democracies at an elaborate, carefully controlled, four-day festival, they could greatly enhance the prestige of the Nazi university, and of the government itself, outside Germany.

In the months prior to the University of Heidelberg's anniversary commemoration, President Conant communicated several times with President Nicholas Murray Butler of Columbia and President James Rowland Angell of Yale, in order to more effectively deflect criticism of their universities' decision to send delegates to the Nazi festival. Each designated as its representative a professor or administrator who was traveling in Europe at the time of the celebration, standard practice when an American university accepted such an invitation from a European counterpart.[87] Harvard was represented by Dr. George D. Birkhoff, dean of the faculty of the College of Arts and Sciences and Perkins Professor of Mathematics. The University of Heidelberg did not invite Princeton University to participate.

This was probably because the Nazis tied the independent Institute for Advanced Study, located in Princeton, New Jersey, to Princeton University. The Institute had provided a faculty position for the refugee physicist Albert Einstein, whom the Nazis fiercely detested.[88]

After taking power in January 1933, the Nazis had quickly tightened party control over all German universities and suppressed all academic freedom, which was widely reported in the American press. German university students were in the forefront of the movement to Nazify German higher education. The German professoriate actively promoted the Nazi project and made vital contributions to it. As historian Max Weinreich has noted, "German scholars from the beginning to the end of the Hitler era worked hand in glove with the murderers of the Jewish people."[89]

The public book burnings staged at universities across the Reich in May 1933 underscored faculty and student support for Nazi antisemitism and anti-intellectualism. Students campaigned to destroy scholarly works they deemed "un-German," including anything written by Jews. About 40,000 people gathered to watch the bonfire near the University of Berlin, in which more than 20,000 books were destroyed. A little more than a week later, the University of Heidelberg staged its book burning, following a torchlight procession in which Nazi storm troopers marched alongside the student dueling corps "in full regalia, booted and sword-belted."[90]

The Nazis swiftly expelled nearly all Jews from university faculty positions, at least 800 in all by the 1934–35 academic year. The Jews forced out of the professoriate included many scholars of international renown, like Albert Einstein, Richard Courant, Max Born, James Franck, and Ernst Cassirer. In April 1933, the German government also passed a law severely limiting the enrollment of Jewish students in universities. Those few who remained were required to carry a red card of "non-Aryanism," while so-called "German" students were issued a "white card of honor." Many German universities initiated severely discriminatory policies against Jews even before the Nazi government required them to do so. Less than three months after the Nazi takeover, for example, the University of Hamburg refused to admit Jews any longer.[91]

By 1936, when the Nazis scheduled the anniversary commemoration, they were in complete control of the University of Heidelberg. The rector, Wilhelm Groh, announced in the summer of 1935 that only professors committed to advancing the Nazi revolution in the universities belonged on the faculty, and that even those Christians who were married to Jews should be removed. Groh habitually wore a military uniform to academic functions.[92] Between 1933 and 1936, the University of Heidelberg discharged forty-four faculty members for "racial, religious, or political reasons." No other faculty there protested these dismissals. Heidelberg required that its students join Nazi party organizations and frequently attend speeches by Nazi officials.[93]

In an action of enormous political significance, the Nazis replaced the statue of Athena, Greek goddess of wisdom, over the entrance to Heidelberg's main classroom building with a large bronze eagle, which they intentionally pointed west toward France, their enemy. The university substituted a new inscription, "To the German Spirit," and a golden swastika in place of the old "To the Eternal Spirit."[94]

The German universities incorporated the Nazi outlook in their curricula, in the sciences as well as the arts. Reich minister of culture and education Bernhard Rust announced in January 1935 that Nazi race theory would constitute the foundation of all university studies. Max Weinreich noted that German scholarship of the mid-1930s "looks like a gigantic assembly line working toward one aim" – the campaign against the Jews and preparation for war.[95] University anthropologists and biologists contributed significantly to the elaboration of a virulently antisemitic "racial science" that the Nazis introduced into school curricula. Law school professors similarly helped the Nazi state fashion and refine antisemitic legislation and provided justification for Nazi legal initiatives. They presented papers at a 1936 conference on "Jewry and Jurisprudence." Richard Evans notes that the University of Heidelberg's Social and Economic Sciences Faculty "focused its research on population, agricultural economics, and the vaguely named 'spatial research' which in fact was focused on accumulating knowledge relevant to the proposed future expansion of the Reich in the pursuit of 'living space.'" Because of the Nazis' exaltation of military force, German university students devoted about one-third of their time to paramilitary exercises and drill.[96]

In 1935, the University of Heidelberg became one of the two principal centers for the propagation of what the Nazis called "Aryan Physics," reflecting the sharp deterioration of educational standards under the Nazis. In December 1935, in a ceremony attended by leading German academics and industrialists that concluded with the Horst Wessel song, the University of Heidelberg Physics Institute was renamed the Philipp-Lenard-Institut, after the school's best-known professor, a Nobel laureate and longtime Hitler supporter. Lenard's mission was to remove what he called "Jewish science" from physics. In the principal speech at the dedication, Dr. Wacker, substituting for Education Minister Rust, who was ill, declared that "[t]he Negro or the Jew will view the same world in a different way from the German investigator."[97]

The next day "an imposing number of German physicists" gathered at the Philipp-Lenard-Institut to declare their commitment to combating "Jewish evil." Professor Dr. Tirala, speaking on "Nordic Race and Science," attributed the principal scientific discoveries since ancient times to "Nordic" investigators. Professor Lenard concluded by declaring that "the Jew is strikingly lacking in appreciation of Truth" and urging those present to "continue energetically the fight against the Jewish spirit."[98]

In early 1936, Lenard published the first volume of his four-volume *Deutsche Physik*, printed in Gothic type to emphasize its "Germanness" (*Deutschtum*).[99] Lenard intended his work to serve as the principal text for university students on Aryan physics. In it, he asserted that "[s]cience ... is racial and conditioned by blood."[100] Heidelberg student leaders embraced Lenard's outlook. For example, in the German academic journal *Deutsche Mathematik*, Fritz Kubach, Reichsleader of the German Student Body in the Department of Mathematics, a national position, demanded that the "fundamental questions of Mathematics" be "handl[ed] ... on a racial basis," which required "the destruction of the ... influence of Jews" in the field.[101]

The leading members of the University of Heidelberg's medical faculty enthusiastically promoted what the Nazis called "racial hygiene," which involved sterilizing people they considered "defective." Professor Hans Runge supervised hundreds of forced sterilizations at the university's women's clinic. Heidelberg professor Carl Schneider became prominent in the Nazi government's "program to systematically murder the mentally ill and handicapped."[102]

All this notwithstanding, Harvard accepted the invitation to participate in the University of Heidelberg's anniversary celebration on March 2, 1936, several days after the leading British universities had publicly announced their refusal. The *New York Times* on February 28 reported that Britain's preeminent universities, Oxford and Cambridge, had refused to send delegates to Heidelberg because of that university's discharge of forty-four faculty members "on the grounds of race, religion, and politics" and its "suppression of academic freedom." They were joined by the Universities of Manchester, Liverpool, Birmingham, London, Edinburgh, and Dublin. The *Times* noted that the scheduling of the ceremony on the date of the 1934 Blood Purge had resulted in "widespread suspicion" in Britain that "the anniversary is intended not to honor Heidelberg, but to glorify the Nazi regime." Moreover, the prestigious British scientific journal *Nature* charged that evidence in the British Museum revealed that the University of Heidelberg's charter had been issued in October 1385 and its first session had begun in October 1386, and thus the upcoming anniversary was not the school's 550th.[103]

In late March, the eminent British medical historian Charles Singer urged President Conant to reconsider his decision to send a Harvard representative to Heidelberg. The University of London professor asserted that "the scandals at Heidelberg have been even above the normal level of German universities both in gravity and number," and that faculty and students at the school shared and often expressed Philipp Lenard's views. Singer informed Conant that leading universities in the Netherlands, including Leyden, Utrecht, and Groeningen, had joined the British universities in refusing to send delegates.[104]

Two Jewish Harvard alumni warned Conant that the German government intended to use the Heidelberg celebration as a vehicle for spreading Nazi propaganda, just as it had at the recently concluded fourth Winter Olympiad held in the twin Bavarian towns of Garmisch and Partenkirchen.[105] Westbrook Pegler, columnist for the New York *World-Telegram*, noted that the Winter Olympics had proven that "the Nazis could not be trusted to refrain from political and military propaganda" when sponsoring international gatherings. The *New York Times* reported that, during the Winter Olympics, Garmisch and Partenkirchen had "become a forest of ... swastika flags," with the Nazi symbol "waving from every roof and draped from almost every balcony," while the flags of other nations were seldom visible. Foreign journalists covering the Winter Olympiad were stunned when State Secretary Funk of the Propaganda Ministry opened the games with a long speech extolling Hitler and Nazism.[106]

Many American observers agreed with William L. Shirer, one of the most experienced foreign correspondents in Germany, that Hitler had scored a major propaganda triumph at Garmisch and Partenkirchen. Shirer reported that the lavish ceremonies, modeled on the Nuremberg rallies, made the Nazis appear administratively efficient. Foreigners had also been impressed with the well-mannered treatment accorded visitors, which to Shirer and other American journalists familiar with the Nazis "of course seemed staged." The *New Republic* commented that the Nazis "unquestionably considered the Games ... as demonstrating international approval of the present regime."[107]

G. E. Harriman, executive secretary of the Non-Sectarian Anti-Nazi League, stressed that the Germans had spread "tremendous Nazi propaganda" at two international scholarly conferences they had recently hosted – the International Prison Congress in Berlin and the Congress for Health and Hygiene. Harriman reported that the foreign delegates attending these conferences had been "inundated with speeches by Nazi officials." In radio broadcasts throughout Germany and abroad, the Nazis had attempted to associate the prestige of "these gatherings of [distinguished] scientists" with the Hitler regime itself.[108]

Conant nevertheless remained steadfast in his commitment to have Harvard represented at Heidelberg, and he received strong support from the *Harvard Crimson*. In a press release announcing Harvard's acceptance of the Heidelberg invitation, Conant had declared that "the ancient ties by which the Universities of the world are united...are independent of...political conditions." He indicated that Harvard had already expressed "strong disapproval" of the "present [German] regime in respect to academic freedom" when it turned down the Hanfstaengl scholarship.[109] Those who wrote to challenge his decision received a standard reply from Conant's secretary insisting that Harvard's relationship with the University of Heidelberg was "purely academic," and that "the matter of politics should not enter." The *Harvard Crimson* similarly editorialized that "Heidelberg University is not the Nazi government" and even claimed that it had opposed Nazi policies. It condemned the British universities that had refused Heidelberg's invitation for "dragging politics in."[110]

Alvin Johnson, director of the New School for Social Research, branded Harvard's idea of an international community of scholars that included Nazi Germany a dangerous delusion. He explained that the Graduate Faculty over which he presided, composed of German exiles, had been established "as an expression...that there is no free German university."[111]

Conant considered Harvard's attendance at the Heidelberg ceremony part of a reciprocal exchange with German universities, whose representatives he had invited to participate in the Harvard tercentenary celebration scheduled for September 1936 and to present papers at the tercentenary conference preceding it. Harvard also planned to award honorary degrees to ten academics from Nazi Germany. These included Werner Heisenberg, who later directed Germany's effort to develop an atomic bomb during World War II, and Friedrich Bergius, whose chemical research proved

highly important to the Nazi war effort.[112] When Dr. Charles Singer
wrote to express strong opposition to sending a delegate to Heidelberg,
Conant replied that the logic of his position would require Harvard to ban
from its tercentenary events "German scientists who . . . have embraced
Nazi policy but nevertheless have remained distinguished members of the
world of scholars." Conant pronounced such a view "absurd."[113]

President Nicholas Murray Butler of Columbia aggressively defended
Harvard's invitation to Nazi academics to its tercentenary, insisting that
"academic relationships have no political implications." To the chairman
of a Columbia student committee established to protest that university's
decision to send a delegate to Heidelberg, Butler sneered, "Perhaps the
Germans might reply that they would send no representatives to the
Harvard Tercentenary Celebration next September because they do not
approve of what the newspapers here call the New Deal."[114]

Albert Einstein took sharp issue with Conant's and Butler's insistence
that academic celebrations had nothing to do with politics. He did not
attend the Harvard tercentenary celebration, although invited, because
he objected to participation by German academics who supported Nazi
policies.[115]

As Conant was making plans for Harvard's participation at Heidelberg, he refused requests from Jewish alumni and the mayor and city
council of Cambridge to reschedule the Harvard tercentenary celebration, which the administration had decided would take place on Rosh
Hashonah. Protests concerning the date had first been presented to the
Harvard administration in December 1934. The Cambridge city council
resolution asking for a change of date, adopted on April 21, 1936, noted
that many of Harvard's Jewish graduates, "from Justice Brandeis down
the ladder of fame have added to the glory and prestige of Harvard."
Conant claimed that the university was limited to only two dates in staging the tercentenary celebration – November 8, equivalent to October
28 on the Julian calendar used in 1636, or September 18, equivalent to
September 8. The former, which marked the passage of the act of the
Massachusetts Bay Colony's General Court that established the college,
fell on Sunday, the Christian day of worship, making it unacceptable to
the administration. It therefore chose September 18. Taking issue with
its Jewish critics, the administration saw nothing in the "dignified ceremonies" it planned that was "incompatible with the proper religious
observance" of the Jewish New Year.[116]

Conant joined with Butler and President Angell of Yale in drafting
a statement to be released if the Nazis at the Heidelberg ceremony

publicly claimed that the presence of delegates from American universities represented an endorsement of the Nazi regime. The statement, mostly Butler's work, criticized the "German government's actions in regard to academic freedom." It praised a long list of men who had made significant contributions to German culture. Butler noted to Conant that he had deliberately included Spinoza, invited to Heidelberg in 1673; Heine; and Mendelssohn, all of whom the Nazis considered Jews. The statement, however, was never issued. The congratulatory greeting that Columbia sent to Heidelberg did not mention any of the latter's Jewish scholars, or even Christians of Jewish ancestry.[117]

The University of Heidelberg anniversary celebration, held from June 27 to June 30, 1936, was highlighted by fiery Nazi speeches delivered by top officials of the Hitler regime and a massive military display. Harvard was represented by Dr. George Birkhoff, dean of the faculty of the College of Arts and Sciences, a mathematics professor who held antisemitic views. At the ceremonies he was in the company of Nazi propaganda minister Josef Goebbels, a Heidelberg graduate, who delivered a welcoming address; Nazi racial theorist Alfred Rosenberg; Education Minister Rust; Ernst Hanfstaengl; and SS chief Heinrich Himmler. As the flags of the participating countries were hoisted in the opening ceremonies, the spectators gave the Nazi salute. A brown-shirted storm trooper was stationed at each flagpole. During the first two days, "military bands and goose stepping...held the center of the stage," and no academic robes were visible.[118]

Following Protestant and Catholic religious services, on the second day, a Sunday, storm troopers drove the foreign guests to a military cemetery overlooking the city of Heidelberg for a memorial ceremony in honor of German soldiers killed during the World War. Presiding was Dr. Schmitthenner, professor of military science at Heidelberg, who proclaimed that Germany's dead had entered Valhalla. He declared that Germany had not been defeated in the World War, and that God had sent her "a great leader, Adolf Hitler, to...liberate the nation." Columbia University's representative, Arthur F. J. Remy, Villard professor of Germanic philology, characterized the service at the war cemetery as "very impressive and dignified."[119]

The anniversary celebration climaxed on June 29 and 30 with lengthy speeches praising Nazi educational policy by Education Minister Rust and Heidelberg philosophy professor Dr. Ernst Krieck, who became rector the next year. Heidelberg presented honorary degrees to foreign professors, including two from Harvard, Kirsopp Lake and Reginald Aldworth Daly.

Rust proclaimed that Germany had discarded forever "the old idea of science" as "abstract intellectual activity" and made scientific research conform to the Nazi outlook. He explained that German universities had removed Jews from their faculties because they belonged to an "alien race," which rendered them unable to understand the "order of nature." The next day Krieck similarly declared that science must be in accord "with the great racial and political task before us."[120]

Back in the United States, Conant remained adamant that Harvard had been "absolutely right" to send a representative. When President Angell wrote to report some alumni concern about the German press coverage, Conant refused to consider issuing the joint statement they had prepared with Butler. He declared, in fact, that the British universities would "live to regret the day when they broke diplomatic relations...with one section of the learned world." Conant considered the harangues by Rust and Krieck "no more absurd than some statements about the aims of education" he had heard expressed in the United States. Conant decided, moreover, that because of the Harvard tercentenary, he would refrain during the next six weeks from making any criticisms of the Nazi regime "out of politeness and good manners." Harvard, after all, was "being host to delegates from German universities."[121]

Harvard's administration remained indifferent to calls to boycott the Olympic Games scheduled to take place in Berlin in late July and August 1936, shortly after the Heidelberg anniversary celebration. As host of such a prestigious international gathering, Nazi Germany presented itself as a respectable, and responsible, member of the world community. The Hitler regime planned to make the Olympics a spectacle that would highlight the vigor and prowess of "Aryan" youth, and Germans' enthusiasm for Nazism. In February 1936, Nazi Germany's *Reichssportführer* (state commissar for sports), Dr. Hans von der Tschammer-Osten, approved publication of a handbook for German athletes that declared they must be "political fighters for Nazism." The German athlete should be fully conversant with Nazi principles and "above all...will be expected to defend convincingly Hitler's racial legislation." The handbook "sternly cautioned" German athletes against the "dangers resulting from inter-racial breeding."[122] Neither President Conant nor his colleagues Presidents Angell of Yale and Butler of Columbia joined the small group of college and university presidents that endorsed a boycott, which included Presidents Tyler Dennett of Williams, Daniel Marsh of Boston University, and Mary E. Woolley of Mount Holyoke.[123]

The Harvard Athletic Association (HAA), in fact, encouraged alumni to support American participation in the Berlin games. When the HAA in September 1935 mailed the ticket applications to that fall's Harvard-Yale football game to 35,000 alumni, it included on the back an appeal for funds to help pay the expenses of American athletes competing in Berlin. William J. Bingham, Class of 1916, Harvard's director of athletics, accused those favoring a boycott to protest Nazi policies of violating "all codes of sportsmanship." He accepted the assurances of Avery Brundage, president of the American Olympic Committee, who had recently visited Nazi Germany, that there was no discrimination there against Jewish athletes.[124] Brundage, an antisemite and later member of the America First Committee, drew this conclusion in part from conversations with German "Jewish leaders," always conducted in cafes in the presence of Nazi "chaperones."[125] Incredibly, Bingham claimed that the Olympics were awarded to a city, not a country, and that the German government had nothing whatsoever to do with the management of the games. In fact, the Hitler government tightly controlled preparations for the Olympics.[126]

Like Bingham, the *Harvard Crimson* supported U.S. participation in the Berlin Olympics and called on American athletes to "suppress their personal feelings about the internal affairs of the host." It declared that "intelligent men with first-hand information believe that the Nazi Government has fulfilled [its] pledges" not to discriminate against Jewish athletes.[127] Contrary to Brundage's claims, however, Americans had reliable information that Nazi Germany was systematically discriminating against and persecuting Jewish athletes.[128]

The Yale Athletic Board, like its Harvard counterpart, raised funds for the American Olympic athletes competing in Berlin. It sponsored a swimming meet in the campus gymnasium for this purpose. President Angell, himself a member of the Yale Athletic Board, defended the use of Yale facilities to provide funds for participants in the Berlin Olympics. He declared that once the American Olympic Committee decided to send a team to Berlin, the issue was settled. Angell noted that both Harvard and Princeton "felt it expedient to contribute to the expenses of the American group" traveling to Nazi Germany.[129]

The *Yale Daily News* and *Daily Princetonian* editorial boards joined the *Harvard Crimson* in opposing the boycott of the Berlin Olympics. The *Yale Daily News* dismissed as "absurd" the call of Jeremiah Mahoney, president of the U.S. Amateur Athletic Union, that the United States withdraw from participation. The *Daily News* argued that it was not clear that Nazi Germany had discriminated against Jewish athletes, and, even if it had, it was "highly questionable whether that would be any concern of the participating nations." Moreover, the Yale editors asserted, boycotting the Olympics implied "that no intercourse of any kind with Germany should be tolerated, that scientists, artists, men of letters, as well as athletes, should have nothing to do with Nazidom."[130]

Princeton's student newspaper contemptuously dismissed what it called "the almost ridiculous protests of those favoring an Olympic boycott." The *Daily Princetonian* declared in an editorial that advocates of a boycott made any "true sportsman or true American righteously ashamed that the United States" included in its population individuals so "narrow and selfish." Their arguments against participation in the Berlin games were "as groundless as they are warped." Just as Presidents Conant, Angell, and Butler had claimed that Nazi policies should not influence relationships among academics, the *Daily Princetonian* editors insisted that "[a]thletics have nothing to do with politics or race."[131]

The Berlin Olympics represented a significant propaganda triumph for Nazi Germany, which used them to project an image of modernism and efficiency. Its athletes accumulated more points than those of the United States, Italy's more than France's, and Japan's more than Britain's. Many concluded from the point totals and the frenzied Nazi crowds in the stadium that the Fascist societies were more dynamic than the seemingly decadent Western democracies, and that they represented the "wave of the future."[132]

Believing that Nazi universities still remained part of the "learned world," President Conant in March 1937 again responded favorably to an invitation from the University of Goettingen to send a delegate to its bicentennial celebration, also scheduled for "Purge Day," June 30, 1937. Goettingen prior to 1933 had been arguably the world's most prestigious university in physics and mathematics, but the Nazi transformation of German higher education had severely damaged its reputation. Goettingen had driven out its Jewish professors under the racial ruling applicable to civil servants. They included several of the world's most eminent scientists, like Richard Courant, Nobel laureate James Franck, and future Nobel laureate Max Born, directors of three of Goettingen's four institutes for physics and mathematics. In late 1933, Franz Boas observed that "the destruction of mathematics in the University of Goettingen ... was accomplished without a protest" from its non-Jewish faculty.[133]

Speaking for Harvard, Conant's secretary, Stephen H. Stackpole, announced that the university planned to be represented at Goettingen for the same reason it had chosen to send a delegate to Heidelberg the previous year. He quoted Conant's June 18, 1936, statement to alumni that "[i]n my opinion it was never more urgent than at the present moment to emphasize the unity of the learned world."[134]

Harvard astronomy professor Harlow Shapley informed Conant that "never in the history of the world has the gutting and disgrace of a scientific school been made so obvious as in the wrecking of the Institute[s] for Mathematical and Physical Sciences at Göttingen." Shapley at that moment was attempting to raise funds to provide for the support of "a brilliant young astrophysicist," Martin Schwarzschild, formerly of Goettingen and at that time exiled in Oslo. The Nazis had barred Schwarzschild from using Goettingen's observatory and library, even though he was the son of Germany's "greatest astrophysicist and astronomer in recent times," who had "loyally helped the Germans murder thousands of Americans during the Great War."[135]

By early April 1937, every English university had announced its refusal to send a delegate to Goettingen, except for Durham, whose chancellor, the Marquess of Londonderry, was considered Nazi Germany's greatest friend in British society. The *New York Times* reported that "Cambridge's refusal was almost a rebuke to Goettingen for having sent the invitation."[136]

Although Harvard's initial reaction to the invitation was favorable, not many American universities expressed interest in sending delegates. Among prestigious universities, only MIT announced it would be represented. Even there, many students fiercely protested their administration's decision. The MIT student newspaper, the *Tech*, bitterly denounced President Karl Compton's position, declaring that, "[i]n lending the name of a leading American scientific school to the Goettingen fete," MIT was "placing a feather in the cap of the educational gangsters... who control the present German system of schooling." The Goettingen bicentennial was not "a scientific meeting" in which MIT sent "a group of professors to exchange technological information and ideas," but a "Nazi celebration."[137]

In early May 1937, President Conant and the Harvard Corporation decided to send greetings to the University of Goettingen instead of a delegate but planned to keep the press from learning that until June. The news was, however, quickly leaked to the Boston *Globe*, which reported it on May 5. Harvard's letter of greeting to Goettingen expressed "sincere sorrow" at not being able to send a delegate and conveyed "the most fraternal of feelings." The Dallas *Morning News* noted that the messages Yale and Princeton sent Goettingen declining their invitations "were much more strongly negative" than Harvard's.[138]

Although President Conant did send Goettingen a warm letter of greeting, Harvard's official alumni publication and the *Harvard Crimson* expressed regret that the university would not be represented at the bicentennial. The *Harvard Alumni Bulletin* in an editorial criticized the administration's decision as "too much like a breaking off of communications." True to form, the *Crimson* declared that the administration had been "downright discourteous" to Goettingen.[139]

Irritated by the *Harvard Alumni Bulletin*'s criticism, Jerome D. Greene, secretary to the Harvard Corporation, insisted in a letter to its editor that the university's not sending a delegate to the Goettingen celebration in no way implied "unfriendliness or disapproval." He explained that the usual procedure when a foreign university staged such an event was to send greetings: "If they can be sent by the hand of a delegate, so much the better." But sending a representative often proved too expensive, and sometimes an appropriate delegate was not available. Greene noted that he was preparing only that week to send cordial greetings to a provincial university in Britain, accompanied by a statement regretting that Harvard was unable to send a delegate. He emphasized that many of the universities that Harvard had invited to its tercentenary events could not afford to be represented by a delegate and just sent "cordial greetings." Greene concluded: "It is annoying to have both the *Crimson* and the *Bulletin* ignore these facts and represent Harvard as having 'refused' to send a delegate" to Goettingen.[140]

Greene repeated to President Conant shortly afterward that it was "the height of absurdity" for the *Crimson*, the *Bulletin*, and the press to have interpreted "the mere fact that a delegate was not going" to the Goettingen celebration as a "refusal." He even noted that Conant's office had informed him that Business School dean Wallace Donham was to be Harvard's delegate to Goettingen, and then a day or two later the office notified him that Donham was unable to go.[141] Greene again emphasized that Harvard's failing to send a delegate to Goettingen should in no way be interpreted as an "insult": "If we sent a delegate to every institution that sends us an invitation for an anniversary . . . we could keep several professors busy the whole year doing very little else."[142]

Representatives of seven American colleges and universities, most notably MIT, were present at the Goettingen bicentennial festivities, held in what the *New York Times* called "a thoroughly National Socialist atmosphere." At the opening ceremony, Goettingen students in Hitler Guard uniforms stood smartly at attention as the swastika was raised to the tune of the Nazi anthem, the Horst Wessel song. The town streets "rang with the tramp of marching Storm Troopers." Goettingen awarded honorary degrees to two American professors, including A. B. Faust, head of Cornell University's German Department, who gave the rector the Nazi salute.[143]

Germany's education minister, Bernhard Rust, wearing the brown uniform of a Nazi party district leader, delivered the two principal bicentennial addresses, both of them intensely antisemitic. In the first, he proclaimed that "the future of science was the principle of race." When he finished speaking, Goettingen's rector rose to exclaim, "We honor and strengthen ourselves in that we cry, 'Our Fuehrer Adolf Hitler, sieg heil!'" The assembled scholars answered him with three lusty "heils." Two days later, Minister Rust lectured the American representatives that commitment to personal liberty invariably led to "dictatorship of the masses," followed by an even worse dictatorship of the Jews. He denounced the Jews as "world wanderers who know no fatherland."[144]

From 1933 through 1937, as the Nazi menace steadily increased and as Germany's savage persecution of Jews was widely reported in the United States, President Conant's administration at Harvard was complicit in enhancing the prestige of the Hitler regime by seeking and maintaining friendly and respectful relations with Nazi universities and leaders. The Harvard administration refrained from supporting protests against fascism and sometimes suppressed them, as when it directed campus police to tear down anti-Nazi fliers posted during Hanfstaengl's visit to the university. Harvard student leaders, notably those associated with the *Harvard Crimson*, on occasion even surpassed the administration in their desire to foster amicable relations between the university and the Nazi regime. When President Conant – who admitted that he "was neither an interventionist nor an isolationist" until well after Germany launched its Western offensive in 1940 – urged U.S. material assistance for Britain, the *Crimson* strongly condemned him, and much of the student body opposed him.[145] Reporting on the waves of violent attacks on Jews that broke out in Berlin in July 1935, *New York Times* correspondent Frederick T. Birchall noted that "[a]nti-Semitism in its worst form is in the saddle" in Germany, and that "there is nothing – save, perhaps, some echo of world opinion – to exercise the least check upon it."[146] It is truly shameful that the administrative, alumni, and student leaders of America's most prominent university, who were in a position to influence American opinion at a critical time, remained indifferent to Germany's terrorist campaign against the Jews and instead on many occasions assisted the Nazis in their efforts to gain acceptance in the West.

3

Complicity and Conflict

Columbia University's Response to Fascism, 1933–1937

On the night of May 10, 1933, shortly after Hitler assumed power in Germany, Nazi students staged massive public book burnings at universities across the Reich, an act that dramatically communicated to the world their opposition to free inquiry and their intense antisemitism. In the capital, students marched in a torchlight parade beside trucks decorated with caricatures of Jews, carrying many of the world's foremost works of scholarship and literature to the bonfire set up before the University of Berlin. The Nazis had spent weeks raiding libraries and bookstores, specifically targeting for confiscation books by Jewish authors, including Sigmund Freud and Albert Einstein, as well as those of non-Jews like Thomas Mann, Erich Maria Remarque, Jack London, and Emile Zola. Sinclair Lewis, at the time the only American to win the Nobel Prize for Literature, declared that the Nazis had condemned to the flames "the noblest books produced by Germany in the last twenty years." As the students, amid Nazi salutes, hurled book after book into the bonfire, Nazi propaganda minister Josef Goebbels proclaimed from a swastika-draped podium, "Jewish intellectualism is dead!"[1]

That night the Nazis burned tens of thousands of books they called "un-German" in sixty "midnight funeral pyres," an event New York *Evening Post* correspondent H. R. Knickerbocker, reporting from the scene in Berlin, compared to the torching of the renowned library in Alexandria, Egypt, in the seventh century C.E. and the Spanish Inquisition's destruction of "heterodox literature." In the West, some of those reading of the German bonfires undoubtedly recalled Heinrich Heine's prescient warning more than a century before: "Where books are burned, in the end people will be burned too."[2]

The *Columbia Spectator*, student newspaper of Columbia University, upon learning of the German bonfires, reported that the Nazis had burned the works of Columbia professor Franz Boas, a world-renowned anthropologist and a Jew who had condemned Nazi theories of Aryan supremacy. Among his works that enraged the Nazis was a 1925 article titled "Nordic Nonsense." Boas had argued that social environment rather than "race" determined a person's intellectual capabilities, and that "German civilization" was the product of "innumerable cultures influencing it." The University of Kiel, where Boas earned a Ph.D. in 1881, removed his books from its library, prior to staging its own book burning. Kiel had awarded Boas an honorary medical doctorate about a year before the Nazis took power, which he, at the time of the book burnings, "with a wave of his hand," announced it could take back.[3]

Columbia students had already staged campus protests against the Nazi regime's violence against Jews, which began as soon as Hitler became Germany's chancellor on January 30, 1933. In March 1933 Columbia's Jewish Students Society (JSS) collected more than 500 signatures on a petition denouncing these outrages, which "recall the blackest hours of the Dark Ages." Columbia's advisors to Protestant and Catholic students both signed the petition, which demanded "concerted action" against Nazi antisemitism. A Columbia student contingent also reserved seating at Madison Square Garden for the mass rally against Nazism that the American Jewish Congress had scheduled for the next week. The *Columbia Spectator* editorial board, alarmed by the German government's recent announced expulsion of fifteen Jews from university faculty positions, called on the Columbia administration to hire them as professors, a proposal the administration did not consider.[4]

Seven months after the book burnings, Columbia's administration, led by President Nicholas Murray Butler, warmly welcomed to campus Dr. Hans Luther, Nazi Germany's ambassador to the United States. Luther had accepted an invitation to lecture on his government's foreign policy, extended by the university's Institute of Arts and Sciences. The Columbia Social Problems Club, a student organization, immediately challenged the administration when it learned of the invitation to Ambassador Luther to speak on campus. It declared that the administration's plan to hold an official reception for Hitler's emissary suggested indifference to Nazi crimes.[5]

Dismissing the student criticism, President Butler indicated that he held Ambassador Luther in high esteem. He declared that Luther "is the official diplomatic representative to the Government of the United

FIGURE 3.1. Nazi Germany's ambassador to the United States, Dr. Hans Luther (front row center), in Washington, D.C., April 21, 1933. With him in the front row, left to right: Dr. Rudolf Leitner, counselor of the German embassy; Gen. Friedrich von Boetticher, military attaché; Richard Southgate, U.S. State Department; and Dr. Johann Lohman, secretary of the German embassy. Courtesy of AP images.

States on the part of the government of a friendly people" and was entitled to "the greatest courtesy and respect." Butler announced that the Nazi ambassador was a "gentleman," and that Columbia would provide him with "a welcome appropriate to his distinguished position." He was pleased to receive any guest like Ambassador Luther who was "intelligent, honest, and well-mannered"; he did not care what his views were.[6]

A year later, in November 1934, the Columbia League for Industrial Democracy, another student group, invited anti-Nazi refugee Gerhart Seger, a former Social Democratic deputy in the German Reichstag, to speak on campus and asked President Butler to join him on the podium and present his views on Nazism. Seger, whom the Nazis had arrested soon after they took power, had escaped from the Oranienburg concentration camp near Berlin after six months' imprisonment. He had changed trains nine times before he managed to slip by storm troopers into the mountains of Czechoslovakia. Shortly afterward, Seger had embarked on a lecture tour of the United States, where he provided Americans with one of the first eyewitness accounts of Germany under Nazi rule. Although President Butler could have used this opportunity to publicly proclaim opposition to Nazism and show his support for a courageous adversary of Hitler, he declined to appear at the presentation, chaired by Professor Reinhold Niebuhr of Union Theological Seminary. An audience of 300 heard Seger declare that "sadism and cruelty" beyond anyone's expectation prevailed in Germany's concentration camps.[7]

From 1933 to 1937, as the Hitler regime savagely persecuted Jews and political opponents, forced many of the world's most prominent scholars into exile, and made Nazi racial ideology the foundation of university studies, Dr. Nicholas Murray Butler, Columbia's president from 1902 to 1945, failed on numerous occasions to take a principled stand against barbarism. As president of the Carnegie Foundation for International Peace, winner of the Nobel Peace Prize in 1931, and head of one of the nation's leading universities, Butler was more widely known to the public than any leader of American higher education during the 1930s. Long prominent in Republican politics and a candidate for that party's presidential nomination in 1920, he often traveled to conferences abroad and met with world leaders. The media gave his comments on international affairs considerable attention. He was therefore in a position to exert significant influence in shaping American views of Nazi Germany.

Although many students and some faculty at Columbia demanded that the university express public opposition to Hitler and assist German exiles, for several years President Butler remained largely indifferent to the Nazis' terrorist campaign against the Jews. Over a year after Hitler became chancellor, the *Columbia Spectator* issued Columbia's president a stinging rebuke: "The reputation of this University has suffered . . . because of the remarkable silence of its President, Dr. Nicholas Murray Butler, with regard to the Hitler government."[8] On several occasions, Butler lashed out viciously against Columbia students who publicly protested Nazi crimes. Butler and leading members of his administration failed to grasp the impact of Nazism on German higher education, and they participated in high-profile events and programs the Hitler regime sponsored to improve its image in the West.

Failing to grasp the nature and implications of Nazism, Butler insisted that it represented a "complete contradiction to the traditions, the interests and the ideals of historic Germany." In July 1934, he claimed that the Hitler regime was a very transient phenomenon and predicted that the "Historic Germany" he so admired was even then reasserting itself. He did not acknowledge any continuity between Germany's earlier authoritarianism, antisemitism, and militarism and that of the Nazis. Nor did he recognize how widespread the collaboration with Nazism was in the German Lutheran and Catholic churches, assuming both to be bulwarks of opposition to Hitler. The next year he expressed hope that if England and France granted Nazi Germany "some concessions to salve its feelings" on such matters as war guilt and the "internal administration of certain German rivers," Hitler might well cooperate in "efforts to settle the problems of Europe." In 1936 he continued to place much of the blame for Nazism's rise on the Allies' alleged lack of fairness at Versailles and the failure of England and France "to disarm."⁹

A longtime admirer of Benito Mussolini, President Butler also sought to establish strong ties between Columbia and Italian Fascist leaders and student emissaries. He aggressively defended the university's Casa Italiana (which housed the Italian Department) when, in late 1934 and 1935, charges by liberals and anti-Mussolini Italian exiles that the Casa constituted a principal center for the dissemination of Fascist propaganda in the United States received national attention.

President Butler's unwillingness to take a principled stand against the Hitler regime when he had the opportunity to do so was influenced both by his antisemitism, privately expressed, and by economic conservatism and hostility to trade unionism. Professor Fritz Stern, a refugee from Nazi Germany who held Columbia's prestigious Seth Low chair and who first encountered Butler in 1943 as a Columbia freshman, called him "a closet anti-Semite."¹⁰ Butler considered Columbia "a Christian institution," and he spearheaded elite universities' efforts to sharply reduce Jewish enrollment during the early twentieth century, a development Upton Sinclair likened to an "academic pogrom."¹¹

Under Butler, Columbia was the first American institution of higher learning to establish an anti-Jewish quota, using nonacademic admissions criteria. During the 1910s, the Butler administration introduced methods to screen out academically qualified Jewish students, such as personal interviews conducted by non-Jewish administrators or alumni, a psychological test, and requiring applicants to list their religion and parents' birthplaces. Columbia also discriminated against public school applicants from the disproportionately Jewish New York City and favored those from boarding schools that excluded Jews. Following this approach,

FIGURE 3.2. Columbia University president Nicholas Murray Butler and his daughter, Sarah Butler. With permission of the University Archives, Columbia University in the City of New York.

within two years Butler reduced by half the percentage of Jews in Columbia's student body in the early 1920s.[12]

Nonetheless, because of Columbia's New York City location and the preference of the elite families there for Harvard, Yale, and Princeton, the percentage of Jewish undergraduates remained larger than that of its peer institutions.[13] This, along with the surrounding urban environment, where the Nazi takeover in Germany immediately sparked highly conspicuous mass protest, explains why student anti-fascist activism at Columbia exceeded that at other leading universities. Several Jewish students became prominent on the *Columbia Spectator*, including two editors-in-chief, Arnold Beichman (1933–34) and James A. Wechsler (1934–35), who went on to distinguished journalistic careers at *PM* and the New York *Post*, both liberal, strongly anti-fascist dailies.

SIRKIN   HOFFMAN   WECHSLER   GERBER   SHERRY

FIGURE 3.3. *Columbia Spectator* managing board, 1934–35. With permission of
the University Archives, Columbia University in the City of New York.

Butler's discomfort with public anti-Nazi activities at Columbia was
influenced in part by the disproportionately Jewish involvement in them.
Strongly committed to upper-class formality and decorum, and repression
of emotion in public, Butler found repellent the intensity and verbal blunt-
ness of student activists, traits he undoubtedly also associated with Jews.
Roger Chase, *Columbia Spectator* editor in April 1936, profiling Butler
as an "Academic Napoleon," reported that he "continually inveighs"
against the "unmannerliness of his students." Chase asserted that Butler,
who deliberately avoided contact with students, was distinctly uncomfortable with grassroots protest, equating it with "mob action."[14]

Eschewing even the least conspicuous forms of anti-Nazi protest, President Butler ignored (and violated) the boycott of German goods and shipping initiated by Jewish organizations soon after Hitler came to power.
In March 1933 the Jewish War Veterans of the United States began the
boycott, which in May was embraced by Samuel Untermyer's League for
the Defense of Jewish Rights (later the Non-Sectarian Anti-Nazi League)
and joined in August 1933 by the American Jewish Congress. In some
European ports, dock workers began refusing to unload ships flying the
swastika flag.[15]

The boycott of German shipping had a significant immediate impact.
In July 1933, the chairman of the executive board of the Hamburg-
American Line, one of Germany's major shipping companies, conceded

that the boycott "has severely hurt the Hamburg-American's business and is continuing to hurt it and German shipping generally." The boycott also inflicted serious financial damage on Nazi Germany's other major shipping line, the North German Lloyd, whose chairman that month acknowledged that traffic was "much shrunken" and "painted a gloomy picture of the near future."[16]

Yet between 1934 and 1937, President Butler regularly booked passage for trans-Atlantic voyages on North German Lloyd liners that flew the swastika flag, and he encouraged Columbia to engage in academic exchanges with Nazi Germany. Butler ignored the German shipping lines' discharge of their Jewish employees in 1933, and U.S. representative Samuel Dickstein's contention that they smuggled Nazi propaganda into the United States.[17]

Columbia and Barnard sent many students to study in Nazi Germany and on tours of the Third Reich, which the Nazis carefully supervised. Although the Hitler government sent to foreign campuses only politically committed Nazis, Columbia and Barnard, like Harvard, Yale, Princeton, and the other Seven Sisters colleges, actively participated in student exchanges with German universities, ignoring the calls by anti-fascists from the very beginning that they be terminated. Less than a year after Hitler came to power, Professor Franz Boas demanded a U.S. Congressional investigation of German exchange students at American universities, charging that they were "appointed agents of Nazi propaganda."[18]

Barnard's German exchange students for both the 1936–37 and 1937–38 academic years energetically championed Nazism there. Ilse Dunst in January 1937 proclaimed in the *Barnard Bulletin* that freedom of speech prevailed in the Third Reich and that Hitler had restored pride to a Germany "broken down in spirit," and she gushed, "We love our leader." Her successor, Ilse Wiegand, told the *Barnard Bulletin* that Jews could only be "guests" in Germany because "Jewish blood" was different from that of Germans. She asserted that anti-Jewish discrimination was justified because Jews had acquired too much control over money.[19]

President Butler's distaste for campus anti-Nazi protestors, and the extremely harsh punishment he inflicted on some of them, was reinforced by his disdain for the labor movement, which conservatives associated with picketing and public protest. Sociologist E. Digby Baltzell stated that Nicholas Murray Butler "loved the rich with a passion."[20] Butler respected Nazi diplomats like Ambassador Hans Luther and enjoyed the company of the Italian Fascist consuls-general in New York, representatives of regimes that had crushed the trade unions. Many Columbia students involved in combating fascism on campus also joined the picket lines of striking campus employees.

As early as May 1933, Columbia students had launched a public protest against their administration's cultivating friendly ties with Nazi Germany's universities, which had immediately expelled Jewish professors and sharply curtailed Jewish student enrollment. A week after the book burnings in German universities, seven Columbia graduate students at the College of Physicians and Surgeons denounced Columbia's New College, the new undergraduate division of Teachers College, for arranging to send a delegation of its students to universities in the Third Reich to study educational techniques. The protesting graduate students, in a statement to the *Columbia Spectator*, declared that the only "educational techniques" the visitors could learn at the Nazified universities were how to suppress "freedom of thought and liberalism in art." They emphasized that Nazi Germany had exiled its leading scholars and banished "the wisdom of the past ... from its libraries," returning the country to "medieval standards." Ignoring the protest, Dean Thomas Alexander continued to send New College students for training in Nazi Germany over the next several years.[21]

Dean Alexander ardently defended some of Hitler's noxious policies and himself visited Nazi Germany in 1934. He tried to persuade the John Day Company to publish a translation he had made of Hitler's speeches, but its editors rejected it as Nazi propaganda. In a January 1934 interview with the *Columbia Spectator*, Dean Alexander expressed "unqualified approval" of the Nazi sterilization policy in Germany. The five members of the genetics division of Columbia's Zoology Department responded by immediately condemning all of the Nazis' sterilization programs, and the *Columbia Spectator* denounced Dean Alexander in an editorial.[22]

The Columbia administration's invitation to Nazi Germany's ambassador Hans Luther to speak on campus sparked angry protests from many students in November and December 1933 and precipitated a massive demonstration the night of the lecture, climaxing in violent clashes as police sought to drive pickets away from the auditorium. Student threats to picket Columbia's Faculty Club caused the university's Deutsches Haus to cancel plans to hold a luncheon there to honor Ambassador Luther.[23]

Seven faculty members – all but one of whom were instructors, lecturers, or assistants – also publicly denounced the administration's bringing Luther to Columbia. They challenged President Butler's claim that the invitation was justified because the Nazi emissary was a "well-mannered gentleman." The faculty members insisted that it was their duty to protest against the persecution and dismissal of professors in Germany, the book burnings, and "the prostitution of such sciences as genetics and anthropology to justify the Nazi philosophy." They also expressed solidarity with "our colleagues in German prisons and concentration camps" and urged that efforts be undertaken to obtain their release.[24]

The day of Luther's speech, the *Columbia Spectator* issued an editorial entitled "Silence Gives Consent, Dr. Butler" that bitterly denounced the Columbia president's failure to criticize the Nazis: "We know of no instance where Dr. Nicholas Murray Butler has forcefully taken a stand on the policies of the Hitler government." It contrasted this with his repeated denunciations of Soviet policies. Calling attention to the Nazis' destruction of democracy, persecution of "non-Aryans," and burning of books, the *Spectator* declared, "This is the government which President Butler by his silence has given the impression that he condones."[25]

That many Columbia students sharply disagreed with their administration's unwillingness to take a public stand against the German government was apparent the night of Ambassador Luther's address at the Teachers College auditorium before an overflow audience of more than 1,200. Outside, where it was so cold that many pickets were unable to hold signs, 1,000 demonstrators, largely students from Columbia, Barnard, and other New York City colleges and universities, expressed vigorous opposition to Nazism. Inside, student protestors were surprised to see that President Butler was absent, and instead Dr. Charles Hyde of Columbia's Institute of Arts and Sciences introduced Luther. (One of the protest leaders later mocked Butler for ducking an exchange with students over a critically important issue in order to attend "an athletic banquet!") The central thrust of Luther's speech was that "the Nazi government was not following a policy of oppression of any type," and that "Germany had exhibited the most peaceful attitude of any nation."[26]

Protestors inside the auditorium did not wait to demonstrate sharp opposition to Nazi educational policies. Early in Luther's presentation, a young woman interrupted him by yelling, "Why has every dissenting professor been exiled from Germany?...Why have the books of Boas and other Columbia professors been burned?...Why are there quotas for Jewish students in German universities?" Policemen promptly seized her and carried her "wriggling" from the hall. Soon afterward, the police forcibly ejected two other women, one of them a Columbia German instructor, for shouting anti-Nazi slogans.[27]

Outside, emotions ran high as the police "repeatedly hurled back charges of the demonstrators," who sought to move closer to the auditorium, precipitating a series of fist fights that threatened to escalate into a riot. The American Civil Liberties Union (ACLU) the next day denounced the police for suppressing speech and for excessively rough treatment of the demonstrators. The ACLU charged that the police had driven cars into the crowd to break it up and had pulled speakers from soapboxes.[28]

Although Luther's claims that Nazi Germany was "democratic" and had only "peaceful intentions" received prominent coverage in the New York press, no Columbia administrator even commented on what he had said, much less criticized his remarks. President Butler maintained his customary silence, while Dean Alexander of Columbia's New College called the anti-Luther demonstration "an example of bad manners." Russell Potter, head of Columbia's Institute of Arts and Sciences, similarly denounced the hecklers as "ill-mannered children."[29] Neither Butler nor any other Columbia administrator showed any interest in the ACLU's charges that the police had violated Columbia students' rights to freedom of speech and assembly and used excessive force against them.

In January 1934, the American Committee Against Fascist Oppression in Germany circulated a letter that bitterly denounced President Butler for failing to speak out in his annual report for 1933 against the massive damage that the Hitler regime had inflicted on Germany's universities, and its anti-intellectualism. The Committee's letter declared that Butler, "noted educator," had been silent when, "[l]ast spring the greatest scientists and scholars of Germany were ousted from their University chairs [and] Nobel prize winners, masters of art, internationally famous authors and dramatist poets, and educators . . . were exiled from their homes." It further noted that, even though "[t]he German government declared itself unalterably opposed to any form of education not designed to further the purposes of a militaristic state,"

Dr. Butler said nothing. His report makes no mention of these matters.
The German government publicly burned the books of its greatest authors.
Dr. Butler said nothing. . . .
At what reality does the President of Columbia gaze?[30]

Two months later, Professor William B. Dinsmoor, executive officer in charge of Columbia's Fine Arts Department, notified Jerome Klein, a Jewish instructor in art history and one of seven faculty members who had signed the appeal against the Luther invitation, that he would not be reappointed. Klein's son recalled that his father had told him that signatures on the petition protesting the Luther visit had been "arranged in a large circle, so none would be first." The purpose of this was to prevent the administration from singling out any individual as responsible for

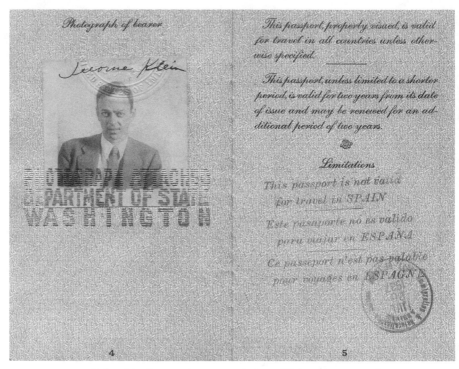

FIGURE 3.4. Columbia fine arts instructor Jerome Klein, whose appointment was terminated by President Nicholas Murray Butler because he protested the administration's welcome to Nazi Germany's ambassador, Hans Luther. Courtesy of George Klein.

leading or initiating the protest. However, "through a student's careless error," Jerome Klein's campus mailbox appeared as "the return address for the petition." According to Klein's son, his father believed that President Butler held him responsible for the petition, and retaliated by having him dismissed. Professor Dinsmoor was vague in explaining why Klein was being discharged, citing only a departmental reorganization.[31]

Jerome Klein had taught at Columbia for seven years and was the only member of the Fine Arts Department who specialized in modern painting. His courses were highly popular on campus. Dinsmoor did not inform Klein that he was not reappointing him until March 1934, after the Barnard catalogue already listed him as scheduled to teach courses open to both Columbia and Barnard students. When Klein learned he would not have a job at Columbia, it was too late for him to secure other academic employment for the next year.[32]

The announcement that Klein would not be reappointed sparked a mass protest at Columbia, spearheaded by his present and former students. The *Columbia Spectator*, under editor-in-chief James A. Wechsler, demanded to know why a "competent, effective member" of the faculty had been discharged "merely at the whim of the head of the department," and it denounced the administration's silence on the matter. Some on campus claimed that "racial prejudice" (meaning antisemitism) had been involved in the dismissal. Dr. Addison Cutler of the Columbia Economics Department, joining Wechsler on the speakers' stand at a protest rally to demand Klein's reappointment, noted that the administration had not dared question Klein's competence. Dinsmoor brushed aside the effort to protect Klein's job, declaring that "the whole question has entirely nothing to do with the *Spectator* or the student body."[33]

Correspondence between Dinsmoor and President Butler several months later strongly suggests that Klein was dismissed for political rather than academic reasons. In a "frank estimate" of the twelve faculty members in the Fine Arts Department, Dinsmoor claimed that few were adequate teachers and identified Meyer Schapiro, later one of the world's most prominent art historians, as its only productive scholar. (Klein was mentioned only as not being renewed.) Dinsmoor found even Schapiro distasteful, a "firebrand... immersed in communistic ideas" and "quite impossible as an undergraduate teacher."[34] Schapiro, then an instructor, had, with Klein, been one of the seven faculty members to sign the appeal against Luther.

In May 1934 President Butler announced that Klein was not needed on the faculty and terminated his academic career. After what his son described as "a very lean year trying to feed himself and a very young child," Klein "began to review art for newspapers, and eventually became the art critic for the New York *Post*." He syndicated his column to 150 newspapers.[35]

Although the Nazis had hurled the works of one of Columbia's most distinguished professors into their bonfires in May 1933, President Butler never assisted in efforts to establish the American Library of Nazi Banned Books, which was inaugurated in December 1934 in Brooklyn, New York. By contrast, during the 1920s he had led the national campaign to rebuild the 300-year-old library of the University of Louvain in Belgium, a major "center of Catholic learning" headed by Cardinal Mercier of Malines, burned by German troops when they invaded that nation in August 1914. Butler, as chairman of the National Committee of the United States for the Restoration of the University of Louvain, for years after World War I energetically solicited funds from 640 American colleges and universities to purchase books and documents and erect a new building to replace what the Germans had destroyed.[36]

Butler involved Columbia directly in the Louvain campaign. He set a quota of $35,000 for alumni to donate "in order to complete Columbia's part of the monument which will be the permanent protest of America's institutions of learning against the wanton destruction of a University Library." He also asked Columbia students each to contribute $1.[37]

To help generate national publicity for his Louvain campaign, President Butler personally bestowed on Cardinal Mercier an honorary Doctor of Laws degree before 10,000 spectators in an elaborate ceremony on the steps of Columbia's Low Library in October 1919. Cardinal Mercier denounced the Germans as "savages" guilty of "crimes against the rights alike of Heaven and humanity."[38]

In 1921 Butler traveled to Belgium to lay the cornerstone for the University of Louvain's new library, amid "the fanfare of trumpets," at a ceremony at which King Albert I presided. The new library's design was replete with Christian symbols. The facade depicted "Our Lady of Victory, supported by St. George and St. Michael crushing the Evil Spirits," and the tower as supported on its four corners by the beasts or symbols of the Evangelists: the Bull, the Eagle, the Angel, and the Lion.[39]

Although eager to cross the Atlantic to lay Louvain's cornerstone and celebrate Catholic learning, Butler would not undertake the much shorter trip across the East River to the Brooklyn Jewish Center to participate in ceremonies launching the American Library of Nazi Banned Books, the first such facility to be established in the United States. Professor Franz Boas, whose own works the Nazis had burned, served on the American Library's Advisory Committee. No Columbia administrator or trustee participated in the effort, even though several had been prominent in assisting Butler in the Louvain campaign. The first "German library of burned books" had been opened in Paris several months before, on the first anniversary of the Nazi bonfires. It contained books the Nazis had "destroyed, censored, or suppressed."[40]

None of New York's college or university administrators were involved in the American counterpart of the Paris library, except Dr. Alvin Johnson, director of the Graduate Faculty at the New School for Social Research, who served on the Advisory Committee. At the inauguration ceremony, Brooklyn Borough President Raymond V. Ingersoll expressed pride to the audience that Brooklyn would be home to the Library of Nazi Banned Books. World-renowned physicist Albert Einstein, one of the first scholars exiled from Nazi Germany, was the principal speaker, and exiled Social Democratic Prussian minister of justice Kurt Rosenfeld sat on the dais.[41]

During Butler's presidency, Columbia's Casa Italiana, which opened in 1927 as a center for the study of Italian culture and which also housed the Italian Department, was controlled by supporters of Premier Benito Mussolini, who used it to propagandize for Fascism. The Casa Italiana also sponsored student exchanges between Columbia and universities in Fascist Italy and arranged many receptions for Mussolini's emissaries, during which his regime was enthusiastically praised. The Mussolini government supplied most of the furniture for the Casa, with President Butler's consent. Mussolini himself in September 1933 wrote to Professor Giuseppe Prezzolini, director of the Casa from 1930 to 1940: "I am following with interest the work done by the Casa Italiana of Columbia University and I am very pleased with what is being accomplished." Prezzolini translated Mussolini's letter and proudly forwarded it to President Butler. Butler responded by thanking Prezzolini for the "charming message from Mussolini" and noted, "It is pleasant, indeed, to know that he is following our work and appreciates it."[42]

Nicholas Murray Butler was a longtime admirer of Premier Mussolini and enjoyed a warm personal relationship with him for many years. In 1931 President Butler startled many when, in his welcoming address to the incoming freshman class, he declared that "the assumption of power by a virtual dictator whose authority rests upon a powerful and well-organized body of opinion" produced leaders "of far greater intelligence, far stronger character and far more courage than does the system of election." Informed listeners understood at the time that it was Mussolini with whom Columbia's president was "conspicuously impressed."[43] The next year Butler maintained that Mussolini's leadership of the Fascist movement had "brought new life and vigor and power and ambition" to Italy.[44] Butler met with the Italian dictator in Rome several times during the late 1920s and 1930s for cordial conversations about international politics. Escorted by Mussolini's federal secretary, Butler was received by the Florence *Fascisti* at their clubhouse, and he donated books to its library. As late as January 1938, Butler was pleased to inform a leading Italian-American donor that Premier Mussolini had recently asked him about the Casa and "was much gratified when I told him the work that was being carried forward."[45]

Butler cultivated Mussolini's friendship despite his suppression of opposition parties and newspapers (completed by 1927) and elimination of academic freedom in Italian universities. In 1931 Mussolini enacted a law requiring all professors in Italian universities to join the Fascist party and take the Fascist oath. Public schools indoctrinated students to promote "national aggrandizement [and] power ... the spiritual essence of fascism." The Fascist government made the teaching of Catholic doctrine the "foundation" of public education, and compulsory in the schools. It introduced standard textbooks for the elementary grades that included passages very hostile to Judaism. As early as 1923, opponents of Mussolini voiced fear that the Fascist educational reforms would drive Jews from the schools, both teachers – because they could not "impart Catholic doctrine" – and students.[46]

Giuseppe Prezzolini, director of the Casa Italiana from 1930 to 1940, and Dino Bigongiari, head of the Columbia Italian Department during the 1930s, were members of the Italian Fascist party (Prezzolini formally joined in 1934). Bigongiari was also a founder in 1923 of the Fascist League of North America and translated the works of leading Italian Fascist theoreticians like Giovanni Gentile and Alfredo Rocco. Prezzolini proudly declared to President Butler in 1935, "I have been for thirty years a friend and admirer of Mussolini."[47]

The other leading members of the Italian Department, Howard Marraro and Peter M. Riccio (whose appointment was at Barnard), were also ardent Fascists. In 1927, Marraro published a book entitled *Nationalism in Italian Education* that proclaimed, "Fascism is the exaltation and ennoblement of all the elements concurring to form and assure the greatness of Italy," and he praised the Fascist program of education instituted by Mussolini's minister of public instruction, Giovanni Gentile. President Butler contributed the book's foreword, which "cordially commended" the work. Upon his return from a 1934 trip to Italy, Marraro declared, "The labor situation in Italy should be a model for the world." He claimed he had not seen in Italy the "distress and suffering" that then prevailed in the United States.[48] Professor Peter M. Riccio's Columbia dissertation, "On the Threshold of Fascism," sought to establish Prezzolini as a leading intellectual progenitor of Italian Fascism. Italian anti-fascists charged that Riccio's work was "one of the worst and most disgraceful dissertations ever written," a crude Fascist polemic that did not meet even "elementary standards of scholarship."[49]

In the fall of 1934, Professor Riccio had a leading role in bringing a delegation of 350 Italian Fascist university students to the United States for a tour of Eastern and Midwestern campuses, and he served as secretary of the committee in charge of the visit.[50] President Butler made Columbia University one of the thirty American colleges and universities sponsoring the tour. The Italian students considered themselves "official ambassadors from Mussolini." *The Nation,* a prominent national liberal weekly magazine, charged that the Italian student tour was "a propaganda move designed to win the friendliness of American university students to the fascist cause."[51]

Docking in New York in September 1934 singing the Fascist anthem "Giovinezza," the Italian student delegation made Columbia its first American university stop. Columbia College dean Herbert E. Hawkes officially greeted the Fascist students on President Butler's behalf at the university's McMillin Theatre. Dean Hawkes declared that Americans had "much to learn" from the Italian delegation.[52] When the Italian students encountered pickets from anti-fascist Columbia student groups, they raised their hands in the Fascist salute and sang the "Giovinezza."[53]

About a month later, the Italian consul-general in New York, at a Casa Italiana ceremony, bestowed on Professor Riccio a medal for his devotion to Italian "culture and ideals." As she introduced the honoree, Dean Virginia C. Gildersleeve of Barnard dismissed the concerns of pickets outside the Casa protesting Riccio's statements in the press that Fascism was the best system of government for Italy. She declared emphatically to the audience, "I don't care what Professor Riccio is."[54]

In November 1934, *The Nation* charged in a series of articles that Columbia's Casa Italiana was "one of the most important sources of fascist propaganda" in the United States. It claimed that the Casa, dominated by Fascist professors, worked closely with Italian government officials to present a favorable image of Mussolini's regime in America. *The Nation* accused the Casa of regularly sponsoring lectures by Fascists, while denying opponents of Mussolini the opportunity to speak, and even forbidding "student gatherings for discussing aspects of fascist rule." It claimed that Professor Arthur Livingston, the only member of the Italian Department opposed to Mussolini, had been transferred to the French Department. According to the *Columbia Spectator,* the reassignment had occurred at the insistence of a Fascist donor.[55]

President Butler angrily denied *The Nation*'s charges, labeling them a "hodge-podge of falsehood, misrepresentation, and half-truth," and assured Casa director Prezzolini that he considered them "nonsensical and untrue." He insisted that the Casa was "without political purpose or significance." Butler praised the Italian Department faculty as "distinguished scholars, so recognized on either side of the Atlantic."[56]

Butler had presided over, and participated in, many events at the Casa Italiana and elsewhere featuring Italian Fascist speakers. He gave the welcoming address for Mussolini's official biographer, Margherita

Sarfatti, at New York's Waldorf-Astoria Hotel, in which he hailed her as a "second Columbus."[57] Butler officially received at the Casa such emissaries of Mussolini as Foreign Minister Dino Grandi (who also spoke at Columbia's Institute of Arts and Sciences); Ambassador Augusto Rosso, who visited Columbia several times between 1933 and 1936; the director of Italians in foreign countries, Signor Parini; and the Italian consuls-general, along with Fascist scholars like Sarfatti and Marchese Piero Misciattelli.[58]

In an effort to discredit *The Nation*'s charges, officers of Columbia's Graduate Club of Italian Studies announced that the club was inviting Gaetano Salvemini, a distinguished historian exiled by Mussolini who was teaching at Harvard at the time, to speak at the Casa Italiana. Salvemini replied to the Graduate Club that, considering *The Nation*'s charges, he would accept the offer only if Professor Prezzolini, as the Casa's director, personally agreed to invite him. He also asked that the Graduate Club inform President Butler of his request, so that he could not dodge responsibility. But Prezzolini refused to invite Salvemini. He explained to the Graduate Club that Professor Salvemini was a "political trouble-maker" whose only purpose in lecturing at Columbia was "to stir up some trouble."[59] As a result, Salvemini, the leading Italian spokesperson for anti-fascism in the United States during the 1930s, never spoke at the Casa Italiana.

Butler shared Prezzolini's desire "to maintain good and friendly relations" with the Mussolini government, which had the support of wealthy Italian-American businessmen whose financial donations to the Casa both men valued highly, and he made no effort on Salvemini's behalf. Prezzolini stated to Butler that had he permitted "anti-Fascist political agitators of the type of Mr. Salvemini" to speak at the Casa, he would not have been able to host Fascists like Margherita Sarfatti and Piero Misciattelli, whom he had invited, he noted, at Butler's own request.[60]

The *Columbia Spectator*, stating that Columbia stood "gravely indicted" by *The Nation*'s charges, demanded that the administration launch an investigation into Fascist control of the Casa Italiana and accused President Butler of evading the key issues. Protesting Butler's refusal to discuss the matter with campus delegations that asked to meet with him, students began picketing his mansion and Low Library, where his offices were located.[61]

In the midst of the controversy, the Casa Italiana sparked more furor when it held a lavish reception to honor Dr. George Ryan, president of the New York City Board of Education, who had just returned from

Rome, which he had visited as guest of the Mussolini government. Dr. Ryan arrived in New York "full of enthusiasm" for Fascist Italy's educational system. The event seemed singularly ill-timed, and *The Nation* suggested that Prezzolini had set it up "under direct orders from Rome." At the Casa, Ryan's Board of Education colleague William Carlin praised Fascist Italy as "the true successor to the glory of Rome," whose "present educational system has the admiration of the world."[62]

Prezzolini objected to the Casa Italiana's being singled out for not hosting anti-Fascist speakers. He pointed out that Columbia's History Department had not been willing to invite Professor Salvemini to speak either. Columbia's Deutsches Haus, which kept a considerably lower profile than the Casa, although maintaining a friendly attitude toward the Hitler regime, had never invited Albert Einstein to give a lecture, although he was then located nearby at the Institute for Advanced Study in Princeton, New Jersey. In fact, as Prezzolini noted, the Deutsches Haus had never invited any German refugee professor to speak.[63]

Returning from Europe in July 1935 on a German liner, President Butler expressed some sympathy for the expansionist designs of Nazi Germany, Fascist Italy, and Japan. He quoted Mussolini as having nearly ten years before personally asked him a "very searching question": must Germany, Italy, and Japan, "because they came later upon the scene" than Britain, France, Russia, and the United States, "be permanently deprived of the opportunities which the other four have long enjoyed?" The former three nations, Butler claimed, unlike the "saturated" ones, needed more territory to provide for population growth and make normal economic development possible. Barnard's Dean Gildersleeve two months later echoed Butler's view, declaring that "the world eventually would be forced to recognize the legitimate needs of Italy and Germany" and permit "their colonization on new land."[64]

Campus protest surpassing even that centering on the Casa Italiana erupted in March 1936 when Columbia's administration immediately accepted the invitation of Germany's University of Heidelberg to send a delegate to its 550th anniversary celebration, scheduled for June 27–30. President Butler had left on February 22 for a five-week trip to the Pacific Coast, and Columbia administrators accepted Heidelberg's invitation in his absence. Frank D. Fackenthal, Columbia's secretary, on March 4 notified Frederick Coykendall, chairman of the Board of Trustees, alumni trustee Archibald Douglas, and Howard McBain, dean of graduate faculties, that the administration was "being bombarded" with protests "from *The Spectator*, *The Columbia Law Review*, Judge Proskauer [later

president of the American Jewish Committee], and Jewish organizations."
Fackenthal noted that Columbia's position was the same as that of
Harvard's president James B. Conant, who had stated the day before
in the *New York Times*: "The President and Fellows [of Harvard] in
accepting the invitation of the University of Heidelberg recognize the
ancient ties by which the universities of the world are united and which
are independent of the political conditions existing in any country at any
particular time." Alarmed by the protests, Fackenthal contacted President
Butler, who telegrammed that he should discuss the matter further with
Coykendall, Douglas, and McBain.[65]

Fackenthal informed Butler on March 7 that he had met with Coykendall, Douglas, and McBain, who all agreed that Columbia should
not withdraw its acceptance. They insisted that "many academic men at
Heidelberg and other German universities" must be "distressed by conditions" in German higher education and would derive "some com-
fort" from "brief companionship" with a "representative from outside."
Fackenthal then noted definite acceptance of the invitation by Harvard,
Yale, Vassar, Cornell, and "a number of other important" American
universities.[66]

Butler then made the decision that Columbia would "stand pat,"
although he and his administration deliberately did not make his involvement in the matter public. Fackenthal, noting the sharp and persistent
protests against acceptance of the invitation from student publications,
Jewish organizations, and individual Jews, reported to Butler three weeks
later that "[e]veryone assumes that the matter was handled in a routine way during your absence and we have done nothing to contradict
that opinion, just so that you might be free to take a fresh start if you
choose."[67]

At Columbia, 1,000 students and faculty members signed a petition
demanding that the university not participate in the Heidelberg festival,
and they were joined by the Student Board (student government) and four
fraternities. Several of Columbia's most distinguished professors signed
the petition, including Franz Boas, who had attended the University of
Heidelberg during the late 1870s; Harold Urey, Nobel Prize winner in
chemistry; and Richard Gottheil, a scholar of Semitic languages, as well
as anthropologist Julius Lips, a non-Jewish exile from Nazi Germany,
who had personally witnessed the 1933 book burning at the University
of Cologne. The *Columbia Spectator* and the *Teachers College News*
also launched editorial campaigns against participation at Heidelberg,

unlike the *Harvard Crimson* and *Yale Daily News*, which supported their universities' decision to send a delegate.[68]

A committee of nine student leaders from Columbia, Barnard, and Teachers College met with President Butler on March 30 to discuss their opposition to the administration's position. Roger Chase, *Columbia Spectator* editor-in-chief, reported after the conference that Butler "made it known that acceptance of the Heidelberg invitation had been carried through in his absence and that he had had nothing to do with it." Chase said Butler had promised the student delegation that he would consider their complaint.[69]

Yet on April 29, after a month during which President Butler spoke no further to students about the matter, the *Columbia Spectator* angrily reported that a "dispatch from Heidelberg" listed Arthur F. J. Remy, Villard professor of Germanic philology, as Columbia's representative at the German university's anniversary celebration. This indicated that Columbia would definitely participate. Roger Chase declared, "The idea of a representative of Columbia University seating himself on the same platform with the monstrous Joseph Goebbels," who would officially greet the delegates, "is utterly obscene."[70]

Butler's choice of Professor Remy as Columbia's delegate to Heidelberg was also provocative. Remy had appeared as a speaker with Nazi Germany's ambassador Hans Luther in December 1933 at an event in which the swastika flag was prominently displayed, the Steuben Society of America's German Day commemoration. New York City's mayor John O'Brien had forbidden the use of a city armory for what he considered a Nazi propaganda celebration.[71]

Franz Boas offered encouragement to the forces opposing Columbia's participation in the Heidelberg celebration when he announced that he would speak at a meeting to commemorate the third anniversary of the Nazi book burnings at the New School for Social Research on May 7. Boas emphasized that his purpose was "to call attention to the situation of science, literature, and art in Germany today." Decades before, Boas had pledged with four fellow Heidelberg students to hold a reunion there on the university's 550th anniversary, but he now declared he would not go to Germany "under any circumstances."[72]

On May 11, the *Columbia Spectator* noted that the semester ended in a week and asked, "Is Dr. Butler intentionally silent until the critics are gone?" Professor Remy was already en route to represent Columbia at a celebration that the *Spectator* charged "will be a glorification of

FIGURE 3.5. Columbia students carry out mock book burning to protest President Butler's sending a delegate to Nazi Germany to participate in the University of Heidelberg's 550th anniversary celebration, May 1936. With permission of the University Archives, Columbia University in the City of New York.

Nazism, of persecution [and] blood." For six weeks, the *Spectator* remarked, Butler had "successfully eluded . . . comment on the [Heidelberg] situation."[73]

When Butler then closed off any discussion by announcing his refusal to see the committee that had met with him on March 30, about 200 students on May 13 staged a mock book burning on campus. Most of them then proceeded to his mansion, where they held a rally and set up a picket line to protest Columbia's participation in the Heidelberg festival.[74]

Responding by letter on May 29 to a student leader wishing to speak to him about Heidelberg, President Butler emphasized that Columbia's relationships with German universities were "strictly academic" and had "no political implications of any kind." Unable to conceal his irritation with the protest, he lectured, "We may next expect to be told that we must not read Goethe's FAUST, or hear Wagner's LOHENGRIN, or visit the great picture galleries at Dresden, or study Kant's KRITIK, because we so heartily disapprove of the present form of government in Germany."[75]

Heidelberg's 550th anniversary celebration when it was held June 27–30 was a well-orchestrated Nazi propaganda festival. Town buildings were draped with swastika flags, and Professor Remy and the other foreign delegates proceeded to the opening ceremony through streets "lined with Storm-Troopers, each holding a flaming torch." The *New York*

Times reported that the celebration began with a Nazi military display, "unexpected... [at] a supposedly academic festival." The *Times* soon learned the reason for this: "A special Propaganda Ministry office has been established here, from which all orders are issued, and it is now responsible for... the scheduled events." The university's rector, Wilhelm Groh, declared the first day that the festival's purpose was to provide guests with "a picture of the spiritual life of the new contented and happy Germany."[76]

Propaganda Minister Josef Goebbels presided at the official welcoming reception and dinner for the foreign delegates, which Arthur Remy found "very enjoyable."[77] Remy reported that Goebbels spoke to the assembled delegates "numerous times," and "each time he made no attempt to disguise his expressions of Nazi philosophy." Goebbels and his wife were "very much in evidence" throughout the entire festival.[78]

When the Heidelberg anniversary celebration was over, Arthur Remy reported to the Columbia administration that it had been "dignified and impressive." He declared that "the presence of black or brown uniforms can certainly not be construed as of sinister significance." Remy concluded, "I... attended a notable academic event and I feel that neither Columbia, nor any one of the American universities that accepted the invitation to be represented, need offer any apology for its course."[79] The *New York Times*, by contrast, summed up the festival as one in which "Nazi troops marched; pre-Hitler Germany was criticized; present-day Germany was praised" and emphasized that the University of Heidelberg was just "another cog in the Nazi machine."[80]

Shortly before the Heidelberg celebration, Columbia College dean Herbert E. Hawkes notified Robert Burke, one of the leaders of the mock book burning at Columbia and of the picket line at Butler's mansion, that he was forbidden to register for classes at Columbia in the fall. The reason the administration gave for Burke's expulsion from Columbia was that he had "conducted a disorderly demonstration in front of the [president's] house" and "delivered a speech in which he referred to the President disrespectfully." It also charged that "members of the assemblage shouted disrespectful, blasphemous, and obscene language" and had left placards "in and about the foyer of the President's house."[81] Burke noted that "Dean Hawkes never questioned my personal behavior" but insisted he was responsible for the alleged behavior of other students because he had led the demonstration.[82]

Burke stated that Dean Hawkes's "action was of a political nature," and that the administration sought to suppress students' freedom of speech and assembly. He noted that the other student who had spoken at the demonstration, when threatened with expulsion, had "repudiated the whole affair, and signed a statement to the effect that he would never again lead or be part of any demonstration which might possibly be distasteful to the administration." Burke himself "could not stomach such a flagrant prostitution of my rights as an American citizen." But President Butler upheld the expulsion.[83]

President Butler, Dean Hawkes, and other Columbia administrators were personally uncomfortable with Burke, a "rugged face[d]" Irish-American from Youngstown, Ohio, who was working his way through Columbia. Burke had become a leader of the radical American Student Union (ASU) on campus, and in March 1936 had led a picket line of Columbia students to support striking building service workers employed by the university. Former *Columbia Spectator* editor-in-chief James A. Wechsler noted that Dean Hawkes "always lamented" that Burke's "manners were not sufficiently elegant."[84]

Burke had struggled to earn his Columbia tuition, working in Youngstown for two years as a truck driver and for one year in a steel mill before he had saved enough to enroll. Burke had developed into a tough amateur boxer good enough to win New York's Golden Gloves middleweight final, and he earned money at Columbia teaching young men to box. Almost alone among Columbia's athletes, he became active in the movement to boycott the 1936 Berlin Olympics. He often worked thirty hours a week outside of class to pay his tuition, "roam[ing] through every conceivable job which promised a dollar or a meal." He washed dogs, and he even sold his blood.[85]

The administration considered Burke's apparently exemplary academic performance irrelevant in expelling him. President Butler insisted that the university was under no contractual obligation to give a diploma for "achievement and excellence" if it disapproved of a person "for any reason whatsoever."[86]

From Youngstown, Burke accused President Butler of using "the methods of fascism" to silence students, and he filed suit to gain readmission to Columbia. He secured the services of Arthur Garfield Hays, one of the nation's preeminent civil liberties attorneys. James A. Wechsler announced that the ASU would organize a nationwide protest against the expulsion, and James T. Farrell, author of the *Studs Lonigan* trilogy and one of America's leading novelists, came to Burke's support.[87]

Butler argued that the disciplinary powers of the president and deans could be "exercised without dispute or debate," and no court had the authority to interfere. In 2008, James A. Wechsler's widow, Nancy Wechsler, herself a participant in the protest against Hans Luther's appearance at Columbia in 1933, recalled that Butler was "a highly egotistical man, not to be disobeyed." John G. Saxe, Columbia's attorney, informed administrators that the university's defense would rest on Burke's having contracted, in enrolling as a student, to abide by Columbia's statutes, which he had violated by leading a disorderly demonstration at President Butler's house. Saxe denounced Arthur Garfield Hays as "one of the agitators of the American Civil Liberties League [*sic*]."[88]

During the 1930s, universities defined academic freedom very narrowly, to cover only professors' statements concerning scholarship in their areas of expertise.[89] Nicholas Murray Butler asserted in 1934 that academic freedom was only for "competent scholars," not students. Academic freedom did not "imply freedom to act in contempt of the accepted standards of morals and good manners."[90] As Robert Cohen noted, this approach "enabled college administrators to justify suppressing any forms of speech which they found distasteful." The courts in this period invariably agreed with university administrators that students were not entitled to academic freedom. They gave them "virtual carte blanche to discipline and even expel troublesome undergraduates and to do so without even a semblance of due process."[91]

Columbia students, joined by those from other New York City campuses, during the fall of 1936 staged a series of rallies to demand Burke's readmission, including a torchlight parade for academic freedom. They set up all-night picket lines in front of President Butler's mansion. At City College of New York, dean of men John R. Turner banned a campus demonstration for Burke because it was not "in good taste." Supporters of Burke held a mock trial of President Butler and his administration on the charge of "willfully undermining the liberties of Columbia students." The judges, who included Dr. Reinhold Niebuhr and playwright Maxwell Anderson, voted that Columbia had "unfairly expelled" Burke.[92]

Because courts accorded university administrators almost unlimited power to discipline students, the protests were of no avail. In October 1937, Burke dropped his lawsuit. During the summer of 1936 he had gone to work for the Committee for Industrial Organization (CIO) in Youngstown. Burke helped lead the CIO's organizing drive at the Republic Steel plant there, during which company thugs beat and injured him. In May 1937 he "came out of the West in a muddy Ford coupe" to again speak at Columbia, this time on "labor, steel, and industrial unionism."[93] When the Columbia Young Communist League chapter announced in

February 1938 that Burke would speak under its sponsorship on "Communism in the CIO," Butler banned him from the campus. The administration shut down the event ten minutes before it was to begin and had him escorted off campus. This sparked a renewed round of campus protests over students' right to free speech.[94]

Columbia was convulsed in conflict in the spring of 1937 when the University of Goettingen in Germany invited it to send a delegate to its bicentennial anniversary celebration, also scheduled for "Purge Day," June 30. President Butler was vacationing in Bermuda when the invitation arrived, and the administration did not indicate whether it would accept. In a forceful editorial on March 15 entitled "Never Again, Dr. Butler," the *Columbia Spectator* urged that Goettingen's invitation be rejected. It argued that it was transparently obvious that Germany's "sudden penchant for celebrating anniversaries in an international fashion" was designed to enhance Nazi prestige in the world. Last year, by participating in the Heidelberg festival, Columbia had "injured its prestige . . . by paying homage to Adolf Hitler." Instead of again "permit[ting] its name to be linked with National Socialism," Columbia must "administer a stinging rebuke" to the Nazis by refusing the invitation.[95]

President Butler was well aware of how severely the Nazis' "racial ruling" regarding civil servants had damaged Goettingen. The British scientific journal *Nature* stated that what had been arguably the world's leading university in mathematics and physics had "ceased in 1933 to be a scientific centre." Only three months after Hitler became chancellor, Franz Boas wrote to President Butler that Dr. Niels Bohr, just arrived in the United States, had informed him "that practically all the mathematicians in Göttingen have been ousted."[96]

Nonetheless, even after the British universities again announced that they would not send delegates, and only the Massachusetts Institute of Technology among the most prestigious American ones accepted its invitation, Butler and his administration remained silent about Columbia's intentions. Many of Columbia's most prominent professors publicly opposed sending a delegate, including sociologist Robert Lynd, anthropologists Franz Boas and Ruth Benedict, philosopher Ernest Nagel, and political scientist Raymond Moley, a leading member of President Roosevelt's Brain Trust. Professor Nagel told the *Columbia Spectator*, "There's no use . . . dressing up . . . Goettingen and pretending that it's alive." Moley stated that "American universities should not participate in any German university celebrations" so long as the Nazis were in power.[97]

On May 7, 1937, the *Columbia Spectator* reported that Dr. Boris Nelson, secretary of the Non-Sectarian Anti-Nazi League, had sent four letters and two telegrams to President Butler asking whether Columbia would accept Goettingen's invitation, but Butler had not acknowledged any of them. Although Goettingen had contacted American universities almost two months before, only Columbia and Syracuse had failed to indicate what they would do. The *Spectator* noted that Columbia College's four class presidents had signed a petition against accepting Goettingen's invitation.[98]

Only on May 9 did Butler announce that Columbia would not send a delegate to Goettingen, undoubtedly influenced by the storm of protest on campus and the failure of all but seven American universities to accept their invitations. Butler also sent a letter of greeting in Latin to Goettingen that, by praising qualities nobody associated with Nazi Germany's universities, implied criticism of the Hitler regime's educational policies: "We wish to mark our appreciation and admiration for that . . . freedom of thought and inquiry, that absence of race and religious prejudice and persecution, which gave to the old Germany the leadership for generations in philosophy, in letters, in science, in the fine arts, in music, and in industry."[99]

Goettingen represented a turning point for Butler, and in September 1937 he opened Columbia's academic year by condemning "the three military dictatorships of Japan, Italy, and Germany," whose expansionist designs posed the most serious threat to world peace. The *Columbia Spectator*, for once, congratulated him for "scrapp[ing] his usual proclivity for generalities" and forcefully denouncing Fascism.[100]

After the horrifying Kristallnacht violence in November 1938, when the Nazis destroyed Germany's synagogues and most of its Jewish-owned shops and sent 30,000 Jews to concentration camps, Butler finally spoke out explicitly against German antisemitism. But his denunciation shortly after Kristallnacht of the "cruel and barbaric treatment of Catholics and Jews now going on in Germany" suggested that he still failed to grasp the uniqueness of the Jews' plight. Like other major university presidents, his response did not go beyond verbal condemnation. He did not join Jewish, labor, and student organizations that called on the United States to lift immigration quotas for Jewish refugees, or to sever diplomatic and commercial relations with Germany. Nor was Butler among the seventeen speakers who addressed the audience of 20,000 that packed New York City's Madison Square Garden after Kristallnacht in a mass protest against Nazi anti-Jewish outrages.[101]

Edward R. Murrow, who actively assisted academic refugees from Nazi Germany almost from the time Hitler came to power, declared in 1935,

"The thing that really concerns me about the situation over here is the general indifference of the university world and the smug complacency in the face of what has happened to Germany."[102] The administration of Columbia University, one of America's foremost universities, under President Nicholas Murray Butler, was determined, at least through 1936, to preserve friendly ties with Nazi Germany, and with Fascist Italy even beyond that, and they reacted angrily to those who challenged this policy. Butler permanently destroyed the academic careers of Robert Burke and Jerome Klein, who recognized that public protest was necessary when elite American universities ignored Nazi and Fascist crimes.

Campus protest against Nazism and Fascism at Columbia was considerably more strident than at other elite universities. This was because Columbia, located in New York City, enrolled a greater proportion of Jewish (and working-class) students than other elite universities, despite President Butler's early and concerted effort to sharply reduce Jewish enrollment. Jewish and working-class students, because of their concern about antisemitism and the plight of trade unions, became disproportionately engaged in opposing Hitler and Mussolini. Asserting their own right to protest in a university environment, they were horrified at the Nazis' destruction of academic freedom and purges of Jewish faculty. Living in New York City, the site of massive demonstrations and rallies against the Nazis in the streets and on the docks, further stimulated their awareness of the fascist threat. At Columbia during the 1930s anti-fascist protest for the first time threatened the centrality that exclusive social activities had traditionally held in student life.

Columbia President Nicholas Murray Butler, whose views on international affairs the press quoted more frequently during the 1930s than those of any other higher education leader, was in a position to heighten public awareness of the menace of fascism. It is lamentable that for several critical years he failed to use his influence against barbarism and chose instead to cooperate with the Hitler and Mussolini regimes in improving their image in the West.

4

The Seven Sisters Colleges and the Third Reich

Promoting Fellowship Through Student Exchange

In January 1935, exiled Reichstag deputy Toni Sender spoke over New York's Jewish radio station WEVD on "How Hitler's 'Aryan' Paradise Enslaves the Women of Germany." Sender had been editor of the German Social Democratic Party's women's magazine *Frauenwelt* before the Nazis came to power. Soon after Hitler became chancellor, Sender donned a disguise and fled on foot into the woods of Czechoslovakia, barely eluding Nazi pursuers intent on murdering her. She had come to the United States on a lecture tour in 1934, presenting to Americans one of the first eyewitness accounts of Germany under Nazi rule. In her radio address, Sender declared that the Nazis believed women to be "incapable of any constructive work," and that they were driving them out of the professions. To restrict female employment options, the Hitler regime had sharply curtailed the number of women permitted to attend universities, imposing a strict 10 percent quota. The Nazis had also denied women opportunities for factory employment, forcing large numbers into misery as servants and prostitutes. Sender emphasized that in Nazi Germany, women's only task was "to marry and to get children – as many as possible."[1]

Joining Sender as a lecturer on Nazi Germany in the United States was her former Reichstag colleague Gerhart Seger, who had made a daring escape from the Oranienburg concentration camp in December 1933. Seger called the Hitler regime "morally insane," strongly condemned its antisemitic campaign and rearmament program, and urged Americans not to trade with or travel to the Third Reich. Speaking at the University of California at Berkeley several weeks after Sender's radio address, he denounced the Nazis for mounting "an insidious campaign of hate" in Germany's schools, designed to prepare the country for another major

FIGURE 4.1. Toni Sender, Jewish Social Democratic Reichstag deputy (1920–33), who narrowly escaped being murdered by the Nazis, forcefully denounced Nazi policies toward women while lecturing in the United States. Courtesy of the Wisconsin Historical Society, Image ID 60527.

war. Denying women access to higher education was part of a larger Nazi campaign to restrict women's lives to "Children, Church, and Kitchen." Two years of Nazi rule had pushed German women "back 100 years."[2]

Later in 1935, Dean Virginia C. Gildersleeve, head of Barnard College, one of the nation's most prestigious women's schools, presented a view of Nazi Germany that differed strikingly from that of the exiled Reichstag deputies. Just returned from her annual European sojourn, Dean Gildersleeve urged Americans to recognize that Nazi Germany's desire to acquire "new land" was "legitimate." She declared that she had been pleased to learn while in Nazi Germany that the Hitler regime, despite the quotas, was allowing women and "a certain proportion of

Jews" to study in universities. Gildersleeve, cofounder of the International Federation of University Women, stated that she could not blame the Nazis for drastically reducing female and Jewish university enrollments because, as she explained, the professions in Germany were overcrowded. She mentioned neither the Nazis' removal of Jewish faculty members from the universities nor the shocking deterioration in academic standards in German higher education. It did not seem to bother her that the Jewish student quota was a minuscule 1 percent. To be sure, Dean Gildersleeve had herself implemented procedures designed to significantly reduce Jewish admissions to Barnard. The College often rejected Jewish applicants from New York City public high schools with excellent scholarly records in favor of finishing school graduates with inferior academic credentials.[3]

President Mildred H. McAfee of Wellesley College, well more than four years after Hitler became chancellor, deliberately placed an aggressive partisan for Nazism on her campus. President McAfee personally invited Lilli Burger to come from Nazi Germany to join Wellesley's faculty for academic year 1937–38, well aware that she was "a staunch supporter of Hitler." Interviewed by the Wellesley student newspaper in January 1938, Burger informed the college that the American press distorted news from Germany, "exaggerat[ing] . . . the persecution of the Jews." She "fervently" praised Hitler's "great work." Burger urged that academic exchanges between the United States and Nazi Germany, already very extensive among elite American women's and men's schools, be increased to further promote friendship between the two nations.[4]

Despite the Nazis' reactionary policies on women and curtailment of their access to a university education, many administrators, faculty, and students at the elite women's colleges known as the Seven Sisters – Vassar, Smith, Mount Holyoke, Wellesley, Bryn Mawr, Radcliffe, and Barnard – shared a sanguine view of Nazi Germany and enthusiastically participated in academic and cultural exchanges with the Third Reich. Such attitudes and behavior were widespread in America's colleges and universities during the 1930s, but the Seven Sisters were particularly influential in shaping American views of the Hitler regime because they were among the most active participants in student exchange programs in Germany. These schools were central to the Junior Year Abroad program that American educators maintained with the University of Munich from 1931 until 1939. Large numbers of students from the Seven Sisters also traveled to the Third Reich for summer study programs at Munich and other Nazified universities such as Heidelberg and Berlin.

American educators involved in administering student exchanges with Nazi Germany shared the outlook of Professor Grace M. Bacon, head of Mount Holyoke College's German Department and a director of the national Junior Year in Munich program, who reported to President Roswell Ham in June 1938 that "[s]tudy in Munich has resulted in a breadth of view, and a tolerance and understanding of another civilization which only direct contact can give."[5] The Seven Sisters sent their students to Europe for the Junior Year in Munich on German ocean liners flying the swastika flag, providing the Nazi government with much-needed foreign currency. The Hitler regime eagerly encouraged such student exchanges, believing them invaluable in disseminating Nazi propaganda in the United States.

The term "Seven Sisters" came into use in the 1920s and referred to the women's colleges that had been for at least two decades considered the nation's most prestigious. During the late nineteenth century these schools had spearheaded the highly controversial cause of higher education for women. To better promote this cause and to coordinate fund-raising, the presidents of Vassar, Wellesley, Smith, and Mount Holyoke established a Four College Conference in 1915, which held regular meetings of administrators and faculty, rotating among the campuses. Bryn Mawr joined in 1925 and Radcliffe and Barnard the next year, making a Seven College Conference. During the 1930s, enrollments ranged from Bryn Mawr's 600 to Smith's 2,000, which made it the nation's largest women's college. Bryn Mawr, the only one of the Seven Sisters with its own graduate school, had arguably the strongest academic reputation.[6]

All seven colleges enjoyed a national reputation for being socially selective, although Barnard and Radcliffe, because of their respective locations in New York City and Cambridge, adjacent to Boston, had more ethnically and economically diverse student bodies. Like the elite men's colleges, the Seven Sisters after World War I restricted Jewish enrollment by requiring on application forms such information as religion, mother's name prior to marriage, and grandparents' birthplaces. The proportion of Jews at Barnard and Radcliffe was nonetheless double to triple that of the other five elite women's colleges. The decision of Barnard and Radcliffe to join the Five College Conference in 1926 was motivated in part by their administrations' desire to make their schools appear more "genteel and gentile."[7] During the Depression, a significant proportion of Barnard and Radcliffe students commuted to school and needed to work to pay their expenses. Radcliffe even arranged training for some of its students in "formal waitress service" and in secretarial work to help them obtain part-time employment.[8]

Wealthier families since the late nineteenth century had encouraged their daughters to travel in Europe to acquire more social polish, and, from the beginnings of the organized Junior Year Abroad programs in the 1920s, the Seven Sisters were prominent in directing them, and they enlisted many of their students as participants. These elite women's colleges gave serious consideration to foreign language instruction, particularly in French, Italian, German, and Spanish, and their students were thus more easily accepted for junior year and summer study at European schools.

The University of Delaware established the nation's first Junior Year Abroad program in 1923, sending some of its own students with those from other colleges to the Sorbonne in Paris. It was influenced by the increased interest in European affairs stimulated by the recent World War. In 1925, Smith College started its own junior year program in France (at Grenoble and Paris), restricted to its own students, which it continued through the 1930s. Beginning in 1931, Smith College also began the first American student exchange program with Fascist Italy. Those participating in Smith's Italian junior year program studied at the University of Florence, with a preparatory month at the University of Perugia.[9]

Delaware had initially assumed that its "educational experiment" would influence other colleges and universities to create their own European junior years abroad, as Smith had, but the cost proved prohibitively expensive. Delaware maintained its European programs only because of financial support from a small group of wealthy patrons, most notably Pierre S. du Pont.[10] As a result, American colleges and universities desiring to send juniors to study at European institutions of higher learning – except for Smith – joined the Delaware program.

The University of Delaware began a junior year in Germany program in 1931, in cooperation with the University of Munich and did not hesitate to continue it after Hitler came to power. During 1933–34, the first full academic year during Nazi rule, fourteen of the nineteen students in the Foreign Study group at the University of Munich were from Seven Sisters colleges.[11] Administrative and faculty members from the Seven Sisters were prominent in directing this effort and its successor, the national German Junior Year, Inc., established in 1936 after Delaware terminated its program. Each American junior enrolled at the University of Munich resided with a German family and attended regular university courses taught by German professors. President William A. Neilson of Smith College was a member of the Executive Council that ran the German program, funded from both American and German sources.

Until 1938, the presidents of the Seven Sisters colleges encouraged students to consider spending their junior year in Munich, without reservation. During academic year 1936–37, three of the seven members of the German Junior Year, Inc., Executive Council were professors at Seven Sisters colleges. Two years later, in 1938–39, President Neilson of Smith was one of four Seven Sisters representatives on the eight-member Executive Council. The liaison between the Executive Council and the Nazi government's *Auslandsstelle* was a Smith College professor.[12] Seven Sisters presidents also strongly endorsed summer study at German universities, and professors at these colleges frequently led student tours to Germany.

Each of the Seven Sisters similarly enrolled exchange students from Nazi Germany. Student newspapers at these colleges regularly published lengthy interviews with these young German women, all members of Nazi youth organizations, in which they effusively praised Hitler and the Third Reich, aggressively championed German rearmament, and often made antisemitic pronouncements.

College administrators and professors never responded to such statements in the school newspapers, and the Seven Sisters presidents regularly reaffirmed their support for German student exchanges. Professor Grace M. Bacon boasted in 1938 that Mount Holyoke College had profited from the "many choice students from Germany" who had enrolled there on exchanges. She commented that "[t]hey have all been very fine types of German young women."[13]

In the early months of Nazi rule, when Americans were forming important first impressions of Hitler's Germany, heads of the Seven Sisters colleges, joined by American administrators from Delaware's Junior Year in Munich program, downplayed reports of antisemitic discrimination and violence, and persecution of political opponents. In April 1933, Dean Virginia C. Gildersleeve, speaking at a Barnard Club luncheon, labeled the situation in the Third Reich "disconcerting" but urged her audience not to judge Germany by American standards. The outlook and behavior of an "alien" people might appear eccentric, but if Americans knew "the circumstances in which seemingly unreasonable actions take place, those actions would seem reasonable." Gildersleeve concluded: "Perhaps if we knew more of the facts we could understand what the German people are feeling and trying and wanting to do."[14] A month later, Smith College president William A. Neilson, returning from a three-month tour of

Germany, Italy, and Spain, reported that he had seen many "scared" people in Germany, but no disorders or "cases of mistreatment."[15]

Seven Sisters presidents also welcomed representatives of the Hitler regime to their campuses and openly fraternized with them. In October 1933, President Henry Noble MacCracken of Vassar hosted Professor Friedrich Schoenemann of the University of Berlin, then on a speaking tour of the United States to promote the Nazi government, and introduced him at his campus lecture on "The New Democracy in Hitler's Germany." Professor Schoenemann compared the Nazi takeover in Germany with the American Revolution and explained that "at bottom [Hitler] is a democrat." Schoenemann claimed that reports of Nazi atrocities against Jews were false, "invented purely for propaganda purposes." He claimed that Jews led the Communist movement and at the same time dominated "all the money-making professions in Berlin." Schoenemann denounced Albert Einstein for not "suspend[ing] his judgment" about the Hitler government "until he knew the facts."[16] Ada Comstock, president of Radcliffe College, accepted the invitation of her school's German Club to celebrate Christmas at a party to honor Hitler's consul-general in Boston, Baron Kurt von Tippelskirch, who addressed the gathering.[17]

Mussolini's Fascist government had decorated President MacCracken in May 1933 for promoting friendship between the United States and Italy. Mussolini's consul-general in New York, Antonio Grossardi, bestowed the Cross of Grand Ufficiale della Corona d'Italia on Mac-Cracken in what he called a "gracious presentation" on the Vassar campus, before "an impressive assembly of faculty in academic dress." Mac-Cracken informed Professor Giuseppe Prezzolini, director of Columbia University's Casa Italiana and an ardent Fascist, that he was "deeply appreciative of the honor."[18]

About a year and a half later, President MacCracken personally welcomed to campus a large delegation of Italian Fascist students on a goodwill tour of the United States. With their commander barking "staccato orders," the Fascist students marched in formation to meet Vassar's president, who accepted a gift from them.[19]

Smith College spent two years searching for a speaker who could present "the pro-Nazi side of the German picture neglected by the American press." In April 1935 it settled on Dr. Hans Orth, a former exchange student from Germany at the University of Cincinnati. Orth charged that the Jews in Germany "had pushed the Aryans out of jobs" and used "key positions" to promote Communism. The Germans had rightly objected to being ruled by "a foreign race." The only blood shed had been that of

FIGURE 4.2. President Marion Edwards Park of Bryn Mawr College. Courtesy of Bryn Mawr College Library.

one hundred Nazis murdered by Communists. One Jew had been killed, but only after he had wounded a Nazi.[20]

The student newspaper at Smith College complained that the audience during the question period after Orth's address had displayed "a singular lack of open-mindedness." The editors were annoyed that it had refused "to listen courteously to the young German's sincere vindication of the Hitler regime."[21]

Only President Marion Edwards Park of Bryn Mawr College among the heads of the Seven Sisters colleges participated in organized public protest against Nazism during the Hitler regime's early months, although it was limited to challenging the discharge of professors considered Jews or political opponents. In June 1933 President Park asked college presidents in her area to sign a statement condemning the dismissals.[22] She also hired three German Jewish refugee scholars to teach at Bryn Mawr, most notably Dr. Emmy Noether (1933–35), then considered the world's most eminent female mathematician. The Nazis had forced Noether to resign from the faculty of the University of Goettingen.[23]

In June 1933, President Park refused to sign the statement circulated among academics by the National Conference of Christians and Jews (NCCJ) about what it called "hostility between Christian and Jewish groups in Germany," mentioned in Chapter 1. Park did not conceal her distaste for the statement, telling NCCJ Director Everett R. Clinchy that it was "confused" and "weak."[24]

Yet President Park actively supported Bryn Mawr student participation in the junior year and summer exchange programs in Nazi Germany's universities. She cooperated with one of her professors, Max Diez of the German Department, who served for several years on the Junior Year in Munich, Inc., Executive Council.[25]

In 1924 President Park had invited Fascist Italy's ambassador to the United States, Prince Gaetano Caetani, to speak at Bryn Mawr on "the spiritual side of the Fascist movement in Italy." Park declared that her purpose in welcoming Prince Caetani to Bryn Mawr was to "renew in this delightful way the connection which the college has always had with Italy." She noted that two of Bryn Mawr's best mathematics graduates were currently studying at the University of Rome. Caetani, accompanied by the Italian consul in Philadelphia, dined with Park before the lecture.[26] In April 1937, Bryn Mawr announced that for the first time, three of its students would join Smith College's junior year program at the University of Florence for the 1937–38 academic year.[27]

One of Bryn Mawr's most distinguished faculty members, Henry Cadbury, professor of biblical literature, expressed views common among the pacifists at that college when he lectured those attending the Central Conference of American Rabbis convention in June 1934 not to fight back against Hitler. Professor Cadbury denounced such nonviolent methods of resistance as the economic boycott, which he called "simply war without bloodshed." He insisted that Jews must display "good will" toward the Nazis and urged them to appeal to the "German sense of justice."[28]

During the early years of the Hitler regime, Seven Sisters colleges often hosted speakers sympathetic to Nazi Germany, who praised Hitler, justified German rearmament and expansionism, and dismissed reports of antisemitic persecution as fabricated. Such speakers included many of the schools' exchange students returning from Germany, members of their faculties who had traveled there, and Nazi officials, professors, and students visiting the United States. Vassar senior Joan Becker of the Class of 1934, who had spent the previous year at the University of Munich with the Delaware group, declared in October 1933 that she admired the energy and "dignity" of the Nazi students and their determination to "clean up Germany." The book burnings that the Nazi students had coordinated at universities across the Reich and carried out in May 1933 impressed her as "a solemn, symbolic ceremony." Mary Ridder, another Vassar senior who had, like Becker, been enrolled at the University of Munich with the Delaware group for her junior year, told the *Vassar Miscellany News* that before arriving in Nazi Germany she had formed an image of Hitler and his Storm Troopers "as a sort of German Ku Klux Klan." But having had the opportunity to speak personally with Hitler in Germany, she was convinced that the Fuehrer was sincerely committed to promoting his country's best interests. She praised the German students as "more socially conscious" than their American counterparts.[29]

The *Vassar Review* "Freshman 1935" issue published a lengthy feature entitled "We Went to Germany," in which four Vassar students explained how living in the Third Reich had led them to dismiss American press accounts of "militarism, terrorism, and bloodshed" there, and to truly appreciate what Germans under Nazi rule had accomplished. Agnes Reynolds, Class of 1938, had traveled to Germany strongly disliking National Socialism "without knowing what it was." Although she found antisemitic publications like the Nazi newspaper *Völkische Beobachter* distasteful, she believed intelligent Germans regarded them the same way educated Americans did subway tabloids. Reynolds considered American criticism of the Third Reich to be "cruel," because the United States had helped make Germany economically insecure and militarily vulnerable. She insisted that "Germany has every right to work out her own destiny in her own way."[30]

Catherine Elliott, Vassar Class of 1936, who had spent her junior year at the University of Munich, reported that Nazi Germany was not remotely like American newspapers described it. Expecting turmoil, Elliott instead found Munich to be "the most orderly and peaceful city in which I had ever had the pleasure to live," a veritable "paradise for students." While uncomfortable with certain Nazi policies (maintaining concentration camps and "ostracizing the Jewish people"), Elliott stated that she could not condemn those policies "without first condemning the world which has forced Germany into her present day situation." Besides, most of the large Jewish stores were doing just as well as before the Nazis came to power. American animosity toward Nazi Germany "can only lead to disaster," Elliott concluded.[31]

Vassar provided another platform for students proclaiming the "merits of National Socialism" at a campus symposium on Germany held in October 1935. Catherine Elliott explained that the abuses of the Versailles Treaty and unstable Social Democratic rule had made the Germans "ready for a revolution." She praised Hitler for achieving "religious unity" and for drastically reducing unemployment. Elliott concluded her presentation by claiming that "Hitler is not militaristic. He is sincerely spoken for peace." Elliott was followed by Em Bowles Locker, who declared that the "New Germany is building – building new houses and new dams – everyone is motivated by a feeling of progress." Locker defended the Nazi sterilization program because it "is eliminating people with inheritable diseases." She noted approvingly that "two doctors and a juror consider each case."[32]

At Wellesley in October 1934, Olga Edmond of the Class of 1936 explained in the school newspaper how visiting Germany for a six-week course at the University of Heidelberg had convinced her that the American press had grossly distorted what that country was really like. She appeared as "satisfied and content" as the Germans she described and seemed intent on trivializing Nazi terror. When Edmond saw her first Nazi brown-shirt she stared at his "polished brown boots" and then moved her gaze slowly up toward his "bright" swastika armband. This was a member of the Storm Troopers, whom American newspapers had told her "ruled Germany in a reign of blood and terror." But the young Wellesley student did not think he looked even "a bit ferocious or terrifying." He was just a harmless boy, resembling a "weary Boy Scout returning from an all-day hike." During the Night of the Long Knives, Edmond claimed that Heidelberg "maintained an air of complete calmness," and the populace had emerged from it with "renewed faith in Hitler's integrity."[33]

Members of Seven Sisters faculties often expressed similar sentiments. In October 1934 Smith College staged a forum at which four of its professors spoke about their recent summer in Nazi Germany. Professor Graham declared that the Weimar Republic had introduced democracy in Germany at the wrong time, and a dictatorship "was the logical solution" to the nation's problems. Graham acknowledged some interference with the press by the Hitler government but insisted that German newspapers presented "the essential facts" to the public. Foreign journalists reporting from Germany had provided distorted accounts of events. Some professors stated that Germany's Jews had controlled the nation's banks, stores, and press until the Nazis came to power. Commenting on Hitler's antisemitic campaign, they asserted that his regime was concerned only with Russian and Polish Communist Jews who had "invaded" Germany after the World War, posing "serious danger to national unity." The Nazis had instituted a Jewish quota in the universities in order to reduce white-collar unemployment. Professors J. C. Hildt (history) and Jacob (English) claimed that Jews in business enjoyed "toleration and acceptance."[34]

Vassar professors who had visited Nazi Germany provided similarly favorable descriptions of the situation there. One claimed she had learned the past summer that the Nazis had not closed down a large number of Jewish shops "as propaganda would lead us to believe." Another contrasted the "enthusiasm and optimism" of Hitler's Germany with the "listlessness and despondency of before."[35]

German exchange students at the Seven Sisters colleges presented the Nazi party version of events in Germany on campus. Emilie Gottschalk of the University of Freiburg, who had spent the academic year 1930–31 at Wellesley College, published a long letter in the student newspaper in May 1933 that denounced "large Jewish and radical organizations" in the United States that had joined with "proverbial German haters" to "maliciously circulat[e] false reports" in the press in an effort to prevent Americans from seeing Hitler's Germany "in the proper light." The demand for a boycott of German goods was part of this insidious propaganda campaign. Just as charges of German atrocities during the World War had been "unfounded lies," so were the claims that in Nazi Germany "the Jewish people are being persecuted and mistreated by the thousands."[36] At Mount Holyoke, Edeltraut Proske, a graduate exchange student, addressing the school's International Relations Club, denounced the "propaganda spread about the Jewish persecutions" in the Third Reich.[37] In the *Vassar Miscellany News*, Henning Freiherr von Dobeneck, a German student at the University of Munich, condemned the German press in the Weimar Republic as the instrument "of the Free Masons and the Jews."[38]

German exchange students also served as propagandists for Nazi women's policy. In November 1934, Dorothy Thompson, the noted newspaper columnist and wife of Sinclair Lewis, whom the Nazi government had expelled from Germany for criticizing Hitler, declared in a speech at Vassar that the Nazis had driven women "out of the universities, out of industry, out of public life."[39] As early as June 1933 in Britain, fourteen nationally organized women's groups had sent a letter of protest to foreign press correspondents in Germany "to rouse the world to a realization of the discriminat[ion]" against women in Germany. The letter charged that the Nazis were making "a very definite attempt... to deprive women of their right to earn," and that "large numbers of women have been turned out of their posts."[40] Yet on the Seven Sisters campuses, administrators, faculty, and students failed to mount any organized protest against the undermining of women's opportunities in higher education and in the public sphere generally.

The Hitler regime defined women's central role as that of mother and homemaker and considered a university education of little importance to women. It promoted the five-child family as the norm and equated those who failed to produce children with military slackers. In January 1934, Dr. Esther Caukin Brunauer, on her return from ten months in Nazi Germany, reported that the regime prohibited women from serving as judges and "made it almost impossible for them to practice law." She stated that hospitals were expelling women physicians and that in Hamburg, where there had been nine female school principals, not one remained. Brunauer declared that Germany's women students "subscribed in large numbers to the Nazi idea of woman's status in the social scheme."[41] The Nazis nearly eliminated women from government. In the first Nazi Reichstag there was not a single woman deputy for the first time since the World War.[42]

The Nazis severely constricted women's opportunities in higher education. The quota limiting women to 10 percent of those admitted caused female university enrollments to drop by 40 percent from 1933 to 1934.[43] In May 1937, Erika Mann, daughter of exiled German novelist Thomas Mann, and herself a refugee, noted that not a single female full professor remained in any German university, and that there were only a few women instructors "in subordinate positions."[44] About the only employment available to women university graduates in Nazi Germany was schoolteaching.[45] Before a woman could enter a university, she had to first perform six months of service in a labor camp, where she was assigned tasks designed to prepare her for marriage and motherhood. Unlike her male counterpart, who went to labor camp to "build roads, regulate rivers, and reclaim land," women's labor service involved such tasks as cooking, sewing, and learning how to care for children. The Washington *Post* called Germany's female labor camps "bride factories."[46]

German exchange students at the Seven Sisters colleges vigorously defended Nazi policy toward women in the campus newspapers. For example, Ursula Engler, an exchange student at Vassar, claimed that the Nazis' sharp reduction in the number of women admitted to universities was the best way to solve Germany's problem of white-collar unemployment.[47] Liselott Strecher, another German exchange student who had recently graduated from Vassar, explained that the Nazis had taken "immediate" and "necessary" action to sharply reduce female and Jewish enrollments in order to alleviate serious overcrowding in the universities and the "misery of a growing academic proletariat." Strecher praised the compulsory labor camps as a screening device designed to solve these problems. She praised the camps' "great educative value," which taught German youth the value of "hand-labor" and "domestic work" and convinced many to embrace "simpler forms of life."[48]

Visiting professors from Germany also made the case for Hitler on campus. At Bryn Mawr College, a school strongly influenced by pacifism, Dr. Fritz Marstein Marx, formerly of the University of Hamburg, was invited to speak in January 1934 on "Hitlerism and Peace." Dr. Marx denounced the American press's "atrocity" stories about the Third Reich and claimed that Hitler was committed to peace, desiring only an equality of armaments with countries that threatened Germany.[49]

Impressionable students were also often influenced by American lecturers who presented a largely favorable view of the Hitler regime during its early years. At Wellesley, for example, Dr. Robert C. Dexter, formerly head of the Brown University Sociology Department and a director of the League of Nations Association, lectured in November 1933 on the "excellent time he [had] enjoyed" in Nazi Germany the previous summer. Dr. Dexter told the students that it was no wonder that the German people backed Hitler, because France was using its superior armaments to build a "wall of steel" around them. The German people were also reacting to the corruption of the Republican governments in the Weimar period. Dexter denounced the press reports of Jewish persecution as "grossly exaggerated" and claimed "that while he was in Germany he had not seen one instance of outright violence." Although he did not approve of the complete exclusion of Jews from civil offices, he explained that there were "extenuating circumstances": the Jews had "held a disproportionate amount of the country's wealth and . . . professional positions." Dexter emphasized that it was most important not to interfere in Germany's internal affairs. The "worst enemies of the German Jew," he pontificated, were not the Nazis, but "the Jews of other countries who are spreading untrue propaganda." This might lead resentful Germans to lash out at Jews to defend their country's honor.[50]

Seven Sisters colleges sponsored social events to promote German-American friendship. Wellesley College arranged a dance and reception for German naval cadets from the battle cruiser *Karlsruhe* when it visited Boston harbor in May 1934 flying the swastika flag on its goodwill tour around the world for the Nazi government. Ignoring the Boston Jewish community's protests against the German warship's visit, Wellesley invited the cadets to campus for a dance. Boston rabbi Samuel Abrams denounced the *Karlsruhe* as an instrument of "hate and darkness." By contrast, the *Wellesley College News* portrayed the cadets as very appealing young blond men "immaculate in flawless black uniforms," whose "friendly grins" made them appear "soft and sincere." Soon after the cadets' arrival, "the floor was filled with dancing couples." Everyone enjoyed the punch and cookies.[51]

Only at Barnard did Seven Sisters students mobilize to protest against Nazi terror in Germany. Barnard had the largest Jewish enrollment and most economically diverse student body among the Seven Sisters. Jews and youth from trade union families displayed more concern about Nazi persecution than did their classmates, as a rule. Addressing a joint meeting of the Barnard and Columbia Menorah Societies, Rabbi Baruch Braunstein vigorously denounced Nazi atrocities against the Jews, a topic that presidents of the Seven Sisters colleges had not explicitly addressed in public. Rabbi Braunstein compared 1933 to the years 70 and 1492, marked by catastrophes that had devastated Jewish life for centuries: the Roman conquest of Judaea and destruction of the Second Temple, which deprived the Jews of their homeland for almost two millennia, and the expulsion of the Jews from Spain, which eliminated Europe's largest and oldest Jewish community.[52]

About six weeks later, Barnard students participated in the aggressive mass picketing of the auditorium at which Nazi ambassador to the United States Dr. Hans Luther spoke, at the invitation of the Columbia University administration. The *Barnard Bulletin* in an editorial denounced Columbia's sponsorship of Luther's lecture, declaring that it provided the barbaric Nazis with "the coveted seal of responsibility."[53]

Students and faculty at the Seven Sisters expressing admiration for the "New Germany" influenced many college youth toward greater sympathy for the Hitler regime. In May 1934, Radcliffe's Debating Council sponsored a debate between the Radcliffe and Brown University teams on whether "Hitlerism is the best thing for Germany." Presenting the affirmative, "the gentlemen from Brown" argued that Hitler had rescued Germany from anarchy and forestalled a Communist takeover. He had ended an ineffective Reichstag's "feudalistic wrangling," stimulated economic recovery, and "restored unity, morale, and self-respect" to a nation exploited by vindictive Allied powers. Hitler's foreign policy did not present a menace to peace. Radcliffe, presenting the negative, declared that Hitler had destroyed German democracy and civil liberties and promoted a belligerent nationalism that would lead to war. Nazi persecution of Jews does not seem to have been mentioned. When the debate was concluded, the Radcliffe audience, acting as judges, granted victory to the Brown team.[54]

Administrators of the Delaware Junior Year in Munich program became alarmed in May 1933 when students at the University of Cincinnati, horrified by the mass public book burnings at German universities, circulated an open letter protesting the suppression of academic freedom in Nazi Germany. University of Cincinnati president Raymond Walters expressed approval of the letter, which called the Hitler government's higher education policy "a menace to the whole world." President Walter Hullihen of the University of Delaware denounced the letter at an assembly of the University of Delaware's Women's College, declaring that stories of Nazi persecution in the American press were "grossly exaggerated, in many cases utterly false." He informed his students that a "majority of the German people" had chosen the Nazi government, and that Americans had "no right to express any protest of opinion to that government about how it handles its purely internal affairs," especially because Americans lacked "any reliable information about conditions in that country." He urged nations participating in an international economic conference scheduled to begin on June 15 to avoid "any unfriendly reference" to Nazi Germany.[55]

President Hullihen instructed directors of the Delaware Junior Year in Munich program to make known to German officials involved in student exchanges with American colleges that the University of Delaware condemned the Cincinnati students' letter.[56] No president or other administrator of a Seven Sisters college, all of which were avid participants in student exchanges with Germany, registered any disapproval of President Hullihen's pronouncements.

Foreign students enrolled at the University of Munich simultaneously sent a statement to American collegians claiming that American newspapers were providing distorted accounts of events in Germany and denying the existence of violence or disorder there. Seven Sisters women made up a majority of the Americans then studying at Munich. They declared "unanimously, of their own free will and accord... that not one single one of them... was, during the entire course of the German national revolution, molested in any manner whatsoever," whether in Munich or elsewhere in Germany. They claimed to be living "as peacefully in Munich as they would have at home."[57]

President MacCracken of Vassar assisted in organizing a tour of Nazi Germany for American college professors and students, sponsored and funded by the Vereinigung Carl Schurz of Berlin, which offered a free trip each way on German ships. Seven Sisters faculty recruited students for the tour, and several took part in it themselves. The *New York Times* explained that those planning the tour were determined that "something definite should be done to correct what they regard as the false attitude toward the new Germany adopted by the greater part of the American public." The Vereinigung Carl Schurz was founded by the German government to promote U.S.-German friendship. To represent the Vassar faculty, President MacCracken selected Professor Dorothy Schaffter of the Political Science Department, later president of Connecticut College for Women.[58]

This summer 1934 tour was the first in which an American group traveled in Nazi Germany under the guidance of Nazi party and government officials. The Americans participating elected as group leader President Homer LeRoy Shantz of the University of Arizona, the only university president making the trip.[59]

The propaganda benefits of the tour for the Nazi government became obvious almost immediately. During the first week in Germany, an awestruck Vassar student wrote to President MacCracken that she had received "the whole-hearted attention of every [Nazi] official in Berlin," and each night she had to choose among three or four invitations. She was pleased to report that on her first night in Berlin she had been seated at dinner opposite Professor Friedrich Schoenemann, the Nazi propagandist whom Hitler had sent on a recent American lecture tour. The student concluded, "I have never in my life had such an exciting... time, nor so much fun."[60]

Upon the group's return, their leader, President Shantz, trumpeted Hitler's achievements, as did Professor Stuart M. Stoke of Mount Holyoke. President Shantz described German agriculture and land use "as the most perfect ever developed" and marveled that "[t]here are not as many weeds in Germany as in 1 square mile in this country." He described the German people as "busy and active." They backed their

Fuehrer much as Americans backed President Roosevelt. Shantz expressed his disapproval of American press coverage of Germany, explaining that it reported "the worst possible events."[61]

The *American Hebrew* summed up President Shantz's remarks by commenting, "on and on he goes, singing the praises of Hitler and Nazism." It noted that Propaganda Minister Josef Goebbels had clearly "figured out the scheme of entertaining American educators and inculcating in them gratitude and appreciation."[62]

Professor Stuart M. Stoke certainly seemed to confirm this by publishing in the *Mount Holyoke Alumnae Bulletin* a description of Nazi Germany every bit as flattering as that of President Shantz. Presenting his German hosts as highly civilized and polite, Professor Stoke stated that they had shown the group "every courtesy and consideration." Everyone in Germany felt secure except the Communists. There was "comparatively little furor" against the Jews. Stoke portrayed Hitler as a reformer like President Roosevelt, who had introduced a "New Deal" in Germany.[63]

Professor Stoke offered a rationale for the Nazis' forcing Jews from the professions, and for their reactionary women's policy. He claimed that 60 percent of Germany's lawyers had been Jews, although they were only 1 percent of the population, and that as a result they had wielded too much power. The Germans insisted that "they were Jews first and Germans second." The Nazi program of teaching women that their place was in the home was designed to solve the problem of male unemployment that had plagued Germany, and to increase the German birth rate. Stoke claimed that German university women supported this policy. He implied that Germany was justified in building up armaments, because the Versailles Treaty had left her defenseless, while her neighbors were "armed to the teeth."[64]

The propaganda value of the tour for the Hitler regime was further enhanced by the distribution of a free film about it on American campuses. The participating Americans had been accompanied while in Germany by cameramen from the state-run Universum-Film Aktiengesellschaft (UFA). The resulting film, entitled *Germany Today*, portrayed the Third Reich as an economically vigorous and harmonious society, thriving under Hitler's dynamic leadership. Its images of German-American amity were designed to counteract "Jewish atrocity propaganda" in the American media.[65]

Professor Dorothy Schaffter, Vassar's faculty representative on the tour, shared her excitement about the film with President MacCracken. She had viewed two reels of *Germany Today* before leaving the Reich and pronounced them "very fine indeed." She wrote to President

MacCracken to suggest that it be shown at Vassar and offered to show the film and talk about it at the Vassar Faculty Club and at the German Club. MacCracken pronounced this a "splendid" idea. He notified the president of the Vereinigung Carl Schurz: "We are awaiting the film with much interest."[66]

During 1934, American university tours of Europe invariably included trips to the fiercely antisemitic passion play at Oberammergau in Bavaria, which celebrated its tercentenary that year. Students from Seven Sisters colleges were even more eager to visit Oberammergau than those from other schools because their curricula gave particular emphasis to theater. Ordinarily, the play was staged throughout the summer preceding the start of each decade, but the Nazi government, excited by how it could be used to present vicious stereotypes of Jews to tens of thousands of visitors, arranged special anniversary performances from May through September 1934. Sponsoring the play aligned the Nazi party closely with Christianity, making it appear more respectable to Western tourists. Adolf Hitler personally attended the Oberammergau Passion Play both in 1930 and as chancellor in 1934, when he spoke with the cast on stage. Hitler strongly endorsed the play, declaring that "never has the menace of Jewry been so convincingly portrayed as in this presentation of what happened in the times of the Romans."[67]

Performed in the village of Oberammergau since 1634, the day-long passion play depicted Jews as an evil race cursed forever for the crime of deicide. The Oberammergau production mixed modern racial anti-semitism with medieval theological antisemitic symbolism. The Jews were clad in yellow, the color of avarice and of prostitution. Their priests wore horned hats, indicating their association with Satan. Jesus was presented as "Nordic"-looking, while actors with swarthy complexions played the Jews, emphasizing their racial difference. The brutal, crucifixion-happy Roman governor of Judaea, Pontius Pilate, was portrayed as "wise and merciful." In 1934 the actors playing Jesus (Alois Lang), the Virgin Mary (Anni Rutz), and eight of the twelve Apostles were members of the Nazi party.[68]

Jews had long denounced the Oberammergau Passion Play as virulently antisemitic. Rabbi Stephen S. Wise, leader of the American Jewish Congress, called the play "a poisonous influence" on Christians, encouraging "every manner of ill-will against the Jews."[69] Well aware of this, the Nazi government enthusiastically promoted the Oberammergau tercentenary, hoping to attract 400,000 tourists to Germany with much-needed foreign currency. The German steamship companies and railroads vigorously promoted the passion play, and the latter provided discounted fares for those traveling to Oberammergau.[70]

Because there was considerable interest among Bryn Mawr College students in that summer's Oberammergau Passion Play, the campus newspaper in February 1930 provided travel and lodging information for those planning to attend, in a lengthy article extolling the "stirring pageant." It remarked that "[n]o one has been able to describe the solemn beauty, the deep and delicate feeling and powerful emotional effect of this event." The article explained that the Fellowship of Reconciliation, a pacifist organization with which many of Bryn Mawr's Quaker administrators had ties, would set up and administer an encampment at Oberammergau from June 1 through September 30, 1930, with the assistance of the World's Student Christian Federation. The encampment's purpose was to enable those who were unable to afford the steep cost of lodging and dining in Oberammergau to attend the passion play.[71]

Marian Hayes of the Mount Holyoke College Art Department in December 1933 informed the student body that the Bureau of University Travel had arranged a student tour that included the next summer's Oberammergau Passion Play. Hayes remarked excitedly that the staging of the play "always means a red letter year for European travelers."[72]

The massive purge that Hitler conducted on the Night of the Long Knives, June 30–July 1, 1934 – when the SS arrested and murdered the leadership of the *Sturmabteilung* (SA), former chancellor Kurt von Schleicher and his wife, and many others – caused panic among administrators of the University of Delaware Junior Year in Munich program and soon after led to its suspension. However, strong support among American colleges and universities for continuing student exchanges with Nazi Germany, much of it mobilized by administrators and faculty at the Seven Sisters colleges, resulted in the establishment of a new national academic organization to carry on this work, known as the Junior Year in Munich, Inc.

President Hullihen of the University of Delaware was already concerned in the spring of 1934 that Jewish opposition to student exchanges with Nazi universities threatened Delaware's German junior year program. He characterized Jewish opinion on this matter as "intensely bitter and inflamed." Hullihen reported to the program's director, Samuel A. Nock of the University of Delaware, that "two of the foremost Jews in America" had visited Dr. Stephen Duggan, director of the Institute of International Education, which promoted student exchanges, and demanded that he terminate involvement with any that included

Germany, or they would "break the Institute for International Education." Hullihen stated that Duggan had replied that the Institute had friends "quite as powerful as the Jews of America" and that he would ignore the demand. Nevertheless, Hullihen told Nock that he was very worried that "the Jews" might pressure the University of Delaware trustees to shut down the Junior Year in Munich program.[73] A few weeks later, President Hullihen wrote to Professor Camillo von Klenze of Stanford University, founder and dean of the Munich program, that he was "very much disturbed by the continually rising tide of condemnation of the present German government in this country."[74]

In early August 1934, President Hullihen was forced to announce that because of "unsettled conditions" in Germany the University of Delaware would not sponsor a student exchange group at the University of Munich for the 1934–35 academic year. He confided to supporters that because wealthy donors had withdrawn the necessary financial commitment that enabled the program to meet overhead expenses, the University of Delaware's trustees had ordered its suspension for the next year. The donors "were all strong German sympathizers," but they were worried about the prospect of continuing instability.[75]

President Hullihen declared that he had until "the very last" opposed suspension of the program, but the trustees' refusal to operate at a deficit had been decisive. He emphasized that "[t]here was no thought at all of expressing disapproval of the present regime in Germany."[76]

President Hullihen explained that the Night of the Long Knives had thrown the Junior Year in Munich program into temporary disarray because Germans prominent in leading or administering it had been murdered by the SS. Hullihen referred to Ernst Roehm, head of the SA, whom he called "one of the warmest supporters of our movement," and Dr. Fritz Beck, director of the University of Munich Studenthaus, where the Foreign Study offices were located. Adolph Morsbach, who Hullihen said "had been interested longer than anyone else in Germany in the Junior Year Plan" and had helped secure scholarships for it from the Deutsche Akademische Auslandsstelle, had been arrested and imprisoned.[77]

Despite the University of Delaware's suspension of its German junior year program, American students continued to study at the University of Munich under the auspices of the Deutsche Akademische Auslandsstelle (Foreign Academic Bureau) during academic years 1934–35 and 1935–36. The Auslandsstelle formed an advisory committee for the junior year program that included Minister Schemm of the Department of Culture and Education, U.S. consul-general Charles Hathaway and his wife, and the rector of the University of Munich. The program was modeled on that developed by the University of Delaware. The University of Delaware student newspaper reported in May 1935 that Professor Edmund E. Miller had resigned from the Modern Languages Department to assume the office of American director under the Auslandsstelle at the University of Munich for 1935–36. It noted that applications had been received from students at seven colleges, including Bryn Mawr, Smith, Vassar, and Wellesley, to study at Munich the next year.[78]

Seven Sisters administrators and professors were prominent in the group that established and directed the new Junior Year in Munich, Inc., for 1936–37, which ran the student exchange program until it was again suspended at the outbreak of World War II.[79] The Junior Year in Munich, Inc., announced that study in Germany promised the best prospect for bringing about "mutual understanding between America and Germany."[80] The Executive Council communicated with the German government through the Auslandsstelle and a consultant appointed by Berlin, Professor Matthias Schmitz of Smith College. Schmitz became "one of Germany's leading propagandists in America during the 1930s."[81]

In October 1935, the Vassar College student newspaper interviewed several faculty members about the College's practice during the last two years of accepting scholarships for its students to study at the Universities of Heidelberg and Munich. Twenty-six Vassar students had received scholarships for the summer of 1935 – eighteen for eight weeks of study at Heidelberg and eight for four weeks at Munich. The professors quoted all favored accepting the scholarships, although two thought Vassar should select for them only "mature" students, not anyone too impressionable. Professor Lilian Stroebe of the German Department commented that Vassar was not forcing any student to accept a scholarship.[82]

In the years following the Oberammergau tercentenary, American students studying in Germany recorded their enchantment with one of the most emotionally charged celebrations of Nazism, the nighttime 9th of November ceremony in Munich, which Hitler staged to honor the sixteen followers killed in his 1923 Beer Hall Putsch. On that date in 1935, the remains of these Nazi martyrs were placed in stone sarcophagi adorned with swastikas, in two temples specially built for them. The remains had been exhumed from cemeteries all over Germany. Frederick T. Birchall, covering the ceremony for the *New York Times*, reported that Munich was "wonderfully garlanded and beflagged for the event," with "ten thousand [Nazi] party banners ... unfurled." A crowd of 150,000 turned out to watch Julius Streicher, editor of the virulently antisemitic *Der Stürmer*, lead the procession to the temples along streets lined with Storm Troopers. Hitler marched with followers in the first ranks, as he had in 1923. Placed along the line of march were 251 pylons surrounded by flaming torches, each bearing the name of a Nazi activist killed in the decade during which the party fought its way to power. Many members of the diplomatic corps were in attendance, but U.S. ambassador to Germany William E. Dodd was conspicuously absent.[83]

In January 1936, Lisa Gratwick of Bryn Mawr, part of the junior year group at the University of Munich, wrote excitedly to her schoolmates about having attended the 9th of November ceremony. She described it as "beautiful to watch," with the "torches all along the main street, Hitler flags at every window." The ceremony was "perfectly solemn and tragic."[84] Mary Anne Greenough of George Washington University, another member of the Junior Year in Munich group, reacted similarly two years later as the Nazis again gathered on November 9th to pay homage to the fallen putschists. Greenough, writing in the Junior Year in Munich, Inc., newsletter, called the ceremony "worthy of our admiration."[85] Still another junior praised the Nazi party for ending "years of inward strife" and expressed pride that he and other members of the program had seen Hitler and "paid our respects" to those slain in 1923.[86]

Having sharply reduced female university enrollments in Germany, the Nazi government was not particularly interested in inviting the American women's colleges to the four-day festival to celebrate the University of Heidelberg's 550th anniversary, but it did ask Vassar to send a delegate. Like the other Seven Sisters, Vassar had regularly sent students to summer programs there. President MacCracken of Vassar in early March 1936 sent the University of Heidelberg his greetings and wished it "many more years of success." He insisted that the "courtesies of university life" had nothing to do with politics and asked, "Shall we cut off communication with those teachers and students who remain in Germany and . . . believe in the mind?" Two Vassar professors announced that they would attend the festival: Lilian Stroebe, a Heidelberg Ph.D., and Ruth Hofrichter, who also held a Heidelberg degree.[87]

The Vassar student newspaper sharply criticized President MacCracken's acceptance of Heidelberg's invitation to celebrate its 550th anniversary. It asserted that "[t]he presence of foreign educators at Heidelberg's anniversary cannot but be interpreted as an approval of the educational principles now ruling there," which were "dictated by the Nazi government." The participation of American academics would inevitably "be hailed as another triumph for Nazi philosophy."[88] Yet a week later, the student newspaper published an editorial praising Hitler's occupation of the Rhineland, which removed the major obstacle to a German invasion of the West.[89]

Professor Max Diez of Bryn Mawr, representing the Junior Year in Munich, Inc., spoke confidently in February 1937 of its vigor, but some of the program's administrators were becoming convinced that continuing Nazi outrages might result in pressure to reduce or even terminate student exchanges. Director Edmund Miller informed President Neilson of Smith that when he came to Germany in 1935 to direct the Munich program he had "hoped that the atrocities were over." But Miller was now becoming concerned that intensifying Nazi repression could precipitate a public outcry in the United States against student exchanges with Germany. He nonetheless reminded Neilson that Professor Diez and another Executive Council member with whom he had spoken were adamant that the German government not be offended. Miller concluded: "we should continue the group in Munich as long as we can."[90]

Professor Grace M. Bacon, who had charge of the student exchange with Germany at Mount Holyoke, reported to President Mary Woolley at the end of the spring semester of 1937 that "[t]he junior year in Germany is becoming more and more popular." She noted that three of Mount Holyoke's juniors would attend the University of Munich during the 1937–38 academic year, and that several more would be enrolled that summer at Munich and at the University of Berlin. Bacon confided to President Woolley that she had expected a decline in the number of Mount Holyoke students majoring in German "due to the prejudice toward Fascist Germany." But Bacon was pleased to report that the next year's registration showed no decline at Mount Holyoke, in contrast to the "New York universities," where "the change is noticeable."[91]

President Neilson carried on Smith's student exchange program with the Fascist-controlled University of Florence from 1931, when it began, through the 1938–39 academic year. In July 1939 Neilson regretfully informed the rector of the University of Florence that because of the "fear of the outbreak of war in Europe," not enough parents were willing to send their daughters to Italy to justify expenses.[92] The Smith College Junior Year in Italy program began the year the Italian universities required professors to take an oath of allegiance to the Fascist government. The twelve who refused to comply were discharged. That same year Fascists in Bologna had assaulted Arturo Toscanini, considered one of the world's greatest conductors, because he refused to begin his concert with the Fascist hymn. The universities strongly encouraged their professors to wear the Fascist black shirt at commencement ceremonies.[93]

The University of Florence program was committed to promoting friendly relations with the Fascist government. The Smith professor who directed the program in Italy, Emma Netti, was an avowed Fascist. She told Smith students that she provided a perspective on Mussolini's Italy rarely presented "in the supposedly unbiased American newspapers."[94] The *Smith Alumnae Quarterly* reported that a representative of the first group of Smith juniors to study in Florence, Laura Marden, "had the honor of a private audience with Mussolini." It proudly noted that "the 'Historical Handbook of Smith College' now reposes in Mussolini's desk."[95] On more than one occasion during the 1930s, President Neilson traveled to Florence to meet the Smith students studying there, and he met personally with its Fascist rector. In November 1937, Neilson again gave Smith students in Florence permission to meet with Benito Mussolini. Netti informed him that when they learned of this, the Smith students "were excited and enthusiastic."[96]

When the Italian government introduced a series of anti-Jewish laws in the autumn of 1938, modeled on those in Germany, defining Jews as a race, President Neilson did not protest to the Italian government, or to the rectors of the Italian universities at which Smith students were enrolled. These "racial laws" forced out any Jewish professors and students remaining in universities, discharged Jewish teachers from public schools, prohibited Jews from attending secondary schools, and segregated Jews in elementary schools.[97] The Italian consul sent Smith College forms asking for the ethnic origin of its students studying in Italy. Neilson did not comment in the American press on the racial legislation. Instead he notified the fathers of the two Jewish students who had been accepted into the Smith Junior Year in Italy program not to send their daughters "without permission from the Italian authorities."[98]

The Kristallnacht of November 9–10, 1938, appeared to put student exchanges with Germany in jeopardy. On that night, in a carefully planned series of pogroms across the Reich, "the Jewish community of Germany went up in flames." Rampaging Nazis destroyed all the nation's synagogues, assaulted thousands of Jews in the streets of every city and town, murdering nearly 100, and wrecked 7,000 Jewish businesses. The Nazis arrested and imprisoned in concentration camps more than 30,000 Jewish men.[99] Kristallnacht pushed Junior Year in Munich, Inc., director Edmund Miller into a "slough of Despond." Miller had hoped after the

September 1938 Munich Conference that Neville Chamberlain's concessions to Hitler ensured "unperturbed development" for the program and "normal enrollment [for] the following year." He now worried about sending American students into "such a depressing environment."[100]

None of the Seven Sisters administrators or faculty members serving on the Executive Council of the Junior Year in Munich, Inc., resigned in protest. Three weeks after Kristallnacht, Henry Hemmendinger, a Jewish academic affiliated with the University Observatory at Princeton, told President Neilson that his participation on the Executive Council enhanced its prestige and urged him to step down. He noted that Smith College's granting credit for courses taken at Nazified universities made a mockery of Smith's academic standards. Hemmendinger lectured Neilson that by not resigning he was responsible for the "moral and scholastic perversion" of Smith College.[101]

American educators after Kristallnacht still wanted to maintain student exchanges with Munich and other universities in the Reich. In April 1939, President Neilson assured a German involved in administering the University of Munich junior year program that Smith College would "put no obstacles of any kind in the way of students who wish to go to Munich," and that it planned to send two or three the next year.[102]

Because some American parents feared that Germany had become too dangerous a place for their daughters, the Executive Council established a separate junior year German program at the University of Zurich in Switzerland, under Edmund Miller's direction. Nevertheless, the Munich program continued under the supervision of Professor Camillo von Klenze, its founder and president of its Executive Council. In March 1939, von Klenze wrote to President Neilson, whom he called "one who has shown concern in maintaining cultural relations between America and Germany," that he had insisted on the continuation of the Munich program. Von Klenze suggested that the Executive Council had created a second German junior year program in Zurich in response to an "unfortunate wave of anti-German sentiment in the United States." Professor Grace M. Bacon of the Executive Council, head of Mount Holyoke's German Department, wrote to her president, Roswell Ham, praising von Klenze for preventing a complete break with Nazi Germany.[103]

Strains were developing among the American administrators of the German junior year program. Edmund Miller from Zurich accused Grace M. Bacon and Professor Matthias Schmitz of Smith of acting as agents of the German government, which was maneuvering to assume complete control over American student exchanges to Germany. He claimed that they were working with Herman Ruoff, stepson-in-law of Mrs. Alfred I. du Pont, and his wife, Madeleine du Pont Ruoff, wealthy benefactors of the Junior Year in Munich, Inc. Ruoff, a German national and member of the Nazi party, was treasurer of the Auslandsstelle. The couple had traveled throughout the United States in 1936 promoting the Junior Year in Munich program and raising funds for it, speaking at university German clubs and at faculty meetings. The Ruoffs entertained the American students participating in the junior year program at their country estate outside Munich.[104]

Professor Max Diez of Bryn Mawr, an influential member of the Executive Council, expressed the ambivalence of many involved in student exchanges with Germany over setting up a program in Zurich. He pointed to American students' enthusiasm about Munich, declaring that few cities in the world could compare with it as a cultural center. Implying that the United States and Germany were equally to blame, Diez asserted that an "incessant press campaign of vituperation on both sides of the water" had caused many colleges to opt for Zurich as a safer environment for their students.[105]

Pressure mounted in the United States for colleges and universities to admit refugee students from Germany. At hastily organized meetings on many campuses, including those of the Seven Sisters, students gathered to raise money to provide scholarships for refugees.[106] Aware that the Seven Sisters' wealthy benefactors would not tolerate more than a token number of Jews at their colleges, administrators were careful to stress that non-Jews were to comprise a significant proportion of any refugees admitted. (See Chapter 8.)

Correspondence between President Henry Noble MacCracken of Vassar and Margaret C. Halsey, a friend who contacted him on behalf of a non-Jewish Polish professor stranded in the United States by the German conquest of his homeland, suggests that MacCracken was not uncomfortable with the prejudice against Jewish refugees common among alumnae. Halsey informed MacCracken shortly after the fall of Poland that Professor and Mrs. Henryk Arctowsky of Lvov, Poland, were in the United States and unable to return to their occupied country. She asked whether Vassar might consider offering Professor Arctowsky a position on its faculty. Halsey told President MacCracken that the Arctowskys "are not Polish Jews" and noted that she had also written to Dr. Frederick Keppel, a dean at Columbia University, "to reassure him" of that. Halsey added, "As you know, Mrs. Arctowsky comes from an American family of social distinction." President MacCracken in his response did not indicate he was in any way displeased with her statement that the Arc-towskys were not Jews. He did not take the opportunity to claim that Vassar hired faculty on merit, not ethnic background. On the contrary, MacCracken informed Halsey that he was passing her request on "at once to the chairman of our committee of the faculty" that considered such appointments.[107]

Despite the outpouring of protest after Kristallnacht, many associated with the Seven Sisters colleges remained unconcerned about Nazi perse-cution of Jews. Students returning from study in the Third Reich at the conclusion of the 1938–39 academic year continued to provide glowing accounts about it to their school newspapers. Blanche Hatfield, Mount Holyoke Class of 1940, for example, reported that she was thrilled when Adolf Hitler himself came into the restaurant where she was having lunch. Her German hosts "could not do enough" to make her stay in the Reich "profitable and enjoyable."[108] In September 1939, with war looming, a "dauntless group" of juniors assembled in New York City eager to sail to Europe for a year of study at the University of Munich; it was prevented from doing so only by the outbreak of hostilities.[109]

The decades-long campaign that Dean Virginia Gildersleeve of Barnard waged against what she called "International Zionism" illustrated the inability of many academic leaders to comprehend the depth and unique-ness of Jewish suffering. In her anti-Zionist tirades, Gildersleeve used code language favored by antisemites. She claimed that the "Zionist control of the media of communication" in the United States made it difficult for the public to obtain accurate information about the Middle East. Politicians' fear of the "Jewish vote" had led them to "bully" Arabs into allow-ing into Palestine a "huge influx of alien foreigners," her term for Jews residing there. Indifferent to the threat six invading Arab armies posed to Jewish survival in 1948, Gildersleeve claimed that they had "entered" Palestine after the Jewish state was proclaimed "to protect their fellow Arabs against such horrors as the Dair Yaseen massacre." Standing up to "Zionist threats and attacks," as she put it, Gildersleeve lobbied against the United Nations plan to partition Palestine into a Jewish and an Arab state, and after 1948 she led groups that attempted to persuade the Gen-eral Assembly "to reconsider its disastrous decision."[110]

In June 1933, New York City's mayor Fiorello H. La Guardia declared to an anti-Nazi gathering of 1,000 delegates from 236 Jewish women's organizations in the city that "the only effective way in which we can voice our protest and get it across to the German people is to make them realize that the American people refuse to deal with Germany as long as Hitler is in power." He strongly endorsed the delegates' commitment to boycott German goods and services in retaliation against the Nazi government's persecution of Jews. Condemning Nazi brutality toward Jews, former U.S. ambassador to Germany James W. Gerard asserted that Germany had returned to the Dark Ages.[111]

By contrast, the administrators and many faculty members at the Seven Sisters colleges remained committed to building and maintaining friendly ties with Nazi Germany's universities, and with its government, into the late 1930s. Such behavior suggested to the American public that the Third Reich was a legitimate member of the community of nations. The Seven Sisters were centrally involved in academic exchanges with Nazified universities right up to the outbreak of World War II. Their students studied under German professors who supported Nazism, in the junior year program at the University of Munich, and in summer courses at the Universities of Heidelberg, Berlin, and elsewhere. Those participating invariably provided favorable accounts of the Third Reich upon their return. Frances Adams of Mount Holyoke, writing from Munich in March 1938, declared that "any account by any junior here is bound to turn into a testimonial."[112] Many Seven Sisters professors who traveled to Nazi Germany similarly became apologists for the regime. Seven Sisters students made frequent visits to the virulently antisemitic passion play at Oberammergau in Bavaria, both in 1930 and during the tercentenary performances in 1934. Their professors encouraged them to attend and often accompanied them to this pageant, which Hitler enthusiastically endorsed for depicting Jews as a depraved race, cursed through the centuries for having committed deicide. The Seven Sisters actively recruited German exchange students who aggressively championed the Third Reich on their campuses.

Like the elite men's universities, the Seven Sisters sought and maintained cordial relations with Nazified universities, through well-organized student exchange programs and tours of the Third Reich that the Hitler regime organized to showcase its "achievements." Participating students, both American and German, celebrated Nazi Germany at campus forums and in the press. Seven Sisters professors returning from travels in the Third Reich often provided support for such views, and, by condemning American press reports of Nazi atrocities as exaggerated, seriously misled the American public. Visiting professors from German universities aggressively propagandized for Hitler and the Third Reich on the Seven Sisters campuses. Oddly, Seven Sisters administrators and faculty remained largely silent as the Nazis drastically reduced opportunities for women in higher education. By encouraging and developing strong relationships with students and faculty from Nazi Germany, and offering them an important forum in which to present their views in the United States, the prestigious Seven Sisters colleges helped the Hitler regime in improving its image in the West as it intensified its persecution of Jews and prepared for war.

5

A Respectful Hearing for Nazi Germany's Apologists

The University of Virginia Institute of Public Affairs Roundtables, 1933–1941

American academia's most prestigious national and international affairs symposium, the University of Virginia Institute of Public Affairs roundtables, held each summer beginning in 1927, contributed to the Hitler regime's efforts to present Germany as a state with legitimate grievances and reasonable objectives. The Institute of Public Affairs often invited scholars and diplomats who rationalized or defended Nazi Germany's foreign and domestic policies to join its roundtables. On some occasions, avowed Nazis either chaired the roundtable or delivered one of the principal addresses.

The Institute of Public Affairs provided a major platform to scholars, polemicists, and German diplomats who advanced the revisionist argument on the origins of the World War, which denied that Germany was primarily responsible for starting it. Revisionist writings and conference presentations caused many Americans to view Germany more sympathetically. Professor Sidney Fay, who held a joint appointment at Harvard University and Radcliffe College, arguably the most influential of the revisionists, asserted in April 1933 that Hitler's "national revolution" was "Germany's answer" to the unfair conditions the victorious Allies had imposed on it at Versailles.[1]

The Influence of the Revisionist Argument on the Origins of the World War on Americans' Response to Nazism

The revisionist historians of the origins of the World War convinced many Americans that either the Allies themselves were primarily to blame for starting the conflict, or that all belligerents were equally to blame. Revisionist arguments appealed to much of the American public as they became increasingly isolationist during the 1920s and resentful of their nation's allies for failing to repay wartime loans. The United States had refused to ratify the Versailles Treaty and would not join its wartime allies in the League of Nations.[2] Many Americans during the interwar period, convinced by revisionist historians that vindictive Allies had imposed unnecessarily harsh conditions and reparations at Versailles on a Germany no more guilty of initiating hostilities than they were, sympathized with Hitler's determination to restore Germany's military strength and lost territories. They credited Hitler with restoring confidence and honor to a prostrated and seemingly unfairly stigmatized nation. By repeatedly disparaging Allied wartime propaganda about German military abuse of civilians, the revisionist scholars, and those who popularized their arguments in the mass media, convinced many Americans that reports of Nazi persecution of Jews were greatly exaggerated or even false.

The pioneering revisionist historians were Sidney Bradshaw Fay and the more strident Harry Elmer Barnes, both of whom were professors at Smith College during the 1920s. In 1929, Fay became the first professor to hold a joint appointment at Harvard and Radcliffe, and he taught there until 1946. Barnes left Smith in 1930 to become an editorial writer with the Scripps-Howard newspaper chain. During 1920 and 1921, Fay published three articles in the prestigious *American Historical Review* arguing that Germany had not intended to go to war and had made concerted attempts to avoid doing so. Fay's two-volume study *The Origins of the World War*, published in 1928, asserted that all the belligerents shared responsibility for the war's outbreak and called for revision of the Versailles Treaty, which had blamed Germany and her allies. *The Origins of the World War* was the most influential scholarly work on the subject in the United States for several decades after its publication.

Harry Elmer Barnes, whom Professor Harold U. Faulkner of the Smith College History Department in 1935 called "the best-known man who has ever been on the Smith faculty," in his book *The Genesis of the World War* (1926) assigned most of the blame for causing the war to the Entente, identifying France and Russia as the "leading precipitators."[3] Barnes's campus presentations received passionate backing from students. In 1926 he delivered a speech to the Harvard Debating Union, arguing the affirmative on "Resolved, that this house favors the revision of the Versailles Treaty in respect to the war guilt of the Central Powers."

The *Harvard Crimson* reported that Barnes "swept [the audience] off [its] feet," presenting "an unanswerable case." He asserted that France, determined to regain Alsace-Lorraine from Germany, and Russia, intent on seizing the Bosporus from Turkey, had together formulated plans "for a sweeping continental war." The Harvard students found Barnes so convincing that there was substantial support for a motion to not even hold a vote. In the end, eighty-one members of the audience voted in favor of Barnes's position, with only twenty-five opposed and twenty-nine not voting.[4]

Although critical of Nazism, Sidney Fay argued that protests against the Nazi regime were counterproductive. He also minimized the support for Nazism among the German people. In April 1933, Fay told the *Harvard Crimson* that what was happening in Nazi Germany was "really none of any other country's business." He pontificated that "[p]rotest meetings such as have been held in this country and in England... merely add fuel to the fire."[5] In January 1935, Fay told an audience at Vassar College shortly after the population of the Saar in a plebiscite voted overwhelmingly to rejoin Germany that the outcome was "a great aid in the cause of peace." He still found 20 percent of Hitler's accomplishments to be "good."[6] Speaking at a mass rally at Radcliffe after the horrifying Kristallnacht pogroms of November 9–10, 1938, Fay declared that protests against the Nazi atrocities "would do no practical good."[7]

During May 1940, as the invading Wehrmacht pushed British troops toward the English Channel and drove into France, Sidney Fay sent an article on "The German Character" to Lester Markel, Sunday editor of the *New York Times*, for consideration for publication; the article revealed that his basic assumptions about Germany remained largely unchanged. Germany had already just conquered Denmark, Norway, the Netherlands, Belgium, and Luxembourg. Fay's major argument in the article was that the majority of Germans were not enthusiastic about the Nazis' domestic or foreign programs. He offered a rationale for much of what they did support. Fay mentioned that only 5 percent of Germans belonged to the Nazi party, and that there were many "terrorized opponents" of Hitler who did not dare speak out. Fay conceded that the vast majority of Germans had backed Hitler's early effort to "decreas[e] the influence of the Jews in Germany," calling the policies he imposed in April 1933 "relatively moderate." These included the 1 percent quota on Jewish university admissions and expulsions of Jews from professions such as law, medicine, and university teaching. But Fay claimed that he doubted whether even 30 percent of Germans approved of the Kristallnacht pogroms. Protestant and Catholic churches were thronged, "but not by Nazis and Nazi supporters." This suggested that Germany's vast church-going population was not in sympathy with the regime.[8]

Fay argued that a significant proportion of Germans turned against Hitler's foreign policy after the Munich crisis of September 1938. He asserted that the majority of Germans had up until then supported Hitler's "successful efforts to get rid of the 'shackles' of the Versailles 'Diktat.'" But Fay claimed that the German "masses" reacted "with revulsion" when they realized how close Hitler had brought them to war over the Sudetenland.

The German people's "doubts as to [Hitler's] wisdom" increased after Germany subjugated the rest of Czechoslovakia in early 1939, signed a nonaggression pact with Stalin later that year, and went to war with Britain and France in the spring of 1940. Fay conceded that the German people almost unanimously supported Hitler "in his determination to break British sea-power," but he ascribed this to their memory of the suffering Britain had inflicted on them by blockading German ports from "1914 to 1920," and to the Allies' "failure to live up to the promises in the Fourteen Points." Even so, Fay claimed that millions of Germans, living on rationed food in May 1940, were still "questioning in their hearts" whether they should support the invasion of France. The great majority of Germans might well turn against the Hitler regime should the Wehrmacht experience "two or three major reverses." Fay concluded by insisting that it was important for Germany to remain a strong nation. It was imperative that any peace settlement "receive her on equal terms into a new concert of Europe."[9]

Lester Markel rejected Fay's article for the *New York Times* because it seemed "almost in the nature of a defense of the Germans." Markel commented that Fay had failed to address key aspects of the German character and mind, including Germany's militarist tradition and anti-semitism. He also sharply criticized as misleading Fay's emphasis on the small percentage of Germans belonging to the Nazi party. Markel was convinced that a large portion of Germany's population was Nazified and noted that the German population appeared united behind Hitler's spring offensive.[10]

Fay conceded to Markel on June 6, 1940, that "under present circumstances," with British and French forces in a desperate rearguard battle against the Wehrmacht, "people would think the article pro-German." But he told Markel that did not worry him. After all, people had considered his *Origins of the World War* "very pro-German" when it was published, but "scholars and many laymen" now rated it "the best book on the subject."[11]

Another of the prominent revisionist historians of the origins of the World War, Charles C. Tansill, professor of American history at American University in Washington, D.C., from 1918 until 1937, and then at Fordham (1939–44) and Georgetown (1944–58), became an outspoken defender of Nazi Germany during the 1930s. Tansill, who received Ph.D. degrees from both Catholic University and Johns Hopkins University, regularly presented papers in diplomatic history at the American Historical Association conventions. The U.S. Senate Foreign Relations committee selected Tansill in 1925 to prepare the Senate's official report on responsibility for the World War. In 1931, Johns Hopkins invited Tansill to deliver the prestigious Albert Shaw lectures in American diplomacy, and during the 1934–35 academic year he served as acting dean of American University's Graduate School. In 1938, Tansill published a major revisionist book, *America Goes to War*, in which he argued that prominent American officials, most notably Secretary of State Robert Lansing and White House advisors Colonel Edward House and Joseph Tumulty, had drawn the United States into the war because they placed British interests above American interests.[12]

Professor Tansill publicly proclaimed his support for the Hitler regime during the summer and fall of 1936 on a visit to Nazi Germany sponsored by the Carl Schurz Society of Berlin, which promoted friendship between the United States and the Third Reich. In September, Tansill was one of fourteen American "honor guests" who participated in the Nazi party's Congress at Nuremberg, an event that U.S. ambassador to Germany William E. Dodd each year refused to attend. On the eve of the Nuremberg Congress, Tansill wrote to Ernest Griffith, who had succeeded him as dean of American University's Graduate School, that the Nazi party rally "should be a great demonstration in honor of Hitler whom I regard as one of the great leaders in German history." Tansill looked forward to meeting Hitler, along with the other "outstanding men of the party." He told Griffith that the Fuehrer "has given a new outlook to the German youth, one of optimism and hope." Tansill also noted how "deeply impressed" he was "with the efficient manner in which everything [in Germany] is conducted." He commented that the German people were "well-fed and well-clothed."[13]

Ambassador Dodd expressed disgust about the 1936 Nuremberg Nazi party Congress and Professor Tansill's participation in it. Dodd would not listen to Nazi leaders make "violent speeches" attacking democratic

nations. He noted that Hitler had gone "so far as to call all democracies 'anarchies.'"[14] Dodd told nationally prominent historian Howard
K. Beale of the University of North Carolina that when "[t]hat Tansill
man" had visited Germany the previous August and September, he did
not see him. He had learned that Tansill at Nuremberg had taken "an
almost worshipful view toward the Fuehrer." Dodd commented that "a
propagandist is not a good professor."[15]

In September 1936, while in Berlin, Tansill was asked by the Nazi
government to broadcast to the United States over shortwave radio his
impressions of the Third Reich. Tansill told Dean Griffith that he considered the invitation "a distinct honor," one he knew Griffith would
appreciate. In Tansill's address, "The New Germany," broadcast on
September 20, 1936, he enthusiastically praised Hitler's accomplishments
and denounced the American press for its critical stance toward Nazi
Germany. Tansill proclaimed that Hitler was "the one man who has
inspired the spirit of the people." Under the Fuehrer, Germany was
"emerging rapidly from the dark cloud that followed Versailles" and
was making "significant advance."[16]

After listening to the broadcast in Washington, D.C., with Tansill's
family, Dean Ernest Griffith wrote Tansill a letter of congratulations. He
declared that it had been a "pleasure" to hear his address on "The New
Germany" and praised "its clarity and vigor."[17]

After his return to the United States, Tansill continued to effusively
praise the Third Reich. In an address before the Presbyterian Ministers Association in Washington, D.C., in November 1936, Tansill proclaimed that under Hitler Germany was "emerging from the shadow of
defeatism and despair into the sunlight of prestige and power." Hitler
had restored to Germany not only law and order but also the self-respect
that the Versailles Treaty had "completely shattered." He claimed that,
in the Third Reich, there were "no breadlines [and] no slums." Tansill
declared that Nazi Germany constituted the "strongest bulwark in Europe
against . . . Communism." He insisted that Germany had no interest in
developing military supremacy in Europe. Germany's military buildup
was "a kind of peace insurance" for all of Europe, because it would
prevent other countries from starting a war.[18] That same month, Tansill denounced the U.S. ambassador to Germany, William E. Dodd, for
holding what he called a "completely unsympathetic attitude" toward the
Nazi government.[19]

When American University Chancellor Joseph M. M. Gray dismissed
Tansill from the faculty in 1937, he denied press speculation that he had

done so because of Tansill's public support for Nazi Germany. Chancellor Gray, of course, after a trip to Germany in 1936, had also highly praised the Third Reich in the press. When Fordham University wrote expressing interest in hiring Tansill, Chancellor Gray described him as "a sound scholar and a brilliant teacher" who deserved a university faculty position. He explained that he had discharged Tansill only because he had become overly concerned with "maintaining his popularity" with students. As a result, Tansill had become "indiscriminate in awarding high grades."[20] Professor Howard K. Beale confirmed to Ambassador Dodd that Tansill's pro-Nazi speeches had not been the cause of his dismissal. Beale explained that Tansill had been "let out for several reasons of personal conduct, one of which was refusal to make any efforts to pay a considerable amount of debts owed to other members of the faculty from whom Mrs. Tansill had borrowed money."[21]

The University of Virginia Institute of Public Affairs Roundtables, 1933–1941: Helping Germany Make Its Case

The University of Virginia Institute of Public Affairs, from 1933 until U.S. intervention in World War II in 1941, provided a major platform and an aura of academic legitimacy for Nazi Germany's supporters and for the propagation of antisemitism. The university established the Institute of Public Affairs in 1927 to answer "sundry charges that the South is backward and provincial." Every year in July the Institute sponsored several days of roundtable conferences on selected topics in national and international affairs. Each roundtable was composed of academics, diplomats, politicians, or other authorities on the subject under consideration, whom the Institute invited to present papers and to participate in discussion. Dr. Charles Gilmore Maphis, dean of the University of Virginia Summer School, was the Institute's director from 1927 until his death in May 1938. The Institute's initial Board of Advisors included four university presidents: Nicholas Murray Butler of Columbia; Harry Woodburn Chase, then of the University of North Carolina; Glenn Frank of the University of Wisconsin; and A. A. Murphree of the University of Florida.[22] Many of the roundtables received national and foreign press coverage.

The Institute's approach was to present "both sides of questions" at conferences, and it gave German Nazis and their American sympathizers considerable opportunity to propagandize for the Third Reich.[23] To secure these speakers, the University of Virginia administration worked closely with Nazi Germany's embassy in Washington, D.C., and with the Carl Schurz Foundation, an organization devoted to promoting friendly relations between the United States and Germany.[24] Institute Director Charles G. Maphis and other University of Virginia administrators accorded great respect to the Nazi spokespersons, some of whom the U.S. government later arrested as seditionists, as unregistered German agents, or for disseminating Nazi propaganda.

Papers by American academic apologists for Hitler at conferences devoted to Nazi Germany in 1934 and 1935 received prominent coverage in the press. Professor Francis W. Coker of the Yale University Political Science Department, chairman of the Institute roundtable on "Dictatorship and Democracy," held July 3–7, 1934, implied that the Nazi position had not received a proper hearing because representatives of the Hitler regime feared that if they accepted his invitation to speak, U.S. representative Samuel Dickstein's committee investigating subversive activities would charge them with disseminating Nazi propaganda.[25] Nonetheless, two of the principal papers were presented by Americans who sympathized with Nazi Germany: Karl F. Geiser, professor of political science at Oberlin College, and W. W. Cumberland of New York. More than 200 Institute members and guests, a particularly large audience for a roundtable, gathered for the first morning's session to hear their addresses.

In his paper, "The German Nazi State," Professor Geiser portrayed Hitler as Germany's savior, "a Siegfried slaying the dragon of communism." Drawing on the more polemical revisionist writings on the World War, Geiser strongly condemned the Allied wartime blockade of German ports, which he claimed had caused 750,000 to 900,000 Germans to starve to death, and what he called unreasonably harsh peace terms. Geiser charged that the Western democracies drew up the Treaty of Versailles in a "mental frame of madness." They forced on Germany "the harshest treaty ever imposed upon a people in modern times." It consigned Germany to "perpetual economic slavery" and impoverished her.[26]

Geiser declared that as a political scientist he admired how Hitler had ended the chaos of Weimar democracy "with its 32 parties," uniting Germans "into one party, for the first time in a thousand years," an achievement impossible without massive popular support. Geiser declared that Germany's "years in bondage" had only strengthened her "discipline and organizing powers," which he hoped would "give her the final victory over the forces of injustice." The *New York Times* reported that the audience applauded Geiser's address.[27]

Delighted with his reception at the University of Virginia, Geiser left immediately after his presentation for Nazi Germany, where he spent the rest of the summer. That fall, he wrote to Institute Director Charles Maphis that he "was charmed . . . by the courtesy of your Southern hospitality."[28]

W. W. Cumberland, who followed Geiser, feared that Nazi Germany, in building up her ground and air forces, was preparing for war, but he found many similarities between her economic programs and those of President Roosevelt. He declared, "Nazi Germany is a counterpart of the United States under the New Deal."[29]

Another member of the roundtable, Dr. Beniamino de Ritis of New York, special correspondent for the *Corriere della Sera* of Milan, described Italy's Fascist regime "in glowing terms," according to the *New York Times*. Mussolini had rescued a nation "on the verge of bolshevism and bankruptcy." For the first time in centuries, a long-divided nation fixated only on vanished ancient glory could look to the future. Mussolini's genius was to create in Italy a new form of state, conceived of "not as an aggregate of groups and individuals" but as "a spiritual entity," in which the individual is "subordinated to society."[30]

During the evening session, Harry Elmer Barnes, then an editor with the Scripps-Howard newspaper chain, presented his revisionist interpretation of the origins of the World War, absolving Germany of "unique blame" for the conflict. Barnes accused the Allies of deceiving the United States in order to draw it into the war, and with having "exacted by fraud vast sums from Germany" in reparations after the Armistice.

Barnes argued at the symposium that democracy had become outmoded as a form of government, making Nazi authoritarianism appear more legitimate. In his view, democracy assumed a "real intellectual equality of men" and an electorate that "carefully scrutinize[d] candidates and platforms." It was designed for a "simple and unchanging rural society" whose political problems were "few and elementary." Yet Barnes claimed that modern psychological research proved that most men were unqualified either to vote or to hold office. The population did not share an approximate mental equality. In fact, "a clear majority range[d] from stupidity (dull normals) to imbecility." Barnes concluded that science and the record of American politics over the previous century had "blown sky-high" the "whole body of assumptions upon which the old democracy rested." What was necessary was a weighted suffrage. Intelligence tests administered to the entire population would allow the government to accord greater voting power to a more intelligent citizen than to one determined to be less intelligent. The government should also require that candidates for political office possess a certain level of "scientific and professional training."[31]

The next year's Institute conference on "American-German Relations" was highlighted by the roundtable chair's dismissal of Nazi oppression of Jews as insignificant; a blatantly antisemitic address by one of the principal speakers, Professor Frederick K. Krueger of Wittenberg College; and defenses of the Nazi government by several other participants. Roundtable chairman Friedrich Auhagen of Columbia University's Seth Low College began the conference by vigorously defending the Third Reich, and he continued to do so at each session. He claimed that Germany could "no longer afford democracy." When roundtable member Dr. Morris Lazaron, a reform rabbi from Baltimore, asked why Auhagen had "so lightly dismissed . . . the religious question in Germany," meaning persecution of Jews, Professor Auhagen replied that "the religious problem" in the Third Reich was not really any different than in any other country.[32]

In a later session, Auhagen announced that the Germans wanted order, which could only be brought about by inflicting suffering on "some" people. Fellow panelist Dr. H. F. Simon of Northwestern University agreed, declaring that "one can not have change without suffering," and that restoring unity to Germany was a worthy goal.[33] Addressing Rabbi Lazaron, who had criticized the Hitler regime, Dr. Simon asked, "Can Dr. Lazaron . . . understand what the German people have gone through since 1914? . . . Hitler is an expression of the proudness of Germany which can not bow to the conditions imposed upon her."[34]

The University of Virginia administration invited Professor Frederick K. Krueger to deliver a major address at the conference fully aware that he had publicly made inflammatory pro-Nazi and antisemitic statements. The *New York Times* reported in early December 1934 that Krueger, who was then lecturing at the National Socialist Academy for Political Sciences in Berlin, had declared: "Some day America will be forced to deal with the problem presented by the Jew." The *Times* noted that the National Socialist Academy for Political Sciences was a "party institution devoted to the inculcation of Nazi theories." Krueger labeled the boycott of German goods "a crime against America," claiming that it harmed U.S. foreign trade. He denounced the American press for misrepresenting what had transpired in Nazi Germany. Krueger declared that American newspapers gave "no sign of an effort to understand the new German soul or to play fair." In his opening lecture at the National Socialist Academy

Krueger had offered Germans advice on how to conduct efficient propaganda in the United States. He explained that "only thoroughgoing National Socialists should be sent to America."[35]

Professor Frederick K. Krueger's address combined vigorous praise of Nazi government policies with a vicious antisemitic diatribe designed to discredit its American critics. Krueger began by declaring that Americans and Germans were "basically of the same racial stock [and] culture." He dismissed the view that liberal democracy was always the most desirable form of government. Krueger claimed that the United States itself had conferred dictatorial powers on its president when confronted with emergencies, "as for instance during the Civil War and the World War." Germany, facing economic crisis and threatened by Communism, had not acted any differently in according Chancellor Hitler such powers. Besides, every nation had the right to choose its own form of government. Americans were also wrong to criticize "so-called German militarism." All Germany wanted was equality in armaments with the nations that surrounded it. The Allies, after all, had violated their pledge at Versailles to reduce their own armaments.[36]

Professor Krueger invoked hoary antisemitic stereotypes to explain why much of American public opinion had turned against the Hitler regime. He claimed that "[t]he American Jews are financially very powerful." They largely controlled the metropolitan press and wielded great power in the movie industry and in radio. Jewish influence over "the organs of public opinion" allowed them to sow hostility to the Nazi government among non-Jewish Americans. Krueger insisted that Nazi Germany's "racial policy" was "its own affair," and that Americans had no right to protest against it. American Jews should "think of the country of their adoption first" and stop "sowing the seed of discord in the United States for the benefit of international Judaism."[37]

Professor H. F. Simon of Northwestern in his address declared that the harsh provisions of the Treaty of Versailles justified what he called "[t]he German Revolution of 1933," which he claimed Americans had very much misjudged. Simon asserted that no nation "would stand the dishonoring and impossible burdens" the "despotic" Allies had imposed on Germany. The Treaty's war guilt provision blaming Germany for starting the war was unfair. Germany was not permitted to rearm, despite being surrounded by "highly armed neighbors." The vindictive Treaty of Versailles had caused the German people to "close ranks" and take refuge "under the strong hands of a trusted and beloved leader," Adolf Hitler. Britain, France, and the United States, "rich in space," smugly preached the status quo, failing to comprehend overpopulated Germany's need to expand.[38]

Still another participant in the roundtable, Ernst Schmidt, in charge of tourist information and promotion for the German Railroads Company in New York, marveled over Nazi Germany's dynamism and modernity. He urged American travelers to see the Third Reich's "sparkling great cities with their stirring business, spotless cleanliness, and efficient administration." Nor should Americans neglect to visit the suburbs and smaller cities, where they could "wonder at the modern architecture and city planning" and "visit the roaring workshops of industry." Any visitor to the Third Reich would have to acknowledge "the rightful eminence of the German people as the most progressive and modern in Europe."[39]

Schmidt portrayed Nazi Germany's "new generation" as far more appealing than their decadent Western counterparts. The young women of the Third Reich combined "good looks" with "genuine culture" and provided "a distinct relief from flappers." The conversation of Germany's young men, who were "full of ideas," contrasted sharply with American youths' "college chatter."[40]

Dr. Henry G. Hodges, associate professor of political science at the University of Cincinnati, criticized American press coverage of Nazi Germany as prejudiced and sensationalistic, ridiculing "hair-trigger editorials whose predictions . . . are belied a week later." He condemned the Jewish-led boycott of German products and services as motivated by a desire for revenge and therefore "contrary to . . . Christian principle." Hodges believed that most Americans considered the Versailles Treaty unjust to Germany. Americans "overwhelmingly" supported Germany's right to rearm. There was also "general sentiment" in the United States that Adolf Hitler had "done as much (and perhaps more) as any of the other European nations to prevent war." Hodges noted that Americans who had traveled to the Third Reich were "more tolerant of her actions, and favorable to her conditions," than those who had not, implying that an "on-the-spot view" would change a person's opinions of Nazi Germany. He quoted one American traveler as commenting that Germany was "courageously facing the problems that we are side-stepping."[41]

Even Virginius Dabney, chief editorial writer for the Richmond *Times-Dispatch*, who had spent six months in Germany and Austria in 1934 and considered himself anti-Nazi, found much to admire in the Third Reich. He claimed that many Americans who had not visited Nazi Germany held a distorted view of it, apparently because of sensational stories about violence in the American press. Many Americans, for example, believed in

March 1933 that "dissident natives were being beaten up on almost every street corner in the Third Reich," and that "murder and mayhem were rife." Yet Dabney claimed that when he visited the Reich the previous year "perfect order prevailed everywhere in public." He reported that 75 percent of the "educated and cultured Germans" had opposed the Hitler regime. Dabney was also convinced that the vast majority of Germans did not want war.[42]

Yet after listing what he found abhorrent about the Hitler regime, Dabney found it "not so difficult to understand why the Nazis became disgusted with democracy." He credited Hitler with significant achievements. To be sure, the suppression of civil liberties, the torture and murder of some political dissenters, the killings during the Night of the Long Knives, and the regimentation of education were "revolting." But Dabney asserted that before Hitler assumed power, Germany had been "going from bad to worse," with more than thirty political parties making for a very unstable situation. Hitler had "promised to put the unemployed to work, to pull the country out of the depression, and to throw off the bondage of Versailles." Dabney declared that Hitler's record was one of "remarkable success." In about two and a half years, he had "made good on some of his most important pledges."[43]

Above all, Dabney urged, Americans must not work themselves "into an anti-German state of mind such as took possession of us from 1914 to 1918." During the World War, Americans had rushed, on the basis of very flimsy evidence, to raise their voices in a "hymn of hate" against Germany. Dabney hoped that Hitler had become "a man of peace" but worried about the intentions of other party chieftains. Still, he told the audience that he remained "tremendously fond of the German people." He described them as "kindly, lovable, and humane." They had much in common with Americans. Perhaps all would work out for the best.[44]

Several days after the conference ended, Institute Director Charles Maphis expressed pleasure that although the roundtable had focused on "a very delicate" subject, attendees' reaction afterward was very positive, and he had received "no severe adverse criticisms."[45] About two years later, in April 1937, Maphis's secretary wrote to University of Virginia president John Lloyd Newcomb that the papers from the July 1935 "American-German Relations" roundtable "have been in constant demand ever since."[46]

Because the University of Virginia was founded by Thomas Jefferson, reports in March 1936 that its administration had accepted the invitation from the Nazified University of Heidelberg to send a delegate to its 550th anniversary celebration were particularly shocking. The *New York Times* contrasted the inscription on Jefferson's tomb at Monticello, overlooking the campus – "Author of the Declaration of American Independence, of the Statute of Virginia for Religious Freedom, and Father of the University of Virginia" – with the Nazis' suppression of civil liberties and academic freedom. The Richmond *Times-Dispatch* urged the University of Virginia to refuse the invitation "in such unmistakable terms that the whole world will listen."[47]

Shortly afterward, University of Virginia president John Lloyd Newcomb declared that the newspaper reports were inaccurate, and that he had in fact declined Heidelberg's invitation "promptly, firmly, and politely." He gave no reason for doing so. Newcomb tempered his denial of the acceptance, however, by adding that, although he personally disliked dictatorships, he did not consider it proper for him "to criticize the German nation for the way it managed its affairs."[48]

Both the University of Virginia student newspaper, *College Topics*, and the Charlottesville *Daily Progress* remained critical of President Newcomb for failing to speak out more strongly against Nazi Germany. *College Topics* stated that whereas university heads around the world had condemned Heidelberg's invitation as an effort to "stifle educational freedom," President Newcomb, "declaring little, [only] denied acceptance." The *Daily Progress*, although pleased that Virginia had declined the invitation, noted that "[o]ther universities have . . . been more outspoken" and had made known their reasons for refusing to send delegates.[49]

That summer, the Institute, by inviting a member of the Hitler Youth to present a paper at its roundtable on "The Emergency and the Long-Run in Education," implied that products of Nazi schooling had insights and suggestions that could be of benefit to American educators. Gerold von Minden was a German exchange student, born in 1914, who had received a B.A. degree from Dickinson College and an M.A. from American University. Von Minden began his address by describing what it was like to grow up in a vanquished nation that experienced foreign military occupation, hyperinflation, and cataclysmic depression. He and his cohort of German youth soon realized that "the Treaty of Versailles and its corollaries" were the cause of their misfortune. They longed for "political unity and spiritual security."[50]

Fortunately, von Minden related, the Nazi movement emerged to rescue a "disintegrating nation." Germany celebrated its own "Fourth of July" with the advent of the National Socialist government. The Hitler

Youth taught von Minden "for the first time what 'Nation' and 'national unity' really meant."[51]

The Nazi educational system ended "the sadness of existence" for von Minden and other German youth and provided "meaning." Schooling under the Nazis was much superior to what the Weimar Republic had offered. During the Weimar period, German schools gave too much emphasis to intellectual training, providing students with too much "superfluous" knowledge. Under Hitler, schools balanced intellect with feeling. They gave much more attention to the study of German, history, geography, and [racial] biology to instill an understanding of Germanic community. A year's compulsory service in a labor camp further contributed to forging a community spirit "so lacking before the National Socialist government came to power." The Hitler Youth movement served as a critical part of Germany's educational system, providing the "action and discipline" that youth craved.[52]

As in 1934, this roundtable included a pro-Mussolini address, this time focusing on Italian Fascist educational policy. John Adams portrayed the Italian Fascist party as moderate, its function "no different from that of an American political party." The Fascist regime had injected no dangerous bias into the Italian classroom. It had introduced Catholic religious teaching and the crucifix to promote national unity, because more than 95 percent of its population was Catholic.[53]

Institute Director Maphis invited several supporters of collective security to speak at the July 1937 conference on a roundtable on international cooperation for world peace, but he also wrote to Dr. Wilbur K. Thomas of the Carl Schurz Foundation, asking him to recommend someone who could discuss "the subject of peace from the viewpoint of the German nation." Maphis was able to secure Dr. Helgo W. Culemann, a former professor at Amherst College, who spoke as a representative of the German embassy in Washington, D.C. In March, Culemann had vigorously defended Hitler's policies as "the salvation of the German nation" in a debate with French journalist Count de Roussy de Sales before the Town Hall of Washington, D.C.[54]

Anti-Nazi speakers on the roundtable included Helen Kirkpatrick, Geneva correspondent of the New York *Herald Tribune*, and Sir Herbert Brown Ames, formerly financial director of the League of Nations secretariat. Both expressed alarm about Germany's rearmament. Kirkpatrick declared that Britain and France had adhered too closely to the disarmament clause of the Versailles Treaty. Reducing armaments had only encouraged Germany to further increase its armed forces. Nevertheless, Kirkpatrick found it unlikely that Germany planned to march on Prague and doubted that there would ever again be a large-scale European war similar to that of 1914–18.[55]

Sir Herbert Brown Ames asserted that Germany would soon have the largest army in Europe, which constituted the greatest threat to peace on that continent. He agreed, however, with Czechoslovakia's president, Dr. Edward Beneš, that peace in Europe would be preserved. Germany was not economically prepared for a long war. The British would certainly come to the aid of Czechoslovakia were Germany to invade her. The destructive power of modern ground and air weapons, as demonstrated in Spain and Ethiopia, would deter any European nation, including Germany, from launching a major war. No nation wanted its civilian population slaughtered on a massive scale in aerial bombardment of its cities.[56]

Helgo W. Culemann's address provided historical justification for Hitler's foreign policy and condemned what he called the "badly disguised imperialistic desires of other European nations." In an interview prior to his presentation, Culemann declared that those who criticized Germany's outlook rarely investigated the reasons for it. They overlooked the Versailles Treaty, which Culemann claimed was intended "to destroy Germany," or at least to permanently reduce her to a second-rate power. Germany, located "in the heart of Europe," had a right to build up an army large enough to protect it against surrounding well-armed neighbors. Defending Germany's system of government, Culemann asserted that "[d]emocracies in many lands have failed for the time being to meet human needs."[57]

University of Virginia professor R. K. Gooch, who became acting director of the Institute of Public Affairs following the death of Charles G. Maphis in May 1938, consulted with the German embassy in Washington to ensure that the Nazi government's position was properly presented at the July 1938 conference on "International Good Will Through Economic Stability." Maphis had hoped to secure as a speaker the strongly pro-Nazi Dr. Friedrich Auhagen, who had chaired the Institute's 1935 roundtable on American-German Relations. In February 1936, Auhagen had received national press attention for delivering a speech in Cleveland endorsing Hitler's "suppress[ing] Jews." Auhagen had justified the removal of Jews from the legal and medical professions, claiming that they had "secured a stronghold" in them and "clos[ed] the doors to thousands of Germans." As it turned out, Auhagen was unable to participate in the 1938 Institute conference, apparently because he was in Germany at the time of the conference.[58]

Paul Scheffer, editor-in-chief of the *Berliner Tageblatt* for four years until January 1937, and its Washington correspondent after that, initially accepted the Institute's invitation to join the roundtable. Scheffer was considered the best-known German journalist abroad. He had largely adhered to the Nazi party line, but Nazi propaganda minister Josef Goebbels had forced his demotion from editor to foreign correspondent because he had shown "occasional independence." Nevertheless, when Scheffer learned that Dr. Ernst Meyer was also to be on the roundtable, he notified the Institute that he would not participate. Meyer, a first secretary at the German embassy in Washington, had resigned from the German Foreign Service in May 1937, and in February 1938 he delivered an address in New York City in which he criticized Hitler. The German embassy responded by declaring that Meyer was a Jew, which he denied.[59]

After Scheffer pulled out of the roundtable, Acting Director Gooch contacted Hans Thomsen, counselor at the German embassy in Washington, asking him to recommend a substitute speaker. Gooch told the Nazi diplomat: "I hope you will agree that it would be unfortunate for the presentation of the German situation to be made only from Dr. Meyer's point of view."[60]

The Institute in 1938 also invited one of America's most notorious antisemites, William J. Cameron, who had edited Henry Ford's *Dearborn Independent*, to present a paper on "The Interdependence of Farm and Industry" at its economic stability roundtable. Cameron had contributed significantly to the *Dearborn Independent*'s vitriolic attacks on Jews during the 1920s. Part of the British Israelite movement that believed the Anglo-Saxons were the real descendants of the Lost Tribes of Israel, Cameron claimed that contemporary Jews were the remnants of a racially distinct and inferior group despised by God. Remaining a top aide to Ford after the *Dearborn Independent* ceased publication in 1927, he cofounded the antisemitic Anglo-Saxon Federation in 1930 and was elected its president. In 1935 Cameron became director of *Destiny*, the Anglo-Saxon Federation organ whose diatribes laid the groundwork for the virulently antisemitic Christian Identity movement. Two weeks after the Institute roundtable, Cameron delivered the keynote address at the ceremony the Nazi government arranged for Henry Ford, at which it presented him with the highest honor it could bestow on a foreigner, the Grand Service Cross of the Supreme Order of the German Eagle.[61]

Despite Cameron's long record of disseminating antisemitism, the Institute of Public Affairs leadership declared that it was honored to have him participate in its roundtable.[62] About three months after the conference, the Institute's acting director expressed to Cameron his "great personal satisfaction and the appreciation of the University and the Institute" for what he said was Cameron's "very important" contribution to the session, about which he had heard "many kind words." Gooch told Cameron that both he and university president John Lloyd Newcomb would be "most grateful" for any suggestions that "might be calculated to improve the conduct of the Institute."[63]

In July 1939, less than two months before Germany launched its invasion of Poland, which began World War II, the Institute again provided the Nazi perspective a respectful hearing. In February, the Institute's acting director, Hardy C. Dillard, invited Nazi apologist Friedrich E. Auhagen to speak at "a morning, afternoon, and night session" at its Foreign Affairs conference. Dillard told Auhagen that the Institute wanted him "to linger with us for as long as you care to remain." He added: "I would count it a pleasure to have you put-up with me."[64] A month later, Dillard asked Auhagen to speak at a weekly Institute seminar to "'enlighten' us on German policy."[65]

In May 1939, Auhagen wrote to Dillard that he was busy establishing a group called the American Fellowship Forum and preparing the first issue of its magazine *Challenge*, which he intended to use to influence American public opinion and foreign policy in a pro-German direction. Anti-Nazi journalist Dorothy Thompson later described the American Fellowship Forum as advocating "precisely the policy advocated by Col. [Charles] Lindbergh and the . . . America First Movement."[66]

Auhagen's evening address dominated press coverage of the July 1939 Institute conference. Several speakers opposed to appeasing Nazi Germany participated, along with Manfred Zapp, New York representative of the Transocean News Service of Berlin, a front for Goebbels's Ministry of Propaganda; Dr. Nika Tucci, a publicist for the Mussolini regime, and William Castle, a former undersecretary of state in the Hoover administration and an isolationist who in 1940 became a leader of the America First Committee. Castle, a Harvard graduate, was a Harvard overseer from 1935 to 1941. U.S. Communist party chairman Earl Browder, another roundtable participant, some six weeks before the Molotov–von Ribbentrop Pact, took strong issue with Auhagen's suggestion that if the Western democracies refused to befriend Germany, she might "get together" with the Soviet Union. Browder answered heatedly that there was as much possibility of that happening as of his being elected president of the U.S. Chamber of Commerce.[67]

Auhagen in his address said that four years ago he had hoped that the United States and Nazi Germany, which he called "the two most progressive-minded nations," would form a friendship, but that unfortunately had not happened. There was no conflict whatsoever between the national interests of Germany and the United States. The strained relations between the two countries resulted only from the United States being a "have" nation and Germany being a "have-not" one. Paradoxically, the United States had "thrown in her lot with her strongest competitor, the British Empire." She championed the interests of Britain, the prime proponent of the status quo, instead of her own. There was no danger that Germany would impose a Nazi political system on the United States, even though the United States had been instrumental in the overthrow of Germany's imperial regime.[68]

William Castle denounced President Roosevelt and Secretary of the Interior Harold Ickes for ignoring "the decencies and amenities of international politics" and "going out of their way to insult Reichsfuehrer Hitler." By doing so they had endangered the security of the United States. Castle declared that Roosevelt and Ickes should look to the British prime minister Neville Chamberlain as their model, a leader who "sticks strictly to his own business" and "does not fling insults about." Castle stated that the British "know that one of their best bulwarks of peace is courtesy."[69]

Samuel K. C. Kopper, a Princeton graduate and assistant leader of the 1939 Foreign Affairs roundtable, promoted appeasement of Nazi Germany in an address shaped by revisionist scholarship on the World War. He warned that the Western democracies, having severely abused Germany at Versailles, were preparing aggressive action against her. The French were planning to "march to Berlin... and complete the work of destruction which they left uncompleted in 1918." The British might join them afterward in "out-Versailles[ing] Versailles."

There was at that time a danger of a European war largely because the West had failed to resolve Germany's grievances by peaceful negotiation. Germany was forced to relinquish Eupen-Malmédy, Memel, and much of Upper Silesia. The French invasion of the Ruhr in 1923 "added insult to injury." In the West, "violently prejudiced" journalists and radio commentators were "whipping up popular anger" against Germany. Kopper urged the Western democracies to use "reason rather than prejudice and hate" to preserve peace with Germany. "When critics were berating

Chamberlain's peace policy last fall," Kopper asked, "were they not being a little Olympian in their attitude?" After all, were Britain and Germany to go to war, 30,000 Londoners would die each day in air raids.[70]

Manfred Zapp delivered a vitriolic antisemitic address in which he proclaimed his ardent support for Nazi Germany. He began by condemning the "one-sided" American press coverage of Germany, which falsely reported that in the Third Reich "the individual has no freedom." Germans actually had "just as much freedom as . . . in other countries, if not more." Unlike in the West, where the rich could "buy more liberties than [were] granted to the poor," each individual in Germany had an equal amount. The Germans had forged a national community, a true "people's state," unlike parliamentary democracies, which were actually ruled by "demagogue politicians." Under the Weimar Republic, Germans were divided by class antagonisms and feared for their safety. Night clubs featuring "nudism and sex" proliferated, undermining the country's moral fabric.[71]

Zapp declared that during the Weimar period a corrosive "Jewish influence . . . became more and more predominant in business and politics." By "preaching freedom of the press, freedom of speech, and freedom of the individual" the Jews "sow[ed] discontent among the German people," fomenting divisions that resulted in twenty-eight different political parties bickering in the Reichstag. Exploiting the chaos they had fomented, the Jews seized control of the nation.[72]

According to Zapp, the Nazi movement arose to liberate Germany from this Jewish-induced decay. It sprang from "German sentiment," grew "on German soil," and was "made for Germans and Germany only." Hitler had restored labor harmony and full employment. Under Nazism, prosperity had returned to Germany, and slums had disappeared.[73]

The conference also heard presentations from several speakers strongly critical of Nazism and Fascism. F. Wilhelm Sollman, former German Reichstag deputy and member of its Committee on Foreign Affairs from 1920 to 1933, declared that a reading of *Mein Kampf* revealed that Hitler aimed to subjugate Eastern and Southeastern Europe. He asserted that Hitler's "drive to the East" did not originate with him but was a continuation of Kaiser Wilhelm II's "power policy." Scholars, politicians, and diplomats had devoted excessive attention to the Versailles Treaty's "injustices" and forgotten that Imperial Germany had imposed severely harsh terms on Romania and Russia in the treaties of Bucharest and

Brest-Litovsk during the World War. Historian Oscar Jaszi, former minister of national minorities in the Hungarian government, recommended fomenting "internal revolution," "tyrannicide" (assassination of Hitler), and the forging of an armed coalition as means of halting Nazi Germany's expansion.[74]

Journalist Louis Fischer "bitterly attacked" Fascist foreign policy in an address that precipitated an angry rejoinder from Nika Tucci. The Fascist propagandist accused Fischer of spreading Communist theory across the United States. Fischer denied the charge, citing his criticism of the Soviet government for suppressing civil liberties.[75]

Dr. Edmund A. Walsh, regent of Georgetown University's School of Foreign Service, who had publicly supported Franco's insurgents in the just-concluded Spanish Civil War, "expressed alarm at the rising tide of anti-Semitism" in the United States. He called for uncompromising opposition to Nazi racial theories.[76]

Even with French forces on the verge of surrender to the Wehrmacht, the 1940 Institute conference, held this time in June, gave isolationists and appeasers of Nazi Germany a significant platform. The conference's theme was "The United States and a World at War." It began only four days after President Roosevelt delivered a strong denunciation of isolationism in his commencement address to the University of Virginia's graduating class. Without mentioning Germany, Roosevelt declared that "the whole of our sympathies" were with the nations fighting "the gods of force and hate." He pledged U.S. material assistance to Britain.[77] The speech became a major subject of controversy at the conference.

At the June 17 session, British writer John Wheeler-Bennett praised President Roosevelt's commencement address as an inspiration for a desperate Britain to "hold on" as it fought for its life. But the *New York Times* reported that none of the American speakers praised Roosevelt's "Charlottesville pledge," and two of them "roundly denounced" it. Lawrence Dennis, a Harvard graduate and former U.S. foreign service officer whom Dorothy Thompson identified as one of Friedrich Auhagen's "leading braintrusters," declared that because of "Germany's imminent triumph over the Allies," President Roosevelt himself had become "America's No. 1 isolationist." His interventionist sympathies had placed the United States in the unenviable position of standing alone against "the four great totalitarian powers." By declaring for the Allies, Roosevelt had disregarded George Washington's warning not to intervene in Europe's quarrels. With Germany on the verge of defeating the Allies, the United

States had lost any prospect that the victor would display goodwill toward her. Dr. Brooks Emeny condemned not only Roosevelt's commencement address but his entire attitude toward European affairs. He claimed that intervention in the European war was not in the national interest.[78]

The next day, Harry Elmer Barnes delivered an address that not only opposed U.S. intervention in the war to stop the Nazi onslaught but expressed lack of confidence that the democratic form of government could persist. He declared that American involvement in the war would result in economic depression and massive loss of life, which would precipitate the sort of crisis in the United States that had brought Hitler to power in Germany. Barnes told the Institute audience that "nose-counting democracy" was breaking down, unable to handle the complex problems resulting from modern industrialization and a communications revolution. He proclaimed that "[t]otalitarianism now menaces representative government and democracy in the same way the Tudors and Bourbons challenged feudalism in the early modern times," implying that an ascendant fascism was likely to prevail over an obsolete American form of government. Frank Kingdon, president of the University of Newark, took issue with Barnes, arguing that the "dynamism of democracy is far more powerful than any totalitarianism can ever be."[79]

During the fall of 1940, the federal government initiated raids that implicated such prominent participants in Institute of Public Affairs roundtables as Friedrich Auhagen and Manfred Zapp as operatives working under German government direction to spread Nazi propaganda in the United States. In November the U.S. House of Representatives Committee on Un-American Activities, chaired by Martin Dies, published a 500-page white paper that demonstrated links between Auhagen and Zapp and German embassy and consular officials. It specifically named Hans Thomsen, chargé d'affaires at the German embassy in Washington, as assisting in disseminating propaganda. The Dies Committee described Transocean News Service as a "Nazi propaganda podium" whose employees had to be approved by the German consulate in New York. The New York *Post* disclosed that in 1938 the German Ministry of Propaganda had dispatched Manfred Zapp, "a highly trusted Goebbels functionary," to New York City to establish Transocean. From a suite of offices on Madison Avenue, Zapp "tirelessly canvass[ed]" the German-language press, persuading editors to run news reports written from the Nazi perspective. Dorothy Thompson reported that Zapp had served as the conduit for funds sent from Germany to Canadian fascist Adrian Arcand to publish his French-language newspaper.[80]

As the press disclosed what the raids had uncovered, it also reported an outcry precipitated by a Colorado State College of Education invitation to both German and British embassy officials to address the 1940 summer session on "War Aims and Peace Plans." The College had invited Hans Thomsen to speak for Germany. Thomsen had to decline but urged the College to invite Manfred Zapp, head of Transocean News Service, in his place. When some members of the board of trustees complained about a Nazi addressing the summer session, and when other citizens protested to the trustees, the College cancelled both the German and British speeches.[81]

Both Zapp and Friedrich Auhagen were arrested as German propagandists. In September 1940, federal agents apprehended Auhagen on the Pacific Coast just as he was preparing to sail for Japan and brought him to Washington, D.C., to be examined by the Dies Committee. In early 1941, federal agents seized him in La Salle, Illinois, on a fugitive warrant from Washington, D.C. Auhagen was indicted in March for failing to register with the State Department as a paid publicity agent of Germany. He was charged with having "lectured, conducted meetings, exhibited movies, and wr[itten] magazine articles to promote Nazi interests."[82]

That same month, the Federal Bureau of Investigation arrested Manfred Zapp and his assistant Guenther Tonn, and a special federal grand jury indicted them and Transocean News Service on charges of violating the Foreign Alien and Registration Act of 1938. When Zapp established a subsidiary of Transocean in the United States in October 1938 he had failed to register as an agent of a foreign government, and he did not do so until January 1939. In registering, he failed to state that "part of his business... was to transmit and disseminate in the United States and numerous countries throughout the world, political propaganda in the interest of the German government and the Nazi party." The indictment also identified Transocean as an arm of the German government. The U.S. government released Zapp and Tonn in a trade for two American journalists held by the Hitler government, and they returned to Germany. When in April 1945, a few weeks before V-E Day, the *New York Times* reported that U.S. Third Army troops had seized Zapp in Germany, it identified him as "the chief Nazi propaganda agent in the United States from 1938 to 1941."[83]

At Auhagen's trial in July 1941, Assistant Attorney-General George McNulty confronted him with his own diary, seized by federal agents when he was arrested in San Francisco, in which he wrote about long conferences with officials of the German Ministry of Propaganda. The

U.S. government contended that Auhagen had traveled to Nazi Germany for that purpose every year since Hitler came to power. The *New York Times* reported that Auhagen's American Fellowship Forum had been linked with the German Library of Information and the German Railroads Information Office as instruments of Nazi propaganda.[84]

A jury in a District of Columbia court found Auhagen guilty on all three counts of the indictment charging him with being a German propagandist. He was sentenced to a term of eight months to two years in the penitentiary and fined $1,000. Auhagen was the first person sentenced for violating the Foreign Alien and Registration Act. In 1947 Auhagen was deported to Germany with a group of other Nazi sympathizers. The U.S. Department of Justice called the deportees a "cargo of human dynamite," too dangerous to be allowed to reside in the United States.[85]

By the time the Institute of Public Affairs held its final conference in June 1941, there was considerably more support among the speakers for American military intervention. Participants included veteran anti-Nazi journalist Edgar Ansel Mowrer and Quincy Howe, who argued that America's joining the war against Nazi Germany was both inevitable and desirable. Institute Director Hardy C. Dillard even lauded Mowrer's address – which branded as defeatist the isolationists' call for the United States to concentrate on defending the Western Hemisphere – as "one of the outstanding addresses of the entire series." U.S. representative John M. Vorys of Ohio, however, did speak in favor of isolationism. He declared that the Germans were "more ready for peace" than assumed.[86]

From 1933 until U.S. entry into World War II, the University of Virginia Institute of Public Affairs conferences on Europe, war and peace, and U.S.-German relations received Nazis and their sympathizers as distinguished guests whose views were entitled to a respectful hearing. Revisionist scholarship on the origins of the World War became highly influential in the United States during the 1920s and caused many Americans, inside and outside of academia, to sympathize with Germany as a country that the victorious nations had severely wronged at the Versailles Peace Conference. The Versailles Treaty was commonly perceived as having been imposed on Germany by vindictive powers that shared equally with her the responsibility for the war's outbreak. It was therefore unfair to deprive Germany of significant amounts of territory, hobble her armed forces, and force her to pay heavy reparations. Many Americans, although uncomfortable with certain Nazi policies, nonetheless became convinced that Hitler's objective was merely to restore Germany's equal stature among the European nations, which they believed to be a commendable goal. They became convinced that his foreign policy was designed only to regain for Germany territory unfairly stripped from her at Versailles, and to ensure that she could defend herself from invasion.

The Institute's directors cooperated closely with the German embassy in Washington, D.C., hardly a body interested in the furtherance of scholarly inquiry and understanding, to guarantee that the Hitler regime was properly represented at the roundtables. As a result, what many speakers presented at the conferences was not reasoned analysis but propaganda celebrating Hitler and Nazism. They obfuscated the actual conditions and developments within Germany and Hitler's real foreign policy intentions.

The Institute of Public Affairs repeatedly presented as authorities on Germany Nazi apologists from within American academia, and from the Third Reich itself, who disparaged democracy and portrayed Hitler as a savior who restored honor, security, and hope to the German people. Many were avowed antisemites. Adolf Hitler in late November 1938 bestowed upon two of the American professors whom the Institute had invited to present major addresses, Karl Geiser and Frederick K. Krueger, the merit cross of the Order of the German Eagle, first class, a very high honor.[87] Speakers routinely denied American press accounts that Jews in Germany were severely persecuted. They justified the discriminatory measures that the Nazis introduced to drive Jews from university faculties and student bodies, and from practicing law and medicine, as necessary to break what they claimed was Jewish control of German academia and the professions. Neither the Institute's directors, nor other University of Virginia administrators, appear to have challenged these participants' unapologetic antisemitism. Indeed, they praised their contributions and asked some to appear again.

6

Nazi Nests

German Departments in American Universities, 1933–1941

University German departments, often staffed by faculty members sympathetic to the Hitler regime, and the German clubs they sponsored, constituted important bases of support for Nazi Germany in the United States. When the Nazi warship *Karlsruhe* docked at Charlestown Navy Yard for its ten-day goodwill visit to Boston in May 1934, German clubs from colleges across New England sent delegations to greet it. German departments at the Universities of Wisconsin and Minnesota became the targets of major anti-Nazi protest when they hosted receptions for Nazi Germany's ambassador to the United States, Hans Luther, during his tour of the Midwest in October 1935. American professors of German were also prominent as foreign delegates at the anniversary celebrations held in Nazi Germany for the University of Heidelberg in 1936 and the University of Goettingen in 1937.

At Rutgers University's New Jersey College for Women (NJC), the administration's termination of the German Department's only anti-Hitler faculty member, upon the recommendation of its strongly pro-Nazi chair, precipitated the nation's most well-publicized academic freedom controversy of the 1930s. It revealed a widespread lack of concern about Nazism among Rutgers administrators and considerable sympathy for the Hitler regime within the faculty and student body.

The Philadelphia *Jewish Exponent* noted in May 1935 that the Nazi government considered American colleges and universities of central importance in shaping public opinion of the Third Reich in this country. Almost immediately after the Nazis assumed power in Germany, they sent propaganda agents to the United States "under the guise of special students, lecturers, or exchange professors" in order "to inject the Hitler virus into the American student body." The "most reprehensible aspect" of this Nazi campus propaganda campaign was the encouragement it received from heads of German language and literature departments.[1]

New England's College German Clubs Welcome the *Karlsruhe*

The Studenten Verbindung Germania, the German club at Dartmouth College, was committed to promoting more friendly relations between the United States and Nazi Germany, two "great countries." It expressed concern that there were groups in the United States that "defame[d]" Nazi Germany and wanted to make her "a social outcast," and it condemned the boycott of German goods. In February 1934, the Studenten Verbindung Germania held its first *Kneipe*, or beer evening, at which its guest was Nazi Germany's consul-general in Boston, Baron Kurt von Tippelskirch.[2]

Dartmouth's German Club helped transform the friendly reception the city of Boston and Harvard University provided for the *Karlsruhe* into a New England–wide event. Twenty-five of its members donned military regalia and traveled to Boston to pay homage to the battle cruiser flying the swastika flag as it lay at anchor there. The *Karlsruhe*'s cadets gave them "a very warm and hearty reception."[3]

The Studenten Verbindung Germania returned the favor the next week by hosting an officer and ten cadets from the *Karlsruhe* at its *Fahnenweihe* at Dartmouth, at which it dedicated its new club flag, the "exact type" that German fraternities used. The ceremony was followed by a banquet of German dishes and dancing. Mingling with the *Karlsruhe* cadets were women from the German clubs of Smith, Bennington, Wellesley, Radcliffe, and Middlebury Colleges, whom the Studenten Verbindung Germania had invited. Forty members of the Dartmouth faculty also attended. Speakers at the banquet included P. C. Hessler, a leading financial sponsor of the Junior Year in Munich program, who donated the new club flag; Professor R. W. Jones, chairman of the Dartmouth German Department; and Stephen Schlossmacher, a member of the department and vice-president of the Interscholastic Federation of German Clubs. Further solidifying the bonds between Nazi Germany and Dartmouth, the North German Lloyd Line selected the Studenten Verbindung Germania band to perform on its ocean cruises that summer.[4]

The University of Wisconsin and University of Minnesota German Departments Host Nazi Germany's Ambassador

In November 1935, Professor A. R. Hohlfeld, chairman of the University of Wisconsin German Department, hosted Nazi Germany's ambassador Hans Luther on a visit to the campus, sparking bitter controversy and nearly provoking a diplomatic incident. Several other members of the German Department socialized with Luther, and University of Wisconsin president Glenn Frank invited him to tea. Representatives of eleven student organizations, including the radical National Student League (NSL), the Hillel, the Newman Club, the Presbyterian Student house, and the Young Women's Christian Association (YWCA), issued a joint statement protesting the Nazi ambassador's visit to campus. The student groups denounced the Hitler regime for exiling "the finest of German scholars," sponsoring violent attacks on Jews and implementing antisemitic legislation, driving women into the kitchen, and diverting youth from universities into labor camps. They noted that Germany's entire educational system, "previously one of the finest in the world," was now "being used to spread the gospels of Hitler and his cohorts." Their statement declared that "the burning of books in 1933 was just a dramatic symbol of the consistent repression of all disagreement, and indeed, of almost all study."[5]

The Nazi ambassador arrived in Madison accompanied by R. L. Jaeger, German consul-general in Chicago. Both men were committed to preventing the circulation of news about Nazi atrocities in the United States. About a year and a half earlier, they had together persuaded Chicago mayor Edward J. Kelly to ban theaters in his city from showing the anti-Nazi film *Hitler's Reign of Terror*. The film was based largely on motion picture footage that Cornelius Vanderbilt Jr. had smuggled out of Germany, and it ended with denunciations of Hitler by Columbia professor Raymond Moley, a leading advisor to President Roosevelt, and U.S. representative Samuel Dickstein. Mayor Kelly shut the film down after a single showing, apparently because of concern that it would endanger friendly relations between the United States and Germany.[6]

Ambassador Luther's stormy eight-hour visit to Madison, Wisconsin, began with a morning press conference that he expected would be routine. When Professor Hohlfeld opened the press conference, two Jewish University of Wisconsin students, Leo Genzeloff of Hackensack, New Jersey, and Daniel Lang of New York City, identifying themselves as reporters for the NSL's *New Student*, demanded to know why the Hitler regime was persecuting Jews and Catholics. Denying that the Nazis mis-treated Catholics, Luther explained that because Jews were not citizens of the German nation, they did not have the rights accorded to citizens. (Germany had introduced the Nuremberg laws that September, strip-ping Jews of their citizenship.) He declared that it was improper for other nations to interfere in Germany's internal affairs. Luther outlined Nazi Germany's triple policy: "peace, good will, and cooperation." He lectured the students that their tone undermined the mutual respect on which understanding between the two nations depended.[7]

When Genzeloff and Lang continued to pepper Luther with hos-tile questions, he "became extremely irritable." The Nazi ambassador pounded the table with his fist and exclaimed, "I am the representa-tive of the German government in the United States." He very quickly "lost his composure" and "abruptly terminated" the press conference. Luther said he did not wish to discuss Hitler's policies with persons who "possessed little understanding of them," and "stalk[ed] out." As he left, Lang shouted, "Down with Hitler!" Later, Luther declared that he had never been treated so disrespectfully anywhere in the United States as at the Madison press conference. There was speculation in the press that he might file an official protest with the U.S. government concerning what he considered the rude treatment to which the students had subjected him.[8]

Although the University of Wisconsin administration and the German Department made every effort to provide the warmest possible recep-tion for Ambassador Luther, tension persisted throughout the rest of his visit. After leaving the press conference, Luther proceeded to luncheon at the University of Wisconsin German House, where university president Glenn Frank, a prominent isolationist, dined with him. Expecting that Luther would be having supper at Professor Hohlfeld's house, anti-Nazi students and members of the community formed a picket line there at 5:00 P.M. and demonstrated for about 45 minutes. However, at the time Luther was having tea with President Frank at his mansion. The pickets, carrying banners and placards denouncing the Hitler regime for persecut-ing and murdering political opponents and Jews, attracted a large crowd of onlookers, including children who shouted "Heil Hitler!" at them.[9]

President Frank, like Nicholas Murray Butler, was undoubtedly drawn to Hans Luther because he considered him a gentleman, a man of high social rank. Professor Hohlfeld had introduced Luther at the press con-ference with the honorific "His Excellency." John D. Hicks, who had attended Northwestern University with Frank and was a professor of his-tory at the University of Wisconsin when Frank was its president in the

1930s, remarked that Frank and his wife had tried to impose in Madison "the high proprieties of New York society." They had hired a butler and a chauffeur and, according to Hicks, "entertained too lavishly," requiring white tie or black tie at many of the social functions they hosted.[10]

Ambassador Luther ended his Madison visit with dinner at the German House, where he was joined by Professor Hohlfeld and German consul-general Jaeger. That night Luther entrained for the Twin Cities, where he was scheduled to make several public addresses and to visit the University of Minnesota in Minneapolis.[11]

The next day, several representatives of University of Wisconsin Christian groups who had signed the statement of protest against Luther's visit distanced themselves from the demonstration at Professor Hohlfeld's house. The Reverend Ezra Young, leader of the university's Congregationalist organization, said that he strongly disapproved of the demonstration and had advised against it. He bore no malice toward Ambassador Luther, whose visit to campus he considered social rather than political. Jane Mond, president of the University of Wisconsin YWCA, stated that her organization's name had been included on the statement protesting Luther's visit by mistake. She asserted that the YWCA did not object to the Nazi ambassador's visit. It believed that "every courtesy and respect should be shown him" as a guest. The Reverend "Shorty" Collins, Baptist leader at the university, also declared that he opposed the picketing.[12]

The *Daily Cardinal* was so angry about the picketing that it declared that the University of Wisconsin owed Luther a "most sincere apology." The editorial board denounced the student "hecklers" at the press conference for subjecting the Nazi ambassador, who "deserved all the hospitality and respect accorded any guest," to a "humiliating experience." Students at the press conference should have shown Luther "the respect that his position warrants." Questioning should have been "polite" and in "good taste." The *Daily Cardinal* declared that being Jewish did not give the "hecklers" the right to express their "prejudices" at the press conference.[13]

The editors proceeded to explain why they had neglected to provide any coverage of the picketing of Professor Hohlfeld's house in the *Daily Cardinal*. They explained that Ambassador Luther was a guest at the University of Wisconsin, and "anything that would mar his visit should have been avoided." The *Daily Cardinal* had refused to publish "anything that would in any way stir up the student body to such an extent that any demonstration would take place."[14]

Upon arriving in the Twin Cities, Ambassador Luther discovered, as the Minneapolis *Journal* put it, that "he had jumped from the frying pan into the fire." He received a friendly reception at the University of Minnesota and from some business and German-American groups, but he met with a storm of protest elsewhere. In Minneapolis, seventy Jewish organizations denounced Luther's appearance before the Minneapolis Civic and Commerce Association. They issued a statement saying that "[o]ur self-respect as Jews and as citizens compels us to assert we consider Mr. Hans Luther's presence in the community as an affront to all freedom-loving citizens, who must refrain from joining in any reception or public hearing given him." The editor of the St. Paul German Catholic newspaper *The Wanderer* issued an open letter saying that Luther was not welcome. The Reverend Henry Scherer, pastor of the Catholic church at nearby New Ulm, Minnesota, also denounced the Civic and Commerce Association for greeting Luther, declaring that "it would be an insult for me or my congregation to be seen at a reception or banquet for Dr. Luther." Branding Nazis as criminal, Rabbi David Aaronson stated that he would "no more care to be seen in the company of a spokesman of Hitler than I would be in the company of the kidnaper of the Lindbergh baby."[15]

A press conference arranged for Twin Cities newsmen to interview Luther turned "fiery" when they pressed him to discuss the persecution of Jews and other minorities in Nazi Germany. L. H. Frisch, publisher of the *Jewish World*, asked the Nazi ambassador about the recent Nuremberg Laws that deprived Germany's Jews of their citizenship. Luther refused to respond to it or to any other specific question. "Plainly annoyed" by the reporters' persistence, Luther's voice at times "rose to ear-shriek proportions." He declared, as he had at the Madison press conference, that the United States had no right to interfere in Germany's internal affairs.[16]

Having been escorted by a police squadron into Minneapolis's Radisson Hotel across a picket line protesting his appearance, Luther spoke about the German economy before an overflow audience that "roundly applauded" him. He also delivered two addresses in St. Paul in German to audiences totaling 800 persons. The Nazi ambassador declared that Germany desired peace and that its rearmament was only for self-defense against neighbors who had refused to disarm. Under Hitler, class distinctions among Germans were disappearing.[17]

Alarmed by the vigor of the protest against Luther's appearances at the University of Wisconsin and in Minneapolis, the University of Minnesota administration and the German Department that hosted him took steps to ensure that he would not be challenged when he visited the campus. It was decided that he would not deliver any address at the university, but only attend a tea sponsored by the German Department. Expecting Luther to speak, anti-Nazi students had prepared and distributed across campus typewritten questions that they hoped people would raise. But their plans to engage the Nazi ambassador in a dialogue about Hitler's policies were frustrated when the German Department admitted to the tea only those whom it had personally invited. When about fifty students appeared at the tea without invitations, Anna Blitz, the University of Minnesota Dean of Women, required them to leave. Campus police forcibly ejected one student who insisted on his right to remain.[18]

Dean Blitz justified her refusal to permit the fifty students to attend the tea by explaining that "this element obviously just wanted to make itself obnoxious." She declared that Ambassador Luther was the university's guest, and it was out of respect for him that she prevented the students from attending the tea. Dean Blitz commented that the student who did not obey her order to leave "was not properly dressed for a tea."[19]

German Departments and German Clubs: Promoting Friendship with the Third Reich

Campus German clubs, consisting largely of students majoring in German, like their sponsoring German departments, entertained Nazi diplomats and sometimes brought them together with university presidents and other administrators. Hitler's consul-general in Boston, Baron Kurt von Tippelskirch, was a frequent guest at German club social functions at New England colleges. He mingled with President Ada Comstock at the Radcliffe German Club Christmas party in 1933, and with the wife of Smith president William Allan Neilson and Smith faculty at a reception and dinner sponsored by that college's German Club in 1935. Von Tippelskirch was the chief speaker at the Harvard German Club's *Abschiedsfeier* in May 1936. His successor as Germany's consul-general in Boston, Dr. Herbert Scholtz, attended the Harvard German Club's dinner-dance in May 1939, to which members of the German clubs at Radcliffe, Wellesley, Dartmouth, and Colby Colleges were also invited.[20]

In December 1934, both the Yale University and Vassar College German clubs invited Dr. Richard Sallet, attaché at the German embassy in Washington, to speak on campus about Hitler's Germany. The Nazi diplomat spoke informally on December 11 to Yale's Germanic Club, which was composed of faculty members and graduate students, on "The New Foundations of the German Commonwealth." Professor Adolph Bennett Benson, chair of Yale's Department of Germanic Languages and sponsor of the Germanic Club, announced that only members of the club would be admitted to Sallet's talk, which was closed to the press. The Yale chapter of the National Student League charged that Sallet's visit was for the purpose of disseminating Nazi propaganda to members of the Yale community.[21] This was certainly Sallet's intention when he spoke several days later at Vassar. He extolled Nazi Germany as a "folk community." The Nazis had abolished all social ranks to create a true "people's fellowship." What solidified it was its exclusivity: a person who had not been born into it could never join it. A person's social or class background mattered not at all, only his or her ancestry. Sallet explained to the assembled German majors and other Vassarites in attendance that because Nazi Germany defined itself in this way it could not annex any non-German territory, "especially Poland." He claimed therefore that Germany was "inherently pacifistic."[22]

Besides influencing their students in the German clubs to adopt a favorable attitude toward Nazism, some prominent professors of German also served as propagandists for the Third Reich in other forums, including Friedrich Auhagen and Frederick K. Krueger, prominent participants in the University of Virginia Institute of Public Affairs roundtables, and Professor Paul H. Curts of the Wesleyan University German Department. In October 1934, Curts explained to a student assembly at Wesleyan that only Hitler could provide Germany with what it needed. Having witnessed the Night of the Long Knives from Hamburg, Germany, Curts reported that most Germans had no objection to "the quick blow of retaliation that the leader made" against what they considered "a radical conspiracy."[23] Speaking at New Haven's Exchange Club about two weeks later as someone who had vacationed several times in the Third Reich, Curts accused the American press of publishing exaggerated accounts of disorder there. Curts declared that the Nazis had no intention of spreading their doctrine outside Germany.[24]

Back in Germany in April 1936, Professor Curts reported that everyone there "believe[d] absolutely in the sincerity of Hitler's offer of non-aggression and peace." He defended the Wehrmacht's march into the Rhineland, claiming it was "an integral part of Germany." Curts endorsed the Nazis' antisemitic policies, declaring that "'Germany for the Germans' is the slogan. Substitute 'America for the Americans' and it sounds quite reasonable."[25]

American professors of German enthusiastically participated in the anniversary celebrations at the Universities of Heidelberg and Goettingen in 1936 and 1937. At Heidelberg, Arthur F. J. Remy, Villard Professor of Germanic Philology, represented Columbia and Professor Ernst Rose, recommended by his department chairman, W. D. Zinnecker, represented New York University. Cornell University president Livingston Farrand appointed Professor A. W. Boesche as that institution's delegate, and Professor Aloysius G. Gaiss represented the University of Michigan. The University of Michigan student newspaper reported that Professor Gaiss was looking forward to the Heidelberg ceremonies "with great excitement." He declared that the presence of delegates from American colleges and universities would improve relations between the United States and Nazi Germany. Gaiss announced that he planned to spend the next seven months after he sailed for the festival on June 11 in Europe, six of them at the University of Heidelberg.[26] The next year at Goettingen, Professor A. B. Faust, chairman of Cornell's German Department, gave the Nazi salute as he accepted an honorary degree at that university's bicentennial celebration.[27]

The Nazi government rewarded several American professors of German for promoting friendship between the United States and Germany with medals that it considered very prestigious. In April 1938, the German consul-general in Los Angeles, Dr. Georg Gyssling, bestowed the Order of the German Eagle on Professor Erwin T. Mohme, head of the German Department at the University of Southern California, for "furthering cultural relationships between Germany and the United States." In presenting the medal, along with a parchment letter of congratulations personally signed by Adolf Hitler, the Nazi consul-general informed Mohme that he was the only man on the Pacific Coast to have received it.[28] In November 1938, about two weeks after the *Kristallnacht*, Adolf Hitler awarded the Order of Merit of the German Eagle, first class, to another American professor of German, William Alpha Cooper, who had retired from Stanford University in 1934.[29]

Professor Max Otto Koischwitz of Hunter College's German Department was so enthusiastic about Nazism that he moved permanently to Germany in 1939, after a fourteen-year career teaching in the United States, and served the Hitler government as a propagandist. In 1939, the Non-Sectarian Anti-Nazi League (NSANL) protested to the New York City Department of Education when the magazine *Literatur*, published in Nazi Germany, carried an article in which Professor Koischwitz denounced American democracy. The NSANL noted that Koischwitz had

FIGURE 6.1. "Axis Sally" (Mildred E. Gillars) leaving U.S. District Court in Washington, D.C., during her trial for treason, February 17, 1949. Courtesy of AP Images.

been under close surveillance as a Nazi propagandist for the previous six years, since Hitler came to power, and had appeared as a guest of honor at meetings of the pro-Nazi German-American Bund.[30] The German-born Koischwitz joined the faculty of Columbia University in 1925, immediately after graduating from the University of Berlin. In 1931, he became a professor of German at Hunter College. Considered a Nazi, according to the *New York Times*, Koischwitz traveled to the Third Reich, allegedly for "study," in 1935, 1937, and 1939. He did not return to the United States after the last trip, on which his wife and three daughters accompanied him.[31]

By 1940, Koischwitz had become a prominent radio official for the Hitler regime and the patron and lover of "Axis Sally" (Mildred E.

Gillars), his former student at Hunter College, whose English-language broadcasts to Allied troops in Europe and North Africa were designed to convince them that it was futile to fight the German armed forces. Koischwitz headed the U.S.A. Zone of German radio, which broadcast by shortwave to the United States and to American soldiers. During World War II, he often met with Germany's foreign minister, Joachim von Ribbentrop, at Hitler's headquarters. Koischwitz and Axis Sally often visited German prisoner-of-war camps to interrogate captured American soldiers and airmen. A District of Columbia grand jury indicted Koischwitz for treason in July 1943.[32]

Although Koischwitz died in Berlin in August 1944, his protégé, Axis Sally, was arrested after the war and convicted of treason in 1949 in a federal court in Washington, D.C. She testified at her trial that Koischwitz had recruited her for Nazi propaganda work in Germany. A federal judge sentenced the "supposedly glamorous radio siren" to serve ten to thirty years in prison (she served twelve). The treason conviction was based on the single count of broadcasting a program entitled *Vision of Invasion* shortly before D-Day, written by Professor Koischwitz. Koischwitz's script began with an announcer intoning: "The D of D-Day stands for doom... disaster... death... defeat." Axis Sally assumed "the role of an American mother who talked to her soldier son in a dream and learned that he had been killed in the [Allied] invasion" of France.[33] Koischwitz had the mother tell her husband that in the invasion "[b]etween 70 and 90 percent of our boys will be killed or crippled the rest of their lives," and that "Roosevelt has no right to go to war."[34]

The Bergel-Hauptmann Case at the New Jersey College for Women

When Friedrich J. Hauptmann, the avowedly pro-Hitler chair of the German Department at New Jersey College for Women (NJC), the women's coordinate college of Rutgers University, in 1935 terminated the employment of his department's only anti-Nazi faculty member, instructor Lienhard Bergel, the resulting controversy focused national attention on the role of German departments and campus German clubs in promoting sympathy for the Third Reich. Hauptmann's dismissal of Bergel received strong backing from the NJC German Department's other faculty members, all of whom were ardent Nazi sympathizers, and from nearly all of the German majors who lived in the NJC German House. NJC's dean and the president of Rutgers upheld Hauptmann's decision. The press described both the German Department and the NJC German House in which most of the majors resided as "Nazi nests." Pressure on the Rutgers University administration from concerned legislators, and adverse publicity in the press, caused Rutgers University president Robert C. Clothier to appoint a special committee composed of five trustees to investigate Bergel's charge that his dismissal was an act of retaliation against him by his chair for refusing to conform to the department's pro-Nazi outlook. This Special Trustees Committee was chaired by J. Edward Ashmead, vice-president of the Rutgers University alumni association. During the lengthy hearings it conducted, the Trustees Committee displayed hostility toward Bergel and others who spoke out forcefully against Nazism and displayed a very complacent attitude toward the German Department's pro-Hitler outlook.

Antisemitism was commonplace in the NJC administration, which imposed a strict quota to limit the admission of Jewish students. In 1930, NJC's acceptance rate for Jewish applicants was about half that of non-Jews: 31 percent as opposed to 61 percent. During the 1920s, the administration implemented measures similar to those used by Harvard, Yale, Columbia, and the Seven Sisters colleges to restrict Jewish admissions. These included requiring applicants to provide place of birth and full names of both parents, along with a photograph, and to list extracurricular activities, including "church work." The administration also gave significant weight to recommendations from principals and alumni that included comments on the candidate's personality and "moral character." It relied on such factors to screen out academically qualified Jewish candidates as not sufficiently "well-rounded."[35]

Mabel Douglass, dean of NJC from its founding in 1918 until 1932, complained that too many Jews had been "inadvertently admitted on academic grading solely." Characterizing many of the Jewish students as "crude," she complained that they had caused the "finest girls" to transfer. Douglass's successor as permanent dean, Margaret T. Corwin, shared her views, and in 1936 she persuaded the trustees to limit the proportion of commuters in the student body to 25 percent. This served to further reduce Jewish enrollment because the percentage of Jewish students who commuted was more than double that of non-Jews: 68 percent as opposed to 30 percent. Corwin's father, Robert N. Corwin, as director of Yale University's admissions board from 1920 to 1933, had been instrumental in developing policies there to restrict Jewish admissions.[36]

Complaints by New Jersey Jews about discrimination against Jewish applicants at Rutgers and NJC caused the Rutgers Board of Regents to hold hearings on the issue in 1931. Ten Jewish organizations representing about 200,000 citizens charged that Rutgers, as a defacto state university that received substantial state appropriations and "the apex of the public school system," had violated New Jersey civil rights law prohibiting discrimination on the basis "of race, creed, or color in furnishing facilities at colleges and universities within the State." A committee representing the Jewish organizations documented in a brief that Rutgers had rejected many Jews from Elizabeth, New Brunswick, and Perth Amboy high schools in favor of non-Jews with much inferior records.[37]

Fraser Metzger, dean of Rutgers College, and other members of the Rutgers University administration emphatically denied that the university had ever discriminated against Jews. Julius Kass, the Perth Amboy attorney who initiated the case, testified that Dean Metzger told him in October 1930 that the administration was determined to maintain a quota limiting Jews to about 15 percent of the student body to prevent Rutgers from becoming "like C.C.N.Y." Kass asked Dean Metzger to consider a hypothetical case in which a Jewish student in the top quarter of his preparatory class and a non-Jewish student in the lower three-quarters both applied for admission when the Jewish quota was already filled, and to tell him which he would admit. Dean Metzger answered "without hesitation" that he would admit only the non-Jewish student. Dr. William B. Gourley, a member of the Rutgers board of trustees, termed Kass's charges "perfect nonsense."[38]

The Rutgers administration insisted it was not discriminating, arguing that it was necessary to preserve geographical balance within the state and to ensure that no ethnic group was admitted in proportions significantly higher than its percentage in the state population. The Nazis used a similar argument in 1933 in restricting Jewish admissions to German universities to 1 percent, their proportion in the German population. The Rutgers administration claimed that Jews, 6 percent of the state's population, composed 12 percent of the student body. Moreover, it maintained that the student body "should be composed of students in fair proportion from all parts of the state." This meant that the administration had the right to reject applicants from northern New Jersey high schools in which Jews were disproportionately represented in favor of those with inferior records from southern New Jersey counties that contained very few Jews. Only the Admissions Committee of Rutgers University possessed the requisite judgment to properly select candidates. The Admissions Committee had been "carefully selected" and its members were "men of high character and long experience." The Jewish organizations' "misunderstanding" arose from their "erroneous assumption that scholastic standing is the sole test" in the college admissions process.[39] Despite the hearings, the Rutgers and NJC administrations maintained this outlook toward Jewish admissions throughout the decade.

NJC and Rutgers discriminated against Jews in faculty hiring as well. There were at most four Jews on the NJC faculty during the mid-1930s, two of whom were German refugees hired in the Music Department in September 1934. There were very few Jews on the faculties of the Rutgers men's colleges. Evalyn Clark, assistant professor of classical languages, in 1935 testified before the Trustees Committee appointed to consider the dismissal of Lienhard Bergel that she had heard NJC dean Mabel Douglass declare that she would not have a Jew on her faculty.[40]

During the 1930s, non-Jewish professors at NJC at times injected crude antisemitic comments into classroom discussions. Marion Siegel Friedman, who attended NJC from 1935 to 1939, recalled in 1986 that she still felt "hatred and revulsion" for her European literature professor because he endorsed in class the medieval charge that Jews ritually murdered Christian children around Easter time to reenact the crucifixion and mock Jesus. The professor had assigned the class the tale of Little Hugh of Lincoln, a Christian boy whom Jews in England had been accused of murdering for this purpose in 1255 C.E. The bizarre Christian ritual murder fantasy, often combined with the blood libel accusation, claiming that Jews extracted the child's blood to mix with matzoh consumed at Passover, resulted in the torture and execution of many innocent Jews. The professor, in discussing the tale in class, had told the students "that there must be some truth to the charge of Jews sacrificing a Christian child for making Passover matzoh."[41]

No sooner had Hitler assumed power in Germany than members of the NJC and Rutgers German departments were extolling Nazi achievements in public forums on and off campus. Dr. Emil Leopold Jordan, instructor in German at NJC, speaking at a meeting of the NJC League of Women Voters in March 1933, declared that Hitler had rescued Germany from a republican system that had left her "worse off than ever." Hitler had unified a nation divided by thirty-six quarreling political parties. He was a man of high moral character, a vegetarian who did not smoke or drink, committed to combating corruption. Jordan concluded his speech by accusing the American press of presenting distorted accounts of German conditions.[42]

Presaging the conflict that later erupted over the NJC German Department's Nazi orientation, Lienhard Bergel, who, in addition to being the only department member opposed to Hitler, was a non-Jewish German native, challenged Jordan's defense of the Nazi government in the question period. According to Bergel, the next day the NJC German department chair, Professor Friedrich J. Hauptmann, "rebuked him for spoiling the good effect of Dr. Jordan's speech." Alice Schlimbach, assistant professor of German and director of the NJC German House, later testified that Bergel's anti-Nazi remarks during the question period had angered students at the German House, precipitating "small riots." She reported that "the girls could not respect a man who spoke in such a disrespectful way about his own country." One student called Bergel "unethical." Another complained that he had made the German department "look like a scrapping place."[43]

Jean M. Earle, who lived in the German House for three years and graduated from NJC in 1934, in 1935 described Dr. Jordan's presentation at the League of Women Voters forum as "a very interesting talk on how Hitler came into power and why the German people were against a certain class of Jews." She said that the students in attendance objected to "hav[ing] that meeting spoiled by Mr. Bergel constantly contradicting Dr. Jordan." The students "had gone to hear Dr. Jordan talk about Hitler and instead had to listen to Mr. Bergel talk against Hitler."[44]

A student who attended the lecture testified in 1935 at the Special Trustees Committee hearings that Jordan had made explicitly antisemitic comments in answer to a question from the floor about Nazi treatment of Jews. The witness had taken notes at the lecture and said that the NJC student newspaper, *Campus News*, had not reported the antisemitic comments. She quoted Jordan as having said that "the Jews should be kept in their place," and that they "should only be employed in the various positions in their proportion to the population." The Special Trustees Committee summary of the hearings stated that "Dr. Jordan said he did not recall" making the remark that "Jews should be kept in their place."[45]

The same evening as Professor Jordan's League of Women Voters presentation, Associate Professor Albert Holzmann of the Rutgers German Department spoke in favor of Hitler at a symposium on the current situation in Germany sponsored by the Rutgers Liberal Club. Holzmann denied that the Nazis had committed antisemitic atrocities, blaming the American press for printing propaganda to besmirch the German people's "fair name." What was remarkable was the very infrequency of antisemitic incidents, considering that a "tremendous revolution" had taken place in Germany. Holzmann credited the Nazi leadership for the alleged lack of violence, claiming that it had ordered its followers "to harm no Jew." He insisted that there was no reason for anyone to protest against the Hitler regime.[46]

Although another speaker, Rabbi Nathaniel Keller, urged that people denounce antisemitic discrimination in Germany, the speaker following him, Dr. Milton J. Hoffman of New Brunswick Theological Seminary, argued that no protest take place until "a thorough investigation of the facts" had been conducted. Hoffman claimed that the Jews were in part responsible for any mistreatment they suffered, because, unlike other "races," they refused to assimilate when they settled in "a foreign country." He declared that "Jews remain Jews and cannot become otherwise."[47]

During the discussion period, NJC German Department chair Friedrich Hauptmann defended Nazi Germany's policy toward Jews, arguing that the Hitler regime was concerned only about Jews who had migrated to Germany from the East after the World War. Hauptmann charged that many of the Jews were contributing to "Socialist and Communist" subversion. Moving into Berlin in large numbers, they rendered many native Germans homeless.[48]

Professor Holzmann aggressively promoted the Hitler regime during the next months. Speaking before the Rutgers chapter of the Phi Beta Kappa Society in early May 1933, he declared that he "was 85 percent in approval of Hitler and the Nazi regime" and praised the Fuehrer for uniting the German people. He told the New Brunswick, New Jersey, *Daily Home News* in late May that Hitler was the savior of Germany, who had put a quarter of a million Germans back to work. Holzmann denounced the German Social Democrats for signing the Treaty of Versailles, which he claimed had "subject[ed] Germany to more humiliating and cruel conditions than any other country in recent civilization has been forced to bear." Ignoring the Nazi students' intense anti-intellectualism, reflected in the massive book burnings they staged that month at universities across the Reich, Holzmann identified the disproportionate involvement of students "and those interested in education" as a particularly impressive feature of the German Nazi party.[49]

NJC students majoring in German who traveled in Nazi Germany during 1933 and 1934 presented glowing accounts of Hitler's achievements in the campus press. Marion Kelley, Class of 1934, returned in the fall of 1933 from fourteen months of study at the University of Berlin impressed with Germany's "earnest and serious" students. She was struck by the "cleanliness and neatness" of German cities, with their "beautiful, well-kept gardens."[50] Margarethe Varga, Class of 1935, who had studied in

Germany during the 1933–34 academic year, told the NJC German Club in September 1934 to disregard American press reports of street violence in the Third Reich. She reported that an "air of peace" prevailed there. Varga said that she had been impressed by the way all Germans, even little children, saluted their friends with the greeting "Heil Hitler," a sign of the national unity the Nazis had forged.[51]

In an April 1936 article published in a Jewish magazine, Lienhard Bergel explained that Nazi faculty in the NJC German Department made special arrangements for the students traveling to Germany for study to maximize their chances of being influenced by Nazi ideology. One of the Nazi NJC professors would personally select a German host family for the student to reside with when abroad that was particularly committed to Nazism. The professor justified his or her personal involvement in the placement by explaining that it was for the purpose of making sure that the student was exposed to a "genuinely German atmosphere."

Bergel considered NJC's financing student travel to the Third Reich by collecting money in the German classes to be the most scandalous aspect of the college's study in Germany program. He noted that "[e]very student in the [German] department is obliged to make weekly contributions for this fund." Although the German Department presented the contributions as voluntary, students were under strong pressure to make them, because the collections were conducted under their professors' supervision. Bergel emphasized that the German faculty expected the Jewish students to contribute along with the non-Jewish. Questions about whether a student really had to contribute, or why the students were not sent to study in a German-speaking country not under Nazi control, like Switzerland or Austria, only "provoke[d] the anger of the teacher" and retaliation against the person asking it.[52]

In December 1934 the NJC student newspaper *Campus News* published sections of a letter it had received from Elaine Zischkau, Class of 1936, the recipient of the 1934–35 NJC German scholarship, who was enrolled at the University of Berlin, full of enthusiasm for the "new Germany." Zischkau extolled Adolf Hitler as a leader "deeply respected by the older people and adored by the younger" in Germany. After years of "growing misery and disunion" under the Social Democrats, the German people had rallied to Hitler, who "offered a new life of which they can be proud." He was determined to forge Germans into one people, and to restore their self-respect. The Nazis were "trying so hard to create a new and better Germany out of the old." They were "so desperately sincere."

To be sure, they had made "occasional errors." But it was impossible "in a revolution of this size" not to do so.[53]

Zischkau angrily denounced the American press for what she called its "savage and unjust attacks" on Nazi Germany. American reporters who had never been to "the new Germany" wrote about it "with absolutely no understanding of the situation." Zischkau singled out a recent *Collier's* editorial that declared that "[i]t was Germany's misfortune and the world's misfortune" that Hitler had assumed power. She strongly resented that such "stupid" and "malicious" articles influenced American perceptions of the Third Reich.[54]

Zischkau became embroiled in a fevered exchange in the *Campus News* when a letter to the editor signed only "Member of '36" denounced her as a propagandist for Hitler. Member of '36 charged that Zischkau could not possibly understand what was really taking place in Germany when the persons with whom she was in contact were "either themselves committing the crimes of the Nazis" or were "in fear of their lives if they tell the truth."[55]

Zischkau responded in the *Campus News* by declaring that she was just "doing [her] part in attempting to destroy this picture of Germany as a land of fear and lies." During her months in the Third Reich she had seen "a government helping its people." The Nazis had united the Germans and made it possible for them "to gain pleasure from music and travel... [and] to gain an equal standing with the people of other nations."[56]

Lienhard Bergel probably had Elaine Zischkau in mind when he wrote in 1936 that it was almost inevitable that a student would return from a year in the Third Reich feeling sympathy for the Hitler regime, given how college study in Germany programs were structured. Arriving in Germany at an impressionable age, the American student came into contact with Nazis almost exclusively. The student's college German Department arranged for her to reside with a pro-Nazi German family. She was enrolled in courses at a German university where "she heard the official Nazi doctrines explained." The professors whose lectures she attended all presented their subjects "from the Nazi angle." No wonder that she "writes letters to the College paper during her stay which are full of praise for the Nazis." Bergel noted that American exchange students continued their pro-Nazi propaganda activities after they returned from Germany. Nazi sympathizers on the German Department faculty referred other students to her to learn "first-hand" about the virtues of the Third Reich.[57]

Professor Emily Hickman of the NJC History Department echoed these paeans to the Third Reich when she returned from the Carl Schurz Tour of Germany that the Nazi government had arranged for American academics for the summer of 1934. Professor Hickman emphasized that "something positive was going on" in the Third Reich and sharply criticized American press coverage as biased and inaccurate. She endorsed the labor camp service the Hitler regime required of students before they entered universities for drawing together youth of different backgrounds, thereby supposedly reducing class divisions. The labor camp also served as an arena in which a prospective student could display character and leadership qualities important in gaining admission to a university. Hickman found much to admire in the Nazi government's higher education policies, which she suggested provided better preparation for modern society's challenges. She explained that "[t]he new [Nazi] system criticizes the highly specialized scholarship of Germany as divorced from life, and believes that higher education should be aimed more nearly at . . . character education and an education fitting the student to deal with the problems met in life." The reduction in the number of students admitted was necessary to alleviate overcrowding in the professions.[58]

The NJC and Rutgers German departments energetically promoted the film of the Carl Schurz Foundation Tour of Nazi Germany that the Hitler government arranged for American academics in the summer of 1934. The film was produced by the Nazi government's Universum-Film Aktiengesellschaft (UFA) studio. The Hitler regime distributed it to American colleges and universities that participated in the tour for campus showings, to present a favorable image of the Third Reich to students and faculty members. The president of Rutgers University, Robert C. Clothier, wrote to Professor Albert Holzmann that he hoped to attend a campus showing. Clothier and Holzmann agreed that proceeds derived from renting the film outside the university would be allocated to send a member of the Rutgers or NJC German Club to study in Germany.[59]

Holzmann informed President Clothier on March 13, 1935, that the first campus screening of the film was "a splendid success." It was "a university affair," sponsored by both the Rutgers and NJC German departments. Professor Hickman assisted the German departments in distributing tickets. According to Holzmann the audience was "large and enthusiastic."[60]

Not only was President Clothier very supportive of the German departments' efforts to expose Americans on and off campus to a Nazi propaganda film produced by the Hitler regime, but several months later he declined an opportunity to publicly support German refugees. In December 1935 Clothier refused Director Alvin Johnson's appeal to join the Advisory Committee he was organizing for the Graduate Faculty of Political and Social Science at the New School for Social Research in New York City. In 1933, Clothier had agreed to be a sponsor of a plan to establish a University in Exile to be staffed by German refugee scholars who had fled to the United States. Serving as a member of the Graduate Faculty's Advisory Committee required no obligation other than to provide occasional advice. All that Johnson really asked of Clothier was his "moral support" for the University in Exile. Nonetheless, Clothier replied to Johnson that it was "inadvisable" for him to join the Advisory Committee.[61]

In the fall of 1933, NJC German Department chair Friedrich J. Hauptmann informed Lienhard Bergel, an instructor hired in February 1932 and the department's lone anti-Nazi, that he would not be retained after June 1935. The Rutgers University trustees had adopted a three-year term limit for instructors during the 1932–33 academic year. Acting NJC dean Albert Meder, who had replaced Mabel Douglass, approved Hauptmann's decision. His successor, Dean Corwin, determined that the German Department could not afford to employ five faculty members, two of whom were instructors, in part because of an anticipated decline in German course enrollments. Hauptmann recommended that the other instructor, the pro-Nazi Emil Jordan, who had been at NJC since 1931, be retained, and not Bergel. After conferring with President Clothier, Dean Corwin wrote to Bergel on May 23, 1934, saying that NJC would terminate his employment in June 1935.[62]

Besides the instructors Bergel and Jordan, the NJC German Department in 1934 consisted of associate professor Hauptmann, chair since 1931; assistant professor Alice Schlimbach; and Marie Hauptmann, the chair's wife, who was classified as "assistant," a temporary position, although she taught at NJC for eight years, until June 1937. Schlimbach had been director of the German House since its establishment in the fall of 1929, and she resided there. All were German nationals educated in Germany. Jordan, who had been in the United States only since 1930, was the only department member with a Ph.D. (in economics, not literature).[63]

Lienhard Bergel's appointment in February 1932 as instructor in the NJC German Department had been arranged by his fiancée, Sylvia Cook, who persuaded Dean Mabel Douglass to turn over Cook's position to him. Bergel came to NJC with "superb recommendations" from the University of Breslau, where he had done his graduate work, and from

Professor William A. Braun of Barnard, under whom Sylvia Cook had studied. Cook, a Barnard alumna and graduate exchange student at the University of Breslau in Germany from 1928 to 1931, began teaching at NJC in the fall semester of 1931. She had met Lienhard Bergel at the University of Breslau, in Professor Paul Merker's seminar on German literature. They became engaged in Germany and were married shortly after Bergel assumed the NJC instructorship. In Breslau, Bergel prepared for his *Staatsexamen*, required of those entering college teaching, and passed it with distinction in 1930.[64]

Cook was one of the few exchange students at Breslau who feared that Nazism constituted a serious long-term threat in Germany, a view Bergel shared. Bergel was not a member of any political party, and Cook described him during his Breslau student days as "having no interest in politics" except that, like Cook, he found Nazism "deeply abhorrent." Neither Bergel nor Cook was Jewish. Bergel had been raised a Lutheran, but neither he nor Cook attended church. Cook's father was a professor at the University of Cincinnati and her mother "an old-fashioned New England type, staunchly Republican."[65]

During the period Bergel and Cook were studying in Breslau, the Nazis became increasingly visible there, and the couple witnessed or heard about Nazi beatings of persons considered a threat to "racial purity." Breslau, situated near Poland, had a significant Jewish population. Cook recalled watching Nazi youths marching in a park near the Coenaculum, a house run by Catholic nuns for women students where she resided, and then fanning out into Breslau, attacking Jews and other "undesirable[s]." The Nazi youths' "weapon of choice" in these beatings was a "*Gummiknuep-pel*," a word Cook said she had not learned in her Barnard German courses – a length of pipe encased in rubber hose.[66]

From the time of Cook's arrival in Breslau in October 1928, she had been deeply disturbed by the chauvinism and militarism expressed by Germans she encountered. Cook, who spoke fluent German, had come to Germany "with happy expectations" shaped by her admiration for German literature, music, and philosophy. The new American exchange student received her first shock when the director of the Coenaculum, a nun called Mutter Bischoff, presiding at a party for Cook, delivered her welcoming address. Mutter Bischoff proclaimed that day a great one for Germany, because it had just launched its first armed cruiser and taken "the first step toward the eventual destruction of England." Cook became "quickly aware of the forces at work around [her]" and read Hitler's *Mein Kampf* carefully, along with the local newspaper, *Breslauer Neueste*

Nachrichten. Foreseeing the "impending catastrophe," Cook arranged to get her fiancé out of Germany to the United States and gave up her position at NJC for him.[67]

Sylvia Cook Bergel recalled in 1992 that German Department chair Friedrich Hauptmann was "jealous and abominated Lienhard [Bergel] from the start," making his life at NJC "a misery." Hauptmann detested Bergel's anti-Nazism and probably felt intellectually intimidated by the younger man.[68]

Hauptmann's academic limitations were clearly revealed when, having received a leave of absence with full pay from the NJC administration, he traveled to Nazi Germany, where the University of Marburg awarded him a Ph.D. for a sixty-nine-page dissertation that he completed, along with some other doctoral requirements, in only five months. He did not even work full time on the dissertation because the leave of absence was granted in part so that he could visit spas in Germany to improve his health. The dissertation, "Eine wissenschaftliche Kritik des Standes des deutschen Unterrichts an den High Schools und Colleges der Vereinigten Staaten" ("A Scholarly Critique of German Instruction at the High Schools and Colleges of the United States"), drew on only "a handful of secondary sources" and some questionnaires Hauptmann mailed to state departments of education, which he may not have used. David Oshinsky, Richard P. McCormick, and Daniel Horn, in their 1989 investigation of the Bergel dismissal, *The Case of the Nazi Professor*, called Hauptmann's dissertation, "a dreadful piece of work." It was "loaded . . . with pro-Nazi statements."[69]

Bergel later described the Rutgers administration's role in the leave of absence as scandalous. He noted that during Hauptmann's five months in Germany he not only wrote his dissertation but prepared for and passed his oral examination "and had still time enough to improve his health in a fashionable watering resort." The worst part of it, he said, was that this had occurred with the administration's full knowledge and approval. It had granted him the leave knowing his expressed purpose and had provided him with his entire salary.[70]

Dean Corwin challenged Lienhard Bergel's assertion that German Ph.D. degrees were equivalent only to American M.A. degrees and claimed that there was "nothing exceptional" in Hauptmann's having completed a dissertation and other doctoral requirements in "only five months." She noted that the University of Marburg had awarded him his degree *cum laude*. Besides, it was "a little difficult to evaluate European degrees."[71]

In justifying Bergel's termination, Hauptmann and Corwin, besides citing the three-year rule for instructors, criticized Bergel's teaching and his lack of attendance at German Department meetings and unwillingness to have meals at the German table in the campus dining hall. In her report to the trustees, Corwin also complained that Bergel, who had been teaching for only three years, had not yet published any of his work. It was in the same report that she defended as academically legitimate Hauptmann's poorly researched sixty-nine-page dissertation from the Nazified University of Marburg. Hauptmann also charged that Bergel had reneged on an agreement that he live in New Brunswick and instead commuted to campus from Cranford, New Jersey, as a result of which he "never participated in social activities," including those of the German Club and German House. Hauptmann and Corwin both claimed that Bergel's anti-Nazism was not a factor in his termination.[72]

In a comment to the Special Trustees Committee, Dean Corwin appeared to dismiss the NJC German Department's Nazi orientation as a matter of concern. She reported that she had been "very much impressed" by a statement of Bergel's that his fiancée had warned him before he came to the United States "of the situation in the German Department of the New Jersey College for Women," and that his experiences during his first few weeks on the NJC faculty had "fully justified the warnings." To Dean Corwin this indicated that Bergel, who while in Germany had seen the Nazis grow into a mass movement, heard their antisemitic invective, and witnessed the impact of their savage violence, "lacked sympathetic understanding" of a college department composed entirely of German-born Nazis. She could not understand how Bergel could have made up his mind about his "colleagues" in the German Department after only a few weeks. Corwin concluded that "[t]he whole statement reinforced me in my opinion that the College should not retain Mr. Bergel."[73]

On April 17, 1935, about a month before the Special Trustees Committee convened the hearings, NJC students met with Dean Corwin to express concern about German Department faculty propagandizing for Nazism in the classroom and Bergel's dismissal. Corwin informed them that a drop in German course enrollment of 20 percent from the 1933–34 to the 1934–35 academic year necessitated the elimination of one position. The students then asked Corwin why Marie Hauptmann, the chair's wife, was not let go instead of Bergel. Corwin refused to answer on the grounds that she would have to share with them confidential faculty salary information. (As aforementioned, Marie Hauptmann was classified as an assistant, a temporary position, although she remained a member of the German Department for eight years, from academic year 1929–30 through 1936–37.)[74] Students returned on May 7 and asked that Dean Corwin appoint a committee to visit all German classes to determine whether Nazi propaganda was being disseminated in them. This Corwin refused to do.[75]

On April 13, 1935, the *Campus News* precipitated student involvement in the Bergel controversy by publishing an editorial that praised his contribution to NJC as a teacher but accepted Corwin's argument that declining German enrollments required the elimination of his position. Several letters to the editor challenged Bergel's termination. One from "A Group of German Students" charged that the German Department's Nazi orientation discouraged many students from enrolling in German courses. In early May, *Campus News* advisor and former acting dean Albert Meder asked the newspaper's editor Marion Short, who had just assumed that office, not to publish letters on the Bergel dismissal, but she refused. Dean Corwin authorized Meder to tell Short that the administration would make no further statement to the *Campus News* on the case. Short also printed letters from students and alumni supporting Hauptmann.[76] The previous editor, Frances Williams, later testified that Meder had summoned her to his office to tell her he was displeased that Short was publishing letters to the editor on the Bergel case, and that he might remove her for doing so.[77]

Alan Silver, a Rutgers student and Bergel supporter, informed reporter Frederick E. Woltman of the New York *World-Telegram* about the controversy, and Woltman produced a story describing the anti-fascist Bergel's isolation in a German Department consisting entirely of Nazis. This generated enormous press interest in the case. Silver also secured an interview for Bergel with the Committee on Academic Freedom of the American Civil Liberties Union (ACLU) in New York, which included Roger Baldwin, Reinhold Niebuhr, Horace Kallen, and Sidney Hook. As a result of the interview, the ACLU decided to investigate and notified President Clothier of its concern. It also suggested that if it determined that the German Department had violated Bergel's academic freedom and had disseminated Nazi propaganda, it would ask the New Jersey legislature to withhold funds from Rutgers. Press coverage, ACLU involvement, and the efforts of the Bergels and their student backers to enlist support from anti-Nazi state legislators and New Brunswick assemblymen brought the case to a wider public.[78]

The five-person Special Trustees Committee that President Clothier selected was dominated by its chair, Newark attorney J. Edward

Ashmead, Class of 1897; New York City attorney and clubman Philip M. Brett, Class of 1892, a former Rutgers football captain and acting president of Rutgers from 1930 to 1932; and John Wycoff Mettler, Class of 1899, founder and president of the Interwoven Stocking Company. Mettler also served on the Board of Managers of the Delaware & Hudson Railroad. All were longtime Rutgers trustees. None of the five members of the committee was a scholar or a teacher. Sylvia C. Bergel in 1988 ridiculed the notion of a man like Mettler, described as "a giant in the field of sock manufacture," serving on the committee. She recalled that Mettler brought socks manufactured in his hosiery mill to the hearings and distributed them to friends.[79]

Sylvia C. Bergel later described the Special Trustees Committee as "an ingrown little group of lawyers and business men closely related to the interests of Rutgers University," and not likely to be objective. In her view it "should have included at least one person of academic experience," as well as someone not affiliated with Rutgers.[80]

Testifying on the first day of the hearings, Bergel charged that Hauptmann's motive in terminating him was his having expressed opposition to Nazism at campus forums, beginning with his challenge to Emil Jordan in March 1933. Bergel said that Hauptmann had told him he would not have hired him in February 1932 if he had known that Bergel would refuse to support Hitler when he became chancellor. He accused Hauptmann of propagandizing for Nazism in the classroom, and of having made antisemitic statements to students. Bergel declared that Dean Corwin had warned him that if he insisted on a hearing to contest his dismissal, the administration would not provide him with letters of recommendation for a position elsewhere.[81]

Testifying himself a few days later, Hauptmann denied that he propagandized in class, but he did state that "there are some good sides to Nazism," and that he had during class "corrected errors in newspaper reports" about Nazi Germany.[82] He told the committee that he was "inclined to discount" many of the American press reports of Nazi atrocities. Hauptmann claimed not to know whether the Nazi government had deprived Jews of civil and political rights, or whether they had removed Jewish professors from universities or burned books by Jewish authors. He praised, however, what he called the Nazis' "destruction of all obscene books in German libraries."[83]

Hauptmann admitted that he had told German Department faculty members not to speak about what was happening in Germany because "there was no first-hand information available." He claimed that only

Bergel disregarded his instructions. Hauptmann informed the committee that he heard that students residing in the German House had said they "were 'disgusted' with Dr. Bergel's criticism of German officials."[84]

Many NJC students made their views known by signing petitions backing Bergel or Hauptmann. A letter signed by "seventy German students," whose names were not listed, was published in the *Campus News* on May 8, denying that German Department faculty propagandized for Nazism in the classroom. Irene Patterson, Class of 1936, who had taken courses with both Bergel and the Hauptmanns and identified herself as the only resident of the German House who was not pro-Nazi, testified that Marjorie Fricke, Class of 1935, president of the German Club, had solicited signatures for the letter in Marie Hauptmann's class. She stated that Ms. Hauptmann had left the room while students passed around the petition, suggesting that German Department faculty had acted in collusion with Fricke to obtain signatures. Evelyn Engle, Class of 1937, testified that the petition was circulated in all the German classes except for Bergel's. Vivien Sigel, Class of 1938, told the committee that in her class Professor Jordan had immediately walked out when Fricke arrived, without speaking with her. Sigel stated that this was a clear indication Jordan knew Fricke was coming.[85]

Bergel's supporters in the NJC student body, responding to the German House letter, secured the signatures of 405 of NJC's 892 students on a petition that praised his teaching and described him as a "thoroughly competent" faculty member. Believing Jewish students had orchestrated the campaign for Bergel, the NJC administration sought to determine how many of those signing the petition were Jews.[86]

During twenty-nine hearings that extended into late July 1935, more than sixty witnesses appeared before the Trustees Committee in support of Bergel, including eleven faculty members, three of whom were department heads (classics, political science, and Italian), as well as students and alumni. About half of these students and alumni were Jewish.[87] Bergel's witnesses, besides testifying to his competency as a teacher, emphasized that chairman Hauptmann and the other pro-Nazi members of the NJC German Department sometimes propagandized for the Hitler regime in class and suppressed criticism of it from students. Some stated that Hauptmann and other department members specifically defended Hitler's anti-semitic policies. The implication was that the German Department would not tolerate an opponent of Nazism on its faculty. Student witnesses described Alice Schlimbach, director of the NJC German House, as a passionate supporter of Hitler who presided over a "Nazi nest." Some also presented specific evidence of Marie Hauptmann's incompetence as a teacher in an effort to convince the Committee that the administration, if it desired to reduce the budget, should have terminated her rather than Bergel.

Faculty witnesses for Bergel described the NJC German Department as a tightly knit group of Nazi sympathizers that tolerated no opposition to the Hitler regime. Frederick E. Woltman, who later won three Pulitzer prizes, reporting on the hearings for the New York *World-Telegram*, declared that the "gravity and sincerity" of some of these witnesses was "so apparent as to make an obvious impression" on those hearing them.[88] Miriam West, professor of economics at NJC for eight years, stated that the German Department, with its chair, Professor Hauptmann, acting as "dictator," was tightly coordinated in the manner of the Nazi government. Professor West testified that Hauptmann had told her that Nazi Germany was right "in shutting out the Jews to prevent them from gaining control of the country." Professor Shirley Smith, head of NJC's Classics Department, charged that Hauptmann ran the German Department with military regimentation.[89] Professor William Oncken, head of NJC's Italian Department, stated that Hauptmann represented "all that is most despicable in Germany" at that time.[90] Evalyn Clark, instructor in classics, testified that she had heard Hauptmann and his wife defend Nazi antisemitism at a dinner party she attended.[91] Mildred Moulton, assistant professor of political science, noted that the concept of academic freedom would be alien to any passionate supporter of Nazism such as Professor Hauptmann.[92]

Several students testified that Hauptmann had injected Nazi propaganda into classroom lectures and discussion and silenced those who tried to rebut it. An NJC senior stated in a letter to the Committee that Hauptmann's propagandizing in class was "very insidious and continuous." It consisted of a "steady flow of remarks." When students protested his claims that Jews had ruled pre-Hitler Germany by controlling its financial system and had no right to live in Germany, he abruptly "closed the discussion." The senior emphasized that the German Department chair became "very emotional and fanatical" when making these allegations. She asserted that Hauptmann's "definite Nazi bias" was "particularly dangerous because he immediately squelches all opposition."[93] Sylvia Silverman, Class of 1934, described Hauptmann bringing German and French newspapers to class to convince the students that the French were building up armaments and that Germany therefore deserved to rearm. When a trustee asked, "Who did most of the discussing?" Silverman replied, "Herr Hauptmann talked and we listened." She also recalled Hauptmann's defending in class the Nazi policy of relegating women to the home.[94]

Adele Lubman, an NJC sophomore, similarly testified to Hauptmann's aggressive championing of Nazism and refusal to tolerate dissent from students. She declared that he spoke in class of how Hitler was making Germany "a strong, good nation," praising "what he was doing for the people." Lubman stated that Hauptmann never showed approval for anything Jews ever did in Germany, although some students tried to bring to his attention significant Jewish contributions to German culture. When Hudson County assemblyman Samuel Pesin, who was permitted to question witnesses, asked Lubman whether any member of the class had tried to ask Hauptmann about Nazi persecution of Jews, she replied, "Yes, but it was impossible to get anywhere." Lubman stated that Hauptmann tried to stifle in class any opinion that he opposed.[95]

Dorothy Venook, Class of 1934, a German minor who had taken four years of German, including courses with both Hauptmann and Bergel, recalled that Hauptmann had condemned in class the March 1934 anti-Nazi rally in Madison Square Garden that had featured presentations by Al Smith, Senator Millard Tydings, Rabbi Stephen S. Wise, Chancellor Harry Woodburn Chase of New York University, and other prominent opponents of Nazism. She testified that Hauptmann had also denounced the Treaty of Versailles and Germany's disarmament in class. Venook asserted that there was "a definite anti-Semitic feeling" in the German Department. She, like the other witnesses who spoke in Bergel's behalf, described him as a "very competent" teacher.[96]

In 1986, Marion Siegel Friedman, who observed Hauptmann both in the classroom and at the German table in the NJC dining hall, recalled his propagandizing for Hitler among students. His manner was aggressive; he "roared frequently," which sometimes terrified the young women. Friedman recalled that Hauptmann insisted to her that "the newspapers lied" about the Third Reich. If she joined the student tour he led to Germany during the summer vacations, he would demonstrate to her that the Nazis were not antisemitic. Friedman refused Hauptmann's "repeated invitation."[97]

Other students testified that Alice Schlimbach, assistant professor of German, behaved in a similar manner to Hauptmann in class and in the NJC German House, which she directed. All German majors were required to live for at least a year in the German House. Naomi Parness, Class of 1934, stated that Schlimbach on several occasions told her

German language class "how wonderful Nazism was," and that she had denied that Hitler was antisemitic. Mary Atwood, who resided at the NJC German House, told the Committee that she had seen several of the students there sing the Nazi party anthem, the Horst Wessel Lied. Atwood testified that the Horst Wessel Lied came first in a book of songs of the *Sturmabteilung* (SA), the Nazi storm troopers, which was available in the German House. Margarethe Varga had obtained the songbook as an exchange student in Germany and brought it back to NJC. She recalled that "about five songs" in the book made "special reference . . . to doing away with the Jewish race in Germany."[98] Atwood stated that because she publicly supported Bergel's reinstatement she had become "an outcast and pariah" at the German House.[99]

Bartlett Cowdrey, Class of 1933, told the Committee that Marie Hauptmann was "the most incompetent instructor" she had ever had at NJC. She expressed astonishment that the administration would terminate Lienhard Bergel, whom she called a "scholar of the first rank," and instead retain Marie Hauptmann, his "inferior both in educational background and as a teacher." Cowdrey had taken intermediate German with Ms. Hauptmann. Two sections of this course were offered, one taught by Ms. Hauptmann and one by Bergel. Cowdrey stated that most of the students were pleased to have been assigned to Ms. Hauptmann's section, because "she was known to be the easiest member of the German department." The class met three days a week, on Tuesday, Thursday, and Saturday, but Ms. Hauptmann often did not show up on Saturday. If she did, most of the students were absent anyway. Ms. Hauptmann made little effort to check student attendance. Even at the end of the year, she was unsure of students' names, and her English was so poor she could only pronounce the German ones. Cowdrey claimed that Ms. Hauptmann's examinations "were a farce" and doubted that she even factored them into the final grade. When a student was shown to be unprepared during class recitation or translation, Ms. Hauptmann never made any comment, even to "habitual offender[s]." Cowdrey noted that the course grades "were exceedingly high for the negligible amount of class room work" Ms. Hauptmann required.[100]

Theresa Kunst, president of the NJC League of Women Voters and senior class advisor, also described Ms. Hautpmann as incompetent. Whereas the chair's wife made "swell cake," as a teacher she "couldn't get it across."[101]

Isabelle Shackell, Class of 1934, a non-Jew, stated to the committee that she believed Ms. Hauptmann may have failed her in a German course because she believed Shackell was Jewish. Shackell later received a high grade when she repeated the course in summer school. Ms. Hauptmann told Shackell when she inquired about her grade that she had missed too many classes during Jewish holidays.[102]

Professor Hauptmann during his nearly five days of testimony presented a very benign view of Nazi Germany. The German Department chair stated that the Hitler regime was not spreading propaganda, explaining that many Americans were confused about this issue because they interpreted the word differently from Germans. He claimed that, in Germany, propaganda meant simply "a statement of facts."[103]

Hauptmann's student witnesses presented similar testimony. Two-thirds of them were members of the German Club and lived, or had lived, in the German House. (Only three of Bergel's student witnesses had lived there.) Margarethe Varga, Class of 1935, an exchange student in Germany during the 1933–34 academic year, told the committee that she cherished a framed etching of Adolf Hitler on display in her room. She liked the Fuehrer both as "a dictator and a man." Varga characterized support for Bergel at NJC as an "organized Jewish" movement. Bergel's counsel, Sidney Kaplan, demonstrated, however, that two of the three NJC students Varga had named as leaders in the campaign against termination were non-Jews. Other pro-Hauptmann students attributed support for Bergel to Jews whose perceptions about Germany were distorted by an excessive sensitivity about antisemitism.[104]

Perhaps the most striking feature of the hearings was the Special Trustees Committee's lack of concern about Nazism in Germany and at NJC, its bias against anti-Hitler witnesses, and its obvious sympathy for Hauptmann. Compounding the problem for Bergel was the denial to his counsel of the right of oral cross-examination. They could only submit questions in writing to the committee, which often chose to rephrase those they asked.[105] About three weeks after the hearings began, Samuel Untermyer, president of the Non-Sectarian Anti-Nazi League and leader of the boycott movement against German goods, told New Jersey governor Harold G. Hoffman that he and many others were "far from satisfied with the impartiality of the Board of Trustees that is now taking evidence."[106] In its report on the hearings, the ACLU stated that "the Chairman and other members of the Committee" were "careful to avoid damaging evidence against Dr. Hauptmann" and had failed to "follow up points."[107] Professor Richard P. McCormick, official historian of Rutgers University and co-author of the only book-length study of the Bergel-Hauptmann case, wrote that the Special Trustees Committee was "obviously hostile" toward Bergel and those who testified in his behalf. He noted that the committee was "not disposed to inquire seriously into [the] actions of the [NJC] German Department."[108]

In questioning witnesses, the trustees appeared indifferent toward the evidence that the German Department faculty acted as advocates for the Third Reich in the classroom. Naomi Parness, Class of 1934, testified that when she challenged Alice Schlimbach's claim in class that the Nazis were not antisemitic by asking her why the Hitler regime had prohibited Jews from practicing law, exiled Jewish scholars such as Albert Einstein, and banned Felix Mendelssohn's music, Schlimbach refused to answer. Special Trustees Committee chair Ashmead then asked Parness whether Schlimbach thought Parness's question was "perhaps, a little outside of the course?" Parness shot back: "Well, the whole discussion was outside of the course."[109] Marjorie Fricke, Class of 1935, a German House resident, told the committee that she did not read newspaper articles about Nazi Germany because Professor Emil Jordan, with whom she studied, "presented the situation [there] fairly" and told his students what they needed to know about it. A smiling Ashmead then asked her whether she believed "the newspaper stories about Germany were untrue and that is why you stopped reading the headlines?" Clearly, he was suggesting that American press accounts about Nazi persecution and violence were inaccurate. Bergel's attorney immediately objected to the manner in which Ashmead was questioning the witness.[110]

Other committee members behaved similarly. When Professor Evalyn Clark testified that Professor Hauptmann had defended Nazi antisemitism in Germany, a trustee dismissed this as irrelevant, exclaiming, "[Y]ou do not mean to say that you have ever found any antipathy towards the Jewish race on this campus?"[111]

In its report upholding Bergel's termination, the Special Trustees Committee found that "none of the classrooms" of the NJC German Department "were ever used for the purpose of spreading pro-Nazi propaganda." Nor had the German Club put forward such propaganda in any of its activities. The committee dismissed the significance of the German House's possessing the *Sturmabteilung* songbook containing the Horst Wessel Lied, which it called "a present-day popular patriotic song of Germany." It claimed that Margarethe Varga, who had brought the songbook to the German House, had never attempted to convert any of its residents to Nazism. The committee praised the students who resided in the German House as "a very intelligent group of young women."[112]

The committee was not bothered that without Bergel the German Department faculty was entirely composed of Nazi enthusiasts. It had "not the slightest doubt that each and every member" of the department was not only professionally qualified, but was a person "of unquestionable character." The committee presented Professor Hauptmann's political views as reasonable and stated that he was "not in the slightest degree anti-Semitic" despite his strong support for Nazism. This suggested that it considered Nazism a legitimate political movement, with some justification for its positions and goals. The committee implied that Hauptmann's opposition to democracy was understandable because the multiplicity of political parties in the Weimar Republic had resulted in instability. It took seriously Hauptmann's argument that he was hostile only to Polish Jews who had migrated into Germany after the World War, and therefore could not be antisemitic. The committee did not criticize his claim that this population was an alien element that did not belong in Germany and a major cause of Germany's economic distress. The trustees declared, moreover, that, having been trained as a Protestant minister, Hauptmann "strongly support[ed] the principle of religious freedom."[113]

The committee blamed not only Lienhard Bergel but Sylvia Bergel as well for causing "a lack of harmony" in the German Department. It took Lienhard to task for failing to participate in the activities of the German House, and for his irregular attendance at the German table in the dining hall, although as a principled opponent of Hitler and antisemitism, he was undoubtedly uncomfortable socializing with faculty and student supporters of Nazism. He did often eat at the French table. As a newly hired instructor, Bergel not only had a very heavy teaching load but needed to devote an enormous amount of time to preparing his courses and engaging in research that would lead to publication. The committee noted that it was "a recognized policy in college administration that in engaging a man consideration is to be given also to the personality of his wife." Like her husband, Sylvia Bergel was an outspoken anti-Nazi, and the committee agreed with Hauptmann that she did not mix well with the other members of the German Department.[114]

Ignoring student testimony to the contrary, the committee declared that "there was no improper limitation of discussion in the classrooms." Professors who had refused to allow students to respond when they praised the Hitler regime in class were only exercising "the proper discretion by the teacher to keep the discussion from becoming so controversial and extraneous as to interfere unreasonably with the regular class work."[115]

Particularly revealing was the committee's assessment of Professor Hauptmann's calling together the German Department faculty members in March 1933, shortly after Hitler had assumed power, and telling them not to comment on conditions in Germany because "the real facts" were not known. The committee, apparently sharing Hauptmann's mistrust of American and British press reports about Nazi Germany, called this "sane advice."[116]

The committee report concluded with a stinging rebuke to those NJC students and faculty members who had criticized the German Department's allegiance to Nazism. The only persons at NJC deserving of criticism, it claimed, were those who had "exhibited a measure of intolerance toward members of the German Department, some of whom have ventured to express a favorable point of view toward the aims and endeavors of the government of the land of their birth."[117]

Rutgers president Robert Clothier and other trustees shared the committee's lack of understanding of Nazism. Trustee August Heckscher of New York City, who had visited Nazi Germany for a month during 1934, wrote to Clothier in September 1935 strongly endorsing the committee's report on the Bergel case. Heckscher declared that his observations in Germany had led him to conclude that there was "much fault on both sides," that is, the Jews and the Nazis were about equally to blame for whatever problems beset Germany. He stated that the Hitler government had been "most harsh and inconsiderate" but had nonetheless solved "a problem that had to be solved." Comparing American Jews to the German Nazis, Heckscher stated that "the Jewish race" had been "almost equally unwise in its aggressive and militant methods," apparently in protesting Nazi persecution in the Third Reich. All that was needed was for "the best of the Jewish race" and the "more tolerant" Nazis, "like Dr. Schacht," to sit down and discuss their differences.[118]

President Clothier replied that he was grateful for Heckscher's letter and called his comments about both Nazism and the Bergel case "highly appropriate." Clothier praised the Special Trustees Committee for conducting its investigation "with painstaking impartiality." He expressed serious concern about the "present spirit of controversy" about Nazism that was "abroad in the land."[119]

Fearing that press coverage of accusations about Nazism on the NJC German faculty might result in the New Jersey legislature reducing appropriations to Rutgers, its administration had Ms. Hauptmann step down from her position as assistant in 1937 and hired Werner Hollmann at the rank of instructor. Dean Corwin hired Hollmann after she received assurances from one of his references, President Ada Comstock of Radcliffe College, that he was not "a strong devotee of one type of government as opposed to another." Comstock explained that Hollmann, son of a Lutheran minister, was not "an adherent" of the Hitler regime but "has found it possible to live under it." She described him as "an exceptionally fine young man,"[120] betraying her own unconcern about Hollmann's apparent indifference toward Nazi depredations and the strangulation of Germany's remaining Jews.

Friedrich Hauptmann himself remained an intransigent Nazi through World War II. In late 1940, with Nazi Germany having conquered most of Europe, President Clothier had Dean Corwin instruct Hauptmann not to speak about "controversial matters" in class. In what had become a very threatening geopolitical climate for the United States, Clothier feared that pro-Nazi statements by German Department faculty members could only severely embarrass Rutgers University. Hauptmann wrote to President Clothier on November 12, 1940, that he understood from his conversation with Dean Corwin that Rutgers "would welcome any renunciation on my part of espousing a cause which seems to me worthy of support" – that is, Nazism. Because he was unwilling to do so, he concluded that the administration wanted him to resign. Hauptmann reiterated that he would not "deny or denounce" Nazi Germany.[121]

Hauptmann's decision to resign was also motivated by his severe financial indebtedness. Even though university trustees and faculty members had already lent him money, he told Corwin that unless the trustees granted him a year's leave with full salary, to be paid into a designated bank account, he would have to declare bankruptcy.[122]

On November 20, 1940, Dean Corwin conveyed to President Clothier her fear that the administration's difficulties with Hauptmann left it in "a very exposed position": "If our present action indicates that the [American] Civil Liberties Union was right in 1935, they will not hesitate to bring it out in the headlines."[123] In 1990, Bergel's widow referred to this correspondence between Corwin and Clothier as the case's "smoking gun."[124]

Hauptmann returned to Germany shortly afterward, his passage paid for at least in part by the Nazi government. There he joined the Nazi party and became the national leader of the Deutsche Akademie (German Academy) for Slovakia. Established to spread German language and culture outside Germany, it disseminated Nazi propaganda during the war. According to the Simon Wiesenthal Center, the Deutsche Akademie "served as a front for intelligence and espionage programs of the

Gestapo." American soldiers arrested Hauptmann shortly after the war's end, and he was briefly imprisoned. He died in obscurity in Austria in 1978.[125]

Although the disclosure of Hauptmann's service to the Hitler regime during World War II revived public interest in the Bergel case, the Rutgers administration refused to reconsider it. President Clothier stated in June 1946 that because the Special Trustees Committee had already "carefully and conscientiously" heard all the evidence on the case in 1935 and dismissed the charges, the university considered it closed.[126] Asked by a reporter in June 1946 to comment on Hauptmann's arrest, former acting NJC dean Albert Meder, who had served as a character witness for the German Department chair when he became a naturalized U.S. citizen in March 1939, replied, "He fooled us," as though his Nazi commitment had not been clear to the administration before.[127]

In the intensely anti-Nazi climate that prevailed during the immediate postwar period, the Rutgers administration reaffirmed its support for NJC German Department chair Emil Jordan, who was on record as having endorsed the Hitler regime on campus. Dean Corwin went so far as to claim that Jordan "had not held Nazi sympathies so far as she knew." Jordan remained chair until his retirement in 1966.[128]

In 1946, the Rutgers German Department did hire the anti-Nazi Claude Hill. Hill, who had arrived in the United States as a refugee from Germany in 1938, remained in the department until about 1980. During World War II, he had analyzed German radio broadcasts for the Voice of America. Hill believed that Rutgers had appointed him "in part to refute the image of the German departments that had taken shape in the 1930s." Hill told historian Richard McCormick in 1985 that the Rutgers administration should not have terminated Lienhard Bergel. He believed it should have acknowledged that it had wronged Bergel and "made some gesture" to him after the press reported that Hauptmann had worked for the Nazis in Germany during World War II. Hill considered Emil Jordan, Alice Schlimbach, and Albert Holzmann pro-Nazi.[129]

The Jewish community lionized Bergel as a man who had risked his career to take a principled stand against Nazism. Even while the hearings were in progress, those attending the Jewish-sponsored "commencement in absentia" in Newark – created for students in Germany who were barred from graduating from school by the Hitler regime's antisemitic legislation – extolled Bergel for his contribution to the larger struggle against Nazism. A capacity audience at the Ezekiel Home adopted a resolution proposed by a committee of Jewish business and professional people that lauded Bergel as a "valiant non-Jewish opponent of Nazism" and demanded his reinstatement.[130] In February 1936, the Women's Division of the American Jewish Congress in New York sponsored Bergel's lecture on "Nazi Activities in American Colleges," a stinging denunciation of the Rutgers administration's tolerance for pro-Hitler propagandizing, which many Jewish newspapers and periodicals reprinted.[131] In April the *Jewish Criterion* of Pittsburgh stated flatly that Rutgers had dismissed Bergel "because of his pronounced anti-Nazi views." It asserted that during the Special Trustees Committee hearings "the infiltration of Nazi propaganda in the University was clearly exposed." Rabbi Stephen S. Wise, a founder of the American Jewish Congress and one of the nation's most prominent Jewish leaders, wrote to President Clothier in 1940 urging him to invite Lienhard Bergel to return to Rutgers. Wise told Clothier that he felt Professor Hauptmann had been "bitterly unjust" to Bergel.[132]

After several years outside of academia, Bergel was able to secure an instructorship in 1938 at the newly founded Queens College in New York City. He remained on its faculty until his retirement in 1974. Bergel earned a Ph.D. from New York University in 1945 and published numerous articles in the course of his career. He also received three Fulbright fellowships and participated in the Columbia University seminar on the Renaissance. Bergel was promoted to full professor in 1958 and received an appointment to the Graduate Center of the City University of New York. Thomas Mann and Benedetto Croce praised his work.[133]

The Bergel-Hauptmann case illuminates the extent of support for Nazism by German Department faculty and students in American universities during the 1930s, and the widespread unconcern about it among university trustees, who were often highly influential business leaders. Members of NJC's German faculty, including its chair, did not hesitate to make their enthusiasm for Hitler's Germany known in public forums, and there is considerable evidence that they spoke favorably about it to their students on many occasions in class. The German Department placed impressionable students in an environment in which they were very susceptible to being influenced by pro-Hitler propaganda. It required its majors to reside for at least a year in the German House, under the supervision of an ardent Nazi faculty member. Nationally prominent Jewish leader Samuel Untermyer asked New Jersey's governor for a legislative investigation of the NJC German Department, which he called "a hotbed of Nazi sedition." The 1935 convention of the New Jersey American Legion unanimously adopted a resolution calling on the legislature to investigate charges that "alien instructors" at NJC were spreading Nazi propaganda.[134]

The issues involved in Bergel's termination are complicated, but what is most alarming about the case is the administration's indifference to having an all-Nazi German Department at NJC, and the Rutgers trustees' obvious hostility to committed opponents of Nazism. Bergel, to be sure, was an instructor on a temporary position with as yet no publications, in a period when the university was experiencing financial difficulty. He had a year's less seniority than the pro-Nazi instructor Emil Jordan, who was retained and promoted to assistant professor. But Bergel was the only member of the department trained in teaching German literature. If the administration needed to eliminate a position from the German Department, a more logical choice might have been Marie Hauptmann, who had far less intellectual capability, training, and teaching ability than Bergel, although she had carried a full fifteen-hour course load since 1930–31. Her salary was $540 less than Bergel's. Two years after terminating Bergel, NJC replaced Ms. Hauptmann, an assistant, with a new instructor, Werner Hollmann, suggesting that by then, at least, it could function on the same budget as when Bergel was employed. The 40 percent decline in German enrollments from 1933–34, the first academic year during which Hitler was in power, to 1936–37 could well be explained by an unwillingness of Jewish and other anti-Nazi students to take courses in a Nazified department. Jews had previously made up a disproportionate number of those enrolled in German courses. French enrollments declined only 10 percent during the same period, and Spanish enrollments increased 23 percent.[135]

During the hearings of the Rutgers Special Trustees Committee, the Philadelphia *Jewish Exponent* declared that investigations at other universities would disclose the "sorry truth" that many German departments resembled NJC's.[136] This was indeed the case, as many German department faculty members and the students they influenced served as campus apologists for Nazi Germany. By writing articles and letters in college newspapers justifying Hitler's policies, and through interviews in metropolitan dailies, they disparaged the Weimar Republic and extolled Hitler as Germany's savior. German departments were centrally involved in promoting student exchanges with Nazified universities and faculty and student tours of the "New Germany." Tightly supervised by Nazi functionaries while in Germany, participants usually returned prepared to propagandize for the Third Reich in the United States. The Hitler government even maintained a list in Berlin of former American graduate exchange students in Germany, assuming that many joined German department faculties in the United States, and regularly mailed them Nazi propaganda.[137] As the major facilitators of social interaction between Nazi diplomats and university administrators, faculty, and students, German departments assisted the Hitler government in its effort to present itself as a legitimate member of a community of nations, with justified grievances and reasonable objectives.

7

American Catholic Universities' Flirtation with Fascism

For the most part sympathetic to Benito Mussolini's Fascist regime, American Catholic universities also helped the new Hitler government project a more favorable image in this country. Catholic institutions of higher learning constituted one of the most important and visible bases of support for the Fascist uprising against the democratically elected government of Spain during that country's civil war. They also provided supporters of Mussolini's invasion of Ethiopia with an important platform to influence Catholics and other Americans. Sentiment for appeasement of Nazi Germany was pronounced on American Catholic campuses until U.S. entry into World War II.

When the Nazis came to power, the Vatican quickly sought to establish friendly ties with the Hitler regime. The Vatican secretary of state, Cardinal Pacelli, negotiated a Concordat with the Nazi government, signed and announced in July 1933 and ratified in September. This constituted Nazi Germany's "first great diplomatic triumph." Pope Pius XI considered the new German regime potentially the Church's most important ally in the struggle against Communism and secular liberalism, which he perceived as the greatest threats to Christianity. In the Concordat, the German Catholic Church and its bishops swore allegiance to the new Nazi state. The Church also agreed not to participate in politics and to disband the Center (Catholic) party. In exchange, the Church, its religious organizations, and its press were permitted to operate without government interference.[1]

Justifying the Concordat to American diplomat James G. McDonald in Rome about five weeks after its signing, Pius XI declared that the Church "did not pick and choose with whom it would negotiate; it dealt with those in power." The pope pointed out, moreover, that "many Catholics," such as former chancellor Franz von Papen, a member of Hitler's cabinet, had "worked earnestly for the Concordat."[2]

By investing its considerable prestige in such a "treaty of cooperation" with Nazi Germany, the Vatican helped enhance the stature of the Hitler regime at a critically important time. Hitler informed his cabinet upon the signing of the Concordat that it had "created an aura of trust" for Germany in Europe that would be of benefit "in the developing struggle against international Jewry."[3]

In August 1933, Vicar General Steinmann, speaking for the Catholic bishop of Berlin, unable to be present because of illness, thanked both Chancellor Adolf Hitler and Pope Pius XI for the Concordat at a mass rally of thousands of Catholic youths of the Berlin Bishopric, who pledged allegiance to Hitler. Vicar General Steinmann cried out from the podium: "Our Chancellor has been appointed by God." He promised that "Catholic youth will help the Fatherland to rise again to greatness and glory."[4]

During the 1930s, the Vatican continued to view the Jews as a people whom God had condemned to live in misery for the alleged crime of deicide, committed nearly two millennia before. The Catholic Church sympathized with Nazi claims that Jews exercised excessive influence in Germany's economic and cultural life, an accusation the Hitler government used to justify the mass expulsions of Jews from the professions, university faculties, newspaper positions, the theater, and the film industry. Neither the Vatican nor the German Catholic Church publicly challenged the removal of Jews from these fields, which was well underway when the Concordat was signed, or the Nazis' national boycott of Jewish businesses staged on April 1, 1933.

Pius XI (Achille Ratti), pope from 1921 until his death in 1939, held strongly antisemitic views. Immediately prior to becoming pope, Ratti had been the Vatican's special ambassador to Poland during the brutal postwar pogroms, in which thousands of Jews were murdered. Ratti had made every effort to ensure that the Vatican took no action to discourage the Poles from slaughtering Jews and burning their homes and synagogues. Some of the pogroms were inspired by blood libel accusations circulated by Poland's Catholic nationalist press – accusations that Jews kidnapped and murdered Christian children to extract their blood to mix with matzoh at Passover. Instead, Ratti warned the Vatican secretary of state of the Jews' disproportionate power in Poland and called the Jews "perhaps the strongest and the most evil" influence in the country. He portrayed the Jews of Poland "as an insidious foreign force eating away at the Polish nation," just as the Nazis later described the Jews of every country. During Pius XI's papacy, the influential Jesuit publication *Civiltà cattolica*, considered "the unofficial voice of the pope himself," embarked on a virulently antisemitic campaign.[5]

James G. McDonald reported that when he asked Pius XI in Rome in August 1933 about the Church's attitude toward the plight of Germany's Jews, "his reply, both the tone and the contents, convinced me that there could be no help expected from that source."[6] When the Concordat was ratified the next month, Pius XI notified the German chargé d'affaires of his concern for German Catholics who had converted from Judaism, or who were descended from persons who had done so, and were suffering discrimination because Nazi antisemitic legislation defined them as racially Jewish. He made no effort on behalf of Jews who had not converted and did not attempt to intervene when the Nuremberg laws of September 1935 stripped them of German citizenship. The Church's position, maintained consistently throughout the Nazi era, was to intervene only on behalf of persons of Jewish background who identified as Catholic. Even then, as Saul Friedländer noted, it generally "submitted to the Nazi measures against converted Jews."[7]

The Catholic Church provided a significant boost for a diplomatically isolated Nazi Germany during the winter of 1934–35, by backing a "Yes" vote in a plebiscite conducted in the Saar, an important coal-mining region, over whether it should again become part of Germany. The Allied powers at the Versailles Peace Conference had assigned the largely German-speaking Saar to France under a League of Nations mandate, with the stipulation that after fifteen years its population would vote whether to join France or Germany. Members of the dissolved Center party allied with Nazis and right-wing Nationalists in a "Deutsche Front" that campaigned to join the Saar to the Third Reich.[8] In Germany, the Catholic bishops of Paderborn, Fulda, and Hildesheim issued a joint statement in December 1934 that all churches in their districts would pray to God for "a plebiscite result favorable to the German nation."[9] When the referendum was held, the Saar's overwhelmingly Catholic population voted by more than 90 percent to become part of Nazi Germany. The Saar's dramatic vote of approval for Nazi Germany energized Hitler, who embarked on a significant expansion of Germany's armed forces.[10]

American Catholic Universities and Nazi Germany

In the United States, the Catholic Church hierarchy, and the top administrators of Catholic universities, kept a lower profile on the issue of Nazi Germany. Criticism of the Third Reich from the American hierarchy was directed mostly at Nazi infringements on Church autonomy, interpreted as violations of the Concordat, and at statements by some Nazi officials considered pagans. Even Catholic spokespersons critical of the Hitler regime almost invariably spoke favorably of Mussolini, especially after his own Concordat with the Vatican, and of Franco's insurgents.

A few prominent lay Catholics in the United States from the outset contributed significantly to heightening public awareness of the Nazis' antisemitic atrocities, but they were not associated with institutions of higher learning. In June 1933, Michael Williams, editor of the Catholic periodical the *Commonweal*, returning from a six-week visit to Germany, declared that the Nazi antisemitic campaign "surpasses any recorded instance of persecution in Jewish history." He reported that the Nazis intended "to absolutely eliminate the Jewish portion of the German nation."[11] Al Smith, former governor of New York, who in 1928, as the Democratic nominee, had been the first Catholic to run for president of the United States, in September 1933 denounced Nazism as a "descent into barbarism" at a dinner to honor Jewish attorney Samuel Untermyer, a leader of the movement to boycott German goods and services. Smith also contributed an essay to one of the first books published in the United States to condemn the Hitler regime, entitled *Nazism: An Assault on Civilization* (1934). Both Smith and Williams appeared as "witnesses" at a mock trial of the Nazi government, accused of "a crime against civilization," in New York City's Madison Square Garden in March 1934, attended by 20,000 people. Catholic labor leader Matthew Woll was a prominent spokesperson for the boycott of Nazi products from 1933 onward.[12]

Throughout the 1930s, however, lecturers and symposia on German affairs at American Catholic universities often sought to emphasize allegedly positive features of the Hitler regime, while downplaying the significance of antisemitism. Campus newspapers sometimes expressed disapproval of the Nazi government's "intolerance" of Jews. Just as common were articles such as the May 1933 *Notre Dame Scholastic* editorial that criticized an American opponent of Hitler for his "one-sided outlook." The *Scholastic* complained that Hitler's critics imputed a sinister motive when he asked for peace. Instead, Americans should give Hitler "the benefit of the doubt." After all, "mutual trust" was "the basis of international amity."[13] In a lecture to the Notre Dame University International Relations Club on "Hitler and Hitlerism" in March 1933, Father Julian P. Sigmar declared at the outset that he would not address the "question of whether the Jews in Germany are really persecuted." He concentrated instead on denouncing the Social Democratic governments of the Weimar Republic, which he claimed had abused Germany's World War veterans. He asserted that Germany's soaring inflation in the early 1920s had been caused by the Social Democrats' pandering to unreasonable demands from the trade unions. The implication was that Hitler had rescued Germany from dangerous instability.[14]

Many American Catholics in and outside of academia complained that the public appeared to be more concerned about Nazi oppression of Jews in Germany than with what they claimed was the more severe persecution of Catholics in Mexico and Spain, and Christians in the Soviet Union. The assistant general secretary of the National Catholic Welfare Conference (NCWC) stated that the resolution Senator Millard Tydings had introduced in the U.S. Senate putting the government on record as denouncing Nazi Germany's persecution of Jews was unsatisfactory because it failed "to have the persecution of Catholic citizens [in Mexico and Spain] condemned quite as heartily."[15] Another NCWC leader was similarly upset when Senator Henry Hatfield in the *Congressional Record* denounced Nazi antisemitism but said "nothing...of the persecution [of Catholics] in Mexico and Spain."[16] In October 1934, an editorial in the *Hoya*, student newspaper of Georgetown University, complained that "in the past year we have heard much of the persecution of Jews in Germany," while nations of the "so-called civilized world" had been extending recognition to the Soviet Union, a country whose objective "is to tear down present-day civilization" and that was "persecuting Christians."[17]

In January 1934, Rev. Dr. Joseph Thorning, S.J., professor of sociology at Georgetown and former foreign correspondent for the Jesuit magazine *America*, credited the Nazi government with significant achievements in a lecture on "Chancellor Hitler, the Man and His Movement," sponsored by St. Joseph's College in Philadelphia, that city's Jesuit institution of higher learning. The president of St. Joseph's College, the Very Reverend Thomas J. Higgins, S.J., personally introduced Thorning, who had recently met with Adolf Hitler in Berlin. Thorning praised the Nazi regime for defeating Communism in Germany and "crushing the materialistic spirit of social democracy." Nazism had brought about "a moral resurrection of the German people." Thorning identified as Nazism's "less favorable results" limitations on individual liberty, an excessively powerful central government, and a "revival of militaristic spirit." He was confident that the Catholic Church could work out any differences with the Nazi government "in a friendly, conciliatory spirit."[18]

Fordham, a Jesuit university and the world's largest Catholic institution of higher learning, with 8,000 students, held an open forum on Hitler's policies in March 1934, the same month the mock trial at Madison Square Garden convicted the Nazi regime for "a crime against civilization." The mood at the Fordham forum was strikingly different, however. The first speaker declared that Hitler had restored stability to Germany and saved it from Communism. He defended the Nazi persecution of Jews as necessary, claiming that Jews were "the mainstay of the Communist Party." After several other students had spoken, the forum reached a consensus: Hitler's policies were justified, with reservations, because the Allied powers had treated Germany unfairly after the war, and a "preponderance of Jews in professional life" allowed a minority disproportionate influence. The professor moderating the forum, in summarizing what had been said, expressed surprise at the students' "defense of Hitler's policies."[19]

About the same time, Heinz Nixdorf, a former German exchange student at Columbia who had chaired its International House's Student Council and was currently employed by the North German Lloyd shipping line, presented a campus lecture praising the Third Reich. Nixdorf denied that the Hitler regime had restricted freedom of speech and accused the American press of providing inaccurate accounts of the situation in Germany. He credited the Nazi government with introducing "many provisions" to benefit students.[20]

Robert Mullen, a Notre Dame junior enrolled at the University of Heidelberg during the 1936–37 academic year, although avoiding political comment, described living conditions in the Third Reich very favorably in a series of articles he wrote for the *Notre Dame Scholastic*. Mullen reported that when he landed in the port of Bremen in September 1936, he "strolled through many beautiful parks," where to his surprise "roses [were] still in bloom." He was struck by "the absolute cleanliness of the town." The people's homes "were really beautiful," each with flower boxes to "decorat[e] the windows." Mullen remarked that "[t]he color, cheerfulness, and cleanliness of the . . . town makes it very inviting and pleasant." Such was his introduction to the Third Reich. Mullen noted that the programs on German radio, a central instrument of Nazi propaganda, were "excellent." He claimed that the university student in Germany was "accorded all the academic freedom possible."[21]

The student newspaper at Boston College, another prominent Jesuit institution, praised Hitler's foreign policy and leadership, as well as his personal qualities, in a March 1935 editorial. It condemned the Allied powers for imposing on Germany "overwhelming indemnities" and the "thoroughly unjust stigma of 'war guilt.'" The editorial also criticized their granting Poland "an agrarian and not a commercial state," a corridor to the sea, which cut East Prussia off from the rest of Germany. Chancellor Stresemann, "who played the puppet for the allies," had done nothing "to alleviate Germany's sad condition." Fortunately, Adolf Hitler had appeared on the scene, "a man of courage" who refused to submit to shame and insisted that Germany be treated fairly. Because it was "surrounded by nations . . . armed up to the teeth," Germany had a right to significantly enlarge its armed forces.[22]

In May 1935, Mgr. James H. Ryan, rector of the Catholic University of America in Washington, D.C., received Dr. Hans Luther, Nazi Germany's ambassador to the United States, at the university's annual alumni banquet and sports award dinner. When Luther was introduced to the audience, it welcomed him with a rousing college cheer, "CU, CU, Luther." The Washington *Post* noted that Mgr. Ryan "was kept very busy" the next day "explaining the significance" of these Catholic University cheers for the Nazi ambassador. Luther invited the college athletes present to attend the next year's Olympic Games in Berlin, hosted by the Nazi government. Football coaches Dick Harlow of Harvard and Jim Crowley of Fordham shared the podium with the Nazi ambassador.[23]

During the 1930s, Anton Lang Jr., professor of German at Georgetown University, served as a leading publicist in the United States for the fiercely antisemitic Oberammergau Passion Play, performed throughout the summers of 1930 and 1934. The play was scheduled to be performed again in the summer of 1940. Anton Lang Jr.'s father had played the role of Jesus from 1900 until 1922 and interpreted the prologue in 1930 and 1934.[24] The senior Lang in 1923 had led a troupe of passion play actors in a six-month tour of the United States to inform Americans about the play and to raise money for Oberammergau.[25] His son, the Georgetown professor, born and raised in Oberammergau, continued this work, presenting lectures and slide shows on "beautiful Oberammergau and the play for which it is famous." Anton Lang Jr.'s wife played Mary Magdalen in the passion play.[26]

The Nazi government also promoted the passion play on American Catholic university campuses, where the religious themes and focus on Jewish deicide exerted strong appeal. In January 1938, the student newspaper at Fordham reported that the campus German Club had been delighted with a film it had just screened depicting the Oberammergau Passion Play, supplied by the government-controlled German railroads.[27]

Robert I. Gannon, S.J., president of Fordham University, later that year built his speech on Jesus, celebrating the reopening of New York City's Church of the Nativity, around the image of venomous, deicidal Jews central to the Oberammergau Passion Play. President Gannon described Jesus returning to the synagogue in which he had worshiped as a youth for the first time since "set[ting] out to find St. John the Baptist." Gannon had Jesus informing the synagogue that he was the messiah of whom Isaiah had spoken. This announcement precipitated an angry response from the Jews, who rushed from their seats and "seized Him [Jesus] roughly." The Jews then took Jesus out of the synagogue to a nearby cliff, planning to murder him by pushing him over the precipice, two years before his crucifixion. But it was too soon for Jesus to die, and to the Jews' "anger, amazement, and confusion," they "suddenly realized that He had disappeared."[28]

Criticism of the Hitler regime in student newspapers at American Catholic universities tended to focus on the oppression of Catholics rather than Jews. The *Notre Dame Scholastic* did publish a passionate denunciation of sending delegates to the University of Heidelberg's 550th anniversary celebration. Its editorial declared that Hitler should limit invitations to those who supported "tyranny, race oppression [a euphemism for antisemitism], and academic slavery" and praised the British universities for their refusal to send delegates. It dismissed the University of Heidelberg as nothing but "a Nazi propaganda school." Professors in Germany who did not "grovel servilly [*sic*] before Hitler" were discharged and sometimes exiled. The editorial did not address the support of the German Catholic Church, and the Lutheran and Evangelical Churches, for many Nazi policies, and it defined Nazism as an "ultra-modern philosophy," suggesting that it was completely disconnected from Christian antisemitism. Although still underestimating the severity of Jewish suffering in Germany, the editorial, unlike much Catholic criticism of Nazism, suggested that Nazi persecution of Jews was worse than that of Catholics. Jews were "baited and hounded"; Catholics and Protestants were "restricted in the exercise of religious liberty."[29]

More typical of Catholic anti-Nazi criticism was that expressed by W. Ralph Schreiner, a German youth beginning his freshman year at Fordham in the fall of 1937, just arrived in the United States. Schreiner described "everywhere" in Germany the "evidence of a nation bound up in a strait-jacket." Parks, theaters, and cafés posted signs forbidding Jews to enter. The Nazis had forced into exile "Jewish scholars...of immense stature," such as Albert Einstein. But Schreiner declared that in Germany "opposition [to] Catholics has been even more far-reaching." He also described the German people as not enthusiastic about Hitler and opposed to war.[30]

Catholic university administrators generally avoided taking any public stand against Nazism. Mgr. James H. Ryan, rector of Catholic University, refused to participate in planning even a symbolic protest against American academic involvement in the University of Heidelberg's 550th anniversary celebration. Bernard A. Grossman, chairman of the Committee on Education of the Federal Bar Association, wrote to Mgr. Ryan in March 1936 asking him to help formulate a plan to express educators' opposition to the upcoming Nazi-sponsored festivities, possibly by organizing a symbolic funeral for the University of Heidelberg to mourn the "death of learning and academic freedom" there. The proposed funeral would close with a period "of general, silent prayer for the restoration" of the pre-Hitler university. On Grossman's letter, P. J. McCormick, Catholic University's vice-rector, wrote, "No reply."[31]

Although concerned about Nazi infringements on the Concordat, the Vatican during the late 1930s publicly promoted friendly relations with the Hitler regime. The *New York Times* reported in February 1937 that Pope Pius XI was very pleased when Hitler sent him a "solicitous message" to congratulate him on the fifteenth anniversary of his coronation. The pope directed the Vatican secretary of state, Cardinal Pacelli, to send Hitler a "cordial reply."[32]

American Catholic Universities and Italian Fascism

American Catholic universities maintained friendly relations with Benito Mussolini's Fascist government, welcoming its diplomats to their campuses and honoring them, and providing an important platform for speakers sympathetic to the regime and its invasion and conquest of Ethiopia in 1935–36. Leading members of the American Catholic Church hierarchy, such as William Cardinal O'Connell of Boston and Patrick Cardinal Hayes of New York, and major Catholic publications, like the

Jesuit organ *America*, spoke approvingly of Fascism's achievements in Italy.[33]

Catholic universities constituted important stops for the 350-member Italian Fascist delegation that came to the United States in September and October 1934 on a "goodwill" tour. Shortly after its arrival, the entire delegation visited Georgetown University in Washington, D.C. The Fascist students then proceeded to the Italian embassy, where Mussolini's ambassador to the United States, Augusto Rosso, welcomed them and spoke about Italo-American friendship. When Ambassador Rosso completed his address, the Italian students cheered Il Duce and the Fascist state. Then the composer of the Fascist hymn "Giovinezza," Giuseppe Blanc, led the black-shirted Italian students in singing it. Rev. Edmund Walsh, S.J., regent of the Georgetown University School of Foreign Service, represented the university at the reception. The Fascist students were also received while in Washington by administrators at Catholic University, who gave them a tour of the campus.[34]

Several days later, a reception committee from the University of Notre Dame Italian Club, headed by two professors and joined by the school band, greeted the Fascist students when they arrived on campus from Chicago, accompanied by the Italian consul-general of that city. Notre Dame's president, Rev. John F. O'Hara, C.S.C., officially welcomed the delegation and spoke about how Notre Dame had greatly benefitted from Italian influence. Giuseppe Blanc presented President O'Hara with a certificate of invitation, signed by Fascist leaders, to visit the Italian universities from which the students were drawn. He also donated a book detailing the history of Italian universities. As the Italians marched to the dining halls, they answered the Notre Dame students' college cheers with the Fascist yell.[35]

When they returned to the East Coast, the Italian students, wearing coats with the *Fascisti* emblem, received a warm welcome at Boston College from its rector, the Reverend Francis J. Mulligan, S.J. Boston College's campus newspaper denounced anti-fascist critics of the visiting Italian Fascist students, declaring, "All biased reports which usually precede these good will tours were stifled by the pleasing and quiet personalities of these men."[36]

Until World War II, a steady stream of speakers at America's Catholic universities praised Mussolini's regime, while administrators fostered cordial ties with its leaders and emissaries. By contrast, Italian anti-fascist exiles received almost no hearing. At Boston College in 1938, J. F. X. Murphy, S.J., described Il Duce as a "surgeon" who had removed the "vicious growths" of "Socialism, Atheism, and Anti-Clericalism" from Italian life. He forcefully denounced the press's "misrepresentation" of "Mussolini and what he has done." The Fascist dictator had reversed his nation's decline, caused by Italy's having "imitat[ed] Protestant England rather than Catholic Spain and France." This "Supreme blunder" had unleashed "a wave of anti-clericalism" that had in turn precipitated the "ruthless march of Freemasons, Socialists, and Communists." Mussolini had defeated these threats to Christianity in Italy and restored her "to the glory of her past."[37]

Leonid I. Strakhovsky, professor of modern European history at Georgetown's School of Foreign Service, returning from a trip to Italy in 1935, described in the Washington *Post* how Mussolini had "clean[ed] the country both physically and morally." He declared that Rome, Florence, Milan, and Naples had become "model communities" without "the dirt [and]...unsanitary conditions" characteristic of pre-Fascist Italy. "Vigor [and] initiative" had replaced "indolence [and] lack of discipline," spurring massive housing and highway construction. Professor Strakhovsky boasted that under Mussolini, the trains now "arrive on schedule." He attributed dramatic improvements in Italy's economic and cultural life to "the untiring building and molding energy of Fascism."[38]

At Notre Dame in 1937, Hazel Chase West, billed as a "noted writer and lecturer" and expert on Italy, similarly celebrated what she alleged were Fascism's spectacular achievements. Reporting on her recent trip to Italy, West showed slides of "smiling, healthy children" and "modern buildings and marvelous roads," all of which, she proclaimed, was "part of the magnificent and modern Italy of Mussolini."[39]

Presidents at American Catholic universities often sought advice and assistance from prominent Fascist officials, who, in turn, sometimes bestowed honors on their professors. In 1937, Mgr. Joseph Corrigan, rector of Catholic University, personally met with Mussolini in Rome to discuss Corrigan's proposal to establish a school of social security at his institution. Corrigan was eager to learn from Mussolini about Italy's current social legislation. He also met with Agostino Gemelli, rector of the Fascist-controlled Catholic University of Milan to discuss its approach to social service education.[40]

When Mussolini learned from his consul-general in New York that Fordham University had no Italian department, the dictator promptly expressed his concern to the Vatican. The Vatican responded by contacting the Father General of the Jesuits in the United States, who wrote to President Gannon of Fordham "expressing his astonishment." As a result,

Fordham established an Italian department in January 1937. It "opened with a flourish," with Fordham conferring an honorary degree on Fascist Italy's ambassador to the United States, Fulvio Suvich.[41]

Nearly a year later, Ambassador Suvich, in a ceremony at the Italian embassy, awarded "the cross" to Domingo Caino de Cancio, professor of Romance languages at Georgetown and founder of the university's Italian Club, and made him Chevalier of the Crown of Italy. Professor Caino was the son of Fascist Italy's consul-general in Puerto Rico. The Georgetown student newspaper reported that the university's "faculty and student body wish to congratulate Professor Caino for the unusual honor bestowed upon him."[42]

When Fascist Italy invaded Ethiopia in 1935, it received strong backing on American Catholic university campuses, as it did from the Church hierarchy in Italy. More than 100 Italian bishops and archbishops issued declarations of support for the invasion and mobilized the public behind it. Diocesan conferences and Catholic student groups regularly made statements endorsing the war effort. Fifteen Italian cardinals participated in Fascist demonstrations during the Italo-Ethiopian war. The Jesuit *Civiltà cattolica* portrayed the invasion as a war of liberation from Coptic rule. Italian victory would bring Jesuit missionaries to Ethiopia, who would convert its population to Catholicism.[43] Gaetano Salvemini, the most prominent anti-fascist Italian exile in the United States, declared that many of America's Italian-speaking priests were "carriers of Fascist propaganda" who encouraged Italian-Americans to back the invasion.[44]

Speakers on American Catholic university campuses portrayed the invasion as a war to civilize a nation of "savage tribes," justified because overpopulated Italy deserved additional natural resources and an outlet for emigration. War correspondent W. W. Chaplin, in an address at Georgetown, praised Mussolini for his determination to achieve these objectives. Mussolini had granted Chaplin an interview in Rome, and the correspondent described Il Duce to his Georgetown audience as "a gentle, witty, clever, and thoroughly human man." He credited him with "put[ting] Italy on its feet."[45] At Notre Dame, visiting history professor Christopher Hollis, in his regular bi-weekly campus lecture, also credited Italy with a civilizing mission in Ethiopia, where murder had been "the normal daily routine of . . . life." He declared that wherever there existed a population consisting of both white and "colored" people, the latter must necessarily be subordinated.[46]

When the Fascist army had completed its conquest of Ethiopia in 1936, Pope Pius XI bestowed his apostolic benediction on Italy's monarch

Victor Emmanuel as "King of Italy and Emperor of Ethiopia."[47] The Church hierarchy's support for the invasion undoubtedly strongly influenced many American Catholic students, who were exposed on campus only to propagandists for Italy. At Fordham in March 1938, the audience at a student debate on whether Britain should recognize Italy's conquest of Ethiopia awarded victory to the team arguing the affirmative.[48]

Rallying Behind Franco's *Cruzada*: American Catholic Universities and the Spanish Civil War, 1936–1939

American Catholic university administrators joined the Church hierarchy in rallying to the support of General Francisco Franco's insurrection to overthrow Spain's republican government. Catholic leaders in the United States and Europe considered Franco's war against the democratically elected Loyalists a religious crusade against Communism. Spain was the land Catholics had devoted seven centuries to wresting back from the Moors, and they attached enormous emotional significance to what they considered a new *reconquista*. In December 1936, Dr. Edmund A. Walsh, S.J., vice-president of Georgetown University, implied that the Spanish Loyalists were an instrument of a Communist movement that posed "the greatest peril to Christian civilization . . . since the Mohammedan invasion of Europe."[49]

The most prominent leaders of the Catholic Church in the United States publicly endorsed Franco's revolt. Patrick Cardinal Hayes of New York City in March 1938 declared that the Spanish republican government was "controlled by Communists and other radicals" and that he was praying for a Franco victory.[50] That same month William Cardinal O'Connell of Boston described the republican government as "nothing but piracy and communism gone rank." Cardinal O'Connell served as honorary chairman of the Spanish Nationalist Relief Committee, which raised money for Franco's cause.[51] The Boston archdiocesan newspaper, the *Pilot*, considered Cardinal O'Connell's mouthpiece, portrayed Franco as a model Catholic ruler who attended Mass every day.[52] The American Catholic hierarchy so emotionally identified with Franco's cause that it intervened in the casting of the movie biography of Knute Rockne because the studio's original choice to play the legendary Notre Dame football coach, Irish-American actor James Cagney, had publicly endorsed the Loyalist cause. Church officials succeeded in denying Cagney the role.[53]

Catholics differed sharply with the overwhelmingly pro-Loyalist American Jewish community over the Spanish Civil War. Many Catholics claimed that "Jewish domination" of the American press explained what they perceived as its pro-Loyalist bias.[54] Jews were drawn to the Loyalists because they were staging the first armed resistance against Fascism. Jews comprised about 30 percent of the volunteers for the International Brigades that came to Spain to defend the republican government, the highest proportion of any ethnic group or nationality.[55]

The Spanish Church's centuries-long tradition of virulent antisemitism and Inquisitorial persecution, and the Falangist statements and acts of aggression against Jews in Spain and North Africa, alarmed many American Jews. The Spanish Church had been instrumental in destroying Europe's largest Jewish community. It encouraged waves of pogroms in 1391 that drastically reduced the Jewish population through murder and forced conversion, and in 1492 it had helped persuade the Crown to permanently expel those who remained. Insurgent general Queipo de Llano declared over the radio in October 1936 that "our war is not a Spanish civil war, it is a war of western civilization against the Jews of the entire world."[56] The major Jewish news service, the Jewish Telegraphic Agency (JTA), described Franco's forces as overtly antisemitic. It reported in August 1936 that the rebels had broadcast over the radio from Seville, a city they held, that "[i]nternational Jewry is definitely siding with the [republican] government." The JTA also stated in the same report that Franco's troops had "arrested and imprisoned in concentration camps the entire Jewish population of Meillua, Spanish Morocco."[57]

Presidents of leading American Catholic universities echoed the views of the prelates and of major diocesan newspapers such as the Brooklyn *Tablet* and Boston's *Pilot*, using the words "Loyalist" and "Communist" interchangeably. They denounced the republican forces as uncivilized and repeatedly accused them of the mass murder of nuns and priests and the burning of churches. The *Pilot* claimed that the "communists" in Barcelona had dug slain nuns out of their graves and placed cigarettes in the corpses' mouths.[58] By contrast, Catholic presidents and prelates equated Franco with George Washington and his troops with the patriots of the American Revolution. President Robert I. Gannon of Fordham in an October 1936 speech, at which Cardinal Hayes presided, declared that the Loyalists adhered not to "the Law, but to their own laws," which he identified as "laws of class greed, laws of class hatred ... unjust, communistic laws." He defined Franco's rebels, in this context, as "glorious outlaws" who fought for God's Law, and he compared them to Washington and Catholic martyrs such as St. Thomas More and those "of the Tower and of Tyburn."[59]

President Joseph M. Corrigan of Catholic University published a strongly pro-Franco letter in the New York *Sun* in October 1937, asserting that the Loyalists had gained control of the Spanish government through "manipulation of elections." The rebels were therefore seeking to overthrow an illegitimate government.[60] President Corrigan approved the proposal of several of his students that he sing a High Mass in the University Shrine for "seminary students and young religious" allegedly "martyred" by Loyalist forces in Spain.[61]

Catholic university presidents, administrators, and professors were prominent among the 175 American Catholic clergymen and laymen who in October 1937 released a statement that defended Catholic support of Franco's rebellion and declared that the Loyalists, if victorious, would establish a Soviet dictatorship in Spain. Their statement supported an open letter the Spanish bishops had issued strongly backing the insurgents. The American Catholics challenged Protestants to explain any support for a republican government "which has carried on a ruthless persecution of the Christian religion since February 1936." Many luminaries in American Catholic higher education joined former New York governor Al Smith, *Commonweal* editor Michael Williams, and Knights of Columbus head Martin H. Carmody in signing the statement. They included the presidents of Catholic University and Fordham, Joseph Corrigan and Robert I. Gannon, respectively; the Reverend Thomas J. Higgins, S.J., president of St. Joseph's College of Philadelphia; the Reverend Raphael McCarthy, S.J., president of Marquette University; the Reverend Harold Gaudin, president of Loyola University of New Orleans; the Reverend Brother Albert, president of St. Mary's College in California; Ignatius M. Wilkinson, dean of Fordham Law School; the Reverend Dr. Peter Guilday, editor of the *Catholic Historical Review*; and Professor Carlton J. H. Hayes of Columbia University.[62]

The Fascist cause in Spain also received very widespread backing from students at Catholic universities, reflected in campus newspaper editorials and presentations at student symposia. Support for the Loyalists was almost never voiced on Catholic campuses, although the republican government had significant support at some elite, non-Catholic institutions of higher learning, and at some state universities. The Fordham *Ram* in October 1937 bitterly denounced a group of what it described as "Protestant clergymen, educators, and laymen" that had published a statement in the *New York Times* challenging the Spanish bishops' recent open letter supporting Franco's insurrection. The *Ram* reported that the Protestants' statement had been drafted by Dr. Guy Emery Shipler, editor of the Protestant Episcopal magazine the *Churchman,* whom the *Ram* identified as "a member of the National Religion and Labor Foundation" allegedly established "to spread communism and socialism in the churches." The *Ram* also identified three Columbia professors who had signed the statement, John Dewey, George Counts, and Franz Boas (a Jew, not a Protestant) as men who "are well known for their atheism and radicalism." Others among the signers had been "taken in hook, line, and sinker" by the Loyalist government's "Red propaganda," which the American press "shamefully... accepted as 'news.'" The Protestant statement repeated "all the old lies," an example of which, according to the *Ram,* was the report that Fascist airplanes had bombed Guernica. It included nothing about "the terrible massacres and horrible torturing of priests and nuns, the burning of churches, and the desecration of graves" by the "Reds and Anarchists."[63]

The Fordham Student Council in January 1937, meeting in extraordinary session, passed a series of resolutions that assailed the Loyalists "as Communist hirelings and denounc[ed] their atheistic activities." The Student Council condemned American newspaper coverage of the Spanish Civil War as strongly biased in favor of the Loyalists. It announced plans to hold a dance to raise funds to buy medical supplies for Franco's troops.[64]

The frequent symposia and lectures on the Spanish Civil War held at Catholic universities provided the Fascist cause with one of its most important platforms in the United States. Invariably, only Franco's side was presented; the conflict was not debated. President Gannon of Fordham presided at a mass meeting on the Spanish war at New York City's Carnegie Hall, sponsored by the Fordham University Alumnae Association and featuring as speakers Fordham professors Hillaire Belloc and the Reverend Jaime Castiello, both strong supporters of Franco. Reflecting the Church's view of the war as a religious conflict, the symposium was titled "A Modern Lepanto," after a sixteenth-century naval battle in which European Christian forces had defeated the Muslim Turks. Cardinal Hayes of New York sent his blessing to the meeting, which raised $5,000 "for the victims of Communism in Spain."[65] Fordham's Freshman Sodality organization sponsored a talk by a student who accused the *New York Times* of publishing "Red propaganda" about the Spanish conflict.[66]

Spanish Civil War symposia often brought students together from several Catholic campuses to promote the Fascist cause. In December 1936, Georgetown University hosted a Catholic Youth convention to formulate a program of action against "atheism and communism," which attracted delegates from Trinity College and numerous Washington, D.C., area Catholic high schools. The main speaker, the Reverend Francis P. LeBuffe, S.J., of New York, associate editor of the Jesuit magazine *America*, compared Franco to George Washington and the insurgents to the American revolutionists. The Fascist troops fought for "life, liberty, and the pursuit of happiness."[67] In February 1938, 125 students met at Providence College for the annual conference of a student branch of the Catholic Association for International Peace. The conference unanimously went on record urging "moral and financial support" for "Franco's Catholic Spain" in its struggle against "Communist Loyalist Spain."[68]

At Fordham in April 1938, an audience of 400 heard student speakers from that university, Notre Dame College of Staten Island; St. Elizabeth's College of Convent Station, New Jersey; New Rochelle College; and St. Peter's College of Jersey City promote Franco's cause in Spain. The Fordham *Ram* described the presentations by Fordham's William Doty and by Collette Golden of Notre Dame College as the symposium's highlights. Doty defended the Fascist bombing of Barcelona and denied as "malicious propaganda" the Spanish government's charge that it constituted a slaughter of innocent women and children. Golden detailed the "persecutions undergone by the Faithful at the hands of the Loyalists, and especially the slaying and mutilation of priests and nuns."[69]

Catholic universities also hosted pro-Franco war correspondents who had traveled behind rebel lines. In July 1937, Fordham Summer School held a symposium on the Spanish conflict, sponsored by *America*, to raise money for the American Spanish Relief Fund, the largest pro-Falange committee in the United States. The symposium's speakers were the Reverend Sylvester Sancho, Spanish Dominican priest, and New York *American* correspondent Jane Anderson, who had been imprisoned by the Loyalists in Spain for forty-three days. An ardent Fascist and anti-semite, during World War II Anderson broadcast pro-Nazi propaganda from Berlin, proclaiming Hitler to be "the great bulwark of 'Catholic civilization.'" Sancho declared that, in the Loyalist capital of Madrid, possession of a crucifix or sacred image was "sufficient grounds for death." Anderson denounced the Loyalists as "nothing but Moscow agents" and called the republican government illegitimate.[70] Seven months later, President Gannon of Fordham appeared on the podium with Jane Anderson when she spoke on "The Truth About Spain" to the annual communion breakfast of the Carroll Club, a Catholic women's organization.[71] Gault MacGowan, Spanish war correspondent for the New York *Sun*, chaired a symposium at Fordham, at which he denounced the Loyalist government for "preventing foreign correspondents from reporting the truth behind the Rebel cause and [rebel] advances."[72]

At the University of Notre Dame, "world famous" Catholic convert Arnold Lunn spoke in October 1937 on "The Background of the Spanish Situation," based on observations made on a three-week tour of Spain the previous summer. He declared that Franco was "fighting for religion and decency against rapine, anarchy, and militant atheism." The Spanish Loyalists were part of a "Red Death . . . spreading like a plague" that would prove far more devastating to Europe than the Black Death of the fourteenth century.[73]

The Newman Club, the Catholic student organization at the University of California at Los Angeles (UCLA), in March 1939 sponsored a lecture by prominent pro-Fascist propagandist Aileen O'Brien, who had served as a nurse for fourteen months in "Nationalist Spain." Franco's army had awarded O'Brien the "coveted Cross of San Fernando, an insurgent medal."[74] O'Brien spoke across the United States under Catholic Church sponsorship to "inform the American public of the true conditions in Spain." She had appeared at a mass rally for Nationalist Spain in Boston the previous year wearing on her sleeve the medallion of an honorary captaincy in Franco's army. Newman Club president Bill Burke, UCLA Class of 1939, declared that the American press presented only the Loyalist side of the Spanish conflict. He was proud to introduce O'Brien, who backed Franco "heart and soul."[75] In her lecture, O'Brien portrayed Franco as a crusader for "God, Catholicism, and right."[76]

Aileen O'Brien gave another speech in Los Angeles on "The Social Reconstruction of Nationalist Spain," sponsored by the Catholic Theater Guild, which resulted in fist fights between Catholic high school youths and supporters of the Loyalists who picketed the lecture hall. Among those sponsoring O'Brien's lecture was John J. Cantwell, archbishop of Los Angeles. Athletes from Los Angeles's Loyola High School used force to break through the picket line, resulting in "scores of hand to hand struggles." These were terminated only when the police discharged tear gas bombs.[77]

At St. Louis University, a Jesuit institution, the administration's discharge of a Jewish professor for publicly endorsing the Loyalist cause precipitated the most significant academic freedom conflict in the United States related to the Spanish Civil War. It began in May 1937 when Dr. Moyer Springer Fleisher, head of the Bacteriology Department at the St. Louis University School of Medicine and a member of the faculty since 1915, joined about thirty other individuals in sponsoring a lecture in St. Louis by an Irish national, the Reverend Michael O'Flanagan, one of the very few pro-Loyalist priests. O'Flanagan was highly critical of the Church's support of the Falange, accusing it of aligning itself with Spain's wealthier classes, which kept "the people in subjection." Church authorities in Ireland had thrice suspended O'Flanagan for his activities on behalf of Sinn Fein.[78]

O'Flanagan, who was touring the United States in an effort to create support for the Loyalists among Irish-American Catholics, denied that he was currently suspended from the priesthood. He stated that his latest suspension, by Ireland's bishop of Eiphin in 1925, had been lifted in 1927 by the diocese's vicar-general while the bishop had been away in Rome.[79]

When it learned that O'Flanagan was coming to lecture on Spain under the auspices of a pro-Loyalist group, the North American Medical Bureau to Aid Spanish Democracy, the Catholic Club of St. Louis promptly issued a letter of protest to the meeting's sponsors objecting to his being identified as a priest in good standing. It also claimed that O'Flanagan was hostile to the Church. The Catholic Club of St. Louis consisted of 150 "prominent Catholic laymen," most of whom were "successful business and professional men." Those wishing to join needed the approval of the archbishop of St. Louis, and most members were friends of his. Before issuing its protest, the Catholic Club had first secured Archbishop Glennon's approval. The archbishop declared that O'Flanagan's sponsors had brought him to St. Louis "under false pretenses," which was "unfair to the Catholic church."[80]

The Reverend Harry B. Crimmins, S.J., president of St. Louis University, in a formal statement to the press, explained that he had fired Fleisher because of "his sponsorship of a lecture on May 25, 1937 by one 'Reverend' Michael O'Flanagan, billed as a 'true representative of Irish Catholicism.'"[81] Because St. Louis University was "a Catholic university under Jesuit control ... it could not countenance one of its faculty members publicly sponsoring a speaker who has taken every occasion to speak offensively of the Catholic church" by criticizing its role in Spain. The university never questioned Fleisher's competence in either teaching or research.[82]

St. Louis University's dismissal of Fleisher caused the American Association of University Professors (AAUP) to launch an investigation. When the administration asked Fleisher to resign, he had refused and demanded a faculty committee hearing. It was the AAUP's position that when asked to resign, a professor had a right to such a hearing. The St. Louis

University administration had also refused an offer of mediation by President Henry Merritt Wriston of Brown University, who was president of the American Association of Colleges.[83]

The AAUP Committee on Academic Freedom and Tenure issued a report in December 1939 that condemned Professor Fleisher's firing as unjust, a violation of academic freedom. It criticized the St. Louis University administration for refusing Fleisher a proper hearing by a faculty committee and stated that the university had shown "no sufficient reason for the extreme penalty of dismissal." The AAUP committee concluded that President Crimmins had discharged Fleisher "after constant pressure on him from outside sources," which explained the year-and-a-half delay. The committee identified the "outside sources" as Archbishop Glennon and the Catholic Club of St. Louis.[84]

The St. Louis *Post-Dispatch* immediately published an editorial that declared: "it is impossible to see that anything in Dr. Fleisher's conduct justified his dismissal." The *Post-Dispatch* agreed with the AAUP that by denying Professor Fleisher a formal hearing to answer its charges, St. Louis University had denied him "the fundamentals of due process essential to academic freedom." After his discharge, the Jewish Hospital in St. Louis hired Fleisher as a medical researcher.[85]

Catholics spearheaded the movement to pressure the United States into recognizing the Nationalist government of Spain in early 1939. In January the newly formed American Union for Nationalist Spain sent President Roosevelt a letter urging him to immediately consider recognizing the Franco government. The group's leaders included President Gannon of Fordham; Ignatius M. Wilkinson, dean of Fordham Law School; and Dr. Joseph F. Thorning, then professor of sociology at Mount St. Mary's College and formerly of Georgetown. Thorning was a prominent propagandist for "White Spain" who had been received by Franco in the Fascist capital of Burgos and in Rome by Mussolini.[86] In March, the Reverend Dr. Joseph Code of Catholic University, speaking before students of Mount St. Mary's College and Seminary and St. Joseph's College for Women, urged immediate U.S. recognition of the Nationalist government. He denounced "the unfriendly attitude of the majority of American newspapers" toward the insurgents.[87]

When the insurgents achieved victory later that month, the Vatican newspaper *L'Osservatore Romano* proclaimed in an editorial that "the victory of Catholic Spain" over the Loyalists was of "incalculable moral" benefit. It expressed "gratitude to God" because the Fascist triumph returned Spain "to the heroic faith of her fathers."[88] In June 1939 Pope Pius XII personally greeted the 3,000 Spanish soldiers of Mussolini's

Italian Arrow Division, accompanied by their Italian officers, at the Vatican's Hall of Benedictions. The pope began by blessing 3,200 rosaries that Spanish monks and nuns had given the Fascist soldiers in Rome. Then, mounting his throne, Pius XII announced to his "most beloved sons" that they had brought him "immense consolation" for fighting in Spain in defense "of the faith and of civilization."[89]

President Gannon's "Exemplary Leader": Antonio de Oliveira Salazar

President Robert I. Gannon of Fordham was as much an admirer of Portugal's rightist dictator Antonio de Oliveira Salazar as he was of Franco, and he awarded him an honorary Doctor of Laws degree in 1938. Gannon frequently gave public lectures praising Salazar, whom he called "the Great Man" and a "brilliant leader."[90] Such praise for Portugal's authoritarian ruler was common among American Jesuits, whose magazine, *America*, published an article in December 1937 that celebrated him as "the Savior of Portugal," a "great Catholic statesman" who had liberated his nation from the "yoke of Masonry and pseudo-liberalism." Salazar had stimulated in Portugal a "social and religious renaissance" and had made it "tranquil and prosperous, an oasis of peace."[91] Fordham's Board of Trustees approved President Gannon's proposal to award Salazar an honorary Doctorate of Laws at the commencement ceremonies in June 1938.[92]

President Gannon made Salazar's honorary doctorate "the center of the Exercises," attended by 6,000 people. Portugal's minister to the United States, Joâo de Bianchi, accepted the degree on Salazar's behalf.[93] In bestowing the degree, Gannon declared that Fordham's rector, its professors, and its students were all "well aware that Your Excellency [Salazar] has become an exemplary leader for the whole world," a champion of "great and eternal ideals."[94]

In 1940, President Gannon asked the Portuguese minister's assistance in raising funds to make a bronze bust or statue of Salazar to occupy a prominent place on the Fordham campus. Gannon called Salazar "one of the really great men of the world, a splendid example of the Catholic scholar and statesman."[95]

Fordham's Danubian Congress

During 1938, a year dominated by German expansion in central Europe, prominent Catholic educators argued vociferously that the Soviet Union rather than Nazi Germany or Fascist Italy represented the primary threat to world peace. Even early during World War II, in February 1941, President Gannon claimed that Nazi Germany was "less dangerous" than the Soviet Union. The Germans, he reasoned, "ha[d] been Europeans for 1500 years," whereas the "Russians are not Europeans yet." The Soviets wanted to "wipe out civilization." As proof, he pointed to their alleged agents, the Spanish Loyalists, who had "sacked the convents... burned the cathedrals, and slaughtered the priests by the thousands."[96] Prominent Catholic educators attempted to maintain friendly ties with German diplomats and served as leading apologists in the United States for right-wing antisemitic dictatorships in Eastern Europe, notably those of Poland, Hungary, and Romania, as they had for Spain and Portugal.

In January and February 1938, Fordham University sought the cooperation of the German and Italian embassies in planning a conference on "The Political and Economic Situation of South Central Europe," designed to stimulate a rapprochement among the six nations of the Danube Valley – Austria, Hungary, Czechoslovakia, Romania, Bulgaria, and Yugoslavia. President Gannon asked that the ambassador or minister of these countries, of Poland, and of the three nations with a "Danubial sphere of interest" – Germany, Italy, and France – each designate a speaker to represent it at the conference. The Reverend Edmund A. Walsh, S.J., head of Georgetown University's School of Foreign Service, agreed to assist President Gannon in securing Nazi Germany's participation.[97]

Gannon and Walsh made every effort to persuade Nazi Germany's embassy to send a representative to the conference, but they agreed that inviting a Soviet diplomat would precipitate widespread anger among American Catholics. Walsh noted that no American Catholic institution had ever invited "the Bolshevik" to a school function. Both men believed that displaying the hammer and sickle banner and playing the "Internationale" at the conference along with the flags and national anthems of the other participating countries would create massive embarrassment for Fordham. Neither Gannon nor Walsh felt that would be the case when Fordham hoisted the swastika flag and played the Nazi anthem.[98]

Gabor de Bessenyey, professor of political science at Fordham and chairman of arrangements, took the opportunity in announcing the conference to defend the autocratic rightist East European governments whose representatives Gannon had invited. Dismissing the American press practice of referring to such countries as Romania, Poland, and Hungary as dictatorships, de Bessenyey claimed that they "safeguard the liberties of their citizens... in the same degree as do the great Democracies of the West." He asserted that "any curtailment of constitutional liberties" in these East European nations was "purely temporary and dictated by the exigencies of the times," that is, justified. Each of these nations remained "democratic in principle."[99]

The Fordham "Danubian Congress," as it was called, held May 6–8, 1938, failed to consider the alarming intensification of antisemitism in Eastern Europe, described in the next chapter. It was highlighted by the Polish representative's denunciation of the Soviet threat to Eastern Europe and the plea of Francis Deak, professor of law at Columbia University, for Hungary's "right of equality... in armament and national defense."[100] Professor de Bessenyey in his speech asserted that an economic or political union of Danubian nations could fill a vacuum left by the collapse of Austria-Hungary and prevent Germany from dominating the region. But he emphasized that if such a union could not be forged, "a Nazi peace through loss of Danubian independence to Germany would be preferable to a 'democratic war.'"[101] The German government instructed its embassy not to send representatives to the conference because it did not wish to reveal its Danubian policy.[102]

Conclusion

Like the American Church hierarchy and the Vatican itself, leaders of American Catholic universities found many of the Hitler regime's objectives and policies appealing, while sharing their concern about Nazi curtailment of Church autonomy. Administrators, faculty, and students at Catholic universities remained largely indifferent to anti-Jewish violence and discrimination in Germany until the Kristallnacht and repeatedly claimed that persecution of Catholics in Mexico and Spain was worse. They expressed resentment over what they considered disproportionate press attention to Nazi oppression of Jews. American Catholic higher education leaders made no criticism of the German Catholic Church's general unwillingness to oppose Hitler's antisemitic measures. They did not denounce the German Church for turning over baptismal, marriage, and other Church records that enabled the Nazis to identify Jews.[103] Most Catholic leaders inside and outside of academia considered the Soviet Union a greater threat to Western civilization than Nazism, causing them to support efforts to appease the Hitler government and even in some cases to sympathize with its expansionist designs. Catholic universities sponsored many speakers who minimized or even justified Nazi anti-Jewish measures, and who provided a rationale for Germany's rearmament and aggressive foreign policy.

Catholic university administrators, faculty members, and students also helped Nazi Germany enhance its image in the United States by providing passionate and highly visible public support for the Fascist regime in Italy and for the German-backed insurgency in Spain. Their endorsement of rightist antisemitic dictatorships in Eastern Europe made many Americans more accepting of Germany's suppression of democratic and Jewish rights. Jesuit enthusiasm for Franco caused St. Louis University to discharge a distinguished professor of bacteriology whom it had employed for twenty-two years, a blatant violation of academic freedom. Catholic university symposia and lectures promoting Mussolini and Franco, and the absence of campus debate over such issues as the Spanish Civil War and Italy's invasion of Ethiopia, caused many Americans to view Fascism more sympathetically.

8

1938, Year of the Kristallnacht

The Limits of Campus Protest

Only in late 1938, after the Kristallnacht pogroms in Germany, did American universities become significantly involved in protest against Nazism. Even then, the initiative came largely from students. College and university administrators remained unwilling to press for strong retaliatory measures against Germany, or to assume much responsibility for raising funds to bring refugees from Nazism to their campuses.

As the plight of Europe's Jews became ever more desperate in the months preceding the Kristallnacht, the campus remained largely quiescent. At the newly established Queens College in New York City, President Paul Klapper cancelled a scheduled lecture by one of the most prominent anti-Nazi refugees and playwrights of the Weimar Republic, Ernst Toller, on the grounds that the majority of faculty and many students considered him too controversial. After the Anschluss, college and university administrations failed to react to the Nazi threat to destroy the Jewish collections at the Austrian National Library in Vienna, although small groups of students on a handful of campuses launched a campaign to rescue the books. The leaders of the World Youth Congress, an international student organization, made major concessions to the Hitler Youth in an ultimately futile effort to persuade it to send delegates to its second biennial convention at Vassar College, even promising to bar criticism of the Hitler government.

American Academia's Reaction to the Polish Ghetto Benches

During 1937 and early 1938, some American educators sought to focus attention on the intensifying antisemitic discrimination in the universities of Poland, the nation with Europe's largest Jewish population, although most of American academia was slow to react. The Fordham Danubian Congress ignored the issue. In 1935, Polish universities began to segregate Jewish students in their classrooms and laboratories. Jews had been ghettoized before in Poland, but universities had never forced them into segregated seating. Many Jews in both Poland and the United States believed that the confinement of Jewish students to "ghetto benches" was intended to prepare the way for their elimination from the universities. This, in turn, constituted an important step toward the economic strangulation of Poland's Jews, as already made evident in Nazi Germany. Indeed, Poland's antisemitic press joyfully proclaimed that the ghetto benches were a "welcome step which shall lead soon to the segregation of Jews in ghettoes in the towns and ultimately force them out of Poland."[1]

Otto Tolischus reported from Warsaw in the *New York Times* on February 7, 1937, that Jews faced disaster in Latvia, Lithuania, Hungary, and Romania as a result of mounting antisemitism, and that the crisis was approaching its "high water mark" in Poland. He noted that the number of Jewish students enrolled in Polish universities was rapidly diminishing. Tolischus declared that Jews in the above-mentioned Eastern European countries, 30 percent of the world's Jewish population, had only two choices: to repeat the Exodus "on a bigger scale than that chronicled in the Bible," a task rendered nearly impossible by immigration barriers erected against them almost everywhere, or to die "a slow death from economic strangulation." In the meantime, Jews were subjected to pogroms in which they were killed or wounded, and their shops wrecked. Antisemites threw incendiary bombs into Jewish tenements at night while the Jews slept. In several Polish towns, they drove Jews from markets and forcibly ejected them from cafes and restaurants. Tolischus concluded by quoting Polish Jews who bitterly commented that, were a Polish Hitler to arise, "there would be little work for him left to do."[2]

Jewish students who refused the humiliation of segregated seating, which was often at the back of the room, and chose to stand were invariably severely beaten by gentile students, fined by the university administration, or expelled from the university entirely. At Warsaw Law School, gentile students stormed into a classroom and assaulted Jews who had taken seats outside the "ghetto" section, injuring six of them. That same month, twelve Jewish students were expelled from the Warsaw Engineering School, which two Jewish-born bankers had founded and funded a half century before.[3]

On October 19, 1937, Poland's Jews staged a nationwide strike against the ghetto benches. Jewish businesses and schools shut down all day across the country, and housewives did no shopping. Jewish students in Warsaw colleges began a strike five days before, when administrators announced that they would discipline students who refused assignment to ghetto benches. The colleges prohibited Jewish students from standing in classrooms or laboratories. On October 15, Jewish students extended their strike to all universities in Poland.[4]

In December 1937, Dr. Stephen Duggan, director of the Institute of International Education, prepared a petition that denounced the ghetto benches, warning that the place of Poland's Jewish students "in the life of scholarship is threatened with extinction." When attempts had been made in Hungary in late 1933 to force Jewish university students "to occupy only the back benches in lecture rooms," sparking antisemitic riots at the Universities of Budapest, Szegeg, and Bebrecen, American academic leaders had remained silent. This was also the case in November 1935, when 500 antisemitic rioters at the University of Budapest physically attacked Jewish students, injuring several of them and smashing the furniture in their rooms.[5]

Duggan was able to secure the signatures of fifty-nine American college and university presidents on the petition, which was published in the *New York Times*. Only one president from the schools of the present-day Ivy League, Henry M. Wriston of Brown, was among the signers. Cornell's former president, Livingston Farrand, also signed. By contrast, four of the Seven Sisters presidents signed – Marion Edwards Park of Bryn Mawr, Ada Comstock of Radcliffe, William A. Neilson of Smith, and Mildred H. McAfee of Wellesley – as did former president Mary E. Woolley of Mount Holyoke. Among the more prominent presidents endorsing the petition were Harry Woodburn Chase of New York University, Frank P. Graham of the University of North Carolina, Daniel Marsh of Boston University, George Norlin of the University of Colorado, R. A. Millikan of the California Institute of Technology, Alexander G. Ruthven of the University of Michigan, and J. L. Newcomb of the University of Virginia.[6]

No presidents of Catholic colleges and universities signed the petition. Nor did any of them speak out against the earlier antisemitic violence and attempts to force Jewish students into segregated seating at Hungarian universities. Catholics prominent in American higher education made no effort to persuade Catholic prelates in Poland or Hungary to use their influence against the persecution of Jews in those nations' universities.

Although antisemitism in Poland and other Eastern European countries was increasing at a frightening rate, President Isaiah Bowman of Johns Hopkins University expressed a view that remained common among presidents of elite universities when, in refusing to sign the petition, he complained that it was time to "protest against the protests." He questioned whether it was wise to "take the initiative in appeals that affect the internal situation" of other countries.[7]

Duggan in January 1938 expressed to President Bowman his deep disappointment about his refusal to sign the petition against the ghetto benches and voiced his irritation at Bowman's suggestion that protest was improper. He asserted that the Polish universities' introduction of ghetto benches was merely the latest in a series of events occurring in Central and Eastern Europe whose objective was "not merely the relegating of the Jews to the ghetto of the medieval times but the destruction of every opportunity for them to secure an education." Moreover, there was "now manifested every desire to drive the Jews out" of Central and Eastern Europe entirely. Duggan noted that because "the doors of practically every other country" were closed to Jews, "such action looks to the destruction of the Jewish race itself." That, Duggan informed President Bowman, constituted "a crime not only against culture but against humanity."[8]

Bowman displayed not only callousness but antisemitism in explaining his refusal to sign the petition to Stephen Duggan. By late 1937, the plight of Poland's Jews was desperate, as Jews were slaughtered in pogroms across the country and as Jewish businesses were picketed and boycotted, synagogues invaded and desecrated, and Jewish stands smashed in the marketplaces. Yet President Bowman declared to Duggan that "[t]here are other minorities than the Jews" and asked, "Do you propose to be as active in their support?" "Or," Bowman continued, "are you responding to the pressure of Jews in New York?" He concluded, "as a friend," by again questioning the propriety of issuing an appeal about such a matter as the ghetto benches, and of "securing signatures and publishing the protest."[9]

The Toller Affair at Queens College: Administration Suppression of Anti-Nazi Speech

In early April 1938, Dr. Paul Klapper, president of Queens College, which had been founded the year before, withdrew an invitation to Jewish anti-Nazi exile Ernst Toller to present a lecture on campus at a symposium on the modern stage, citing opposition by faculty and students. The invitation had been issued by assistant professor Dwight Durling. The Nazis had burned Toller's books in May 1933 and revoked his German citizenship in August 1933. In early 1934, he published an autobiography in the United States entitled *I Was a German* that denounced "infatuated nationalism" as "the madness of this epoch." Toller was in Switzerland when the Nazis invaded his home and confiscated virtually everything he owned. He remained an exile until his death by suicide in New York in 1939. One of the Weimar Republic's premier dramatists, Toller was guest of honor at the dinner of the P.E.N. Club, the leading international association of writers, in London in 1925, to which he was welcomed by William Butler Yeats. In June 1934, Toller traveled to the Twelfth International Congress of P.E.N. in Edinburgh, Scotland, to join his fellow "men without a country" – German Jewish writer Emil Ludwig, whose books the Nazis had also burned the previous year, and Dr. Rudolf Olden, former editor of the Berliner *Tageblatt*.[10]

Toller charged that President Klapper had cancelled his lecture on "Social Drama," scheduled for April 8 at Queens College, for "political and racial reasons," meaning that as a Jewish opponent of Nazism Klapper considered him too controversial. Toller asserted that Professor Durling had informed him, two days after he issued the invitation to speak, that Queens College could not allow the lecture because "the majority of the faculty felt that I was known internationally as an anti-Nazi, and because many students and constituents of the Borough of Queens were of the first and second generation of [German] extraction." Toller asked Durling to explain why the college considered his political views relevant, as it had asked him to speak on a literary topic. Durling "replied that the subject [of the lecture] would probably arouse discussion and that [Toller] might, in response to a question, introduce a point which could cause resentment." Toller expressed to the press his shock at this statement.[11]

President Klapper even denied to the press that the college had invited Toller to speak, claiming that it had "merely sounded [him] out about a speech," but conceded that he opposed inviting him. Both Klapper and Durling expressed concern to the Queens College student newspaper, the *Crown*, that "Toller might deviate from the topic and enlarge upon his political philosophy," which they considered "unsuitable at a discussion on the 'Social Drama.'" Klapper also stated that because Toller "was not known to the New York theatregoer" and "was an ardent propagandist," it was not appropriate for him to speak on "Social Drama" at Queens College.[12]

President Klapper's refusal to permit Toller to present his lecture on campus precipitated a storm of criticism from liberal, trade union, and radical groups not affiliated with Queens College, including the League of American Writers, the New York College Teachers Union, the American Society for Race Tolerance, and the New Theatre League. The New York Civil Liberties Committee called on the New York City Board of Higher Education to take action "to preserve academic freedom and free speech in New York colleges." Toller accepted the invitation of the New York College Teachers Union to present his lecture on social drama to its Washington Square College Chapter at New York University (NYU).[13]

The Communist *Daily Worker* called "ludicrous" Klapper's stated desire for "a speaker more familiar with America." It noted that the college had substituted as a speaker in Toller's place at the symposium Paul Vincent Carroll, who had been in the United States for only one month. Toller, by contrast, had established permanent residency in New York, had applied for American citizenship, and had spoken on social drama before numerous audiences throughout the United States.[14]

John W. Gassner, Queens College professor and member of the New York Drama Critic Circle, who was also scheduled to speak at the Queens College symposium, announced his withdrawal in protest against the administration's cancellation of Toller's presentation. Gassner planned instead to present an address to Queens College students on "Why Ernst Toller Is So Prominent on the Social Stage."[15]

Embarrassed by the adverse publicity in the press, President Klapper rescinded his cancellation of the invitation to Toller. Disputing Toller's charge, he claimed he had not intended to deny a platform to an anti-Nazi speaker. The whole controversy had been "an unfortunate misunderstanding." Toller, however, notified Klapper that he would participate only if the administration sent him a written invitation. Just as Toller was about to speak at the meeting sponsored by the New York College Teachers Union at NYU, a messenger arrived from Queens College to deliver the written invitation.[16]

Toller assailed the Hitler regime in his Queens College address, renamed "The Theatre as a Social Force," before a capacity audience of 600. He traced the history of drama over 2,500 years, telling his listeners that the theater "must serve not national but international interests; not war but peace; not race hatred but understanding." He contrasted artistic freedom in the United States with the stifling of artistic expression in Germany.[17]

The Queens College student newspaper was primarily concerned with defending President Klapper's handling of the controversy, which it claimed had been "grossly mistreated by the daily press." In an editorial, it denounced as "absurd" the press's "double-barreled charge" that the administration had used "Fascistic tactics" against Toller, and that it stood "in the way of free expression of opinion." But the *Crown*'s only argument was that President Klapper was a "man of calibre" whose "vast record of achievements and thoughts have consistently shown him to be of broadly liberal leanings."[18]

The Queens College administration's cancellation of Toller's lecture, and its duplicity in denying it had ever invited him, may well have contributed to the depression that led to his suicide in a New York City hotel room in May 1939, at the age of forty-six. In its obituary of Toller, the *New York Times* cited friends who "attributed much of his depression" not only to his "gloomy view" of recent events in Europe but also to the "threat he saw of the extension of totalitarianism to the American continent."[19] After all, Toller, a Jewish refugee from Nazism, had accused Queens College of cancelling its invitation to him to speak because it might upset pro-Hitler German-American students and residents of Queens. He might have perceived an American college's suppression of academic freedom, and desire to placate Nazi sympathizers, as a sign of incipient totalitarianism.

The Campaign to Prevent the Burning of Jewish Books at the Austrian National Library

Later that April, immediately after Germany's Anschluss with Austria, students at three of America's elite men's colleges – Yale, Princeton, and Williams – initiated a movement to rescue Jewish and other "non-Aryan" books in the Austrian National Library in Vienna that many feared the Nazis planned to burn. College and university administrations took no part in this effort. The *New York Times*, New York *Herald Tribune*, Chicago *Tribune*, and other major American newspapers reported on April 24, 1938, that the Nazis had sent the Austrian National Library's chief librarian a list of books they wanted removed for burning from among the 1.2-million-volume collection housed in the Hofburg, the palatial former home of the Habsburgs. The *New York Times* noted that as soon as the Nazis assumed power in Austria, the bookstores had removed from circulation "all volumes likely to prove objectionable to the new rulers" and had destroyed many of them.[20]

Students on three campuses reacted the next day by starting a fund-raising campaign to purchase the books in the Austrian National Library that the Nazis intended to burn and to transport them to the United States. At Williams College, a small group, including James MacGregor Burns, Class of 1939, editor of the college newspaper and literary monthly, and Woodrow W. Sayre, Class of 1940, grandson of Woodrow Wilson, sent a cablegram to the Austrian National Library's chief librarian offering to purchase all the books the Nazis intended to burn. Four juniors at Princeton sent Hitler a telegram asking him to donate the books to the new library that their university was building, an act they thought "would mark a friendly gesture from Germany to America." One of the students was chairman of the *Daily Princetonian*, the campus newspaper, which editorialized that the "destruction of the books contravenes our ideas of liberal education."[21] The *Yale Daily News* also joined the campaign to prevent a book burning, publishing an editorial that called on its university to "administer a well-justified backhand slap" against the Nazis, "while adding to its intellectual equipment" by acquiring books targeted for destruction.[22] Brooklyn borough president Raymond V. Ingersoll cabled the Austrian National Library as well, offering to pay for the transportation of the books to the Brooklyn Public Library.[23]

Taking sharp issue with the *Yale Daily News*, the head librarian for Yale University's Sterling Memorial Library, Professor Andrew Keogh, denied that the Nazi takeover of Austria endangered Jewish books. He emphatically declared that "under no circumstances would the Yale Library buy non-Aryan books" from the Vienna collection. Keogh announced: "I must stay clear of politics." He claimed that Yale's purchasing literature banned by the Nazis constituted "a political violation," because the Hitler regime prohibited exporting the books. Professor Keogh insisted that "European bonfires are never so serious as the newspapers would make them" and suggested that they resulted merely from "students letting off steam."[24] The *Yale Daily News* identified Keogh as "one of the country's best known librarians." Two weeks earlier, when Keogh had announced that he planned to retire in June 1938, after thirty-nine years of service at Yale, the *Yale Daily News* editorial board had lamented "the loss of a man who was excellently fitted for [the] very important position" of head librarian at Yale.[25]

Harvard University showed little interest in becoming involved in the campaign to save the Austrian National Library's Jewish books. The chairman of the *Yale Daily News* sent the *Harvard Crimson* a telegram asking its cooperation in acquiring the threatened books for the "Big Three" university libraries, but the *Crimson* only acknowledged receipt and withheld comment. Authorities at Harvard's Widener Library stated that "we are willing to purchase any worthwhile books that we do not have" but expressed doubt that the Austrian National Library had many books they could use.[26]

The campaign to save the Jewish books precipitated what the campus newspaper called a "riotous campus civil war" at Williams College, as 500 undergraduates "turned the Berkshire quadrangle into a shambles." One group of students prevented the burning of a brown-shirted effigy of Hitler that was to have provided the centerpiece for a campus anti-Nazi rally. When the anti-Hitler collegians sought to substitute a huge red swastika emblem, their opponents brought out two fire hoses to protect it. The *Williams Record* dismissed any suggestion that the resulting "free-for-all" possessed political significance. It compared it to the nineteenth-century cane rushes, a rite of spring that permitted the student body "to get winter out of its veins," and it noted that "a good time was had by all." But the *Record* did praise the attempt to acquire the "non-Aryan" books that the Nazis had "consigned to the flames of bigotry" as "a magnificent gesture from a liberal college to an intolerant state."[27]

The publicity that the campaign to save the Jewish collection generated may have prevented a public book burning of the Austrian National Library Jewish collection. The Library announced it would not consider American offers to purchase the books, calling them insulting. It would not destroy the books but instead remove them from public access and lock them in special rooms.[28]

The 1938 Convention of the World Youth Congress at Vassar College

The second biennial convention of the World Youth Congress (WYC), which promoted contacts among student leaders across national boundaries as a means of fostering international understanding, revealed that one of academia's most liberal organizations was very reluctant to isolate Nazi Germany. The convention of the Geneva-based WYC, held from August 16 to 24, 1938, at Vassar College, brought together more than 700 representatives, mostly college and university students, from fifty-four nations on six continents. Among the principal issues it scheduled for discussion were whether an international system to maintain peace could work without all nations participating and how to stop the arms race.[29]

The WYC leadership failed to secure Nazi Germany's participation in the convention, although it offered to concede almost everything the Hitler Youth demanded. International secretary Elizabeth Shields-Collins of Britain announced that the WYC's leaders had decided unanimously to prohibit criticism of the Hitler regime at the convention, to deny representation to anti-Nazi refugee groups, and to make German the language of the convention. The WYC balked only at the fourth request, that no Communists be included in other nations' delegations. The denial of the fourth request was not acceptable to the Hitler Youth, and it refused to participate.[30]

Henry Noble MacCracken, president of Vassar, who delivered the welcoming address, informed his college's board of trustees at the end of the convention that he considered it a success, although he stated that it "may . . . be criticized for having omitted to make clear that the matter of Soviet Russia is just as much a dictator as the leaders of Germany and Italy." He also believed that had conservative organizations in the United States officially appointed delegates, as Britain's appeasement-oriented Conservative Party did, the American delegation "would have been more truly representative of the total public opinion in this country."[31]

The American delegation divided over the issue of collective security, with a majority favoring "concerted action, by boycotts and embargoes" as "the only practical and quick way to a peace." However, a significant minority of the Americans participating, undoubtedly pro-appeasement conservatives, isolationists, and pacifists, argued that any "aggressive attitudes" nations displayed were caused by "injustices" that had been inflicted on them. These delegates asserted that "a lasting peace" could not be achieved "by a condemnatory attitude toward any nation," meaning that they opposed criticism of Nazi Germany, Fascist Italy, or Japan and believed that their foreign policies were at least partly justifiable.[32]

The WYC convention was sharply criticized by the acting mayor of Poughkeepsie, where Vassar was located, and by the American Catholic Church, reflecting deep mistrust of efforts to promote collective security against fascism. The acting mayor refused to officially greet the convention because he claimed that it promoted "internationalism."[33] The Church was suspicious that the convention would be heavily influenced by Communists. In June 1938, Archbishop Michael J. Curley, chancellor of Catholic University in Washington, D.C., called the upcoming convention an "international meeting of Communism."[34] The administrative board of the National Catholic Welfare Council appealed to Catholic youth groups not to participate in the convention, arguing that it provided "an opportunity for the fostering of irreligion and . . . the class hatreds of sovietism."[35] The Right Reverend Msgr. Edward J. Maginn, vicar general of the Albany Catholic Diocese, declared after the convention that it had been dominated by "Atheistic Communism."[36]

Although the Hitler Youth had not sent delegates to Vassar, the WYC, which had made "valiant efforts" to include them, vowed to maintain contact. The WYC announced after the convention, "We refuse to be cut off from the youth of Germany and Italy," and sent the Hitler Youth and the Italian Fascist youth organization messages of good will.[37]

Universities Respond to the Kristallnacht

The horrifying Kristallnacht pogroms of November 10, 1938, for the first time sparked widespread protest against Nazism in the American campus mainstream. Students, faculty members, and some administrators added their voices to those of several prominent politicians and labor leaders, and many ordinary Americans. But although the Kristallnacht precipitated a significant student-initiated movement to raise funds to enroll refugee youth in American institutions of higher learning, academia did not join those pushing for reducing immigration barriers or economic sanctions on the Third Reich.

The assassination on November 7, 1938, of a German diplomat, Ernst vom Rath, in Paris by a seventeen-year-old Jewish youth, Herschel Grynszpan, provided the Hitler regime with a pretext for launching a violent and sweeping attack on Germany's entire Jewish population. Hitler the previous month had ordered the expulsion from Germany of more than 12,000 Polish-born Jews, who for many years had been legal residents of Germany. In a single night, these Jews were driven out of their homes into trains bound for the Polish border. The Nazis permitted each Jew to take only one suitcase, forcing them to permanently abandon their homes and nearly everything they owned. Herschel Grynszpan, then residing in Paris, determined to exact revenge against the Nazis after he received a postcard from his sister, informing him that she and his parents were trapped at the Polish border. The Nazis had taken everything they had, and they were penniless, with nowhere to go.[38]

The highly coordinated pogroms across Germany that the Hitler regime unleashed during the early hours of November 10 resulted in the destruction by fire of more than 1,000 synagogues, leaving almost none remaining anywhere in the Third Reich. Nazi storm troopers, joined by many ordinary Germans, smashed up 7,000 Jewish shops and businesses, whose broken window-glass gave the pogroms their name, Kristallnacht (Night of Broken Glass). In every part of the country, the Nazis physically assaulted Jews, killing about 100, and ransacked Jewish homes, burning the furniture and books inside. They seized 30,000 Jewish men, about one-quarter of those who remained in Germany, and imprisoned them in concentration camps. The German government compelled the already-impoverished Jews to pay a substantial fine for the damage that the Nazis had caused to Jewish property.[39]

The Kristallnacht sparked considerable outrage in the United States, as leading newspapers provided detailed coverage and issued strong editorial condemnations. Hitler's ambassador to the United States, Hans Dieckhoff, reported to Berlin from Washington, D.C., on November 14 that "a hurricane is raging here."[40] That day, President Roosevelt recalled the U.S. ambassador to Germany, Hugh R. Wilson, as a "dramatically framed method of protest," according to the *New York Times*, "calculated to be more emphatic than any diplomatic note could be." In a press conference that day, Roosevelt declared that he "could scarcely believe that such things could occur in a twentieth-century civilization." The *Times* noted that Roosevelt had rebuked Nazi Germany for the Kristallnacht in language as strong as an American president had ever used to a "friendly" nation.[41]

Other prominent Americans immediately denounced the Hitler regime for the pogroms. Former New York governor Al Smith and New York City district attorney Thomas E. Dewey spoke out in a radio broadcast sponsored by the Non-Sectarian Anti-Nazi League. Dewey called the Kristallnacht "sickening" and appealed "to world opinion to rebuke a dictatorship gone mad." Governor Charles F. Hurley of Massachusetts assailed Nazi "bestiality."[42] American Federation of Labor (AFL) president William Green declared that words could not express "his deep sense of horror" over the Nazis' brutality toward Jews.[43] Speaking over nationwide radio, he urged all of the AFL's affiliated trade unions to intensify their efforts to make the boycott of German goods and services fully effective. AFL vice-president Matthew Woll called for "a moral ring around Germany" and denounced Nazism as "savagery." In New York, 600 members of the theatrical profession staged an anti-Nazi protest meeting at which Orson Welles, Raymond Massey, and Manchester *Guardian* reporter Robert Dell spoke.[44]

Journalist Dorothy Thompson, whom Hitler had expelled from Nazi Germany in August 1934, tried to rally non-Jewish Americans to appeal to the French government to spare the life of Herschel Grynszpan. She asserted over the radio that the Nazis' brutal antisemitic persecution had provoked his desperate act. Thompson told her listeners that she felt she knew Grynszpan, because she had met many Jews who had suffered what he had:

He read that Jewish children had been stood on platforms in front of a class of German children and had had their features pointed to and described by the teacher as marks of a criminal race. He read that men and women of his race, amongst them scholars and a general decorated for his bravery, had been forced to wash the streets, while the mob laughed.

Thompson declared that the entire Christian world was on trial, along with "the men of Munich," who had recently signed a pact with Hitler ceding to him the Sudetenland, "without one word of protection for helpless minorities." She concluded her radio appeal for Grynszpan with the words: "We who are not Jews must speak, speak our sorrow and indignation and disgust in so many voices that they will be heard."[45] Thompson's appeal generated almost no response on American campuses.

On November 17, 1938, several presidents of major universities "added their voices" to the public condemnation of the Nazis' Kristallnacht rampage. President Conant of Harvard declared that American educators "may well unite in expressing their horror at this latest example of the barbaric spirit of the present German government." Also speaking out were the presidents of Yale, the University of Wisconsin, the University of Chicago, Stanford, the University of North Carolina, and the University of Rochester.[46] None of the university presidents, however, called for changes in U.S. immigration policy or mentioned the boycott of German goods and services, nor did any of them endorse Dorothy Thompson's appeal on behalf of Herschel Grynszpan. They did not join in the picketing of German consulates or of German liners at the New York City docks.

University presidents were not among the seventeen speakers at New York City's massive "protest against Nazi outrages" at Madison Square Garden on November 21. A capacity audience of more than 20,000 people, with 2,000 more listening over loudspeakers in the streets outside, heard Dr. Harry F. Ward of Union Theological Seminary call for an international conference of democratic nations to evacuate the Jews from Germany. He proposed that the cost be paid by the Hitler regime, collected by impounding any money democratic nations owed to German citizens and by instituting a trade embargo against Germany. Vito Marcantonio of the International Labor Defense declared that Nazism "must be smashed... with guns." Dorothy Thompson spoke about her appeal for Grynszpan, announcing that Nazi Germany must be made the defendant at his upcoming murder trial in Paris.[47]

Two days after the Madison Square Garden rally, 30,000 merchants in New York City shut their grocery stores, butcher shops, bakeries, drug stores, and other retail establishments between noon and 1:00 P.M. in a coordinated protest against antisemitic persecution in Germany. In some sections of the city, stores remained closed for as long as two or three hours. In the Bronx, the County Pharmaceutical Association and the Retail Drug Store Employees Union Local 1199, CIO reported "virtually 100 percent" cooperation between the drug store owners and the employees in the protest.[48]

Within academia, protest was student-initiated, beginning at Harvard and quickly spreading to a multitude of other colleges and universities. On November 16, 1938, 500 Harvard and Radcliffe students attended a meeting called by eleven undergraduate organizations to express outrage over the Kristallnacht. They formed a committee to raise funds to bring to Harvard refugee students from Germany, Austria, or the Nazi-occupied Sudetenland. This Harvard Committee to Aid German Student Refugees planned to bring twenty refugee students to Harvard by soliciting donations from the university's faculty, students, and alumni and persuading the administration to waive the tuition. U.S. immigration law permitted some "properly accredited" foreign students to enter the country on a non-quota basis, provided that an American college or university admitted them and arranged to cover their expenses.[49]

The *Harvard Crimson* identified the refugees to be assisted as "Catholic and Jewish victims of Nazi persecution."[50] This suggested that the *Crimson* and others involved in the project either did not understand the uniqueness of the Jews' plight, or that they did not consider it feasible to rally administration and alumni support behind a cause that focused primarily on the rescue of Jews.

A delegation from the newly formed committee, including leaders of the liberal American Student Union and the Zionist Avukah, met with President Conant to discuss its plan. Conant received the group "very cooly" but was eventually persuaded to endorse its plan. The Harvard Corporation voted $10,000 to establish twenty scholarships for qualified refugee students, with the provision that the student committee provide funds for living expenses. Half of the money that the Harvard Corporation earmarked for scholarships, $5,000, had been donated by the wealthy Boston reformer Elizabeth Glendower Evans.[51]

The Harvard administration indeed would not acknowledge that Germany's Jews faced a uniquely dangerous predicament. It announced to the press that "a large number of the recipients of these scholarships would be young men who were refugees from Germany for reasons other than the Nazi persecution of racial minorities," meaning non-Jews.[52]

The Harvard administration almost immediately clashed with the students' Harvard Committee to Aid German Student Refugees. It denied the committee permission to distribute pledge cards and collect contributions at its mass meeting to raise funds for the refugee students' living expenses, which was scheduled for Harvard's Sanders Theater on December 6, 1938. The administration justified its action by citing a Harvard Corporation rule that prohibited the collection of money at meetings without written permission in advance.[53]

Nonetheless, more than 2,000 people jammed into Sanders Theater to inaugurate the fund-raising campaign. The meeting's featured speakers were Massachusetts governor-elect Leverett Saltonstall and Jewish comedian Eddie Cantor, who pledged $1,000.[54]

Bryn Mawr students, also quick to react to the Kristallnacht, held an emergency mass meeting on November 17, 1938, and voted to raise funds to pay for the room and board of two refugee students. They raised $1,700 "almost overnight," with 357 of 450 undergraduates, 40 of 70 resident graduate students, and more than 50 faculty members contributing. In addition, President Marion Edwards Park provided not only tuition for one graduate student but the funds to cover her other expenses for one year. Bryn Mawr's campaign precipitated a similar one at nearby Swarthmore College.[55]

Alarmed by the Kristallnacht, students at numerous colleges and universities prodded their administrations to take action on behalf of refugee students from Nazi Germany. Among the first to do so were Yale, MIT, Barnard, Radcliffe, Wellesley, and Vassar. At Yale, a group of law students almost immediately began a collection to aid refugees, and several days later graduate students established a committee for the same purpose.[56] College and university administrations invariably implemented plans similar to Harvard's, in which they covered tuition but required the students to raise the funds for living expenses.

At Yale, undergraduates were slower to display interest in the movement to assist refugee students. The *Yale Daily News*, which strongly supported fund-raising for refugees in the weeks after the Kristallnacht, complained in an editorial on December 2, 1938, that there had as yet been "no practical demonstration of humane feeling on the part of the [undergraduate] students." On December 14, it reported that Yale undergraduates had contributed more than $300 to a newly formed Committee for Refugee Students, whose purpose was "to bring to Yale a small number of . . . graduate students . . . driven from Germany for religious, racial, or political reasons." It said that the amount raised did not compare favorably with that collected at other colleges.[57]

Impeding the fund-raising efforts at Yale was an indifference or hostility toward Jewish refugees widespread among the undergraduates. The *Yale Daily News* editorialized on December 14 that "[o]ne of the sobering features of the present undergraduate drive to raise money for German Jewish refugees is the prejudice and narrowness of outlook which it is uncovering right here on the Yale campus." The editorial bluntly identified antisemitism as a serious problem in the student body, declaring that "an all too large group of students has said: 'We don't like Jews.'"[58] The *Daily News* had a short time before interviewed Yale undergraduates who expressed sympathy for the Hitler regime, or argued that press reports of Kristallnacht atrocities were exaggerated. Jack Arrington, Class of 1939, declared that American newspapers gave "far too much attention . . . to the more spectacular and cruel aspects" of Nazi treatment of Jews. Eugene Metz, Class of 1941, endorsed measures he said the Hitler government considered "necessary to building a strong united race."[59]

In January 1939, a new *Yale Daily News* editorial board warned that the anti-Nazi feeling that had resulted in mass meetings and petition campaigns since the Kristallnacht had "ominous aspects." Lacking "the control of reason and balance," such "moral fervor" could "do little but harm." The anti-Nazis' efforts might well "stir up a hornet's nest of hate and anger," which could prove impossible to control.[60]

Most college and university presidents appeared reluctant to devote much energy to the campaign to bring refugee students to the United States. President Robert Maynard Hutchins of the University of Chicago refused several requests by students to speak at protest meetings, although he publicly expressed his outrage at the Nazis' Kristallnacht atrocities. On November 15, President Hutchins declined to see a delegation of his students who were "very anxious" to speak with him about arranging a campus protest meeting on "the Jewish situation in Germany." During the next ten days, he turned down invitations to speak in Detroit and in Ann Arbor, Michigan, at mass meetings convened to denounce the Nazi persecution of Jews. Hutchins had the previous year responded to the Non-Sectarian Anti-Nazi League's request that he become a member by informing it that "I have an iron clad rule that I will not join organizations or committees of any kind."[61] Dean Virginia Gildersleeve, head of Barnard College, emphasized to her students that tuition waivers for refugees would require denying scholarships to needy Americans.[62]

Efforts to assist refugees were limited by the determination of trustees and administrators not to identify their colleges and universities too openly with the rescue of European Jewry. Mount Holyoke president Roswell Ham reported strong trustee reservations about the student refugee campaign. He stated that the trustees opposed granting refugee scholarships exclusively to Jews, and he expressed doubt about the college's ability to assimilate more than three refugee students. The trustees required the college to have commitments to all the funds needed to support the refugee students before accepting any students. Mount Holyoke's Committee for Giving Aid to Refugees from Germany in January 1939 announced that it would not ask the college's trustees for any money, and it stipulated that "not more than half of those aided by the college shall be Jews." The committee reported that New York alumnae had sent a letter of protest "reflecting the sentiment prevailing in New York against encouraging refugees of Jewish faith to come to the United States."[63]

President Robert C. Clothier of Rutgers University also was equivocal in his support for the refugee campaign. He refused the request of the Rutgers student committee for refugee scholarships that he affiliate with it as a sponsor. Clothier claimed it was improper for a university president to sponsor what he called a student project. Dean Fraser Metzger of Rutgers College recommended that he decline the invitation. President Clothier informed the chair of the student committee, John H. Ludlum, that "while we all have profound sympathy for [the refugees] there are those who feel that our first responsibility is to our young people here in America." Ludlum reminded Clothier that the plight of Germany's Jews was especially desperate: "[T]he American student's handicap is economic only, whereas the handicap of the students to be helped is racial and religious, or other arbitrary discrimination."[64]

Although Rutgers and New Jersey College for Women each accepted one refugee student, President Clothier was not significantly involved in the effort to bring them to the university. He declined the invitation to speak at the campus rally for German Student Refugee Aid in April 1939, on the grounds that he had an appointment in New York that evening.[65]

The Rutgers administration relied heavily on Jews, both on and off campus, to provide the funds to support the refugees. One Jewish fraternity at Rutgers provided the male refugee student, Walter Sokel, with a free room, and another promised free meals, for his four years at the university. His tuition was paid by Newark department store magnate Louis Bamberger, who was Jewish, and anonymously by Chester I. Barnard.[66]

President Clothier could not even remember who Walter Sokel was when Sokel wrote in May 1941, prior to graduating from Rutgers, to thank the university for its assistance. Clothier wrote the following note to a member of his staff: "Before I reply to Walter Sokel's letter, can you get some information on him for me? Is he a graduate student, what's his field, has he been an undergraduate student, where did he come from?"[67]

Because college and university administrations were almost always unwilling to cover any of the refugee students' expenses besides tuition, Jewish fraternities and sororities became especially involved in the campaign on many campuses. Hillel, the Jewish student organization, often assisted them. Such cooperation among Jewish students on behalf of the refugees occurred on such campuses as the University of Illinois, Cornell University, Pennsylvania State University, the University of Southern California, and the University of Texas, along with Rutgers. The University of Texas Hillel raised $40,000 for refugee students by persuading movie houses throughout the state to donate a percentage of their income for the cause.[68]

Students at the nation's only Jewish liberal arts college, Yeshiva University in New York City, and at the overwhelmingly Jewish "subway colleges" there, such as City College of New York (CCNY) and Brooklyn College, worked vigorously to bring refugee students to the United States. By June 1939, Yeshiva had taken in fifteen refugee students and faculty from Nazi Germany, and twenty-seven students were enrolled in October 1941. Raising funds for the refugees was a "continuous activity" at Yeshiva. In early 1939, Yeshiva's president, Bernard Revel, organized a large dinner to benefit the school's refugee aid campaign, which President Roosevelt's son James addressed. New York City movie executives provided strong backing for the dinner and fund-raising effort. Students at CCNY donated the proceeds of its basketball game with Brooklyn College to its refugee fund. Brooklyn College raised a considerable amount for refugee students through cake sales and rallies.[69]

In protesting the Kristallnacht pogroms, college and university students and faculty often suggested that Nazi persecution of Jews was not significantly different from that experienced by other groups, and they absolved the German people from responsibility for Nazi atrocities. Helen Douglas, Vassar Class of 1940, writing in her college newspaper in January 1939, declared that "[a]lthough the desperate plight of the Jews in Nazi Germany is most before the public eye at present, we must remember that students of other faiths and nationalities are equally a prey to persecution."[70] A week after the Kristallnacht, the faculty council of CCNY's College of Liberal Arts and Sciences passed a resolution that strongly condemned the Hitler government's "persecution of Catholics, Protestants, and Jews."[71] President Karl Compton of MIT presided at a campus rally billed as a protest against the "persecution of Jews and Catholics in Germany."[72] The editors of the *Wellesley College News* on November 23, 1938, lectured the student body that it "will do well to remember that disapproval of a government's policy should not bring unfriendly action toward the people who happen to be ruled by that government."[73]

Professor Philip H. Davis of the Vassar Greek Department circulated a petition at a mass meeting at Poughkeepsie High School that called on President Roosevelt to cut off all trade with Nazi Germany but also displayed a failure to grasp the uniqueness of the Nazis' persecution of Jews. The petition assumed that the German people were the unwilling victims of a dictatorship whose outlook most of them did not share, and it overlooked the complicity of the Catholic and Protestant churches in Nazi rule. It condemned the "brutality exercised against the Jewish people and Christian churches of Germany by the Nazi government." Ignoring the German public's overwhelming backing of the Hitler regime's antisemitic policies, it called the Nazi Kristallnacht pogroms "an attack upon all civilized people, including the great majority of Germans themselves." Professor Davis insisted that the Germans "are not a Nazi people...but a people like us, separated from us only by a wall of tyrannical repression."[74]

At the initiative of students from Harvard and Bryn Mawr, delegates from 35 of the 100 colleges and universities that had established committees to aid student refugees met in New York City during the winter vacation on December 27–28, 1938, and formed the Intercollegiate Committee to Aid Student Refugees (ICASR). Headquartered in New York City, its purpose was to extend and coordinate the campaign to assist "students who are the victims of racial and religious persecution in fascist countries." It planned to establish a national fund to permit students who could not persuade their administrations to provide tuition scholarships to send the money they raised to another college that would cover tuition but lacked the funds to pay for living expenses. The ICASR also provided information to colleges about the visas and affidavits that refugees needed. Ingrid Warburg, a Jewish refugee from Germany and member of the wealthy banking family, paid the ICASR's initial office rent.[75]

Despite the hopes engendered by the formation of the ICASR, a poll taken in December 1938 by the Student Opinion Surveys of America revealed that the overwhelming majority of students at American colleges and universities believed that "Jewish refugees should not be admitted to the United States in great numbers." Asked whether the United States should "offer a haven in this country for Jewish refugees from Central Europe," only 31.2 percent of undergraduates responded "Yes," whereas a whopping 68.8 percent said "No." The *Harvard Crimson* commented that students clearly wanted "Uncle Sam [to] come to the aid of oppressed German minorities in some way, perhaps by the offering of homes in United States possessions."[76]

In February 1939, Harvard president James B. Conant resisted an appeal from Bryn Mawr president Marion Edwards Park to use his influence to persuade the State Department and the Labor Department's Immigration and Naturalization Service to encourage U.S. consulates to exercise more flexibility in granting visas. Park told Conant that U.S. consular officials in London refused to grant a visa to the second recipient of Bryn Mawr's refugee student scholarship, a resident of England for two and a half years, because she could not meet the requirement of identifying a permanent residence to which she could return after completing her studies.[77] Since 1933, the State Department had instructed American consulates to apply very strictly the clause of the Immigration Act of 1917 permitting exclusion of "persons held liable to become public charges."[78] The consulates used refugee student applicants' inability to identify a permanent residence in Europe to which they could return to claim that they risked becoming financially dependent, even though their educational level would be significantly higher than that of most Americans. Park stated that the American Friends Service Committee had reported to her that about fifty students to whom American colleges and universities had awarded refugee scholarships were unable to obtain visas for this reason.[79]

Conant replied that he was aware that U.S. immigration barriers made it very difficult for many of the recipients of refugee scholarships to enter the country. He noted that the immigration quotas from central European nations were already filled, in several cases, for a number of years in advance. Conant was also well aware that the State Department had granted to American consuls "absolute power to decide" individual cases.[80]

Nevertheless, Conant declared to President Park that "it would be very unfortunate for college presidents, either individually or collectively, to attempt to exert any pressure on the State Department or the Labor Department." He believed that the consuls were "doing the best they can in the very difficult and awkward circumstances." Conant told Park he was satisfied that the students had made "the moral gesture" of initiating a call for refugee student scholarships. He found it sufficient that colleges and universities could grant an estimated one hundred scholarships to the refugee students "trickling into this country."[81]

The campus refugee aid movement of 1938–39 was able to assist only a relatively small number of students from Nazi Germany and Nazi-dominated parts of Europe because of U.S. immigration restrictions and insufficient donations by college and university administrators and alumni. Although Harvard's alumni included many of the nation's wealthiest men, written appeals that the Harvard Committee to Aid German Student Refugees sent to 10,000 of the university's graduates had brought in only $2,300 by February 1939, as opposed to $11,000 from Harvard students and faculty. Many of the students that the movement assisted were not Jewish. Although Harvard, which had initiated the refugee campaign, had planned to award twenty refugee scholarships, the largest of any university, it provided only fourteen in the end.[82]

Conclusion

American academia remained largely quiescent for most of 1938, as Jews faced economic strangulation, or worse, not only in Germany but in much of Central and Eastern Europe. In December 1937, many American university presidents had at least been willing to engage in a limited verbal protest against the Polish universities' segregation of Jewish students in their classrooms. But none of them pressed for firmer measures, such as reducing immigration barriers to permit Polish Jews to take refuge in the United States. Several of America's most prominent university presidents, such as James B. Conant of Harvard and Nicholas Murray Butler of Columbia, did not sign the petition. President Isaiah Bowman of Johns Hopkins remarked testily that he saw no point in any protest on behalf of European Jewry.

President Paul Klapper's cancellation of Ernst Toller's lecture at Queens College in April 1938 reflected an insensitivity concerning Nazi persecution of Jews then prevailing in much of American academia. Rather than educating the American public about the increasingly precarious situation of Europe's Jews, President Klapper questioned the legitimacy of inviting one of the most prominent anti-Nazi exiles, a distinguished playwright, dismissing him as a propagandist.

Although some students at Williams, Princeton, and Yale made a brave effort after the Anschluss to protect Jewish books housed at Austria's National Library at Vienna, college and university presidents declined to speak out. At Williams College, a large body of students aggressively protected an effigy of Adolf Hitler and a swastika emblem. Administrators at the nation's leading university library, Widener at Harvard, expressed very little interest in the Vienna collection that the Nazis threatened to destroy.

University administrators' unwillingness to extend protests against the Kristallnacht beyond verbal condemnation of the pogroms, or to acknowledge the uniqueness of the Jews' plight, seriously limited the impact of the first large-scale national campus protests against Nazism, which students initiated. Most importantly, without a lowering of immigration barriers preventing the entry into the United States of Jews and other anti-Nazi refugees, only a handful would ever make their way onto the campus. In his account of growing up in Nazi Berlin, Peter Gay, a Jew who witnessed the Kristallnacht and escaped from Germany with the last group of refugees allowed to land in Cuba, recalled that the protests abroad against the November pogroms "sounded very good" to him and other German Jews but were "completely hollow." He emphasized that "[n]one of this verbal onslaught led to the action we needed: a place to go."[83] University presidents would not endorse the *Vassar Miscellany News*'s call to drastically revise U.S. immigration laws and sever commercial relations with Germany.[84] On the very eve of the Holocaust, universities sharply limited the proportion of refugee scholarships that they granted to Jews.

Moreover, the college and university administrations provided only tuition scholarships for the refugees. They required that students and others sympathetic to the refugees' plight raise the funds for all their living expenses and often for transportation. Sometimes faculty members provided a room in their homes and some meals for a refugee student. It was left to the Jewish community, including the campus Hillel and the Jewish fraternities and sororities, to raise much of the necessary money to support the refugees.

Epilogue

James B. Conant and the Parole of Nazi War Criminals

James B. Conant was significantly involved in paroling vast numbers of Nazi war criminals, including those who engaged in the most heinous atrocities, when he served as U.S. high commissioner for Germany from 1953 to 1955, and as U.S. ambassador to the Federal Republic of Germany (West Germany) from 1955 to 1957. He resigned as president of Harvard in January 1953.

During the last year of Conant's presidency, Harvard hired the formerly high-ranking Nazi physicist Carl Friedrich von Weizsaecker to teach a course on scientific method during the summer session. Von Weizsaecker was a leader, along with his mentor Werner Heisenberg, of the team of Nazi scientists assigned to develop an atomic bomb during World War II. He was the son of Baron Ernst von Weizsaecker, Hitler's deputy foreign minister and wartime ambassador to the Vatican. An Allied military court at Nuremberg convicted the senior von Weizsaecker of war crimes, including officially approving the deportation of 6,000 Jews from France to the gas chambers at Auschwitz. It sentenced him to seven years in Landsberg prison.[1]

After World War II, Carl Friedrich von Weizsaecker was the prime architect of the myth that Nazi Germany's scientists chose not to build an atomic bomb but devoted their efforts instead to developing peaceful applications for atomic energy. The Americans, by contrast, focused on creating a "ghastly weapon of war." In his study of German scientists during World War II, John Cornwell labeled von Weizsaecker's claim a "full blown assertion of [Nazi scientists'] moral superiority." For several months after V-E Day, the Allies detained von Weizsaecker and other leading German physicists who participated in Hitler's wartime nuclear research program at Farm Hall in England. Cornwell noted that the Farm Hall detainees "shared in common the remarkable fact that they failed to acknowledge moral responsibility for their collusion with the Nazi regime."[2]

In the early 1950s, von Weizsaecker persuaded one of his father's defense attorneys at Nuremberg to intervene in the case of convicted Nazi war criminal Dr. Martin Sandberger, sentenced first to hang and then to life imprisonment, in an effort to reduce his punishment. Sandberger, an SS officer, had commanded a Nazi mobile killing unit that annihilated Estonia's Jewish population in 1941–42.[3]

While teaching at Harvard, von Weizsaecker openly revealed his virulent antisemitism and racism. Marie Allen, Harvard's first African-American secretary, described to me in 2008 her chilling encounter with von Weizsaecker in 1952. She was then working in a Harvard office that handled typing and other secretarial work for professors and students. When von Weizsaecker entered the office with some letters he wanted to dictate and have transcribed, he was directed to Allen. Allen recalled that when von Weizsaecker saw that she had been assigned his work, he "was visibly surprised, disturbed, and clearly did not want to acknowledge me in any way." Von Weizsaecker deliberately spoke very rapidly while dictating the letters. Several times he asked Allen "to repeat what he had dictated," which she "did without any trouble whatsoever." Then, "for the first time, [he] looked at me and said, 'Here's a letter from a dirty kike.'" Allen responded with "a stony glare." She stated, "When Professor von Weizsaecker came back into the office to pick up his neatly and perfectly typed letters, he seemed annoyed that he couldn't find one error in them." Allen concluded: "I've had many poignant uncomfortable moments in my life, but this one was particularly cutting to my soul."[4]

As U.S. high commissioner to Germany and as ambassador, Conant served as public apologist for the clemency boards that released most of the convicted Nazi war criminals that Allied courts had tried immediately after World War II. He invariably endorsed the boards' decisions to parole those imprisoned after they served only a fraction of their sentences, often for directly ordering or participating in mass murder. In November 1953, the World Jewish Congress, alarmed by the rapid release of Nazi war criminals, pleaded with U.S. secretary of state John Foster Dulles not to extend further clemency, but to no avail.[5] In the spring of 1950, the Western allies – the United States, Britain, and France – had held 3,649

Nazi war criminals in prison. By January 1955, 3,300 had been released.[6] With Conant's support, the United States paroled 250 Nazi war criminals from Landsberg prison in the eighteen months prior to June 1955, leaving only forty-two behind bars. Conant, then U.S. ambassador, expressed confidence in July 1955 that the new clemency board would "act promptly to consider the cases of all those who remain in confinement."[7]

As U.S. high commissioner, Conant approved the release from Spandau prison in November 1954 of Konstantin von Neurath, Hitler's foreign minister from 1933 to 1938 and Reich protector of Bohemia and Moravia from 1939 to 1941, after he had served only eight years of a fifteen-year sentence. Conant did not comment when delirious Germans gave von Neurath what the Los Angeles *Times* called a "hero's welcome" upon his return to his ancestral home. Von Neurath was the first paroled of the seven top Nazi leaders held at Spandau, all of whom had escaped hanging at Nuremberg. The Chicago *Tribune* noted that "[n]one ever had been expected to see the outside again."[8] When von Neurath returned home, "[c]hurch bells pealed" and villagers lined the streets to cheer him. As the Nazi leader rode by in a flower-bedecked sedan, "men doffed their hats and women wept," while "little girls waved bouquets of flowers."[9]

In March 1954, American Jewish organizations, Representative Jacob Javits of New York, and the International League for the Rights of Man challenged High Commissioner Conant's approval of the West German government's appointment of former Nazi diplomat Peter Pfeiffer to be its observer at the United Nations (UN). UN secretary-general Dag Hammarskjold initially acquiesced in the appointment on the grounds that he had to respect Conant's favorable recommendation of Pfeiffer to the U.S. State Department. Pfeiffer, who directed the Personnel Department of West Germany's Foreign Office, had joined the Nazi party in 1940 and served as Hitler's consul-general in Algiers during World War II.[10] In July 1952, a West German Bundestag committee, responding to the *Frankfurter Rundschau*'s charges that many former Nazis held positions in the Foreign Ministry, recommended to Chancellor Konrad Adenauer that Pfeiffer not be sent on missions abroad.[11] As a result of the protests, the West German government withdrew Pfeiffer's appointment as UN observer but reassigned him to a new post at the ambassadorial level.[12]

In May 1955, Judge William Clark, chief justice of the Allied Appeals Court in Nuremberg from 1948 to 1953, testified before the U.S. Senate Foreign Relations Committee against High Commissioner Conant's confirmation as U.S. ambassador to West Germany, accusing him of "encouraging the release of German war criminals."[13] Several months later, Judge Clark declared that Ambassador Conant was implementing a policy that amounted to a massive prison release of Nazis guilty of "murder, torture, and general brutality." Clark noted that one of Conant's early acts as high commissioner was to appoint Henry Shattuck, Harvard's former treasurer and trustee, who had no criminal law experience, to head a mixed American-German clemency board that considered cases of Nazi war criminals. As a result, Clark stated, "a lot more murderers and torturers were let out." The former chief justice also charged that, in an effort to avoid criticism, Conant had "imposed a censorship" on the releases of Nazi war criminals. This, Clark asserted, "led to the absurd situation" of the West German press interviewing a paroled Nazi war criminal at his home "while the High Commissioner refused to acknowledge that he was out."[14]

Judge Clark sharply differed with Ambassador Conant on the release in October 1955 from Landsberg prison of the "monstrous" Waffen SS general Josef "Sepp" Dietrich, the "Butcher of Malmédy," who had ordered the massacre of several hundred unarmed American prisoners-of-war and Belgian civilians in a series of atrocities during the Battle of the Bulge. A nine-man U.S. military court sentenced Dietrich to life imprisonment for war crimes, reduced in 1951 on recommendation of the War Crimes Modification Board to twenty-five years imprisonment.[15] An early follower of Hitler who participated in the 1923 Munich Beer Hall Putsch, Dietrich "won favor" in the Nazi party "through his prowess in fighting at political meetings and in the streets" during the 1920s. In 1931, Hitler appointed Dietrich to head his bodyguard. Dietrich directed the SS firing squad that executed six leaders of the *Sturmabteilung* (SA) at Munich's Stadelheim prison during the Night of the Long Knives.[16] William L. Shirer, who knew Dietrich personally when he was a correspondent in Nazi Germany, described him as "one of the most brutal men of the Third Reich."[17] During World War II, Dietrich had supervised the annihilation of the Jewish population of Kharkov, in the Ukraine.[18]

Ambassador Conant supported Dietrich's parole after only ten years in prison in part because a joint American-German clemency board in which he "had such confidence" recommended it. Conant insisted that U.S. authorities should release any Nazi war criminal "serving a thirty-year sentence . . . whose record in prison and plans for parole were satisfactory" after ten years. The United States should honor the sovereignty of West Germany, whose government favored leniency toward most war criminals.[19]

Conant was angered when the American Legion and the Veterans of Foreign Wars (VFW), America's two leading veterans' organizations, and Senator Estes Kefauver of Tennessee forcefully condemned the paroling of Dietrich. Timothy Murphy, the VFW's national commander, denounced Dietrich as "one of Hitler's most vicious killers" and declared that he was "shocked beyond words" by his release.[20] Kefauver, who had served on the three-member subcommittee of the U.S. Senate Armed Services Committee that investigated the Malmédy Massacre, warned Secretary of State John Foster Dulles that releasing Dietrich would send a signal that convicted murderers "are to be forgiven for their crimes." Moreover, it would open the way for the parole of several of Dietrich's lieutenants, men "who [had] violated every principle of the Geneva convention," such as Joachim Peiper, a Waffen SS colonel who had ordered his tank crews to machine-gun American soldiers after they surrendered.[21]

Conant, alarmed that the criticism from veterans' groups and Senator Kefauver was "damaging German-American relations," asked the State Department to arrange a meeting so that he could justify the paroling of Nazi war criminals to the U.S. Senate Foreign Relations Committee.[22] He believed that committee members would be sympathetic to Chancellor Adenauer's pleas "to have as many of the war criminals released as possible at this time." Conant considered this especially desirable because West Germany had recently become sovereign and was "in the process of building up a new army."[23] He was willing to trivialize Nazi war crimes and let those who had committed atrocities go free after serving minimal time in prison, in order to promote U.S. friendship with a rearmed West Germany.

After his parole, Dietrich remained an unreconstructed Nazi who addressed a reunion of the Waffen SS. In 1957, a West German court tried him for supervising the executions of six SA leaders during the Night of the Long Knives. At the beginning of the proceedings, Dietrich praised the men who had served in the Waffen SS: "If you study their careers in and after the war, you will have to agree that they were a respectable, clean, and loyal lot." The court sentenced him to eighteen months in prison for the killings. The court's position was that it was illegal to execute imprisoned political opponents without trial. Dietrich admitted his role in the executions, but his attitude was that "[m]y Fuehrer [did] not give illegal orders." The presiding judge, in issuing sentence, declared that he had taken Dietrich's military career into consideration, as a point in his favor. He declared that the defendant's "bravery and comradely bearing are generally recognized."[24] Conant criticized neither the judge's extreme leniency nor his praise of the Waffen SS general who had ordered the execution of American prisoners-of-war.

As Senator Kefauver had predicted, Joachim Peiper was paroled not long after Dietrich, with Ambassador Conant's approval. His death sentence, pronounced by an American military court in July 1946, had later been commuted to life in prison. The panzer unit Peiper commanded was known as the "Blowtorch Battalion" for having burned Russian villages to the ground earlier in World War II, with flamethrowers mounted on halftracks.[25] Peiper's release drew angry protests from American veterans' organizations, and from Senator Kefauver. Kefauver called Peiper "the worst kind of sadistic murderer" and declared that his parole "would destroy any hope" of deterring "similar atrocities in the future."[26]

In January 1958, having recently stepped down as U.S. ambassador to West Germany, Conant presented a series of three lectures at Harvard University before audiences that included prominent politicians and educators, in which he emphasized that "[contemporary] Germany today repudiates the Nazi past."[27] Later that year, Conant published the lectures as a book entitled *Germany and Freedom*. In it, Harvard's president emeritus declared that persons who had not lived in a totalitarian society had no right to condemn the German people for their behavior when Hitler was in power. He dismissed any threat of a neo-Nazi revival in Germany and implied that neither Germans nor Americans need dwell any longer on the Nazi era. Conant approvingly cited the distinction many contemporary Germans made between persons who had joined the Nazi party under Hitler but were "never 'real Nazis,'" and "*terrible* Nazis." He did not explain why as ambassador he had supported the parole of persons even he would admit were "terrible Nazis," such as Sepp Dietrich and Joachim Peiper. Conant called on "former resistance sympathizers and former [Nazi] party members (not terrible Nazis)" to work together to build a new Germany. Seemingly still defensive about Harvard's relations with Nazified universities during his presidency, Conant claimed that [the] "universities of Germany have been blamed (perhaps unduly) for much that has happened in the past."[28]

During the late 1950s and early 1960s, Conant, often cited in the American press as an authority on German affairs, remained indifferent about the rehabilitation of Nazi war criminals and their reentry into influential positions in government, education, and the military. Chancellor Adenauer's chief personal aide from 1953 to 1963, Hans Globke, state secretary of the West German Chancellery, had headed the Office of Jewish Affairs in Hitler's Ministry of the Interior and co-authored the official

FIGURE E.1. Retiring U.S. ambassador to West Germany James B. Conant (left) shakes hands with Dr. Hans Globke in Bonn, February 19, 1957. Courtesy of AP Images, photo by Horst Faas.

Nazi commentary on the Nuremberg race laws, introduced in September 1935.[29] Globke was responsible for having the passports of Jews stamped with the letter "J," facilitating their apprehension, confiscation of their property, and deportation to death camps.[30] Theodor Oberlaender, who became Adenauer's minister for refugees in 1953, was a former SS officer who became a Nazi party member in 1933. He served as national chief of the Federation German East, which carried out Nazi Germany's territorial policy in Eastern Europe. Oberlaender had signed articles in Nazi organs calling for the "expulsion and resettlement" of the non-German inhabitants of lands into which the Third Reich expanded and for "racial purity."[31]

Frederick Wallach accused Conant in the *New York Times* of having followed a "policy of moral amnesia" as high commissioner.[32] Critics charged that by endorsing the process of rapid release of Nazi war criminals, Conant encouraged the Germans to minimize, and even forget, Nazi crimes. In 1960, Minister for Refugees Oberlaender left the cabinet amid charges that in 1941 he had directed a massacre of Jews and Poles in Lvov, as an officer in the infamous "Nightingale" battalion of Hitler's army. The *New York Times* noted that "the mass of Germans" took no interest in a former Nazi serving in the cabinet: "They have long since given up trying to evaluate their fellow citizens on the basis of their pasts, possibly because so many of them were members of the Nazi party or possibly because they see so many who were higher-ranking Nazis than the Minister in top-paying non-governmental jobs."[33]

Differing sharply with Conant's sanguine view of West Germany, William L. Shirer, author of the recently published *The Rise and Fall of the Third Reich*, in 1961 declared in a lecture at Boston's Ford Hall Forum that Adenauer's Foreign Ministry was "shot through and through with Nazis." He stated that a Nazi past was not a handicap to anyone's career in West Germany. Shirer also emphasized that antisemitism remained "fairly strong" there. He found most appalling the refusal of West Germany's schools "to inform students concerning the atrocities of the Third Reich."[34]

Mircea Eliade: Iron Guardist Honored by American Universities

The honors that many American universities bestowed on Mircea Eliade, a leading supporter during the 1930s of Romania's virulently anti-semitic Legion of the Archangel Michael, also known as the Iron Guard, reflected widespread indifference in academia after World War II about the Fascist past. Established by Corneliu Codreanu in 1927, the Legion considered Romanian nationalism intrinsically linked with the Eastern Orthodox Church. It viewed Jews as foreigners contaminating Romania's "Dacian-Roman" racial structure. Marta Petreu noted that antisemitism was "the most conspicuous and violent component of the Legion's all-encompassing chauvinism."[35] The cover of the Legion's magazine *Pământul stramoşesc* (Land of Our Fathers) displayed the image of the warrior St. Michael, venerated by the Orthodox Church, and a map of Romania that showed "with black spots, the extent of the Jewish invasion."[36] The Legion conceived of its struggle as one between its patron saint and the Jewish dragon. Its main goal "was to eliminate the Jews from Romania."[37] Legionnaires were prohibited from any contact with Jews: "They could not enter a Jewish home or shop; they could not shake hands with a Jew."[38]

Eliade was drawn to the Legion in the late 1920s at the University of Bucharest, where he studied with its leading ideologist, Professor Nae

Ionescu. In his autobiography, Eliade acknowledged that Ionescu became his spiritual guide: "I considered him my 'master.'"[39] Drawn to Eastern religious thought and mysticism, Eliade received his Ph.D. in 1932 after completing a dissertation on yoga, which he researched in India. Inspired by Mussolini, Eliade traveled to Italy and established contact with Fascist theorists Giovanni Papini, Giovanni Evola, and Giuseppe Tucci, whose writings he admired.[40]

During the 1930s, Eliade propagandized for the Legion in Romanian rightist newspapers, including *Cuvântul* (The Word), which his mentor Ionescu edited. He condemned both Jews and Western influence, sometimes conflating them, as when he expressed outrage at "the Judaic spirit of the French."[41] He considered Jews an invasive and destabilizing presence in Romania, intent on dominating it: "Jews have overrun the villages of Maramures and Bucovina, and have achieved an absolute majority in all the cities of Bessarabia."[42] In the face of this Jewish "onslaught," he warned, "Romanian villages are disappearing."[43] Like his mentor Ionescu, Eliade considered democracy a dangerous Western import. In 1935, voicing "disgust" with "Europe," by which Eliade meant Western liberal thought and the heritage of the revolutions of 1848, he wrote that he wished Romania did "not actually belong to the continent that discovered profane science, philosophy, and social equality."[44]

A strong supporter of Franco's insurrection in Spain, Eliade in January 1937 published an article in which he extolled as martyrs two Romanian Iron Guardists, Ion Moța and Vasile Marin, killed in combat against Loyalist forces. Eliade knew both men personally. Underscoring Moța and Marin's status as fascist martyrs, the ministers of Nazi Germany and Fascist Italy attended their funeral in Bucharest. An early collaborator with Codreanu in the founding of the Legion, Moța was fiercely antisemitic. While a student at the University of Cluj in 1923, he translated into Romanian from French the *Protocols of the Elders of Zion*, a czarist secret police forgery that purported to demonstrate a Jewish conspiracy to conquer the world.[45] Marin, a University of Bucharest Ph.D. who joined the Legion in 1932, was also an antisemitic ideologue, who polemicized against universal suffrage and what he called Romania's "putrefying democracy." In his writings, Marin claimed that "international finance," "masonic lodges," and the "Jewish press" constituted a "democratic octopus" that held Romania in a stranglehold.[46] Eliade's article appeared in *Vremea* (The Times), a Bucharest newspaper "under Iron Guard influence" that regularly printed antisemitic caricatures. In the article, Eliade accorded "mystic significance" to the "volunteer death" of Moța and Marin, calling it a "sacrifice in the name of Christianity."[47]

A year after Moța and Marin were "martyred" in Spain, Eliade declared in *Vremea* that it was his generation's destiny to "start a revolution like no other" in Romanian history. Helping to bring about this "Christian revolution, set in motion by the Legionary movement," to eradicate Jewish and other foreign "contamination" in Romania gave his life "a precise and greater purpose."[48]

In 1938, King Carol II, fearing the Legion's destabilizing influence, imprisoned many of its members and sympathizers, including Nae Ionescu and Eliade. Eliade noted in the second volume of his autobiography: "I had been tracked down and arrested for my friendship with Nae Ionescu and because I was a contributor to his newspaper." He refused the inspector of security's repeated requests to sign declarations dissociating himself from the Legion. Eliade was released after a few months' confinement. Remaining intensely loyal to Nae Ionescu, Eliade was one of four pallbearers at his funeral in March 1940.[49]

During World War II, when Romania was allied with Nazi Germany, Eliade served it in diplomatic posts. Having become friendlier with the Legion of the Archangel Michael during the spring of 1940, King Carol II's government appointed Eliade cultural attaché in London, although the British Foreign Office objected, aware that he was an Iron Guard supporter. British intelligence called Eliade the "most Nazi member of the [Romanian] Legation."[50] After General Ion Antonescu, a friend of Hitler, and the Iron Guard forced King Carol II to abdicate in September 1940, the new regime appointed Eliade press and propaganda attaché at Lisbon, where he remained until September 1945. During this period he wrote an admiring biography of Portuguese dictator Antonio de Oliveira Salazar, celebrating his opposition to "democratic chaos." Eliade considered Salazar "the ideal model of a Christian leader."[51]

The Romanian regimes Eliade served participated enthusiastically in forcing the Jews into ghettoes, and then in their genocide. The Iron Guard launched a savage pogrom in January 1941, months before the German invasion of the Soviet Union, when the Einsatzgruppen began their mass executions. In Bucharest, the Iron Guardists sang hymns as they butchered Jews and hung them on hooks in a slaughterhouse.[52] Romanian-Jewish writer and physician Emil Dorian, who witnessed the pogrom in Bucharest, wrote in his diary on January 24, 1941, that the Iron Guardists' atrocities "cover the complete range of a demented imagination – Jews forced to drink gasoline with Epson salts – crosses cut on the skin of their back – torture and killing – on and on." Sometimes before killing the Jews, the Iron Guardists gouged out their eyes, cut out their tongues, and broke their limbs. They left Jewish corpses in the street to be chewed up by dogs.[53] Lucy S. Dawidowicz noted that Romanian army units collaborating with Einsatzgruppe D in southern Russia "dismayed the Germans with their passion for killing and their disregard for disposal of the corpses." By late 1942, almost two-thirds of the at least 200,000 Jews Romania had deported to Transnistria had died from epidemic disease or starvation.[54]

Emigrating to the United States after eleven years in Paris, Eliade developed a highly successful professional career as a professor of comparative religion. The *New York Times* Sunday book review in 1981 called Eliade a "Renaissance man" and "one of the greatest scholars of religion in our times."[55] Had Eliade returned to Romania after the war, he would have been tried for collaborating with Antonescu's fascist regime, toppled in August 1944, immediately prior to that nation's surrender to the Allies.[56] But his academic career flourished in the United States. In December 1955, Eliade was appointed Haskell Lecturer and visiting professor at the University of Chicago for the academic year 1956–57. The university paid the entire cost of his travel from Paris to Chicago. The next year Eliade became a permanent professor at the University of Chicago and chair of the Department of the History of Religion of the Federated Theological faculty, which included the Divinity School. According to the Washington *Post*, Eliade's visiting lectures so impressed the University of Chicago administration that it "created a department for him to direct."[57]

When the University of Chicago administration learned that it had brought Eliade and his wife to the United States on a visa that stipulated that he leave the country after its expiration for at least two years before reentering, it went to great lengths to persuade the federal government to waive that requirement. It prevailed on University of Chicago trustee James H. Douglas, then assistant secretary of defense in the Eisenhower administration, to have the government declare Eliade's work at the Divinity School "indispensable to the security and welfare of the United States." The Defense Department had a special waiver prepared for the State Department that on May 1, 1961, permitted Eliade and his wife to remain in this country indefinitely.[58]

The University of Chicago expressed the deepest pride in having Eliade on its faculty. In 1963 it made him the Sewell L. Avery Distinguished Service Professor at the Divinity School. He taught a joint seminar with Paul Tillich on theology and the history of religion for two years.[59] The

administration waived the mandatory retirement age of sixty-five for
Eliade and allowed him to teach for many more years. His department,
in petitioning the provost for the extensions, noted that "[o]ther schools
are already soliciting Professor Eliade in anticipation of his retirement
from the University of Chicago."[60] Eliade taught at the Divinity School
until 1983, when he was seventy-six. In 1981, University of Chicago
president Hanna Holborn Gray wrote to Eliade to congratulate him on
the publication of the first volume of his autobiography. She declared:
"You have had a fascinating life, and I'm delighted that you've put it down
to inform and instruct all of us. It's a wonderful story." She concluded:
"The Divinity School and the entire University are honored to have you
among us."[61]

In the second volume of his autobiography, begun at the University of Chicago in 1963, Eliade remained favorable to the Legion of
the Archangel Michael, describing it as "the only Romanian political
movement [in 1938] which took seriously Christianity and the church."
He portrayed the Legion as the victim of King Carol II's brutality and
continued to justify his involvement in it during the 1930s, explaining,
"I could not conceive of dissociating myself from my generation in the
midst of its oppression, when people were being prosecuted and persecuted unjustly."[62]

In 1972, Eliade visited the dying Vasile Posteuca in Chicago's Columbus Hospital, having maintained contact with the prominent Iron Guard
activist since his arrival at the University of Chicago.[63] Active in the
Iron Guard when it wielded power in Romania in 1940–41, Posteuca
had assumed a position in the National (Phantom) Government that its
leader Horia Sima established in Vienna after Romania's capitulation to
the Allies in August 1944.[64] In 1955, the FBI had evidence that Posteuca,
who immigrated to Canada after World War II, had assumed leadership
of that country's Iron Guard exiles.[65] The exiled Iron Guardists disseminated antisemitic propaganda, including the "theory that the U.S.A. is led
and controlled by Jews and Freemasonry." Posteuca was a professor of
language arts at Mankato State University in Minnesota from 1966 until
1972.[66]

In 1985, a year before his death, the University of Chicago paid tribute
to Eliade by establishing an endowed chair in his name in the history of
religions. It was the first time that the Divinity School had named an
endowed chair in honor of a faculty member. Divinity School dean Jerald
C. Brauer wrote that "[f]or almost thirty years Mircea Eliade has brought
honor and distinction both to the University and to its Divinity School."[67]

Eliade's death elicited glowing tributes from the University of Chicago. At a memorial service following Eliade's death in 1986, University of Chicago religion professor Martin E. Marty, in a eulogy entitled "That Nice Man," declared that those who had gathered to toast him "agreed that he was the only true genius we had known."[68] In a letter of condolence to Eliade's widow, President Gray wrote that "Mircea was truly a great figure in the history of our University." She praised Eliade for promoting "an understanding of mankind's deepest yearnings and cultural differences and relationships." President Gray concluded: "His was a full life and his presence will remain among us as long [as] our University endures, an example to those of us who knew him and those of us who learned from him."[69]

Several other American universities bestowed honorary degrees on Eliade. Loyola University of Chicago (1970), Oberlin College (1972), and George Washington University (1985) presented him with honorary Doctor of Humane Letters degrees, and Ripon College gave him a Doctor of Sacred Theology degree.[70] Canada's University of Windsor gave Eliade the Christian Culture gold medal for 1968, presented each year "to an outstanding lay exponent of Christian ideals."[71] In 1966, President Kingman Brewster Jr. of Yale University, as he bestowed an honorary Doctor of Humane Letters degree on Eliade, proclaimed: "You belong to the world.... [Y]ou have helped to find a human language for eternal truth."[72]

Yale in 1964 had invited Eliade to address a university-wide audience, under the sponsorship of its prestigious Woodward Lectureship. The university's Department of Religious Studies, awaiting his acceptance "with keen anticipation," informed him that its faculty was "eager to . . . solicit your advice about our own program in the History of Religions."[73]

Mircea Eliade's obituaries did not mention his Iron Guard past, but Saul Bellow made a point of raising the issue in his novel *Ravelstein*, published in 2000. Bellow clearly based the character Radu Grielescu, a scholar of religion and myth, on Eliade. The novel's principal character, Abe Ravelstein, a professor at a Midwestern university modeled on the University of Chicago, tells the narrator that Grielescu was "an Iron Guardist connected with the Romanian prewar fascist government. . . . a follower of Nae Ionescu," who became "something of a cultural big shot in London" and then "in Lisbon under the Salazar dictatorship." Ravelstein continues: "Grielescu is making use of you. In the old country he was a fascist. He needs to live that down. The man was a Hitlerite."

The narrator responds, "Come, now...."

"Has he ever denied that he belonged to the Iron Guard?"

"It's never come up."

"You haven't brought it up. Do you have any memory of the massacre in Bucharest when they hung people alive on meat hooks in the slaughterhouse and butchered them – skinned them alive?"

Grielescu's past was forgotten. But Ravelstein notes that "The record...shows what [Grielescu] wrote about the Jew-syphilis that infected the high civilization of the Balkans," and he urges the narrator to "[j]ust give a thought now and then to those people on the meat hooks."[74]

Notes

1. Germany Reverts to the Dark Ages: Nazi Clarity and Grassroots American Protest, 1933–1934

1. *Jewish Advocate*, March 7, 1933.
2. *New York Times*, March 13, 1933.
3. Ibid., March 20, 1933.
4. Manchester *Guardian*, March 10, 1933.
5. *New York Times*, March 21, 1933.
6. Ibid., March 20, 1933.
7. *Jewish Chronicle* [London], May 19, 1933.
8. Manchester *Guardian*, March 25, 1933. American journalists reporting from Germany "who understood the true nature of Nazism and its fanatical hatred of Jews" included H. R. Knickerbocker of the New York *Evening Post*, Edgar Ansel Mowrer of the Chicago *Daily News*, Sigrid Schultz of the Chicago *Tribune*, Otto Tolischus of the *New York Times*, Ralph Barnes of the New York *Herald Tribune*, Pierre van Paassen of the New York *World*, and William Shirer of CBS radio. Deborah Lipstadt, *Beyond Belief: The American Press and the Coming of the Holocaust, 1933–1945* (New York: Free Press, 1986), 28. The Manchester *Guardian* from Britain provided extensive coverage of Nazi atrocities.
9. Manchester *Guardian*, March 27 and April 4, 1933.
10. Ibid., April 8, 1933.
11. New York *Evening Post*, April 1, 1933.
12. John Haynes Holmes to H. R. Knickerbocker, April 6, 1933, box 1, H. R. Knickerbocker Papers, Columbia University Rare Book and Manuscript Library [hereafter CURBML], Butler Library, New York, N.Y.
13. New York *Evening Post*, April 1, 1933, and Manchester *Guardian*, April 1, 1933.
14. Richard Breitman, Barbara McDonald Stewart, and Severin Hochberg, eds., *Advocate for the Doomed: The Diaries and Papers of James G. McDonald, 1932–1935* (Bloomington: Indiana University Press, 2007), 33.

15. *New York Times*, April 2, 1933.
16. Richard J. Evans, *The Third Reich in Power* (New York: Penguin, 2005), 14–15.
17. Martha Dodd, *Through Embassy Eyes* (New York: Harcourt, Brace, 1939), 294–97.
18. *New York Times*, April 24, 1933.
19. Ibid., May 12, 1933.
20. Ibid., May 8 and September 23, 1933.
21. Ibid., March 16, 1933; Manchester *Guardian*, April 1 and 12, 1933.
22. Manchester *Guardian*, April 12, 1933.
23. Breitman, Stewart, and Hochberg, eds., *Advocate for the Doomed*, 30, 38.
24. Ibid., 48, 65.
25. Manchester *Guardian*, May 17, 1933.
26. *New York Times*, September 22, 1933.
27. Ibid.
28. Ibid., June 14, 1933; Ismar Elbogen, *A Century of Jewish Life* (Philadelphia: Jewish Publication Society of America, 1944), 645.
29. *New York Times*, June 19, 1933.
30. Gulie Ne'eman Arad, *America, Its Jews, and the Rise of Nazism* (Bloomington: Indiana University Press, 2000), 111, 113.
31. Boston *Herald*, October 9, 1933.
32. *New York Times*, September 10, 1933.
33. Ibid., March 28 and April 6, 1933.
34. Ibid., March 17, April 2, and November 21, 1933; Fritz Stern, *Einstein's German World* (Princeton, N.J.: Princeton University Press, 1999), 153–54; John Stachel, "Albert Einstein" in Stephen H. Norwood and Eunice G. Pollack, eds., *Encyclopedia of American Jewish History* (Santa Barbara, Calif.: ABC-CLIO, 2008), vol. 2, 744.
35. Stachel, "Einstein" in Norwood and Pollack, eds., *Encyclopedia of American Jewish History*, vol. 2, 744; Jamie Sayen, *Einstein in America: The Scientist's Conscience in the Age of Hitler and Hiroshima* (New York: Crown Publishers, 1985), 10.
36. Sayen, *Einstein in America*, 7, 57–59, 61; *New York Times*, June 8, 1930, and October 6, 1940.
37. *New York Times*, October 27, 28, and 30 and November 2, 1933; Washington *Post*, October 30, 1933.
38. *New York Times*, October 28 and 30, November 2, 3, and 6, 1933; Washington *Post*, October 30, 1933; London *Times*, October 27, 1933.
39. *New York Times*, December 24, 1933.
40. Ibid.
41. Boston *Herald*, October 9, 1933.
42. Pierre van Paassen, "Silence Is Criminal," *Opinion*, November 1933, 8–9.
43. Dorothy Thompson, "Germany Is a Prison," *Opinion*, March 1934, 16; New York *Evening Post*, May 6, 1933.
44. Pierre van Paassen and James Waterman Wise, eds., *Nazism: An Assault on Civilization* (New York: Harrison Smith & Robert Haas, 1934), 310.

45. Robert Dell, *Germany Unmasked* (London: Martin Hopkinson, 1934), 13.
46. Los Angeles *Times*, April 27, 1934; London *Times*, May 2, 10, and 11, 1934.
47. London *Times*, May 10, 1934.
48. Ibid., May 11, 1934.
49. London *Times*, May 11, 1934; *New York Times*, May 12, 1934.
50. "Report from Nuremberg," Easter 1934, folder H2, James G. McDonald Papers, Herbert Lehman Suite, CURBML.
51. *New York Times*, May 20, 1934.
52. London *Times*, May 22, 1934; *New York Times*, May 29, 1934.
53. *New York Times*, March 20, 1933.
54. Boston *Herald*, March 22, 1933.
55. New York *Evening Post*, March 22, 1933.
56. *New York Times*, March 24, 1933.
57. Boston *Herald*, March 27, 1933.
58. *Hitlerism and the American Jewish Congress: A Confidential Report of Activities* (New York: American Jewish Congress, 1934), 2–3, container 43, William E. Dodd Papers, Library of Congress [hereafter LC], Washington, D.C.; *Christian Science Monitor*, March 28, 1933; *New York Times*, March 28, 1933; Chicago *Tribune*, March 28, 1933.
59. *New York Times*, March 28, 1933.
60. New York *Evening Post*, March 28, 1933.
61. *New York Times*, March 29 and 30, 1933.
62. Baltimore *Sun*, March 31, 1933.
63. Edgar E. Siskin to President James Rowland Angell, March 24, 1933, and James Rowland Angell to Rabbi Edgar E. Siskin, March 25, 1933, box 116, President's Office: James Rowland Angell Papers, Sterling Library, Yale University, New Haven, Conn.
64. *Tech*, March 31, 1933; Boston *Herald*, March 31, 1933.
65. Boston *Herald*, April 4, 1933; *Jewish Advocate*, April 4, 1933.
66. Boston *Herald*, April 5, 1933; Boston *Globe*, April 7, 1933.
67. Boston *Globe*, April 6, 1933.
68. New York *Evening Post*, April 15, 1933.
69. Ibid., April 15, 1933.
70. *New York Times*, May 8, 15, and 16, 1933; Richard A. Hawkins, "Hitler's Bitterest Foe: Samuel Untermyer and the Boycott of Nazi Germany, 1933–1938," *American Jewish History* 93 (March 2007): 23, 26.
71. Non-Sectarian Anti-Nazi League to Champion Human Rights, "Visit Germany This Year and See," n.d., Addenda I, box 108, Robert Maynard Hutchins Papers, Special Collections Research Center [hereafter SCRC], Regenstein Library [hereafter RL], University of Chicago [hereafter UC], Chicago, Ill.
72. Hawkins, "Hitler's Bitterest Foe," 41; *New York Times*, March 30, April 7, and July 14, 1934.
73. G. E. Harriman, "Anti-Nazi Boycott Circular Letter," 1933 in Robert H. Abzug, ed., *America Views the Holocaust, 1933–1945: A Brief Documentary History* (Boston: Bedford/St. Martin's, 1999), 34.
74. *New York Times*, May 16, 1933.

75. Ibid., May 13, 1933; Leo F. Wormser to Hon. William E. Dodd, April 27, 1934, container 45, Dodd Papers, LC.
76. *New York Times*, July 7, 1934; Chicago *Tribune*, August 29, 1937.
77. *Harvard Crimson*, May 22, 1935.
78. *Daily Maroon*, March 12, 1936. For a similar advertisement, see *Yale Daily News*, April 23, 1938.
79. *Hitlerism and the American Jewish Congress*, 3, container 43, Dodd Papers, LC; *New York Times*, May 10–11, 1933; New York *Evening Post*, May 10, 1933; "Items of Interest," *The Jewish Veteran*, 22, May 1933, Julius Klein Archives of the National Museum of American Jewish Military History, Washington, D.C.
80. Chicago *Tribune*, May 11, 1933; Philadelphia *Inquirer*, May 11, 1933.
81. Richard E. Gutstadt, circular letter, June 8, 1933, reel 35, Franz Boas Papers, microfilm edition, LC.
82. New York *Evening Post*, March 24, 1933; *New York Times*, June 6 and 8, 1933; "American Hebrew Medal to Toscanini," *American Hebrew*, February 4, 1938, 5, 24.
83. "Hail Toscanini!," *American Hebrew*, August 7, 1936, n.p.; "Toscanini's Artistic Integrity Calls Attention to Nazi 'Gleichschaltung,'" *American Hebrew*, January 8, 1937, 746; "American Hebrew Medal," 5, 24.
84. *New York Times*, June 11, 1933.
85. Everett R. Clinchy to President Marion Edwards Park, and attached untitled statement, June 8, 1933, Marion Edwards Park Papers, Bryn Mawr College Archives, Bryn Mawr, Pa.; *New York Times*, July 5, 1933.
86. Chicago *Tribune*, July 2 and 4, 1933; *New York Times*, July 2 and September 10 and 11, 1933.
87. Chicago *Tribune*, July 2, 4, and 6, 1933; *New York Times*, September 10, 1933.
88. *New York Times*, September 11, 14, and 16 and October 4, 17, and 19, 1933.
89. Philadelphia *Public Ledger*, February 20, 1934.
90. *New York Times*, March 6, 1934.
91. Ibid., September 2 and 8, 1934.
92. Ibid., July 21, 1933; London *Times*, July 21, 1933.
93. *New York Times*, August 14, 1933.
94. Chicago *Tribune*, August 12, 1933.
95. San Francisco *Chronicle*, September 28, 1933.
96. *New York Times*, October 14 and 22, 1933.
97. Ibid., December 14, 1933.
98. Boston *Evening Transcript*, November 23, 1933; Boston *Globe*, April 3, 1944.
99. *New York Times*, October 25, 1933.
100. Frank W. Buxton to Ambassador William E. Dodd, July 6, 1933, container 40, Dodd Papers, LC.
101. Boston *Herald*, November 27, 1933; Boston *Globe*, November 27, 1933; Boston *Post*, November 27, 1933.

102. Boston *Herald*, November 27, 1933; Boston *Globe*, November 27, 1933; Boston *Post*, November 27, 1933.
103. Boston *Herald*, November 27, 1933; Boston *Post*, November 27, 1933; Boston *Globe*, November 27, 1933; *New York Times*, November 27, 1933.
104. American Committee Against Fascist Oppression in Germany, "International Inquiry into Hitler Oppression," Addenda I, box 5, Hutchins Papers, SCRC, RL, UC; *New York Times*, July 3 and 4, 1934; Washington *Post*, July 3, 1934.
105. Lewis S. Feuer, "The Stages in the Social History of Jewish Professors in American Colleges and Universities," *American Jewish History* 71 (June 1982): 455, 462; Leonard Dinnerstein, *Anti-Semitism in America* (New York: Oxford University Press, 1994), 88.
106. R. M. Hutchins to Mr. [Alvin] Johnson, May 25, 1933, Addenda I, box 105, Hutchins Papers, SCRC, RL, UC; Chicago *Tribune*, May 28, 1933.
107. Peter M. Rutkoff and William B. Scott, *New School: A History of the New School for Social Research* (New York: Free Press, 1986), 84, 92; Claus-Dieter Krohn, *Intellectuals in Exile: Refugee Scholars and the New School for Social Research* (Amherst: University of Massachusetts Press, 1993), 62, 69; *New York Times*, May 13, 1933.
108. Alvin Johnson to President Hutchins, May 27, 1933, Addenda I, box 105, Hutchins Papers, SCRC, RL, UC.
109. *New York Times*, August 19, 1933.
110. Krohn, *Intellectuals in Exile*, 69, 71.
111. *New York Times*, September 2, 1933.
112. Dan A. Oren, *Joining the Club: A History of Jews and Yale* (New Haven, Conn.: Yale University Press, 1985), 125.
113. Statement by Isaiah Bowman concerning his correspondence with Alvin Johnson, n.d. Series 2, box 2.23, Isaiah Bowman Papers, Records of Office of the President [hereafter ROP], Milton S. Eisenhower Library, Johns Hopkins University [hereafter JHU], Baltimore, Md.
114. Alvin Johnson to President Isaiah Bowman, November 18, 1935, Bowman Papers, Series 2, box 2.23, ROP, JHU.
115. Marjorie Lamberti, "The Reception of Refugee Scholars from Nazi Germany in America: Philanthropy and Social Change in Higher Education," *Jewish Social Studies* 12 (Spring/Summer 2006): 164–66; Krohn, *Intellectuals in Exile*, 27–28. The EC's major donors were the New York Foundation, the Nathan Hofheimer Foundation, the American Jewish Joint Distribution Committee, Jewish philanthropist Felix Warburg, financier Henry Ittleson, and the family of Jewish philanthropist Julius Rosenwald. Lamberti, "Reception of Refugee Scholars," 167.
116. Lamberti, "Reception of Refugee Scholars," 167; Krohn, *Intellectuals in Exile*, 29; Rutkoff and Scott, *New School*, 94.
117. James M. Stifler to Alexander Brin, December 31, 1934, Addenda I, box 59, Hutchins Papers, SCRC, UC.
118. Stifler to Morton M. Berman, January 29, 1938, Addenda I, box 59, Hutchins Papers, SCRC, UC.

119. Oren, *Joining the Club*, 124.
120. Brooks Mather Kelley, *Yale: A History* (New Haven, Conn.: Yale University Press, 1974), 416.
121. Stephen Duggan to Felix Frankfurter, July 18, 1933, and Harlow Shapley to E. R. Murrow, August 7, 1933, box 113, Emergency Committee in Aid of Displaced Foreign Scholars Papers [hereafter ECADFS Papers], Manuscripts and Archives Division [hereafter MAD], New York Public Library [hereafter NYPL], New York, N.Y.; Morton Keller and Phyllis Keller, *Making Harvard Modern: The Rise of America's University* (New York: Oxford University Press, 2001), 153–54.
122. Breitman, Stewart, and Hochberg, eds., *Advocate for the Doomed*, 327.
123. Keller and Keller, *Making Harvard Modern*, 154; *New York Times*, January 30, 1934.
124. President Conant to E. R. Murrow, February 12, 1934, box 113, ECADFS Papers, MAD, NYPL.
125. James Waterman Wise, *Swastika: The Nazi Terror* (New York: Harrison Smith and Robert Haas, 1933), 114.

2. Legitimating Nazism: Harvard University and the Hitler Regime, 1933–1937

An earlier version of this chapter was published as Stephen H. Norwood, "Legitimating Nazism: Harvard University and the Hitler Regime, 1933–1937," *American Jewish History* 92 (June 2004): 189–223.

1. William M. Tuttle Jr., "American Higher Education and the Nazis: The Case of James B. Conant and Harvard University's 'Diplomatic Relations' with Germany," *American Studies* 20 (Spring 1979): 54, 61, 66; Morton Keller and Phyllis Keller, *Making Harvard Modern: The Rise of America's University* (New York: Oxford University Press, 2001), 49, 153–55. Claus-Dieter Krohn noted that the New School for Social Research, which hired many anti-fascist refugee scholars, served as an excuse for many American universities' "inaction," and that that was "especially true of Harvard." Claus-Dieter Krohn, *Intellectuals in Exile: Refugee Scholars and the New School for Social Research* (Amherst: University of Massachusetts Press, 1993), 76.
2. James G. Hershberg, *James B. Conant: Harvard to Hiroshima and the Making of the Nuclear Age* (New York: Alfred A. Knopf, 1993), 86.
3. Ibid., 96–97.
4. Washington *Post*, August 22, 1936; *New York Times*, December 20, 1937.
5. *New York Times*, June 17, 1922.
6. Hershberg, *James B. Conant*, 58; Marcia Graham Synnott, *The Half-Opened Door: Discrimination and Admissions at Harvard, Yale, and Princeton, 1900–1970* (Westport, Conn.: Greenwood Press, 1979), 202; Jerome Karabel, *The Chosen: The Hidden History of Admission and Exclusion at Harvard, Yale, and Princeton* (Boston: Houghton Mifflin, 2005), 168–73. Karabel notes that "[e]ven at the height of a war against a fanatically racist,

anti-Semitic enemy, it seemed that nothing – not even the reports of the extermination of European Jews already making their way into the newspapers –
could dislodge Harvard's policy of restricting Jewish enrollment." Karabel,
The Chosen, 180.

7. Harriet Zuckerman points to chemistry's "longstanding inhospitality to
Jews." Harvard chemistry professor Albert Sprague Coolidge testified to
a Massachusetts legislative committee in 1945 that his department did not
award scholarships to Jews because "there were no jobs for Jews in chemistry." Harriet Zuckerman, *Scientific Elite: Nobel Laureates in the United
States* (New York: Free Press, 1977), 76. Dan A. Oren, *Joining the Club: A
History of Jews and Yale* (New Haven, Conn.: Yale University Press, 1985),
357; Alan D. Beyerchen, *Scientists Under Hitler: Politics and the Physics
Community in the Third Reich* (New Haven, Conn.: Yale University Press,
1977), 49. Harvard's chemistry department had no "self-identified Jewish
professors" during Conant's presidency, which lasted until 1953. Keller and
Keller, *Making Harvard Modern*, 97.

8. E. K. Bolton to Dr. James B. Conant, September 8, 1933, and James B.
Conant to Dr. E. K. Bolton, September 13, 1933, box 31, James B. Conant
Presidential Papers [hereafter JBCPP], Harvard University Archives [hereafter
HUA], Pusey Library, Cambridge.

9. Obituary of Max Bergmann, *New York Times*, November 8, 1944.

10. Sir William J. Pope to President Conant, October 2, 1933, and Conant to
Pope, October 18, 1933, box 31, JBCPP, HUA. Fritz Haber had converted
to Christianity more than forty years before, in 1892. Fritz Stern, *Einstein's
German World* (Princeton, N.J.: Princeton University Press, 1999), 73.

11. *Jewish Advocate*, November 10 and 14, 1933.

12. *New York Times*, January 9, 1934; Washington *Post*, February 7, 1934;
"Speech of Senator Millard E. Tydings," March 7, 1934, Series II, box 2,
Millard E. Tydings Papers, Archives and Manuscripts Department, Horn-
bake Library, University of Maryland, College Park.

13. Tuttle, "American Higher Education," 66–67; *New York Times*, May 15,
October 14 and 22, 1933; *Jewish Advocate*, November 14, 1933.

14. *Harvard Crimson*, October 25, 1934; William L. Shirer, *The Rise and Fall
of the Third Reich* (New York: Simon & Schuster, 1960), 222–23; Karl
Dietrich Bracher, *The German Dictatorship* (New York: Praeger, 1970),
239. Shirer notes that at the 1957 Munich trial of individuals accused of
carrying out executions in the June 30 "Blood Purge" a figure of more
than a thousand slain was presented. Former Social Democratic Reichstag
deputy Gerhart Seger, who had escaped from the Oranienburg concentration
camp in December 1933 and lectured in the United States about conditions
inside Nazi Germany, charged in November 1934 that in excess of one
thousand had been slaughtered in the June 30 Blood Purge. Chicago *Tribune*,
November 22, 1934.

15. *New York Times*, March 7, 8, and 9, 1934; *Harvard Crimson*, October 11,
1934.

16. *Harvard Crimson*, March 11, 1936.

17. Boston *Herald*, May 12 and 13, 1934.

18. Ibid., May 12 and 13, 1934; Boston *Post*, May 12, 1934.
19. Boston *Herald*, May 12, 1934; *Jewish Advocate*, December 29, 1933.
20. Boston *Herald*, May 12, 1934. The Women's International League for Peace and Freedom also protested against the official celebration of the *Karlsruhe*'s visit. Boston *Evening Transcript*, May 15, 1934.
21. Boston *Herald*, May 12 and 13, 1934; Boston *Post*, May 17 and 20, 1934.
22. Ferris Greenslet to Felix Frankfurter, November 10, 1933, reel 102, Felix Frankfurter Papers, Library of Congress [hereafter LC], Washington, D.C.; Boston *Post*, May 17 and 19, 1934; *Harvard Crimson*, November 26, 1934, and April 28, 1936.
23. Boston *Evening Transcript*, May 15, 1934; *Harvard Crimson*, June 6, 1934; Boston *Herald*, May 18, 1934.
24. Boston *Post*, May 18, 1934; *Christian Science Monitor*, May 18, 1934; *Tech*, May 18, 1934.
25. Boston *Post*, May 18, 1934.
26. Boston *Post*, May 18, 1934; Boston *Globe*, May 18, 1934; Boston *Herald*, May 18, 1934; *Harvard Crimson*, May 18, 1934.
27. Boston *Post*, May 21, 1934; *Harvard Crimson*, May 21, 1934. Several of those arrested charged that the police had severely beaten them after booking them at the station. Boston *Post*, May 25, 1934; *Harvard Crimson*, May 22, 1934.
28. *Harvard Crimson*, May 24 and June 11, 1934, and May 8, 1936. The MIT student newspaper agreed that a demonstration "aimed... at the discomfort" of the *Karlsruhe*'s crew was "out of place." *Tech*, May 18, 1934. Dartmouth College hosted a contingent of *Karlsruhe* officers and cadets, who journeyed to the Hanover, New Hampshire, campus at the invitation of the German Department. *New York Times*, May 20, 1934.
29. Boston *Herald*, May 30, 1934; *Tech*, June 5, 1934; Alfred H. Hirsch to James B. Conant, November 13, 1934, box 32, JBCPP, HUA.
30. James A. Wechsler, *Revolt on the Campus* (Seattle: University of Washington Press, 1973 [1935]), 341; *Tech*, May 18, 1934.
31. Boston *Post*, May 18, 1934; *Harvard Crimson*, May 18 and 19, 1934. Boston College administrators invited the *Karlsruhe* crewmen to a track meet and baseball games on their campus. Boston *Post*, May 12, 1934.
32. *Jewish Advocate*, May 18, 1934; Boston *Post*, May 18, 1934; Boston *Globe*, May 18, 1934; obituaries of John Walz in *New York Times*, April 17, 1954, and *Harvard Crimson*, April 20, 1954.
33. Boston *Post*, May 17 and 20, 1934; Boston *Evening Transcript*, May 19, 1934.
34. Boston *Evening Transcript*, May 21, 1934; *Harvard Crimson*, May 22, 1934; Boston *Globe*, May 22, 1934.
35. *New York Times*, June 19, 1934.
36. Boston *Post*, May 23, 1934; New York *Post*, March 5, 1936.
37. Los Angeles *Times*, June 24, 1937, and April 11, 1940; *New York Times*, December 31, 1936, June 24, 1937, and April 13, 1940; Chicago *Tribune*, April 15, 1940; William L. Shirer, *Berlin Diary: The Journal of a Foreign Correspondent* (New York: Alfred A. Knopf, 1941), 315; "Ships

of the German Navy: *Karlsruhe* (Light Cruiser, 1929–1940)," Department of the Navy – Naval Historical Center, www.history.navy.mil/photos/sh-fornv/germany/gersh-k/karlsru3.htm.

38. Morton Keller and Phyllis Keller state that Harvard Treasurer Henry L. Shattuck, "a Brahmin of Brahmins," was the most influential member of the Harvard Corporation, the university's major governing board, during the 1930s, and that all of its members besides Conant himself "were part of or...had close ties to the Boston Brahmin elite." Keller and Keller, *Making Harvard Modern*, 18.

39. Gerhard L. Weinberg, *The Foreign Policy of Hitler's Germany: Diplomatic Revolution in Europe, 1933–1936* (Chicago: University of Chicago Press, 1970), 11; Erika Mann and Klaus Mann, *Escape to Life* (Boston: Houghton Mifflin, 1939), 119. Ron Rosenbaum notes that Hanfstaengl "may have been as close to [Hitler] as anyone in the 1920s." Ron Rosenbaum, *Explaining Hitler* (New York: HarperCollins, 1998), 125.

40. Bracher, *German Dictatorship*, 117; Peter Conradi, *Hitler's Piano Player: The Rise and Fall of Ernst Hanfstaengl, Confidant of Hitler, Ally of FDR* (New York: Carroll & Graf, 2004), 45, 63.

41. Conradi, *Hitler's Piano Player*, 44; *Harvard Crimson*, December 12, 1978; William E. Dodd and Martha Dodd, *Ambassador Dodd's Diary, 1933–1938* (New York: Harcourt, Brace, 1941), 360.

42. Richard Breitman, Barbara McDonald Stewart, and Severin Hochberg, eds., *Advocate for the Doomed: The Diaries and Papers of James G. McDonald, 1932–1935* (Bloomington: Indiana University Press, 2007), 27–28, 69; *New York Times*, April 22, 2004. Edgar Ansel Mowrer, Berlin correspondent for the *Chicago Daily News* and a non-Jew, recalled that Hanfstaengl tried to discredit his reports of antisemitic outrages in the early months of Nazi rule by accusing him of being a "secret Jew." Edgar Ansel Mowrer, *Triumph and Turmoil: A Personal History of Our Time* (New York: Weybright and Talley, 1968), 219. James G. McDonald noted in his diary on April 3, 1933, that Hanfstaengl insisted to him that both Mowrer and H. R. Knickerbocker of the New York *Evening Post*, another American journalist in Berlin critical of the Nazis, were Jewish. Breitman, Stewart, and Hochberg, eds., *Advocate for the Doomed*, 28.

43. *Harvard College 25th Anniversary Class Report, Class of 1909*, 277–78, HUA.

44. *New York Times*, September 11, 1933; February 4, March 29, and May 28, 1934; Conradi, *Hitler's Piano Player*, 135; Erika Mann, *School for Barbarians: Education Under the Nazis* (New York: Modern Age Books, 1938), 65; Boston *Evening Transcript*, March 30, 1934; *Jewish Advocate*, March 30, 1934. Because of the Jews' lack of familiarity with the Communist salute, the bent arm and clenched fist, the parade scene had to be rehearsed repeatedly. *New York Times*, September 11, 1933.

45. Conradi, *Hitler's Piano Player*, 144–45; *Harvard College 25th Anniversary Class Report, Class of 1909*, n.p., HUA; *Jewish Advocate*, April 6, 1934.

46. Boston *Evening Transcript*, March 30, 1934; Conradi, *Hitler's Piano Player*, 145. Halpern's protest deeply impressed Golda Meyerson [Meir], who

proposed that he be appointed secretary general of Hechalutz, "the world organization of Jewish youth for pioneering work in Palestine." Marie Syrkin, "Ben: A Personal Appreciation," in Frances Malino and Phyllis Cohen Albert, eds., *Essays in Modern Jewish History* (Rutherford, N.J.: Fairleigh Dickinson University Press, 1982), 10–11.

47. William Leland Holt to Dr. James B. Conant, March 30, 1934, box 32, JBCPP, HUA.

48. Secretary to Dr. William L. Holt, April 3, 1934, box 32, JBCPP, HUA; Boston *Post*, June 12, 1934.

49. *Harvard Crimson*, May 8, 1934; Conradi, *Hitler's Piano Player*, 145; Boston *Evening Transcript*, March 30, 1934.

50. *Harvard Crimson*, June 13, 1934; *New York Times*, June 13, 1934; Conradi, *Hitler's Piano Player*, 149. Morton and Phyllis Keller describe the *Harvard Crimson* as "fashionably antisemitic in its recruitment until after" World War II. Keller and Keller, *Making Harvard Modern*, 300.

51. Baltimore *Sun*, June 18, 1934.

52. Conradi, *Hitler's Piano Player*, 145; New York *World-Telegram*, June 15 and 16, 1934.

53. Boston *Globe*, June 18 and 19, 1934; Boston *Herald*, June 18 and 19, 1934.

54. Boston *Globe*, June 19, 1934; Boston *Herald*, June 19, 1934; Boston *Post*, June 19, 1934; James B. Conant, *My Several Lives: Memoirs of a Social Inventor* (New York: Harper and Row, 1970), 141.

55. Boston *Globe*, June 20, 1934; Boston *Post*, June 19, 1934.

56. Boston *Post*, June 20, 1934.

57. Boston *Herald*, June 20, 1934; obituary of Frederick H. Prince, *New York Times*, February 3, 1953.

58. Boston *Evening Transcript*, June 18, 1934; Boston *Evening Globe*, June 18, 1934; *The Day*, June 24, 1934.

59. Boston *Globe*, June 19 and 20, 1934.

60. Ibid., June 19, 1934; Boston *Post*, June 19, 1934.

61. Boston *Herald*, June 22, 1934; Boston *Globe*, June 22, 1934; Boston *Post*, June 22, 1934.

62. *The Day*, June 24, 1934.

63. Boston *Herald*, June 22, 1934; Boston *Post*, June 22, 1934; Boston *Globe*, June 22, 1934. One demonstrator chained to the fence, Alice Stearns Ansara, narrowly escaped arrest. Merri Ansara, her daughter, noted, "In the family story the demonstration covered all of Harvard Square, with people perched even atop the Out of Town News Kiosk." When the police "ran to get blow-torches to cut [my mother] down ... her comrades rushed to her side with the key and bustled her away across the street to their apartment ... where they watched the continuing melee." Ansara emphasized that her "mother and father always considered this demonstration a success in helping to bring attention to ... the Nazi threat." Merri Ansara to Stephen Norwood, November 14, 2004.

64. Eugene D. Bronstein, et al., "An Open Letter to President Conant," n.d., James B. Conant to Professor H. M. Sheffer, November 7, 1934, and Mrs.

Joseph Dauber to Dr. James B. Conant, November 14, 1934, box 32, JBCPP, HUA; *Harvard Crimson*, October 24, 1934.

65. H. M. Sheffer to President James B. Conant, November 6, 1934, and James B. Conant to Professor H. M. Sheffer, November 7, 1934, box 32, JBCPP, HUA.

66. Mrs. Dauber to Conant, November 14, 1934, box 32, JBCPP, HUA; Conant, *My Several Lives*, 142. The seven demonstrators were released after they had served thirty-six days of their sentences. Boston *Evening Transcript*, November 28, 1934.

67. Washington *Post*, September 5, 1934.

68. *New York Times*, September 18 and October 4, 1934; Conant, *My Several Lives*, 141, 144.

69. H. B. Peirce to President James B. Conant, October 15, 1934, box 12, Translation from *Berliner Boersen Zeitung*, October 13, 1934, box 32, Dr. K. O. Bertling to President James B. Conant, October 9, 1934, box 32, and J. C. White to Hon. Secretary of State, October 12, 1934, box 32, JBCPP, HUA; *New York Times*, October 13, 1934; Chicago *Tribune*, October 13, 1934.

70. Translation from *Deutsches Nachrichtenbüro*, October 9, 1934, box 32, JBCPP, HUA.

71. Dallas *Morning News*, October 9, 1934. Roscoe Pound, Diary, Part II, entry for September 17, 1934, reel 41, Roscoe Pound Papers, microfilm edition, LC; Boston *Evening Transcript*, September 17, 1934.

72. "Memorandum of Conversation with Pound and President Conant regarding an invitation from Pound," September 14, 1934, reel 55, Felix Frankfurter Papers, LC.

73. Roscoe Pound, Diary, Part II, entry for July 11, 1934, reel 41, Roscoe Pound Papers, microfilm edition, LC.

74. *Paris Herald*, August 4, 1934, clipping, reel 55, Frankfurter Papers, LC.

75. "Memorandum of Conversation," reel 55, Frankfurter Papers, LC.

76. Ibid.

77. Ibid.; Invitation from the German Ambassador to Professor Felix Frankfurter, reel 55, Frankfurter Papers, LC.

78. *Harvard Crimson*, October 1 and 6, 1934. President Angell was delighted to welcome the Italian delegation to Yale and to "salute the young Fascisti," as he put it. James R. Angell to Mr. Lohmann, September 25, 1934, box 116, James R. Angell Presidential Papers [hereafter JRAPP], Sterling Library [hereafter SL], Yale University [hereafter YU], New Haven, Conn. After the welcome, the Italian students gave President Angell the Fascist salute and shouted, "Viva Mussolini!" *Yale Daily News*, October 11, 1934. The Yale administration invited the Fascist students to be its guests at the Yale-Columbia football game, and to parade in their college uniforms into and around the stadium, giving the Fascist salute. The Yale band serenaded the Italian Fascist students with "a tumultuous rendition of the Fascisti anthem *Giovinezza*." C. Lohmann to Mr. President, September 15, 1934, and David L. Clendenin to Dr. James R. Angell, October 8, 1934, box 116, JRAPP, SL, YU; *Yale Daily News*, October 6, 1934; *New Haven Evening Register*, October 7, 1934.

79. *Harvard Crimson*, October 1, 1934; Boston *Herald*, October 6, 1934.

80. *Harvard Crimson*, October 1 and 3, 1934; *Tech*, October 5, 1934.

81. Boston *Post*, March 18, 1935; *Harvard Crimson*, March 19, 1935. When Harvard built the chapel in 1931, it had not included the names of its alumni killed fighting for Germany on a plaque honoring the university's war dead. The *Harvard Crimson* led a campaign to add the names of the Germans to the plaque. As a compromise, the university placed a separate tablet for the German soldiers in the chapel. There was no such controversy after World War II. The name of the Harvard Divinity student killed fighting in the Nazi army was included on the plaque honoring Harvard men slain during World War II. It remains there today. *Harvard Crimson*, November 23, 1951, and November 6, 2003.

82. *Harvard Crimson*, May 1, 1935.

83. Boston *Globe*, May 1, 1936; Stephen Duggan to Professor Walter F. Willcox, September 24, 1937, box 118, Records of the Office of the President [hereafter ROP], Milton S. Eisenhower Library [hereafter MSEL], Johns Hopkins University [hereafter JHU], Baltimore.

84. *New York Times*, April 25, 1936, and August 27, 1937; "Nazis: Exchange Students End Training for Foreign Service," *Newsweek*, September 6, 1937, clipping in box 118, ROP, MSEL, JHU.

85. Duggan to Willcox, September 24, 1937, box 118, ROP, MSEL, JHU.

86. *New York Times*, July 24, 1935; Weinberg, *Foreign Policy of Hitler's Germany*, 239–40, 253–61.

87. Stephen H. Stackpole to Walter M. Hinkle, April 6, 1936, box 59, JBCPP, HUA; James R. Angell to James E. G. Fravell, March 7, 1936, JRAPP, box 100, SL, YU.

88. Nicholas Murray Butler to President James R. Angell, April 9, 1936, box 100, JRAPP, SL; Keller and Keller, *Making Harvard Modern*, 106, 156.

89. Steven P. Remy, *The Heidelberg Myth: The Nazification and Denazification of a German University* (Cambridge, Mass.: Harvard University Press, 2002), 1, 3; Max Weinreich, *Hitler's Professors: The Part of Scholarship in Germany's Crimes Against the Jewish People* (New Haven, Conn.: Yale University Press, 1999 [1946]), 9.

90. Michael Stephen Steinberg, *Sabers and Brown Shirts: The German Students' Path to National Socialism, 1918–1935* (Chicago: University of Chicago Press, 1977), 138–40; *New York Times*, May 11 and 19, 1933.

91. Beyerchen, *Scientists Under Hitler*, 15; Saul Friedländer, *Nazi Germany and the Jews*, vol. 1: *The Years of Persecution, 1933–1939* (New York: Harper-Collins, 1997), 30; *New York Times*, April 26 and October 8, 1933, and February 11, 1934; Memorandum on Official Discrimination Against Jews in Germany, box 153, Emergency Committee in Aid of Displaced Foreign Scholars Papers [hereafter ECADFS Papers], Manuscripts and Archives Division [hereafter MAD], New York Public Library [hereafter NYPL].

92. Remy, *Heidelberg Myth*, 15; Charles Singer to President Conant, May 27, 1936, box 59, JBCPP, HUA. After the U.S. army occupied Heidelberg in 1945 "American investigators dismissed 70 percent of the faculty [of the university] for having Nazi ties, and kept a close watch on those who remained there."

Victor Zarnowitz, *Fleeing the Nazis, Surviving the Gulag, and Arriving in the Free World: My Life and Times* (Westport, Conn.: Praeger, 2008), 91–92.

93. Friedländer, *Nazi Germany and the Jews*, vol. 1, 51; Singer to Conant, March 24, 1936, box 59, JBCPP, HUA; Charles Grant Robertson, "University of Heidelberg – Dismissal of Staff" in *Heidelberg and the Universities of America* (New York: Viking Press, 1936), 23.

94. Remy, *Heidelberg Myth*, 50; *New York Times*, June 28, 1936; Tuttle, "American Higher Education," 61.

95. *New York Times*, January 20, 1935; Weinreich, *Hitler's Professors*, 67–68; Remy, *Heidelberg Myth*, 25, 34; L. G. Montefiore, "The Spirit of the German Universities" (London, n.d.), 5, enclosure in Singer to Conant, May 27, 1936, box 59, JBCPP, HUA.

96. Weinreich, *Hitler's Professors*, 17, 38–39; Remy, *Heidelberg Myth*, 25, 34; Richard J. Evans, *The Third Reich in Power* (New York: Penguin, 2005), 293, 315.

97. "Philipp-Lenard-Institut at Heidelberg," in *Heidelberg and the Universities of America*, 47; Weinreich, *Hitler's Professors*, 11; *Tech*, March 3, 1936.

98. "Philipp-Lenard-Institut at Heidelberg," in *Heidelberg and the Universities of America*, 48–49; Montefiore, "Spirit," enclosure in Singer to Conant, May 27, 1936.

99. Montefiore, "Spirit,"enclosure in Singer to Conant, May 27, 1936.

100. Correspondent, "Heidelberg, Spinoza and Academic Freedom," in *Heidelberg and the Universities of America*, 52.

101. Montefiore, "Spirit," enclosure in Singer to Conant, May 27, 1936.

102. Remy, *Heidelberg Myth*, 45, 72.

103. *New York Times*, February 23 and 28 and March 3, 1936; "U.S. Colleges Arouse Protests by Accepting Nazi Bid," *The Anti-Nazi Economic Bulletin*, March 1936, box 114, ECADFS Papers, MAD, NYPL; M. Gardiner, "Heidelberg, Spinoza, and Academic Freedom," in *Heidelberg and the Universities of America*, 53.

104. Singer to Conant, March 24, 1936. Amsterdam University almost immediately afterward announced it would not participate in the anniversary ceremony. The Universities of Stockholm and Oslo also refused their invitations. *New York Times* clipping, March 25, 1936, in box 114, ECADFS Papers, NYPL; *Columbia Spectator*, March 24, 1936; Tuttle, "American Higher Education," 61. In Switzerland, the Basel canton government forbade students at Basel University from sending a delegation to Heidelberg. Manchester *Guardian*, June 8, 1936.

105. Ronald D. Hoffman and Arnold Hoffman to Dr. James B. Conant, March 3, 1936, box 59, JBCPP, HUA.

106. New York *World-Telegram*, February 26, 1936; *New York Times*, February 5, 1936.

107. Shirer, *Berlin Diary*, 46–47; Richard D. Mandell, *The Nazi Olympics* (Urbana: University of Illinois Press, 1987 [1971]), 104–05; *New Republic*, March 18, 1936, 152.

108. G. E. Harriman to Frank E. Robbins, March 12, 1936, box 134, Non-Sectarian Anti-Nazi League Papers [hereafter NSANL] Papers, Columbia University Rare Book and Manuscript Library [hereafter CURBML], New York.
109. James B. Conant, press release, March 3, 1936, box 59, JBCPP, HUA.
110. See, for example, Stephen H. Stackpole to Roger Baldwin, April 6, 1936, Stackpole to Hinkle, April 6, 1936, and Stackpole to Lewis Eldridge, April 6, 1936, box 59, JBCPP, HUA; *Harvard Crimson*, March 3, 1936. The *Yale Daily News* agreed with the *Harvard Crimson* in an editorial: "To refuse stiffly such a well-meant gesture of international friendship might easily place Yale in an indefensible position of bigoted hostility to a friendly nation." *Yale Daily News*, March 5, 1936.
111. Alvin Johnson to G. E. Harriman, March 9, 1936, box 134, NSANL Papers, CURBML.
112. *New York Times*, May 27, 1936, and April 1, 1949; Dr. Friedrich Bergius to Professor Dr. James Bryant Conant, October 23, 1936, box 96, JBCPP, HUA.
113. Charles Singer to President Conant, May 27, 1936, and Conant to Singer, June 23, 1936, box 59, JBCPP, HUA.
114. Nicholas Murray Butler to Hubert Park Beck, May 29, 1936, Central Files [hereafter CF], Columbia University Archives – Columbiana Library, Low Library [hereafter CUACL].
115. Tuttle, "American Higher Education," 64; Jamie Sayen, *Einstein in America: The Scientist's Conscience in the Age of Hitler and Hiroshima* (New York: Crown Publishers, 1985), 101–02.
116. John D. Lynch to President and Fellows, Harvard College, April 24, 1936, and Jerome D. Greene to Hon. John D. Lynch, April 28, 1936, box 70, JBCPP, HUA. In 1915, President Lowell had brushed aside Jewish objections when Harvard scheduled its entrance examinations on Yom Kippur. Complaints about Harvard's scheduling of important events on the Jewish High Holidays continued into the 1950s. Synnott, *Half-Opened Door*, 45–46.
117. Nicholas Murray Butler to President James R. Angell, April 9, 1936, Butler to Conant, April 24 and 28, and May 11 and 14, 1936; Conant to Butler, April 27, May 4, 7, and 12, 1936; "Proposed Form of Statement in re Heidelberg," box 59, JBCPP, HUA; "Suggested Revision of Proposed Form of Statement in re Heidelberg To be Revised if Thought Necessary About June 30," CF, CUACL. The congratulatory greeting that Columbia sent to the University of Heidelberg praised "the notable achievements of Bunsen in the field of chemistry, of Kirchhoff in physics, of Helmholtz in physiology . . . of Gervinus in literature, of Schlosser and Hausser in history, of Bluntschli in international law, of Rothe in theology, of Zeller and Fischer in philosophy." "Report of the President of Columbia University for the Year Ending June 30, 1936" in *Annual Report of the President and Treasurer to the Trustees with Accompanying Documents for the Year Ending June 30, 1936*, CUACL.

118. G. D. Birkhoff to James B. Conant, July 1, 1936, box 59, JBCPP, HUA; Arthur F. J. Remy, "A Report of the Celebration of the 550th Anniversary of Heidelberg University, June 27th to July 1st, 1936," CF, CUACL; *New York Times*, June 28 and 29, 1936; Keller and Keller, *Making Harvard Modern*, 65, 106, 238. Yale University was represented at Heidelberg by Dr. Hans Oertel, formerly dean of Yale Graduate School, who was then a professor at the University of Munich. James Rowland Angell to James Fravell, March 7, 1936, box 100, JRAPP, SL, YU.

119. Remy, "Report"; *New York Times*, June 29, 1936; Chicago *Tribune*, June 29, 1936; *Columbia Spectator*, April 29, 1936.

120. Remy, *Heidelberg Myth*, 58, 79; *New York Times*, June 30 and July 1 and 5, 1936.

121. James R. Angell to President James B. Conant, August 13, 1936; Conant to Angell, August 17, 1936, box 59, JBCPP, HUA.

122. Chicago *Tribune*, February 5, 1936.

123. *New York Times*, December 2, 1935.

124. Maxwell Steinhardt, letter to editor, *Harvard Alumni Bulletin*, September 27, 1935, 22; Chicago *Tribune*, November 6, 1935.

125. Mandell, *The Nazi Olympics*, 73.

126. *Harvard Crimson*, September 26 and November 26, 1935.

127. Ibid., October 24 and November 5, 1935.

128. Mandell, *The Nazi Olympics*, 73.

129. *Yale Daily News*, February 11 and 12, 1936.

130. *New York Times*, November 4 and 5, 1935.

131. *Daily Princetonian*, December 7, 1935.

132. Mandell, *The Nazi Olympics*, 280.

133. Stephen H. Stackpole to H. U. Brandenstein, April 21, 1937, box 83, JBCPP, HUA; *New York Times*, April 19, 1937; Beyerchen, *Scientists Under Hitler*, 15; Friedländer, *Nazi Germany and the Jews*, vol. 1, 50; "Renowned Scientist Against the Enslavement of the Spiritual Life of Fascist Germany," *Bulletin No. 6*, November 1933, box 153, ECADFS Papers, NYPL; "American Scholars and Göttingen," *New Republic*, April 28, 1937, 346.

134. Non-Sectarian Anti-Nazi League to Champion Human Rights, "American Universities Snub Hitler," press release, March 30, 1937, Addenda I, box 108, Robert M. Hutchins Papers, Special Collections Research Center, Regenstein Library, University of Chicago, Chicago, Ill.

135. Harlow Shapley to Conant, April 16, 1937, box 83, JBCPP, HUA.

136. Ernest L. Meyer, "As the Crow Flies," box 83, JBCPP, HUA; *New York Times*, April 19 and 20, 1937; Chicago *Tribune*, April 2, 1937. The University of Durham decided not to participate at the last moment, leaving Glasgow the only British participant. *New York Times*, June 26, 1937.

137. *New York Times*, May 4, 1937; *Tech*, April 23 and 30, 1937.

138. Arthur Held to James B. Conant, May 5, 1937, box 83, JBCPP, HUA; Boston *Evening Globe*, May 5, 1937; Boston *Globe*, May 8, 1937; Dallas *Morning News*, May 5, 1937. See also *The Day*, April 30, 1937.

139. Boston *Evening Transcript*, May 14, 1937; *Harvard Crimson*, May 8, 1937.

140. Jerome D. Greene to John D. Merrill, May 18, 1937, box 83, JBCPP, HUA.
141. Greene to James B. Conant, June 1, 1937, box 83, JBCPP, HUA.
142. Greene to Conant, May 24, 1937, box 83, JBCPP, HUA.
143. *New York Times*, June 26, 27, and 28, 1937. The American schools represented included MIT, Haverford College, Temple University, University of Idaho, Wittenberg College, and the University of Alabama. *New York Times*, June 26, 1937. Clara Evans, representing Temple University, was the first American delegate at the ceremonies to return the Nazi salute. "Germany: The Goettingen Celebration," *American Hebrew*, July 2, 1937, 22.
144. *New York Times*, June 27 and 29, 1937.
145. Conant, *My Several Lives*, 209, 214, 222. On May 31, 1940, a *Harvard Crimson* editorial declared that "sober analysis throws much doubt" on President Conant's comment that the United States could not "live at peace with a victorious Germany." It asserted that U.S. entry into the European conflict "offers nothing but disaster for us." *Harvard Crimson*, May 31, 1940. A Harvard senior, John F. Kennedy, took sharp issue with the *Crimson* in a letter to the editor. He asserted that Britain's failure to build up armaments might well prove disastrous and concluded: "Are we in America to let that lesson go unlearned?" *Harvard Crimson*, June 9, 1940.
146. *New York Times*, July 24, 1935.

3. Complicity and Conflict: Columbia University's Response to Fascism, 1933–1937

An earlier version of this chapter was published as Stephen H. Norwood, "Complicity and Conflict: Columbia University's Response to Fascism, 1933–1937," *Modern Judaism* 27 (October 2007): 253–83.

1. New York *Evening Post*, May 11, 1933; Chicago *Tribune*, May 11, 1933; *New York Times*, May 10 and 11, 1933; *Christian Science Monitor*, May 12, 1933; Richard J. Evans, *The Coming of the Third Reich* (New York: Penguin, 2003), 427, 429–30.
2. New York *Evening Post*, May 11, 1933; Evans, *Coming of the Third Reich*, 430–31.
3. *Columbia Spectator*, May 10, 1933; New York *Evening Post*, May 5, 1933.
4. *Columbia Spectator*, March 24 and 27 and April 21, 1933.
5. *New York Times*, November 20, 1933; *Columbia Spectator*, November 23 and 24, 1933.
6. *Columbia Spectator*, November 20, 1933; James A. Wechsler, *The Age of Suspicion* (New York: Random House, 1953), 54–55.
7. "Mr. Gerhart Seger Lectures," n.d., box 24, Papers of Non-Sectarian Anti-Nazi League, Columbia University Rare Book and Manuscript Library [hereafter CURBML], New York, N.Y.; *Columbia Spectator*, November 15 and 19, 1934; *New York Times*, October 31, 1934, and March 31, 1935.
8. *Columbia Spectator*, March 9, 1934.

9. *New York Times*, July 17, 1934, and March 20, 1935; San Francisco *Chronicle*, March 10, 1936.
10. Fritz Stern, *Five Germanys I Have Known* (New York: Farrar, Straus and Giroux, 2006), 162.
11. Robert A. McCaughey, *Stand, Columbia: A History of Columbia University in the City of New York, 1754–2004* (New York: Columbia University Press, 2003), 266; Upton Sinclair, *The Goose-Step* (Pasadena, Calif.: privately published, 1923), 356.
12. McCaughey, *Stand, Columbia*, 268; Michael Rosenthal, *Nicholas Miraculous: The Amazing Career of the Redoubtable Dr. Nicholas Murray Butler* (New York: Farrar, Straus and Giroux, 2006), 332–43; Jerome Karabel, *The Chosen: The Hidden History of Admission and Exclusion at Harvard, Yale, and Princeton* (Boston: Houghton Mifflin, 2005), 129–130; E. Digby Baltzell, *The Protestant Establishment: Aristocracy and Caste in America* (New York: Vintage Books, 1964), 211. In 1914, President Butler had proposed that Columbia give significant attention in evaluating students to their "character, personality, and general bearing," which he believed would put Jews at a disadvantage. Karabel, *The Chosen*, 584.
13. McCaughey, *Stand, Columbia*, 257; Karabel, *The Chosen*, 87.
14. Roger Chase, "Academic Napoleons No. III: Nicholas Murray Butler," *The Student Advocate*, April 1936, 20–21.
15. *New York Times*, May 8 and 23, 1933.
16. Ibid., July 27 and 28, 1933.
17. *New York Times*, July 16 and 17, 1934, February 8 and July 15, 1935, July 16, 1936, and July 16, 1937. Representative Dickstein reported that the Hamburg-American liner *New York*, for example, "had been organized as a floating unit of the Nazi party." *New York Times*, November 1, 1933.
18. *Columbia Spectator*, October 27, 1933.
19. *Barnard Bulletin*, January 15 and December 10, 1937.
20. Baltzell, *Protestant Establishment*, 211.
21. *Columbia Spectator*, May 18, 1933; *New York Times*, June 24, 1934, and May 19, 1935.
22. *Columbia Spectator*, January 10, 11, and 16, 1934.
23. Wechsler, *Age of Suspicion*, 54–55; *Barnard Bulletin*, November 14, 1933; *Columbia Spectator*, December 12, 1933.
24. *Columbia Spectator*, November 29, 1933.
25. Ibid., December 12, 1933.
26. Ruth Rubin, "I Heckled Luther," *Student Review*, January 1934, 8; New York *Herald Tribune*, December 13, 1933; *Columbia Spectator*, December 13, 1933.
27. Rubin, "I Heckled Luther," 8; New York *Evening Post*, December 13, 1933; *Columbia Spectator*, December 13, 1933.
28. Wechsler, *Age of Suspicion*, 55; *Columbia Spectator*, December 13 and 15, 1933.
29. *Columbia Spectator*, January 10 and 16, 1934; *New York Times*, December 13, 1933; New York *Herald Tribune*, December 13, 1933.

30. K[atherine] Perry to Robert M. Hutchins, January 25, 1934, and attached statement of American Committee Against Fascist Oppression in Germany, Addenda I, box 5, Robert M. Hutchins Papers, Special Collections Research Center, Regenstein Library, University of Chicago, Chicago, Ill.

31. George Klein to Stephen H. Norwood, November 10, 2006.

32. Klein to Norwood; *Columbia Spectator*, April 30 and May 2, 1934; *Barnard Bulletin*, May 15, 1934.

33. *Columbia Spectator*, April 27 and 30, May 4, and May 15, 1934.

34. William Bell Dinsmoor to President Nicholas Murray Butler, October 20, 1934, box 375, Central Files [hereafter CF], Columbia University Archives – Columbiana Library, Low Library [hereafter CUACL], Columbia University, New York, N.Y.

35. *Columbia Spectator*, May 18, 1934; "Dictated by the President," May 16, 1934, box 487, CF, CUACL; Klein to Norwood, November 10, 2006.

36. Columbia University Committee, "The Proposed Library for Louvain," and Corey Ford, "The Drama of Louvain," World War I Collection, CF, CUACL; Larry Zuckerman, *The Rape of Belgium: The Untold Story of World War I* (New York: New York University Press, 2004), 30; *New York Times*, October 2, 1919, and April 5, 1922.

37. "The Columbia Committee for Participation in the Restoration of the Library of the University of Louvain, Destroyed by the Germans in 1914," March 4, 1924, John Hassinger to Chairman Student Organization, n.d., World War I Collection, CF, CUACL; *New York Times*, April 5, 1922.

38. *Columbia Spectator*, October 6, 7, and 9, 1919; *New York Times*, October 8, 1919; Zuckerman, *Rape of Belgium*, 128.

39. Ford, "Drama of Louvain," and Carlos Contreras, "The Architecture and Symbolism of the Louvain Library," World War I Collection, CF, CUACL; *New York Times*, June 26, 1921.

40. "Library of Banned Books Inaugurated Here," *American Hebrew*, December 28, 1934, 139; London *Times*, March 27 and May 11, 1934; *New York Times*, March 27 and May 11, 1934. Heinrich Mann was president of the Paris library, and Lion Feuchtwanger, André Gide, and Romain Roland were honorary presidents.

41. "Library of Banned Books," *American Hebrew*, 139; *New York Times*, December 23, 1934.

42. Giuseppe Prezzolini to Philip M. Hayden, October 1, 1934, Prezzolini to Nicholas Murray Butler, September 20, 1933, and Butler to Prezzolini, September 26, 1933, box 357, and Prezzolini to President Butler, October 31, 1933, box 551, CF, CUACL. John Diggins states that the Italian department "functioned as something of an overseas branch of Italy's Ministry of Culture and Propaganda." Diggins, *Mussolini and Fascism: The View from America* (Princeton, N.J.: Princeton University Press, 1972), 255.

43. Wechsler, *Age of Suspicion*, 16.

44. Rosenthal, *Nicholas Miraculous*, 381.

45. Nicholas Murray Butler to Joseph Paterno, January 3, 1938, box 551, CF, CUACL; *New York Times*, April 11, 1930, and March 15, 1934.

46. Michele Sarfatti, *The Jews in Mussolini's Italy: From Equality to Persecution* (Madison: University of Wisconsin Press, 2006), 43, 45–46, 48, 53, 65; *Columbia Spectator*, February 11, 1935.

47. Dino Bigongiari to President Nicholas Murray Butler, October 31, 1934, box 375, and Prezzolini to Butler, March 14, 1935, box 357, CF, CUACL; *New York Times*, March 21, 1923; Diggins, *Mussolini and Fascism*, 255.

48. Howard R. Marraro, *Nationalism in Italian Education* (New York: Italian Digest & News Service, 1927), ix, 94–96; William Leonard, "Italy's Second Embassy," *The Student Review*, December 1934, 14.

49. Special Investigator, "Fascism at Columbia University," *The Nation*, November 7, 1934, 531.

50. Gustavus T. Kirby to Dr. Nicholas Murray Butler, August 7, 1934, box 14, Peter M. Riccio Papers, CURBML.

51. Kirby to Butler, August 7, 1934; "Exchange Visit of Italian University Students to American Universities," September 26, 1934, box 14, Riccio Papers, CURBML; *New York Times*, September 26, 1934; Special Investigator, "Fascism at Columbia," 530.

52. *New York Times*, September 21, 1934.

53. "Unity Against Fascism," *The Student Outlook*, October 1934, 4.

54. Clippings from Johnstown, Pa., *Evening Tribune*, October 13, 1933; New York *American*, October 21, 1934; and *Il Progresso Italo-Americano*, October 25, 1934, in box 10, Riccio Papers; *Columbia Spectator*, October 24, 1934.

55. Special Investigator, "Fascism at Columbia," 530–31; *Columbia Spectator*, November 1 and 8, 1934.

56. "President Butler and Fascism," *The Nation*, November 14, 1934, 550; Butler to Prezzolini, March 22, 1935, box 357, CF, CUACL. Butler also told Bigongiari not to pay any attention to the charges. Butler to Bigongiari, April 15, 1935, box 375, CF, CUACL.

57. *New York Times*, April 13, 1934.

58. "The Case of the Casa," n.d., box 10, Riccio Papers; *New York Times*, October 13, 1931.

59. "Correspondence: Salvemini and the Casa," *The Nation*, January 30, 1935, 129–30; "The Case of the Casa." Gaetano Salvemini was professor of history at the Universities of Messina, Pisa, and Florence from 1901 to 1925. Fleeing Fascist Italy in 1925, he taught at several British and American universities from 1925 until 1933. In 1933, Harvard appointed him to give the Lauro De Bosis lectures on the history of Italian civilization, a position established under the provisions of an anonymous gift to honor a recently deceased young anti-fascist Italian poet who had taught at Harvard in 1926. Salvemini was renewed in this low-paying lectureship many times, holding it until after World War II. H. Stuart Hughes noted that Salvemini's courses at Harvard "avoided the contemporary topics that might have tempted him into controversy." Boston *Herald*, December 20, 1933; *Harvard Crimson*, September 23, 1935; H. Stuart Hughes, *The Sea Change: The Migration of Social Thought, 1930–1965* (New York: McGraw-Hill, 1975), 94–95.

60. Prezzolini to Butler, March 14, 1935, box 357, CF, CUACL; Rosenthal, *Nicholas Miraculous*, 388.
61. *Columbia Spectator*, November 1–2, 5, 8, 12, 14–15, 1934.
62. Ibid., February 11–12, 1935; *Nation*, February 27, 1935, 234.
63. Prezzolini to Butler, March 14, 1935.
64. *New York Times*, July 16 and September 11, 1935.
65. Frank D. Fackenthal, "Memorandum for Mr. Coykendall, Mr. Douglas, and Dean McBain," March 4, 1936, and "Memorandum for the President," March 7, 1936, box 481, CF, CUACL.
66. F. D. F., "Memorandum for the President," March 7, 1936, box 481, CF, CUACL.
67. Ibid.; F. D. F., "Memorandum for the President," March 26, 1936, CF, CUACL.
68. *Columbia Spectator*, March 27, 30, and 31 and May 5, 1936; *Harvard Crimson*, March 3, 1936; *Yale Daily News*, March 5, 1936.
69. *Columbia Spectator*, March 30 and 31 and April 29, 1936.
70. Ibid., April 29, 1936.
71. *New York Times*, December 2 and 7, 1933.
72. *Columbia Spectator*, May 5 and 8, 1936.
73. Ibid., May 11 and 12, 1936.
74. Ibid., May 12 and 13, 1936.
75. Nicholas Murray Butler to Hubert Park Beck, May 29, 1936, box 549, CF, CUACL.
76. *New York Times*, June 28, 1936; Arthur F. J. Remy, "A Report of the Celebration of the 550th Anniversary of Heidelberg University, June 27th to July 1st, 1936," box 549, CF, CUACL.
77. *New York Times*, June 29, 1936; Arthur F. J. Remy, "A Report."
78. *Columbia Spectator*, October 7, 1936.
79. Arthur F. J. Remy, "A Report."
80. *New York Times*, July 5, 1936.
81. Supreme Court: NY County. Robert Burke, Plaintiff, against the Trustees of Columbia University in the City of New York, Defendant. Answer.... ([submitted by] John Godfrey Saxe, attorney for the defendant), box 668, CF, CUACL.
82. *Columbia Spectator*, May 4, 1937.
83. Ibid.
84. New York *World-Telegram*, March 10, 1936; James A. Wechsler, "The Education of Bob Burke," *The Student Advocate*, October–November 1936, 12.
85. Wechsler, "Education of Bob Burke," 12.
86. Nicholas Murray Butler to John Godfrey Saxe, September 16, 1936, box 668, CF, CUACL.
87. Washington *Post*, June 30, 1936; James T. Farrell, "An 'International Showcase,'" *The Student Advocate*, December 1936, 23.
88. Butler to Saxe, September 16, 1936, and J. G. S., Memorandum for Committee on Legal Affairs, March 10, 1937. Subject: Robert Burke v. University, box 668, CF, CUACL. Nancy Wechsler quoted in *Jewish Press*, April 4, 2008 [Brooklyn, N.Y.].

89. Robert Cohen, *When the Old Left Was Young* (New York: Oxford University Press, 1993), 104.
90. *New York Times*, May 12, 1935.
91. Cohen, *When the Old Left Was Young*, 105, 107.
92. *Washington Square College Bulletin*, October 5 and 8, 1936; *New York Times*, October 6, 8, 9, 13, and 21, 1936; Washington *Post*, October 22, 1936.
93. *Columbia Spectator*, May 5 and October 5, 1937.
94. *New York Times*, February 22 and 26, March 2, 1938; *Columbia Spectator*, February 18, 21, 24, and 25, March 1, 2, and 4, 1938.
95. *Columbia Spectator*, March 15, 1937.
96. "Centenary of the University of Göttingen," *Nature* 139 (April 24, 1937): 703; Franz Boas to President Nicholas Murray Butler, May 3, 1933, box 318, CF, CUACL.
97. *Columbia Spectator*, March 30, April 29 and 30, 1937.
98. Ibid., May 7 and October 5, 1937.
99. "Report of the President of Columbia University for the Year Ending June 30, 1937," 39–41, CF, CUACL.
100. *Columbia Spectator*, September 23, 1937; *New York Times*, September 23, 1937.
101. *Barnard Bulletin*, November 22, 1938; *New York Times*, November 19, 22, and 28, 1938; Los Angeles *Times*, November 23, 1938.
102. Murrow quoted by Marjorie Lamberti, "The Reception of Refugee Scholars from Nazi Germany in America: Philanthropy and Social Change in Higher Education," *Jewish Social Studies* 12 (Spring/Summer 2006): 167.

4. The Seven Sisters Colleges and the Third Reich: Promoting Fellowship Through Student Exchange

1. Toni Sender, *The Autobiography of a German Rebel* (New York: Vanguard Press, 1939); *New Leader*, January 12, 1935; Stephen H. Norwood, "Toni Sender" in Stephen H. Norwood and Eunice G. Pollack, eds., *Encyclopedia of American Jewish History* (Santa Barbara, Calif.: ABC-CLIO, 2008), vol. 1, 388–90.
2. Chicago *Tribune*, November 22, 1934; Los Angeles *Times*, December 22, 1934; and *Daily Californian*, January 31, 1935.
3. *New York Times*, September 11, 1935; Upton Sinclair, *The Goose-Step* (Pasadena, Calif.: privately published, 1923), 360.
4. *Wellesley College News*, January 27, 1938.
5. Grace M. Bacon, "German Department Report to President," June 1, 1938, Series B, folder 1, LD 7092.6, German Language and Literature Department [hereafter GLLD] Papers, Mount Holyoke College Archives [hereafter MHCA].
6. Elaine Kendall, *"Peculiar Institutions": An Informal History of the Seven Sisters Colleges* (New York: G. P. Putnam's Sons, 1976), 29; Henry Noble MacCracken, *The Hickory Limb* (New York: Charles Scribner's Sons, 1950), 43, 143; Arthur C. Cole, *A Hundred Years of Mount Holyoke College: The Evolution of an Educational Ideal* (New Haven, Conn.: Yale

University Press, 1940), 319–20; Margaret Farrand Thorp, *Neilson of Smith* (New York: Oxford University Press, 1956), 149; Liva Baker, *I'm Radcliffe! Fly Me!: The Seven Sisters and the Failure of Women's Education* (New York: Macmillan, 1976), 2, 6.

7. Rosalind Rosenberg, *Changing the Subject: How the Women of Columbia Shaped the Way We Think About Sex and Politics* (New York: Columbia University Press, 2004), 140. In 1947, Wellesley's president Mildred McAfee Horton and the college's board of trustees opposed a Massachusetts Fair Educational Practices Act that would have prohibited colleges and universities from requiring information on religion and race on application forms. Bruce Bliven, "For 'Nordics' Only," *New Republic*, December 8, 1947, 18. Bliven listed Bryn Mawr and Mount Holyoke as examples of "well known American colleges [that] have enrolled conspicuously small proportions of Jews."

8. Morton Keller and Phyllis Keller, *Making Harvard Modern: The Rise of America's University* (New York: Oxford University Press, 2001), 53; Marian Churchill White, *A History of Barnard College* (New York: Columbia University Press, 1954), 128; Alice Duer Miller and Susan Myers, *Barnard College: The First Fifty Years* (New York: Columbia University Press, 1939), 138–39; *New York Times*, January 13, 1935.

9. "The Junior Year Abroad," February 27, 1933, Foreign Study [hereafter FS] 1933, Walter Hullihen Papers, University of Delaware Archives [hereafter UDA], Newark, Del.; Laura Marden, "The First Junior Year in Italy," *Smith Alumnae Quarterly*, November 1932, 23, 25; William Allan Neilson, "The Juniors Abroad," *Smith Alumnae Quarterly*, May 1937, 241.

10. "The Junior Year Abroad," Foreign Study Records [hereafter FSR], UDA.

11. "1933–34 German Foreign Study Group," Hullihen Papers, FS 1933, UDA.

12. "Announcement of Junior Year in Munich," December 1936, and "Announcement of the Junior Year in Munich, 1938–39," box 32, Records of the Foreign Study Plan, UDA.

13. Grace M. Bacon, "Data for the Archives," GLLD Series A, folder 1, MHCA.

14. *New York Times*, April 30, 1933.

15. Ibid., June 1, 1933.

16. *Vassar Miscellany News*, October 28, 1933.

17. *Radcliffe News*, December 15, 1933.

18. Henry Noble MacCracken to Nobile Comm. Antonio Grossardi, May 10, 1933, and MacCracken to Director [Giuseppe Prezzolini], April 28, 1933, folder 94.8, Henry Noble MacCracken Papers, Vassar College Archives [hereafter VCA], Poughkeepsie, N.Y.; *Vassar Miscellany News*, May 13, 1933.

19. *Vassar Miscellany News*, October 3, 1934.

20. *Smith College Weekly*, May 1, 1935.

21. Ibid.

22. Stephen P. Duggan to Marion Edwards Park, June 12, 1933, and Marion Edwards Park to Dr. Stephen P. Duggan, June 15, 1933, Marion Edwards Park Papers, Bryn Mawr College Archives [hereafter BMCA], Bryn Mawr, Pa.

23. Marion Edwards Park to Mrs. Eisenhart, October 11, 1933, and Secretary to the President to Richard Hertz, December 26, 1939, Park Papers, BMCA; *Bryn Mawr College News*, October 11, 1933. Noether's hiring was made possible by a joint grant from the Institute of International Education and the Rockefeller Foundation.
24. Everett R. Clinchy to President Marion Edwards Park, June 8, 1933, and Marion Edwards Park to Everett R. Clinchy, June 17, 1933, Park Papers, BMCA.
25. "Announcement of the Junior Year in Munich, Eighth Year, 1938–39," box 32, Records of Foreign Study Plan, UDA.
26. Marion Edwards Park to His Excellency, Prince Gaetano Caetani, January 29, 1934, and Italian Ambassador to Park, February 2, 1924, Park Papers, BMCA.
27. *Bryn Mawr College News*, April 28, 1937.
28. *New York Times*, June 15, 1934.
29. *Vassar Miscellany News*, October 11, 1933.
30. Agnes Reynolds '38, "We Went to Germany," 6, 16–17, *Vassar Review*, Freshman 1935, VCA.
31. Catherine Elliott '36, "We Went to Germany," 7, 20, *Vassar Review*, Freshman 1935.
32. *Vassar Miscellany News*, October 9, 1935.
33. *Wellesley College News*, October 4, 1934.
34. *Smith College Weekly*, October 31, 1934.
35. *Vassar Miscellany News*, October 14, 1933.
36. *Wellesley College News*, May 4, 1933.
37. *Mount Holyoke College News*, November 4, 1933.
38. *Vassar Miscellany News*, March 3, 1934.
39. Ibid., November 3, 1934.
40. *Christian Science Monitor*, June 7, 1933.
41. *New York Times*, September 10, 1933; Washington *Post*, January 26, 1934.
42. Alice Hamilton, "Woman's Place in Nazi Germany," *Advance*, February 1934, 20.
43. Chicago *Tribune*, February 14, 1935.
44. *Vassar Miscellany News*, May 15, 1937.
45. Los Angeles *Times*, February 25, 1934.
46. *New York Times*, September 10, 1933; Washington *Post*, February 17, 1934.
47. *Vassar Miscellany News*, May 15, 1937.
48. Ibid., April 14, 1934.
49. *Bryn Mawr College News*, January 17, 1934.
50. *Wellesley College News*, November 2, 1933.
51. Ibid., May 24, 1934.
52. *Barnard Bulletin*, October 27, 1933.
53. Ibid., December 12 and 15, 1933.
54. *Radcliffe News*, May 4, 1934.
55. Walter Hullihen, "Suggested Protest by American College Students," Hullihen Papers, FS 1933, UDA; *New York Times*, May 21, 1933.
56. Hullihen, "Suggested Protest."

57. *Notre Dame Scholastic*, May 12, 1933.
58. President MacCracken to Professor Schaffter, April 4, 1934, and Dorothy Schaffter to President MacCracken, April 6, 1934, folder 72.28, MacCracken Papers; *New York Times*, May 29 and August 18, 1934.
59. *New York Times*, May 29, 1934; *Arizona Daily Star* [Tucson], July 25, 1934.
60. Harriet [Trowbridge] to Mr. MacCracken, July 11, 1934, folder 72.28, MacCracken Papers, VCA.
61. *Arizona Daily Star*, August 25, 1934.
62. "Arizona Plagued by Nazi Apologist," *American Hebrew*, March 29, 1935, 402.
63. Stuart M. Stoke, "Germany in the Summer of 1934," *Mount Holyoke Alumnae Quarterly*, November 1934, 157–58.
64. Ibid., 158–60.
65. Robert Edwin Herzstein, *Roosevelt and Hitler: Prelude to War* (New York: Paragon House, 1989), 133; Der Präsident, Vereinigung Carl Schurz E.V., Berlin to Mr. President, Vassar College, December 15, 1934, and Vice-President, Vereinigung Carl Schurz E.V. to Mr. President, December 22, 1934, folder 72.28, MacCracken Papers, VCA.
66. Dorothy Schaffter to President MacCracken, December 27, 1934, MacCracken to Miss Schaffter, January 3, 1935, and MacCracken to President, Vereinigung Carl Schurz, January 9, 1935, folder 72.28, MacCracken Papers, VCA.
67. "Bulletin of the University of Delaware, Foreign Study Plan, Junior Year in Germany, Financial Arrangements and Registration for 1934–1935," box C, FSR, UDA; Saul S. Friedman, *The Oberammergau Passion Play: A Lance Against Civilization* (Carbondale and Edwardsville: Southern Illinois University Press, 1984), 114.
68. Friedman, *Oberammergau Passion Play*, 86–88, 122; James S. Shapiro, *Oberammergau: The Troubling Story of the World's Most Famous Passion Play* (New York: Pantheon, 2000), 88; *New York Times*, May 19, 1930, and March 8, 1960. Performances of the play lasted from 8 A.M. until 6 P.M., with a two-hour intermission. Barbara E. Scott Fisher, "Notes of a Cosmopolitan," *The North American Review*, March 1934, xi.
69. *New York Times*, May 19, 1930.
70. Ibid., March 23, 1923, May 19, 1930, and December 25, 1933; Friedman, *Oberammergau Passion Play*, 119–20.
71. *Bryn Mawr College News*, February 26, 1930.
72. *Mount Holyoke College News*, December 9, 1933.
73. Walter Hullihen to S. A. Nock, March 27, 1934, Hullihen Papers, FS 1934, UDA.
74. Hullihen to Professor Camillo von Klenze, April 16, 1934, Hullihen Papers, FS 1934, UDA.
75. Hullihen to Madeleine Rowe, July 26, 1934, and Hullihen to Mrs. Richard Y. FitzGerald, August 6, 1934, Hullihen Papers, FS 1934; Wilmington [Del.] *Evening Journal*, August 9, 1934, UDA.
76. Hullihen to FitzGerald, August 6, 1934, and Hullihen to Adam Bernhard, November 13, 1934, Hullihen Papers, FS 1934, UDA.

77. Hullihen to Rowe, July 26, 1934, Hullihen Papers, FS 1934; Chicago *Tribune*, July 6, 1934, clipping in Hullihen Papers, FS 1934, UDA.
78. Akademische Aulandsstelle e.V. Münschen, August 16, 1934, and Hullihen to Dr. Bert E. Young, October 5, 1934, Hullihen Papers, FS 1934, UDA; *Review*, May 22, 1935.
79. The German Junior Year, Inc., "Binding the Cultural Ties Closer," n.d., box 51, William Allan Neilson Papers, Smith College Archives [hereafter SCA], Northampton, Mass.; Jessie Douglass, "Report for the Junior Year Committee," February 9, 1935, and "Announcement of the Junior Year in Munich," December 1936, UDA.
80. "Binding the Cultural Ties," n.d., box 51, Neilson Papers, SCA.
81. William Allan Neilson, "The Juniors Abroad," 241; David M. Oshinsky, Richard P. McCormick, and Daniel Horn, *The Case of the Nazi Professor* (New Brunswick, N.J.: Rutgers University Press, 1989), 144.
82. *Vassar Miscellany News*, October 26 and November 2, 1935; *New York Times*, May 14, 1935.
83. *New York Times*, November 9 and 10, 1935.
84. *Bryn Mawr College News*, January 15, 1936.
85. Mary-Anne Greenough, "The Celebrations on the Ninth of November," *Junior Year Newsletter*, November 18, 1937, box 51, Neilson Papers, SCA.
86. John W. Richards (Springfield College), "November 9th," *Junior Year Newsletter*, November 18, 1937, box 51, Neilson Papers, SCA.
87. *Vassar Miscellany News*, March 4 and 7, 1936.
88. Ibid., March 7, 1936.
89. Ibid., March 14, 1936.
90. *Bryn Mawr College News*, February 10, 1937; Miller to Neilson, August 1, 1937, box 51, Neilson Papers, SCA.
91. Grace M. Bacon, "Report to the President. Department of German, 1936–1937," Series A, folder 1, GLLD Papers, MHCA.
92. William A. Neilson to Al Magnifico Rettore, University of Florence, July 22, 1939, box 51, Neilson Papers, SCA.
93. Max Ascoli, "The Press and the Universities in Italy," *Annals of the American Academy of Political and Social Science* 200 (November 1938): 251; Gaetano Salvemini, "Such Things Happen" in Frances Keene, ed., *Neither Liberty nor Bread: The Meaning and Tragedy of Italian Fascism* (New York: Harper & Brothers, 1940), 123.
94. *Smith College Weekly*, January 15, 1936.
95. Marden, "First Junior Year in Italy," 25.
96. Emma Netti to President William A. Neilson, November 15, 1937, Neilson to Netti, November 29, 1937, and Netti to Neilson, December 30, 1937, box 51, Neilson Papers, SCA; "The Juniors Abroad," *Smith Alumnae Quarterly*, May 1931, 302; Neilson, "The Juniors Abroad," 241.
97. M. H. Nicholson to President W. A. Neilson, n.d., box 51, Neilson Papers, SCA; David I. Kertzer, *The Popes Against the Jews: The Vatican's Role in the Rise of Modern Anti-Semitism* (New York: Alfred A. Knopf, 2001), 282.
98. Nicholson to Neilson, n.d, box 51, Neilson Papers, SCA.

99. Lucy S. Dawidowicz, *The War Against the Jews, 1933–1945* (New York: Bantam, 1975), 100–02, 196; Martin Gilbert, *Kristallnacht: Prelude to Destruction* (New York: HarperCollins, 2006), 13.

100. Miller to Max Diez, November 27, 1938, and Miller, "Report to the National Advisory Committee, Junior Year in Munich," February 21, 1939, box 51, Neilson Papers, SCA.

101. Henry Hemmendinger to President William Allan Neilson, December 4, 1938, box 51, Neilson Papers, SCA.

102. William A. Neilson to Frau Lili Eidam, April 28, 1939, box 51, Neilson Papers, SCA.

103. Camillo von Klenze to President W. A. Neilson, March 11, 1939, box 51, Neilson papers, SCA; Bacon, "Report to the President; 1938–1939," Series A, folder 1, GLLD Papers, MHCA.

104. Miller to Executive Council, March 12 and April 10, 1939, and Max Diez to President William A. Neilson, December 5, 1938, box 51, Neilson Papers, SCA.

105. *Bryn Mawr College News*, February 15, 1939.

106. *Radcliffe News*, November 18, 23, and 25, 1938; *Barnard Bulletin*, December 6, 1938; *Vassar Miscellany News*, November 16, 1938; *Mount Holyoke College News*, November 18, 1938; *Bryn Mawr College News*, November 16 and 30, 1938; *Wellesley College News*, November 23, 1938.

107. Margaret C. Halsey to President Henry N. MacCracken, October 11, 1939, and Henry N. MacCracken to Mrs. Halsey, October 14, 1939, folder 45.22, MacCracken Papers, VCA.

108. *Mount Holyoke College News*, September 29, 1939.

109. Grace M. Bacon, "Report to the President," June 1940, GLLD Papers, Series A, folder 1, MHCA.

110. Virginia C. Gildersleeve, *Many a Good Crusade* (New York: Macmillan, 1954), 182–86, 406–12.

111. *New York Times*, June 28, 1933.

112. Frances Adams '39, "Junior Year in Munich," *Mount Holyoke Alumnae Quarterly*, May 1938, 21, MHCA.

5. A Respectful Hearing for Nazi Germany's Apologists: The University of Virginia Institute of Public Affairs Roundtables, 1933–1941

1. *Harvard Crimson*, April 18, 1933.

2. Robert Edwin Herzstein, *Roosevelt and Hitler: Prelude to War* (New York: Paragon House, 1989), 73.

3. *Smith College Weekly*, June 19, 1935; *Harvard Crimson*, April 9, 1926; *New York Times*, May 27, 1926.

4. *Harvard Crimson*, December 1, 1926.

5. Ibid., April 18, 1933.

6. *Vassar Miscellany News*, January 19, 1935.

7. *Radcliffe News*, November 18, 1938.

8. Sidney Fay, "The German Character," box 2, Sidney Fay Papers, Harvard University Archives [hereafter HUA], Pusey Library, Cambridge, Mass.

9. Ibid.
10. Lester Markel to Professor Sidney Fay, May 30, 1940, box 2, Fay Papers, HUA.
11. Sidney Fay to Lester Markel, June 6, 1940, box 2, Fay Papers, HUA.
12. Washington *Sunday Star*, clipping, [1938] in personnel file of Charles Tansill, American University Archives [hereafter AUA], American University; Washington *Post*, August 19, 1934, and November 13, 1964; *New York Times*, December 29, 1935; Charles C. Tansill to Joseph M. M. Gray, December 8, 1936, Tansill personnel file, AUA.
13. Washington *Post*, November 17, 1936; Charles C. Tansill to Ernest S. Griffith, September 7, 1936, Tansill personnel file, AUA.
14. William E. Dodd to Frederick W. Wile, December 11, 1936, container 50, William E. Dodd Papers, Library of Congress [hereafter LC], Washington, D.C.
15. William E. Dodd to Howard K. Beale, March 19, 1937, container 50, Dodd Papers, LC.
16. Tansill to Griffith, September 7, 1936, Tansill personnel file, AUA; Washington *Post*, September 21, 1936.
17. Ernest S. Griffith to Charles C. Tansill, September 21, 1936, Tansill personnel file, AUA.
18. Washington *Post*, November 17, 1936.
19. Ibid., March 9, 1937.
20. Joseph M. M. Gray to the Rev. G. Dumas, S.J., May 1, 1939, Tansill personnel file, AUA.
21. Howard K. Beale to William E. Dodd, March 3, 1937, container 50, Dodd Papers, LC.
22. *New York Times*, July 31 and August 8, 1927.
23. R. K. Gooch to Hans Thomsen, June 18, 1938, box 100, Institute of Public Affairs [hereafter IPA], Office Administrative Files [hereafter OAF], Accession RG-2/4/1.891, Manuscript Department, Alderman Library, University of Virginia [hereafter UVA], Charlottesville, Va.
24. Charles G. Maphis to Dr. [Karl F.] Geiser, December 21, 1934, box 78, IPA, OAF, UVA.
25. *New York Times*, July 8, 1934.
26. Karl F. Geiser, "The German Nazi State," July 3, 1934, box 32, IPA, OAF, UVA.
27. Ibid.; *New York Times*, July 4, 1934.
28. Karl F. Geiser to Dr. Charles G. Maphis, October 11, 1934, box 78, IPA, OAF, UVA.
29. *New York Times*, July 4, 1934.
30. Dr. Beniamino de Ritis, untitled address, July 3, 1934, box 32, IPA, OAF, UVA; *New York Times*, July 4, 1934.
31. Harry Elmer Barnes, "The Critical Period of Democracy and Capitalism," July 2, 1934, box 32, IPA, OAF, UVA; *New York Times*, July 4, 1934.
32. "Secretary's Summary, Round Table – American-German Relations," July 8, 1935, box 37, IPA, OAF, UVA.
33. "Secretary's Summary," July 12, 1935, box 37, IPA, OAF, UVA.

34. "Secretary's Summary," July 9, 1935, box 37, IPA, OAF, UVA.
35. *New York Times*, December 9, 1934.
36. Frederick K. Krueger, "Present and Future Political and Diplomatic Relations Between the United States and Germany," July 13, 1935, box 37, IPA, OAF, UVA.
37. Ibid., *New York Times*, July 14, 1935.
38. H. F. Simon, "Cultural Relations between 1912–1932," July 9, 1935, box 37, IPA, OAF, UVA.
39. Ernst Schmidt, "Americans in Germany," July 12, 1935, box 37, IPA, OAF, UVA.
40. Ibid.
41. Henry G. Hodges, "American Opinion of the New Germany," July 10, 1935, box 37, IPA, OAF, UVA.
42. Virginius Dabney, "The Germany of Hitler Looks at the United States," July 10, 1935, box 37, IPA, OAF, UVA.
43. Ibid.
44. Ibid.
45. Charles G. Maphis to Rabbi Morris S. Lazaron, July 20, 1935, box 83, IPA, OAF, UVA.
46. Marjorie McLachlan to Dr. John Lloyd Newcomb, April 9, 1937, box 7, subseries III, Accession RG 2/1/2.491, Institute of Public Affairs folder, President's Office papers, Manuscript Department, Alderman Library, UVA.
47. *New York Times*, March 13, 1936; Richmond *Times-Dispatch*, March 15, 1936.
48. *New York Times*, March 15, 1936; Richmond *Times-Dispatch*, March 15, 1936; "U.S. Colleges Arouse Protests by Accepting Nazi Bid," *The Anti-Nazi Economic Bulletin*, March 1936, box 114, Emergency Committee in Aid of Displaced Foreign Scholars Papers, Manuscripts and Archives Division, New York Public Library, New York, N.Y.
49. *College Topics*, March 24, 1936; *Daily Progress* [Charlottesville, Va.], March 16, 1936.
50. Gerold von Minden, "Education in Germany," July 16, 1936, box 41, IPA, OAF, UVA.
51. Ibid.
52. Ibid.
53. John Adams, "The Emergency in Italy II," July 16, 1936, box 41, IPA, OAF, UVA.
54. Maphis to Wilbur K. Thomas, April 19, 1937, box 7, subseries III, President's Office Papers, UVA; Washington *Post*, March 15, 1937.
55. Helen Kirkpatrick, "Additional Summary of an Address by Miss Helen Kirkpatrick," July 8, 1937, box 42, IPA, OFA, UVA.
56. Sir Herbert B. Ames, "Does German Rearmament Necessarily Mean War?" July 13, 1937, box 42, IPA, OAF, UVA.
57. Helgo W. Culemann, "Is Healthy Competitive Spirit of German People an International Felony?" July 13, 1937, and "Excerpts from an Interview With Dr. Helgo W. Culemann," July 13, 1937, box 42, IPA, OFA, UVA; *New York Times*, July 14, 1937.

58. Marjorie McLachlan to Herr Hans Thomsen, May 10, 1938, box 100, IPA, OAF, UVA; Washington *Post*, February 2, 1936.
59. *New York Times*, January 3, 1937, and February 25, 1938. Meyer stated that he was a member of the Lutheran church. He had "some Jewish blood" in his "paternal ancestry," but not enough to disqualify him from government service under the Nuremberg laws. *New York Times*, February 25, 1938.
60. R. K. Gooch to Hans Thomsen, June 18, 1938, box 100, IPA, OAF, UVA.
61. Marjorie McLachlan to W. J. Cameron, May 21, 1938, box 100, IPA, OAF, UVA; Neil Baldwin, *Henry Ford and the Jews: The Mass Production of Hate* (New York: Public Affairs, 2001), 265–67, 283–84, 307.
62. McLachlan to Cameron, May 16, 1938, box 100, IPA, OAF, UVA.
63. R. K. Gooch to W. J. Cameron, November 7, 1938, box 100, IPA, OAF, UVA.
64. Hardy C. Dillard to Dr. Frederick Auhagen, February 13, 1939, box 105, IPA, OAF, UVA.
65. Dillard to Auhagen, March 25, 1939, box 105, IPA, OAF, UVA.
66. Auhagen to Dillard, May 13, 1939, box 105, IPA, OAF, UVA; Washington *Post*, October 23, 1940.
67. Ibid., July 6, 1939, December 12, 1940, and October 14, 1963. Castle's *New York Times* obituary noted that he "pleaded for strict neutrality as World War II approached and was especially critical of the United States aid to Britain at the start of the war." *New York Times*, October 14, 1963.
68. Friedrich Auhagen, "America and Germany: Contrasts or Conflicts?" July 5, 1939, box 45, IPA, OAF, UVA.
69. Washington *Post*, July 9, 1939.
70. Samuel K. C. Kopper, "Plain Sanity or Vain Insanity in International Thought," July 6, 1939, box 45, IPA, OAF, UVA.
71. Manfred Zapp, "The Position of the Individual in Germany," July 13, 1939, box 46, IPA, OAF, UVA.
72. Ibid.
73. Ibid.
74. F. Wilhelm Sollmann, "Germany's Drive to the East," July 7, 1939, box 46, IPA, OAF, UVA; Washington *Post*, July 6, 1939.
75. Washington *Post*, July 4, 1939.
76. Ibid., July 9, 1939.
77. Ibid., June 11, 1940; *New York Times*, June 11, 1940.
78. *New York Times*, June 18, 1940; Washington *Post*, October 23, 1940.
79. *New York Times*, June 19, 1940; Washington *Post*, June 19, 1940.
80. Washington *Post*, October 23 and November 21, 1940; Los Angeles *Times*, October 13 and November 22, 1940.
81. *New York Times*, November 22, 1940.
82. Washington *Post*, October 23, 1940; Chicago *Tribune*, March 4, 1941.
83. *New York Times*, March 12 and July 15, 1941, and April 16, 1945.
84. Washington *Post*, July 10, 1941, and *New York Times*, July 12, 1941.
85. Ibid., July 12, 1941, and June 4, 1947.

86. Nelle Swan to Ann C. Yates, June 5, 1941, and Hardy C. Dillard to Edgar Ansel Mowrer, July 10, 1941, box 115, IPA, OAF, UVA; *New York Times*, June 25, 1941.
87. *New York Times*, November 25, 1938; Chicago *Tribune*, November 25, 1938.

6. Nazi Nests: German Departments in American Universities, 1933–1941

1. Philadelphia *Jewish Exponent*, May 31, 1935.
2. *Dartmouth*, May 17 and June 15, 1934.
3. Ibid., May 12 and 14 and June 15, 1934.
4. Ibid., May 15, 16, and 19, 1934.
5. *Capital Times* [Madison, Wis.], November 17, 1935; *New York Times*, November 17, 1935.
6. "Chicago Bars Film Showing Hitler Terror," *Jewish Criterion*, April 27, 1934, 4; *New York Times*, April 22 and 27 and May 1, 1934; Chicago *Tribune*, April 24 and 27, 1934.
7. *Capital Times*, November 18, 1935; Chicago *Tribune*, November 18, 1935; *New York Times*, November 18, 1935.
8. *Capital Times*, November 18, 1935; Chicago *Tribune*, November 18, 1935; *New York Times*, November 18, 1935; *Daily Cardinal*, November 19, 1935. Earlier that year, Ambassador Luther had encountered trouble from student demonstrators when he visited the University of Texas campus as the luncheon guest of its president, H. Y. Benedict. Luther was then on a speaking tour of Texas. The *Jewish Criterion* of Pittsburgh, in an editorial entitled "They're Not All Cowpunchers," congratulated University of Texas anti-Nazi students for their vigorous protest against Luther's campus visit. *Jewish Criterion*, February 1, 1935. University of Texas German professor W. E. Metzenthin was listed as toastmaster at a banquet to honor Luther in Austin the evening before his campus visit, and associate professor of history R. L. Biesele greeted him there in German. *Daily Texan*, January 18 and 19, 1935.
9. *Capital Times*, November 18, 1935; Chicago *Tribune*, November 18, 1935.
10. John D. Hicks, *My Life with History: An Autobiography* (Lincoln: University of Nebraska Press, 1968), 204.
11. *Capital Times*, November 18, 1935.
12. *Daily Cardinal*, November 19, 1935.
13. Ibid., November 19, 1935.
14. Ibid., November 19, 1935.
15. Minneapolis *Journal*, November 18, 1935; Chicago *Tribune*, November 16, 1935.
16. Minneapolis *Journal*, November 18, 1935.
17. Ibid., November 19 and 20, 1935.
18. *Minnesota Daily*, November 20, 1935.
19. Ibid., November 20, 1935.
20. *Radcliffe News*, December 15, 1933; *Smith College Weekly*, October 16, 1935; *Harvard Crimson*, May 20, 1936, and May 12, 1939.
21. *Yale Daily News*, December 11, 1934; *New York Times*, December 12, 1934.

22. *Vassar Miscellany News*, December 19, 1934.
23. *New York Times*, October 28, 1934.
24. Hartford *Courant*, November 15, 1934.
25. Ibid., April 18, 1936.
26. W. D. Zinnecker to H. O. Voorhis, March 6, 1936, box 46, Harry Woodburn Chase Papers, New York University Archives, Bobst Library, New York, N.Y.; *Cornell Daily Sun*, March 4, 1936; *Michigan Daily*, March 5, 1936.
27. *New York Times*, June 28, 1937.
28. Los Angeles *Times*, April 6, 1938.
29. *New York Times*, November 25, 1938; Washington *Post*, November 25, 1938.
30. "Nazi Propagandist at Hunter College," *News from the Boston Chapter Non-Sectarian Anti-Nazi League*, August 18, 1939, box 217, Non-Sectarian Anti-Nazi League Papers, Rare Book and Manuscript Library, Columbia University, New York, N.Y.
31. *New York Times*, July 27, 1943; Washington *Post*, February 25, 1949.
32. *New York Times*, July 27, 1943; Washington *Post*, February 11, 16, 17, and 25, 1949.
33. *New York Times*, July 27, 1943, October 28, 1947, February 1 and March 26, 1949, July 11, 1961, and July 2, 1988; Washington *Post*, February 25, 1949.
34. Washington *Post*, February 1, 1949.
35. Michael Greenberg and Seymour Zenchelsky, "Private Bias and Public Responsibility: Anti-Semitism at Rutgers in the 1920s and 1930s," *History of Education Quarterly* 33 (Fall 1993): 300–08; New Jersey State Board of Regents. In the Matter of Race Discrimination at Rutgers University. Brief for Complainants. Submitted June 22, 1931, by Joseph Siegler, William Newcorn, Max J. Kohler, of Counsel, box 32, Robert C. Clothier Papers, RG/MC no. 04/A14, Special Collections and University Archives [hereafter SCUA], Alexander Library [hereafter AL], Rutgers University [hereafter RU], New Brunswick, N.J.
36. Greenberg and Zenchelsky, "Private Bias," 300, 307, 318; Dan A. Oren, *Joining the Club: A History of Jews and Yale* (New Haven, Conn.: Yale University Press, 1985): 42–45. Corwin, who served as executive secretary of the Yale University Graduate School for sixteen years before coming to NJC, was at Yale with her father for many years. *New York Times*, February 21, 1983.
37. New Jersey State Board of Regents. In the Matter of Race Discrimination at Rutgers University, box 32, Clothier Papers, SCUA, AL, RU; David M. Oshinsky, Richard P. McCormick, and Daniel Horn, *The Case of the Nazi Professor* (New Brunswick, N.J.: Rutgers University Press, 1989), 34–35; Greenberg and Zenchelsky, "Private Bias," 312–14.
38. *Targum*, October 14 and 18, 1930; Testimony of Julius Kass, October 27, 1930, and clipping from Newark *Evening News*, March 26, 1932, in box 32, Clothier Papers, SCUA, AL, RU.
39. J. Edward Ashmead to New Jersey State Board of Regents, April 1931, box 7, Trustees, Personal Papers, J. Edward Ashmead, RG 3/B3/1, SCUA,

AL, RU; Oshinsky, McCormick, and Horn, *Case of the Nazi Professor*, 35.

40. New York *World-Telegram*, May 22, 1935, clipping in box 5, Papers of the Board of Trustees Committee Investigation of the Charges of Lienhard Bergel, 1935 [hereafter BTCI], RG 3/CO/2, SCUA, AL, RU; *New York Times*, May 23, 1935; Greenberg and Zenchelsky, "Private Bias," 300; Oshinsky, McCormick, and Horn, *Case of the Nazi Professor*, 33, 35, 37. Oshinsky, McCormick, and Horn list the two German refugees in the Music Department as the only Jewish faculty members at NJC. Rutgers trustee Philip Brett claimed in 1935 that there were four Jews on the NJC faculty, all recently hired. New York *Evening Journal*, May 23, 1935, clipping in box 5, BTCI, SCUA, AL, RU.

41. Marion Siegel Friedman to Dr. [Richard P.] McCormick, October 9, 1986, box 19, Richard P. McCormick Papers, SCUA, AL, RU.

42. *Campus News*, March 31, 1933; Oshinsky, McCormick, and Horn, *Case of the Nazi Professor*, 15.

43. "Report of Investigators for the American Civil Liberties Union on Trustees' Investigation into Dismissal of Lienhard Bergel from the German Department at the New Jersey College for Women," 18, August 1935, box 6, Lienhard Bergel Papers, Columbia University Rare Book and Manuscript Library [hereafter CURBML], Butler Library [hereafter BL], New York, N.Y.; Michael Greenberg and Seymour Zenchelsky, "The Confrontation with Nazism at Rutgers: Academic Bureaucracy and Moral Failure," *History of Education Quarterly* 30 (Fall 1990): 335.

44. Jean M. Earle to J. Edward Ashmead, May 27, 1935, box 1, BTCI, SCUA, AL, RU.

45. "In the Matter of the Investigation of the Charges of Lienhard Bergel, Report of Special Trustees' Committee," *Rutgers University Bulletin*, Series XII, No./2B, August 1935, 33, box 7, Bergel Papers, CURBML, BL.

46. *Targum*, April 1, 1933.

47. Ibid.

48. Ibid., Oshinsky, McCormick, and Horn, *Case of the Nazi Professor*, 15–16.

49. *Targum*, May 3, 1933; Oshinsky, McCormick, and Horn, *Case of the Nazi Professor*, 17; New Brunswick *Daily Home News*, May 25, 1933, clipping in box 18, McCormick Papers, SCUA, AL, RU.

50. *Campus News*, October 10, 1933.

51. Ibid., September 26, 1934.

52. Lienhard Bergel, "Nazi Activities in American Colleges," *Jewish Criterion*, April 3, 1936, 73–74.

53. *Campus News*, December 8, 1934.

54. Ibid.; Greenberg and Zenchelsky, "Confrontation," 336.

55. *Campus News*, February 2, 1935.

56. Ibid., April 17, 1935.

57. Bergel, "Nazi Activities," 73.

58. *Campus News*, October 3 and 17, 1934; Oshinsky, McCormick, and Horn, *Case of the Nazi Professor*, 33.

59. Robert C. Clothier to Albert W. Holzmann, March 6 and 19, 1935, and Holzmann to Clothier, March 13, 1935, box 89, Clothier Papers; Robert Edwin Herzstein, *Roosevelt and Hitler: Prelude to War* (New York: Paragon House, 1989), 133.

60. Holzmann to Clothier, March 13, 1935, box 89, SCUA, AL, RU.

61. Alvin Johnson to President Robert C. Clothier, December 10, 1935; Johnson to Clothier, December 31, 1935, box 48, Clothier Papers, SCUA, AL, RU.

62. Oshinsky, McCormick, and Horn, *Case of the Nazi Professor*, 22, 26–28; Greenberg and Zenchelsky, "Confrontation," 326.

63. Oshinsky, McCormick, and Horn, *Case of the Nazi Professor*, 28; "In the Matter of the Investigation of the Charges of Lienhard Bergel, 7–8, box 7, Bergel Papers.

64. Sylvia C. Bergel, "Observations related to the Bergel-Hauptmann matter at Rutgers University in 1935," September 1991, box 5, Bergel Papers, CURBML, BL; Oshinsky, McCormick, and Horn, *Case of the Nazi Professor*, 12.

65. Sylvia C. Bergel to Michael Greenberg, October 20, 1990, and Sylvia C. Bergel to Michael Greenberg, August 18, 1987, box 5, Sylvia C. Bergel to Seymour Zenchelsky, August 24, 1994, and Sylvia C. Bergel to Elie Wiesel, June 18, 1985, box 6, Bergel Papers, CURBML, BL.

66. Sylvia C. Bergel, "Observations," box 5, Bergel Papers, CURBML, BL.

67. Ibid.; Sylvia C. Bergel to Michael Greenberg and Seymour Zenchelsky, May 21, 1992, box 5, Bergel Papers, CURBML, BL.

68. Sylvia Cook Bergel to Greenberg and Zenchelsky, May 21, 1992; *Case of the Nazi Professor*, 31.

69. Oshinsky, McCormick, and Horn, *Case of the Nazi Professor*, 31–33, 130.

70. Bergel, "Nazi Activities," 74.

71. "Miss Corwin's Statement. Report to the Trustees Committee," box 18, Richard P. McCormick Papers, R-MC 050, SCUA, AL, RU.

72. "Miss Corwin's Statement"; *Targum*, June 8, 1935; Oshinsky, McCormick, and Horn, *Case of the Nazi Professor*, 64.

73. "Miss Corwin's Statement."

74. "Miss Corwin's Statement"; Alan Silver, "The Bergel Case: Rutgers' Dreyfus Affair," box 19, McCormick Papers and Alan Silver, "The Economic and Administrative Considerations in the Bergel Case," draft of April 10, 1987, SCUA, AL, RU. Ms. Hauptmann began with a six-hour teaching load in 1929–30 and assumed a full fifteen-hour teaching load in 1930–31.

75. "Miss Corwin's Statement," box 18, McCormick Papers, SCUA, AL, RU.

76. "In the Matter of the Investigation," 40–41, box 7, Bergel Papers, CURBML, BL; Oshinsky, McCormick, and Horn, *Case of the Nazi Professor*, 44–45; *Campus News*, April 13 and 24, May 1, 1935.

77. *New York Times*, May 24, 1935.

78. Oshinsky, McCormick, and Horn, *Case of the Nazi Professor*, 51–53; "In the Matter of the Investigation," 46, box 7, Bergel Papers, CURBML, BL.

79. Sylvia C. Bergel to Michael Greenberg, March 13, 1988, box 5, Bergel Papers; Oshinsky, McCormick, and Horn, *Case of the Nazi Professor*, 57; *New York Times*, May 11, 1926, October 31, 1930, November 25, 1936, and July 3, 1960.

80. Sylvia C. Bergel to Alan Silver, September 9, 1986, box 19, McCormick Papers.

81. Oshinsky, McCormick, and Horn, *Case of the Nazi Professor*, 58–59; *New York Times*, May 22, 1935.

82. *New York Times*, May 26, 1935.

83. "In the Matter of the Investigation," 11; Newark *News*, June 7, 1935, clipping in box 5, Board of Trustees Committee. Investigation of the Charges.

84. *New York Times*, May 28, 1935.

85. *Campus News*, May 8, 1935; Committee Hearings: Notes Made by Miss Miriam L. E. Lippincott, Committee Member, May 23, 1935, box 1, BTCI, SCUA, AL, RU; *New York Times*, May 24, 1935.

86. Oshinsky, McCormick, and Horn, *Case of the Nazi Professor*, 45–46.

87. Ibid., 60, 62; New York *World-Telegram*, May 23, 1935, box 5, BTCI, SCUA, AL, RU; "Report of Investigators for American Civil Liberties Union," 6.

88. New York *World-Telegram*, May 23, 1935, box 5, BTCI, SCUA, AL, RU.

89. Newark *Star-Eagle*, May 23, 1935; New Brunswick *Home News*, May 23, 1935, box 5, BTCI, SCUA, AL, RU.

90. Ibid.

91. *New York Times*, May 23, 1935.

92. Unidentified clipping, May 23, 1935, box 5, BTCI, SCUA, AL, RU.

93. Letter from "senior at N.J.C.," box 1, BTCI, SCUA, AL, RU.

94. Testimony of Sylvia Silverman, May 21, 1935, box 1, BTCI, SCUA, AL, RU.

95. Testimony of Adele Lubman, May 21, 1935, box 1, BTCI, SCUA, AL, RU.

96. Testimony of Dorothy Venook, May 23, 1935, box 1, BTCI, SCUA, AL, RU.

97. Friedman to McCormick, October 9, 1986, McCormick Papers, SCUA, AL, RU.

98. Testimony of Naomi Parness, May 24, 1935, and of Mary Atwood, recalled for further direct examination, box 1, BTCI, SCUA, AL, RU; "In the Matter of the Investigation," 30, box 7, Bergel Papers, CURBML, BL; Greenberg and Zenchelsky, "Confrontation," 335.

99. Alan Silver, "Some Evidence of the Prejudicial Atmosphere of the Trustees Hearings of 1935," Alan Silver folder, Bergel/Hauptmann Case, SCUA, AL, RU.

100. Bartlett Cowdrey, "To the Committee Investigating the Dismissal of Dr. Bergel," May 26, 1935, box 1, BTCI, SCUA, AL, RU.

101. Newark *Star-Eagle*, May 22, 1935.

102. Long Branch, N.J., *Record*, May 23, 1935, clipping in box 5, BTCI, SCUA, AL, RU.

103. Newark *Star-Eagle*, June 13, 1935.

104. New Brunswick *Sunday Times* clipping, June 16, 1935, box 18, McCormick Papers, SCUA, AL, RU; "Report of Investigators for American Civil Liberties Union," 7–8; Oshinsky, McCormick, and Horn, *Case of the Nazi Professor*, 66–67.
105. Newark *Evening News* clipping, August 20, 1935, box 1, BTCI, SCUA, AL, RU.
106. *New York Times*, June 9, 1935.
107. "Report of Investigators for American Civil Liberties Union," 5, Bergel Papers.
108. "Administration-Trustee Shortcomings" [handwritten notes], n.d., box 18, McCormick Papers, SCUA, AL, RU.
109. Testimony of Naomi Parness, May 24, 1935, box 1, BTCI, SCUA, AL, RU.
110. *New York Times*, May 31, 1935.
111. New York *World-Telegram*, May 22, 1935, box 5, BTCI, SCUA, AL, RU.
112. "In the Matter of the Investigation," 29–31.
113. Ibid., 9, 11.
114. Ibid., 15, 20–21; Oshinsky, McCormick, and Horn, *Case of the Nazi Professor*, 71; Greenberg and Zenchelsky, "Confrontation," 338.
115. "In the Matter of the Investigation," 39.
116. Ibid.
117. Ibid., 41.
118. A. Heckscher to Dr. Robert C. Clothier, September 27, 1935, box 23, Rutgers University. Board of Trustees. Minutes and Enclosures 1935 [hereafter RUBTME], SCUA, AL, RU.
119. Clothier to Heckscher, September 28, 1935, box 23, RUBTME, SCUA, AL, RU.
120. Oshinsky, McCormick, and Horn, *Case of the Nazi Professor*, 80, 88–89.
121. Friedrich Hauptmann to President Clothier, November 12, 1940, and Margaret Corwin to President Clothier, November 16, 1940, box 88, Clothier Papers, SCUA, AL, RU.
122. Hauptmann to Clothier, November 12, 1940.
123. Margaret Corwin to President Clothier, November 20, 1940, box 88, Clothier Papers, SCUA, AL, RU; Oshinsky, McCormick, and Horn, *Case of the Nazi Professor*, 92–93.
124. Sylvia C. Bergel to Michael Greenberg, October 20, 1990, box 5, Bergel Papers, CURBML, BL.
125. Office Memorandum to Director, FBI from Guy Hottel. Subject: German Archives, Dr. Friedrich Johannes Hauptmann, May 15, 1946, box 7, Bergel Papers, CURBML, BL; Aaron Breitbart to Sylvia C. Bergel, November 19, 1985, and Sylvia C. Bergel to Simon Wiesenthal Center, September 11, 1985, box 6, Bergel Papers; Oshinsky, McCormick, and Horn, *Case of the Nazi Professor*, 93, 99, 104–07.
126. Newark *Evening News*, clipping, June 12, 1946, box 19, McCormick Papers, SCUA, AL, RU.
127. Alan Silver, "Some Evidence." Hauptmann became a U.S. citizen in order to keep his job on the NJC faculty. His wife chose not to become a U.S. citizen. Oshinsky, McCormick, and Horn, *Case of the Nazi Professor*, 89.

128. Newark *Evening News* clipping, June 12, 1946, box 19, McCormick Papers, SCUA, AL, RU; George Schmidt, *Douglass College: A History* (New Brunswick, N.J.: Rutgers University Press, 1968), 98.

129. Memo from Richard McCormick, October 7, 1985, box 19, McCormick Papers, SCUA, AL, RU.

130. Newark *Evening News* clipping, June 28, 1935, box 1, BTCI, SCUA, AL, RU.

131. See, for example, Philadelphia *Jewish Exponent*, March 13, 1936, and *Jewish Criterion*, April 3, 1936.

132. *Jewish Criterion*, April 3, 1936, 18; Stephen S. Wise to Robert C. Clothier, March 21, 1940, box 88, Clothier Papers, SCUA, AL, RU.

133. "Lienhard Bergel Career Information," box 6, Bergel Papers, CURBML, BL; Michael Greenberg and Seymour Zenchelsky, "Letter to the Editor," *History of Education Quarterly* 31 (Summer 1991): 318.

134. *New York Times*, June 9 and September 8, 1935.

135. Silver, "Economic and Administrative Considerations," draft of April 10, 1987, SCUA, AL, RU.

   In the wake of President Reagan's visit to a cemetery in Bitburg, Germany, where members of the Waffen SS were buried in 1985, Alan Silver succeeded in reviving media interest in the Bergel-Hauptmann case. As a result of pressure from the media and Silver, President Edward Bloustein of Rutgers appointed a committee of three historians, chaired by David Oshinsky and including Richard P. McCormick and Daniel Horn, to conduct a new investigation. Some criticized the choice of three Rutgers professors on the grounds that they could not be impartial in conducting an investigation of the university that employed them. Richard P. McCormick had also published a history of Rutgers University in 1966 that endorsed the administration's interpretation of the affair and praised President Robert C. Clothier in glowing terms. The committee released an Interim report in December 1986 and published its analysis and view of the case in a book entitled *The Case of the Nazi Professor* (New Brunswick, N.J.: Rutgers University Press, 1989). It found that the principal reasons for Bergel's termination were financial cutbacks suffered by Rutgers, declining enrollments in German courses, and the rule limiting instructors to three years. The committee concluded that under these conditions the university was able to retain only one of the two instructors, Bergel or Emil Jordan. It felt that Jordan was the logical choice because he had been hired a year before Bergel, participated in extracurricular activities, and was completing a textbook that was published in 1935. The committee did state that "[p]olitical considerations probably played a role in this decision." It also asserted that the conclusions of the Special Trustees Committee in 1935 "had been marred by their prejudices." Oshinsky, McCormick, and Horn, *Case of the Nazi Professor*, 74, 113–14. On McCormick's earlier assessment of the Bergel-Hauptmann case and of Clothier, see McCormick, *Rutgers: A Bicentennial History* (New Brunswick, N.J.: Rutgers University Press, 1966), 225–26, 238–39.

   Lienhard Bergel and Sylvia C. Bergel denounced the Oshinsky committee's conclusions as a whitewash of the Rutgers administration and trustees, as did Alan Silver. New Brunswick *Home News*, December 18, 1986 and Richard P. McCormick to Sylvia Bergel, March 13, 1988, box 5, Bergel Papers, CURBML, BL. Sylvia C. Bergel made sure after her husband died in 1987 that his papers went to Columbia University rather than to Rutgers.

In 1987, Arthur F. Burns, who had served as chairman of the Board of Governors of the Federal Reserve System and as U.S. ambassador to West Germany and who was an associate professor of economics at Rutgers at the time of the Bergel-Hauptmann case, wrote to Alan Silver that although "the Oshinsky Committee went about its difficult task in a thoroughly professional manner," its report "does not analyze thoroughly the economic factors surrounding the Bergel dismissal." As a result, Burns stated: "I cannot... accept the main conclusion of the Oshinsky Report." Burns in 1985 had told Silver, who had been his student, that "I do indeed recall the dismal events surrounding the Bergel case," and that it was to Silver's credit that he invited others "to remember the injustice." Arthur F. Burns to Alan Silver, June 10, 1985, and Burns to Silver, March 10, 1987, box 19, McCormick Papers, SCUA, AL, RU. The principal critique of the Oshinsky committee's findings is Greenberg and Zenchelsky, "Confrontation," 325–49.
136. Philadelphia *Jewish Exponent*, May 31, 1935.
137. Bergel, "Nazi Activities," 19.

7. American Catholic Universities' Flirtation with Fascism

1. Daniel Jonah Goldhagen, *A Moral Reckoning: The Role of the Catholic Church in the Holocaust and Its Unfulfilled Duty of Repair* (New York: Alfred A. Knopf, 2002), 43, 77–78.
2. Richard Breitman, Barbara McDonald Stewart, and Severin Hochberg, eds., *Advocate for the Doomed: The Diaries and Papers of James G. McDonald, 1932–1935* (Bloomington: Indiana University Press, 2007), 90–91.
3. Goldhagen, *Moral Reckoning*, 43; Saul Friedländer, *Nazi Germany and the Jews*, vol. 1: *The Years of Persecution, 1933–1939* (New York: Harper-Collins, 1997), 48–49.
4. *New York Times*, August 21, 1933.
5. David I. Kertzer, *The Popes Against the Jews: The Vatican's Role in the Rise of Modern Anti-Semitism* (New York: Alfred A. Knopf, 2001), 135, 246, 250–51, 260, 273.
6. Breitman, Stewart, and Hochberg, eds., *Advocate for the Doomed*, 91.
7. Friedländer, *Nazi Germany and the Jews*, 47.
8. Richard J. Evans, *The Third Reich in Power* (New York: Penguin, 2005), 623–24.
9. *New York Times*, December 31, 1934.
10. Chicago *Tribune*, February 4, 1935; Evans, *Third Reich in Power*, 627.
11. *New York Times*, June 14, 1933.
12. Ibid., September 11, 1933, and March 8, 1934.
13. *Notre Dame Scholastic*, May 12, 1933.
14. Ibid., March 31, 1933.

15. Assistant General Secretary to Mr. [William F.] Montavon, February 9, 1934, box 37, National Catholic Welfare Conference [hereafter NCWC] Papers, The American Catholic History Research Center and University Archives [hereafter ACUA], The Catholic University of America, Washington, D.C.

16. William F. Montavon to Fr. Burke, Fr. Ready, Miss Regan, Mr. Caravati, D. J. Ryan, June 12, 1933, box 37, NCWC Papers, ACUA.

17. *Hoya*, October 31, 1934.

18. Ibid., January 31, 1934.

19. Fordham *Ram*, March 15, 1934.

20. Ibid., February 16, 1934.

21. *Notre Dame Scholastic*, December 4, 1936, and April 9, 1937.

22. *Heights*, March 22, 1935.

23. *New York Times*, May 2, 1935; Washington *Post*, May 3, 1935. Crowley had been one of the Notre Dame football team's legendary Four Horsemen in the 1920s.

24. Los Angeles *Times*, May 19, 1938; *New York Times*, May 29, 1947.

25. James S. Shapiro, *Oberammergau: The Troubling Story of the World's Most Famous Passion Play* (New York: Pantheon, 2000), 26.

26. *Hoya*, November 17, 1937; Washington *Post*, March 13, 1939. Anton Lang Sr. was especially pleased to be entertained by Henry Ford, America's most prominent antisemite, when visiting Detroit in 1930. *Hoya*, November 17, 1937.

27. Fordham *Ram*, January 21, 1938.

28. Speech of Robert I. Gannon, S.J., at Re-Opening of the Church of the Nativity, New York City, October 9, 1938, box 15, Robert I. Gannon Papers, Fordham University Archives [hereafter FUA], New York, N.Y.

29. *Notre Dame Scholastic*, March 13, 1936.

30. Fordham *Ram*, October 8, 1937.

31. Bernard A. Grossman to Dr. [James H.] Ryan, March 20, 1936, box 36, Records of President/Rector, ACUA.

32. New York Times, February 13, 1937.

33. John P. Diggins, *Mussolini and Fascism: The View from America* (Princeton, N.J.: Princeton University Press, 1972), 183, 185–86.

34. *Hoya*, October 3, 1934; Washington *Post*, September 24, 1934.

35. *Notre Dame Scholastic*, September 28 and October 5, 1934.

36. *Heights*, October 10, 1934.

37. Ibid., March 25, 1938.

38. Washington *Post*, July 21, 1935.

39. *Notre Dame Scholastic*, April 16, 1937.

40. Washington *Post*, February 18, 1937.

41. Robert I. Gannon, *Up to the Present: The Story of Fordham* (Garden City, N.Y.: Doubleday, 1967), 213.

42. *Hoya*, December 15, 1937.

43. Gaetano Salvemini, "The Vatican and the Ethiopian War" in Frances Keene, ed., *Neither Liberty nor Bread: The Making and Tragedy of Italian Fascism* (New York: Harper & Brothers, 1940), 191–93; Richard A. Webster, *The*

Cross and the Fasces: Christian Democracy and Fascism in Italy (Stanford, Calif.: Stanford University Press, 1960), 123.

44. Salvemini, "Mussolini's Empire in the United States" in Keene, ed., *Neither Liberty nor Bread*, 342.

45. *Hoya*, March 11, 1936.

46. *Notre Dame Scholastic*, March 6, 1936.

47. *New York Times*, February 13, 1937.

48. Fordham *Ram*, March 11, 1938.

49. Washington *Post*, December 5 and 6, 1936.

50. *New York Times*, March 24, 1938.

51. Donald F. Crosby, "Boston's Catholics and the Spanish Civil War: 1936–1939," *New England Quarterly* 44 (March 1971): 84; Boston *Globe*, May 4, 1938.

52. Crosby, "Boston's Catholics," 87.

53. Robert Sklar, *City Boys: Cagney, Bogart, Garfield* (Princeton, N.J.: Princeton University Press, 1992), 107.

54. J. David Valaik, "In the Days Before Ecumenicism: American Catholicism, Anti-Semitism, and the Spanish Civil War," *Journal of Church and State* 13 (1971): 467–68.

55. Albert Prago, "Jews in the International Brigades in Spain," A *Jewish Currents* reprint, 1979, 4, 19.

56. Ibid., 3.

57. Washington *Post*, August 4, 1936.

58. "National Catholic Welfare Conference Annual Report 1936, Social Action Department," NCWC Papers, ACUA; Crosby, "Boston's Catholics," 85–86.

59. The Very Rev. Robert I. Gannon, S.J., "The Majesty of the Law," October 13, 1936, box 15, Gannon Papers, FUA.

60. John B. Snow to Right Rev. Mgr. Joseph M. Corrigan, October 18, 1937, box 66, Papers of Rector/President, ACUA.

61. Fr. A. Walsh to Rt. Rev. Mgr. Joseph Corrigan, October 12, 1936, and Mgr. Patrick J. McCormick to Mgr. Corrigan, October 17, 1936, box 66, Papers of Rector/President, ACUA.

62. *New York Times*, October 14, 1937; "Open Letter," *Time*, October 11, 1937, 27.

63. Fordham *Ram*, October 8, 1937.

64. Ibid., January 22, 1937.

65. *New York Times*, February 28, March 14 and 20, 1937.

66. Fordham *Ram*, January 21, 1938.

67. Washington *Post*, December 5 and 6, 1936.

68. *New York Times*, February 27, 1938.

69. Fordham *Ram*, April 8, 1938. A similar symposium featuring speakers from the same schools was held shortly before Fordham's, at St. Peter's College. Fordham *Ram*, April 1, 1938.

70. *New York Times*, July 22, 1937; *Harvard Crimson*, February 23, 1938; Washington *Post*, December 9, 1945. Jane Anderson's wartime broadcasts from Berlin earned her the nickname "Lady Haw Haw." After World War II,

she was indicted for making treasonable broadcasts. She had made statements that the Nazis were fighting for "religious freedom and social justice" and that "Jews and not the Japanese had destroyed the Pearl Harbor [U.S. naval] vessels" on December 7, 1941. Washington *Post*, October 28 and December 9, 1947.

71. *New York Times*, February 26, 1938.

72. Fordham *Ram*, April 8, 1938.

73. *Notre Dame Scholastic*, October 8, 1937.

74. *UCLA Daily Bruin*, March 16, 17, and 20, 1939.

75. Ibid., March 16 and 17, 1939; Boston *Globe*, May 4, 1938.

76. *UCLA Daily Bruin*, March 20, 1939.

77. Los Angeles *Times*, March 8, 1939; *UCLA Daily Bruin*, March 17, 1939.

78. St. Louis *Post-Dispatch*, May 24–26, 1937, and January 26, 1939.

79. Ibid., May 24 and 25, 1937.

80. Ibid., January 26 and 27, 1939; "Academic Freedom and Tenure: St. Louis University" in *Bulletin of the American Association of University Professors*, vol. XXV, no. 5, December 1939, 521.

81. St. Louis *Post-Dispatch*, January 27, 1939.

82. Ibid., January 27, 1939; "Academic Freedom and Tenure," *Bulletin*, 531.

83. St. Louis *Post-Dispatch*, January 27, 1939.

84. Ibid., December 11, 1939; *New York Times*, December 11, 1939; "Academic Freedom and Tenure," *Bulletin*, 532–35.

85. St. Louis *Post-Dispatch*, December 11, 1939.

86. *New York Times*, January 28, 1939; Washington *Post*, January 28 and February 25, 1939.

87. Washington *Post*, March 7, 1939.

88. Chicago *Tribune*, March 30, 1939.

89. *New York Times*, June 12, 1939.

90. Robert I. Gannon to Hon. V. E. Verdades de Faria, February 16 and March 22, 1938; Jean R. Levis to Gannon, March 19, 1938; and Gannon to Joseph D. Fragoso, March 22, 1938, box 13, Gannon Papers, FUA.

91. Laurence K. Patterson, "Salazar, the Inspirer of Portugal's New State," *America*, December 18, 1937, 249–50.

92. Robert I. Gannon to Hon. V. E. Verdades de Faria, April 9, 1938, box 13, Gannon Papers, FUA.

93. Robert I. Gannon to Hon. V. E. Verdades de Faria, March 22, 1938, and Joâo de Bianchi to Fr. Gannon, June 7, 1938, box 13, Gannon Papers, FUA.

94. Statement on Salazar, no title, n.d., box 13, Gannon Papers, FUA.

95. Robert I. Gannon to His Excellency, Joâo de Bianchi, September 6, 1940, box 13, Gannon Papers, FUA.

96. "Address by the Reverend Robert I. Gannon, S.J.," February 1, 1941, box 9, Gannon Papers, FUA.

97. Robert I. Gannon to Edmund A. Walsh, January 19 and February 9, 1938; Ambassador Dieckhoff to Walsh, February 4, 1938, and Gannon to Constantin Fotitch, January 11, 1938, box 3, Gannon Papers, FUA.

98. Walsh to Gannon, February 15, 1938, and Gannon to Walsh, February 17, 1938, box 3, Gannon Papers, FUA.

99. Dr. Gabor de Bessenyey, "A Statement on the Forthcoming Danubian Conference," *Fordham University News Bulletin*, February 20, 1938, box 3, Gannon Papers, FUA.

100. *New York Times*, May 8, 1938. Exiled German novelist Thomas Mann did speak briefly to the conference on the need to preserve "the genius of the Danubian peoples." *New York Times*, May 9, 1938.

101. Ibid., May 9, 1938.

102. New York *Herald Tribune*, April 24, 1938.

103. On the German Church's cooperation in providing such records to the Nazi government, see Daniel Jonah Goldhagen, *Hitler's Willing Executioners: Ordinary Germans and the Holocaust* (New York: Alfred A. Knopf, 1996), 110–11.

8. 1938, Year of the Kristallnacht: The Limits of Campus Protest

1. Joel Cang, "The Academic Ghetto," *American Hebrew*, January 3, 1936, 239, folder H29, James G. McDonald Papers [hereafter JGMP], Herbert Lehman Suite and Papers [hereafter HLSP], Rare Book and Manuscript Library [hereafter RBML], Columbia University [hereafter CU], New York, N.Y.; Chicago *Tribune*, December 15, 1935.

2. *New York Times*, February 7, 1937; William Zukerman, "Jews and the Fate of Poland," *Nation*, April 2, 1938, 381.

3. Cang, "Academic Ghetto," 239, JGMP, HLSP, RBML, CU; *New York Times*, November 10 and 18, 1937.

4. Ibid., October 16 and 20, 1937.

5. *New York Times*, November 30, December 8 and 14, 1933, and December 20, 1937; Washington *Post*, November 20 and 21, 1935.

6. *New York Times*, December 20, 1937.

7. Isaiah Bowman to Stephen Duggan, November 23, 1937, and Bowman to Duggan, January 28, 1938, box 118, Records of the Office of the President [hereafter ROP], Special Collections [hereafter SC], Milton S. Eisenhower Library, Johns Hopkins University [hereafter JHU], Baltimore, Md.

8. Duggan to Bowman, January 27, 1938, box 118, ROP, SC, JHU.

9. Bowman to Duggan, January 28, 1938, box 118, ROP, SC, JHU. President Bowman, a geographer, had received an honorary diploma from the Nazis' Verein für Geographie und Statistik in Frankfurt in December 1936. George A. Makinson to Dr. Isaiah Bowman, December 16, 1936, box 158, ROP, SC, JHU.

10. *New York Times*, April 1 and June 18, 1934, and obituary, May 23, 1939; London *Times*, August 26, 1933; Flushing *Journal*, April 6, 1938, Queens College Archives [hereafter QCA], New York, N.Y.; Washington *Post* obituary of Ernst Toller, May 23, 1939.

11. Flushing *Journal*, clipping, n.d., QCA; *New York Times*, April 5, 1938.

12. New York *Post*, April 5, 1938; *New York Times*, April 5, 1938; *Crown*, April 8, 1938, QCA.

13. *New York Times*, April 5 and 6, 1938; unidentified clipping, n.d., QCA.

14. *Daily Worker*, April 6, 1938, clipping in QCA.

15. *New York Times*, April 7, 1938; Washington *Post*, April 7, 1938; unidentified clipping, n.d., QCA.

16. New York *Post*, April 7, 1938, and *Long Island Star*, April 8, 1938, clippings in QCA; *Crown*, April 8, 1938.

17. New York *Post*, April 9, 1938, and unidentified clippings, n.d., QCA.

18. *Crown*, April 8, 1938, QCA.

19. *New York Times* obituary, May 23, 1939.

20. Ibid., April 24 and 27, 1938; New York *Herald Tribune*, April 24, 1938; Chicago *Tribune*, April 24, 1938.

21. *Daily Princetonian*, April 25, 1938; *Christian Science Monitor*, April 26, 1938; *New York Times*, April 26, 1938; New York *Herald Tribune*, April 26, 1938.

22. *Yale Daily News*, April 26, 1938; *Christian Science Monitor*, April 26, 1938.

23. *New York Times*, April 26, 1938; New York *Herald Tribune*, April 26, 1938.

24. *Yale Daily News*, April 27, 1938.

25. Ibid., April 11 and 12, 1938.

26. Boston *Globe*, April 26, 1938; *Christian Science Monitor*, April 26, 1938; *Harvard Crimson*, April 27, 1938.

27. *Williams Record*, April 30, 1938.

28. *New York Times*, April 27 and July 13, 1938; Washington *Post*, April 27, 1938.

29. Marguerite Kehr, "Comments on the World Youth Congress Held at Vassar College, August 16–24, 1938," subject file 27.59, Henry Noble MacCracken Papers, Vassar College Archives [hereafter VCA], Poughkeepsie, N.Y.; *New York Times*, July 3 and August 18, 1938.

30. Washington *Post*, July 16, 1938.

31. "Second World Youth Congress. Report by President Henry Noble Mac-Cracken to the Board of Trustees," August 23, 1938, subject folder 76.4, MacCracken Papers, VCA.

32. Eleanor Finney, "The World Youth Congress: Impressions of an A.A.U.W. Observer," *Journal of the American Association of University Women*, October 1938, 31, in subject folder 27.59, MacCracken Papers, VCA.

33. Poughkeepsie *Star-Enterprise*, August 15, 1938, clipping in subject folder 27.61, MacCracken Papers, VCA; *New York Times*, August 16, 1938.

34. Joseph Cadden to Archbishop Michael J. Curley, June 25, 1938, subject folder 76.8, MacCracken Papers, VCA.

35. *New York Times*, July 2 and August 16, 1938.

36. Albany *Knickerbocker News*, October 10, 1938, clipping in subject folder 27.59, MacCracken Papers, VCA.

37. Kehr, "Comments," MacCracken Papers, VCA.

38. Martin Gilbert, *Kristallnacht: Prelude to Destruction* (New York: Harper-Collins, 2006), 23–26.

39. Ibid., 13; Daniel Jonah Goldhagen, *Hitler's Willing Executioners: Ordinary Germans and the Holocaust* (New York: Alfred A. Knopf, 1996), 99–103; William L. Shirer, *The Rise and Fall of the Third Reich* (New York: Simon & Schuster, 1960), 430–34.

40. Shirer, *Rise and Fall of the Third Reich*, 433. Deborah Lipstadt notes that the American press was nearly unanimous in denouncing the Kristallnacht atrocities. *Beyond Belief: The American Press and the Coming of the Holocaust, 1933–1945* (New York: Free Press, 1986), 104.

41. *New York Times*, November 16, 1938.

42. Los Angeles *Times*, November 12, 1938; Washington *Post*, November 17, 1938.

43. *Christian Science Monitor*, November 14, 1938.

44. *New York Times*, November 19, 1938.

45. Washington *Post*, November 15, 1938.

46. *New York Times*, November 18, 1938.

47. Ibid., November 22, 1938.

48. Ibid., November 24, 1938.

49. Gerhard Sonnert and Gerald Holton, "'The Grand Wake for Harvard Indifference': How Harvard and Radcliffe Students Aided Young Refugees from the Nazis," *Harvard Magazine*, September–October 2006, 50–51; Mount Holyoke Faculty. "Committee on Refugee Students Survey," December 9, 1938, LD 7092.2 MHC, Mount Holyoke College Archives.

50. *Harvard Crimson*, November 18, 1938.

51. Sonnert and Holton, "Grand Wake," 51; *New York Times*, November 30, 1938; *Harvard Crimson*, November 30, 1938.

52. *Harvard Crimson*, November 30, 1938.

53. *Christian Science Monitor*, December 5, 1938; *Harvard Crimson*, December 5, 1938.

54. *Christian Science Monitor*, December 5, 1938; *New York Times*, December 7, 1938.

55. Marion Edwards Park to Miss [Caroline] Newton, December 3, 1938, Marion Edwards Park Papers, Bryn Mawr College Archives [hereafter BMCA], Bryn Mawr, Pa.; *Bryn Mawr College News*, November 30, 1938; *New York Times*, December 2, 1938.

56. *Yale Daily News*, November 17 and 23 and December 2, 1938.

57. Ibid., December 2, 7, and 14, 1938.

58. Ibid., December 14, 1938.

59. Ibid., November 23, 1938.

60. Ibid., January 20, 1939.

61. Typed note, November 15, 1938, Robert Maynard Hutchins to Charles Easton, November 22, 1938, penciled note, November 21, 1938, and typed note, November 25, 1938, Addenda I, box 76, and Hutchins to Dr. Boris E. Nelson, May 17, 1937, Addenda I, box 108, Robert Maynard Hutchins Papers, Regenstein Library, University of Chicago, Chicago, Ill.

62. *Barnard Bulletin*, December 13, 1938.

63. "Minutes of Committee for Giving Aid to Refugees from Germany," January 4, 1939, Series B Minutes, folder 1, LD7092.2, Mount Holyoke Faculty Papers, Mount Holyoke College Archives, South Hadley, Mass.

64. J. Ludlum to Dr. Robert C. Clothier, n.d., Robert C. Clothier to John H. Ludlum, March 23, 1939, Statement by President Clothier to Board of Trustees, n.d., box 56, Robert C. Clothier Papers, Special Collections and University

Archives [hereafter SCUA], Alexander Library [hereafter AL], Rutgers University [hereafter RU], New Brunswick, N.J.

65. Clothier to Ludlum, April 6, 1939, box 56, Clothier Papers, SCUA, AL, RU.

66. Clothier to Board of Trustees, n.d., note attached to Walter Sokol to President Robert C. Clothier, May 22, 1941, and Clothier to Louis Bamberger, June 23, 1939, box 56, Clothier Papers, SCUA, AL, RU.

67. Note attached to Walter Sokel to President Robert C. Clothier, May 22, 1941, box 56, Clothier Papers, SCUA, AL, RU.

68. International Committee to Aid Student Refugees. "Summary of Progress, January to June 1939," folder 94.7, MacCracken Papers, VCA.

69. Ibid., MacCracken Papers, VCA; Michael Zylberman, "Concern from Afar: The Participation of 'Yeshiva' Students and Faculty in World War II Service and Holocaust Relief and Rescue Efforts, 1936–1947," *Chronos*, 2000.

70. *Vassar Miscellany News*, January 11, 1939.

71. Washington *Post*, November 18, 1938.

72. *Tech*, November 22, 1938.

73. *Wellesley College News*, November 23, 1938.

74. *Vassar Miscellany News*, December 3, 1938.

75. Catherine Deeny to MacCracken, January 6, 1939, Intercollegiate Committee to Aid Student Refugees. Report of Activity, January to June, 1939, "Intercollegiate Committee to Aid Student Refugees," n.d., folder 94.7, MacCracken Papers, VCA; Sonnert and Holton, "Grand Wake," 52–53.

76. *Harvard Crimson*, December 14, 1938.

77. Marion Edwards Park to James B. Conant, January 9, 1939, and Conant to Park, February 20, 1939, Park Papers, BMCA.

78. D. W. MacCormack to Dr. Isador Lubin, August 23, 1933, container 41, William E. Dodd Papers, Library of Congress, Washington, D.C.

79. Park to Conant, January 9, 1939, Park Papers, BMCA.

80. Conant to Park, February 20, 1939, Park Papers, BMCA.

81. Ibid.

82. Sonnert and Holton, "Grand Wake," 53–54; *Harvard Crimson*, February 6, 1939.

83. Peter Gay, *My German Question: Growing Up in Nazi Berlin* (New Haven, Conn.: Yale University Press, 1998), 140.

84. *Vassar Miscellany News*, November 16, 1938.

Epilogue

1. *Harvard Crimson*, November 16, 1957; Norbert Frei, *Adenauer's Germany and the Nazi Past: The Politics of Amnesty and Integration* (New York: Columbia University Press, 2002 [1997]), 150–51; Washington *Post*, April 14–15, 1949.

2. John Cornwell, *Hitler's Scientists: Science, War, and the Devil's Pact* (New York: Penguin, 2003), 397–98, 400–01, 405.

3. Frei, *Adenauer's Germany*, 226–27.

4. Marie Allen to Stephen H. Norwood, April 27, 2008.

5. *New York Times*, November 22, 1953.

6. Ibid., January 13, 1955.

7. Walter Dowling to Ridgway B. Knight, June 23, 1955, and James B. Conant to Joseph Cardinal Frings, July 29, 1955, box 164, Security-Segregated General Records, 1953–1955, Records of Foreign Service Posts of the Department of State [hereafter FSPDS], Record Group [hereafter RG] 466, National Archives [hereafter NA], College Park, Md.

8. Los Angeles *Times*, November 8, 1954; Chicago *Tribune*, November 7, 1954.

9. Los Angeles *Times*, November 8, 1954.

10. *New York Times*, March 10, 13, 14, and 25 and May 20, 1954; Chicago *Tribune*, May 20, 1954.

11. *New York Times*, July 15, 1952.

12. *New York Times*, May 20, 1954; Chicago *Tribune*, May 20, 1954.

13. Washington *Post*, May 6, 1955; *New York Times*, June 19, 1954, and October 11, 1957.

14. *New York Times*, January 5, 1956.

15. Memorandum of Pertinent Data on Case of Sepp Dietrich (Josef), Estes Kefauver to John Foster Dulles, November 8, 1955, and John Foster Dulles to Estes Kefauver, November 17, 1955, box 165, FSPDS, RG 466, NA; *New York Times*, January 5, 1956.

16. Chicago *Tribune*, May 16, 1946; *New York Times*, July 17, 1946; London *Times*, October 25, 1955, and July 29, 1957, and obituary of Sepp Dietrich, London *Times*, April 25, 1966.

17. William L. Shirer, *The Rise and Fall of the Third Reich* (New York: Simon & Schuster, 1960), 222.

18. T. H. Tetens, *The New Germany and the Old Nazis* (London: Secker & Warburg, 1962), 103.

19. Conant to Livie (Livingston T. Merchant), December 20, 1955, box 164, FSPDS, RG 466, NA.

20. Los Angeles *Times*, October 25, 1955.

21. Estes Kefauver to Hon. John Foster Dulles, November 8, 1955, box 165, FSPDS, RG 466, NA.

22. Conant to Merchant, telegram, November 30, 1955, and Conant to Livie, December 20, 1955, box 164, FSPDS, RG 466, NA.

23. Ibid.

24. London *Times*, May 7, 11, and 15 and August 3, 1959.

25. *New York Times*, July 17, 1946; Washington *Post*, December 23, 1956; and April 28, 1985.

26. Ibid., December 28, 1955.

27. Tetens, *The New Germany*, 19–20.

28. James Bryant Conant, *Germany and Freedom* (Cambridge, Mass.: Harvard University Press, 1958), 10, 12–13, 17–19, 30.

29. Tetens, *The New Germany*, 37–38; *New York Times*, February 13, 1957.

30. *New York Times*, January 8, 1961; Washington *Post*, March 9, 1958.

31. Ibid., January 5, 1960.

32. Ibid., February 20, 1960.

33. Ibid., April 8, 1960.

34. *Harvard Crimson*, October 2, 1961.

35. Marta Petreu, *An Infamous Past: E. M. Cioran and the Rise of Fascism in Romania* (Chicago: Ivan Dee, 2005), 71.
36. Ibid., 32–33.
37. Leon Volovici, *Nationalist Ideology and Antisemitism: The Case of Romanian Intellectuals in the 1930s* (Oxford: Pergamon Press, 1991), 66; Adriana Berger, "Fascism and Religion in Romania," *Annals of Scholarship* 6 (1989): 458.
38. Volovici, *Nationalist Ideology*, 66.
39. Radu Ioanid, "Mircea Eliade and Fascism – Myth and Reality" (unpublished manuscript), n.d., 3; Mircea Eliade, *Autobiography*, vol. 2: *1937–1960, Exile's Odyssey* (Chicago: University of Chicago Press, 1988), 6.
40. Obituary of Mircea Eliade, *New York Times*, April 23, 1986; Berger, "Fascism and Religion," 456.
41. Berger, "Fascism and Religion," 457; Ioanid, "Mircea Eliade and Fascism," 8.
42. Norman Manea, "Happy Guilt: Mircea Eliade, Fascism, and the Unhappy Fate of Romania," *New Republic*, August 5, 1991, 33.
43. Berger, "Fascism and Religion," 457.
44. Petreu, *Infamous Past*, 208.
45. Hans Rogger and Eugen Weber, eds., *The European Right: A Historical Profile* (Berkeley and Los Angeles: University of California Press, 1966), 521, 527, 549; Eliade, *Autobiography*, vol. 2, 65 (translator's note).
46. Petreu, *Infamous Past*, 47.
47. Ioanid, "Mirea Eliade and Fascism," 4–5.
48. Petreu, *Infamous Past*, 70.
49. Eliade, *Autobiography*, vol. 2, 4, 63–64, 66.
50. Berger, "Fascism and Religion," 459–60.
51. Ibid., 460; Ioanid, "Mircea Eliade and Fascism," 10.
52. Seymour Cain, "Mircea Eliade, the Iron Guard, and Romanian Anti-Semitism," *Midstream* 35 (November 1989): 29; Manea, "Happy Guilt," 30.
53. Emil Dorian, *The Quality of Witness: A Romanian Diary, 1937–1944* (Philadelphia: Jewish Publication Society of America, 1982), 139.
54. Lucy S. Dawidowicz, *The War Against the Jews, 1933–1945* (New York: Bantam, 1975), 385.
55. Robert S. Ellwood Jr., review of Mircea Eliade, *Autobiography*, vol. 1: *1907–1937, New York Times* Sunday book review, November 22, 1981.
56. Berger, "Fascism and Religion," 460.
57. Robert M. Strozier to Professor Mircea Eliade, December 12, 1955, box 26, Mircea Eliade Papers, Special Collections Research Center [hereafter SCRC], Regenstein Library [hereafter RL], University of Chicago [hereafter UC], Chicago, Ill.; Chicago *Tribune*, July 11, 1957, and April 23, 1986; Washington *Post*, May 12, 1961; *New York Times*, April 23, 1986; Jerald C. Brauer, "Mircea Eliade and the Divinity School," *Criterion*, Autumn 1985, 26.
58. Brauer, "Eliade and the Divinity School," 25.
59. Chicago *Tribune*, September 27, 1962; Brauer, "Eliade and the Divinity School," 23, 26.

60. Joseph M. Kitagawa to John T. Wilson, July 14, 1970, box 1 and Edward H. Levi to Professor Mircea Eliade, August 26, 1974, box 2, Eliade Papers, SCRC, RL, UC.

61. Mac Linscott Ricketts, translator's preface, Eliade, *Autobiography*, vol. 2, xi; Hanna Holborn Gray to Mircea Eliade, December 18, 1981, box 2, Eliade Papers, SCRC, RL, UC.

62. Eliade, *Autobiography*, vol. 2, 65–66.

63. Mircea Eliade, *Fragments d'un Journal II, 1970–1978* (Paris: Gallimard, 1981), 92–93; Vasile Posteuca to Mircea Eliade, March 3 and April 11, 1957, box 26, Eliade Papers, SCRC, RL, UC. Posteuca signed one of these letters to Eliade "with great love."

64. Report by G. Maylon Miller, November 15, 1954, and Report by Paul E. Bowser Jr., May 10, 1955, Classification 105, Foreign Counterintelligence [hereafter FC], box 187, Federal Bureau of Investigation [hereafter FBI] Records, Record Group [hereafter RG] 65, NA, College Park, Md.

65. Report by Bowser.

66. Dean Milhovan to Federal Bureau of Investigation, January 8, 1990, Classification 105, FC, box 187, FBI Records, RG 65, NA; obituary of Posteuca, *New York Times*, December 7, 1972.

67. Obituary of Eliade, *New York Times*, April 23, 1986; Brauer, "Mircea Eliade and the Divinity School," 23.

68. Martin E. Marty, "That Nice Man," May 14, 1986, box 76, Eliade Papers, SCRC, RL, UC.

69. Hanna Holborn Gray to Mrs. Mircea Eliade, April 24, 1986, box 79, Eliade Papers, SCRC, RL, UC.

70. Honorary degrees, box 68, Eliade Papers, SCRC, RL, UC.

71. Chicago *Tribune*, April 14, 1968.

72. "Yale University Commencement," June 13, 1966, box 64, Kingman Brewster Jr. Records. Office of the President. Sterling Library, Yale University, New Haven, Conn.

73. Jaroslav Pelikan to Mircea Eliade, November 10, 1964, box 2, Eliade Papers, SCRC, RL, UC.

74. Saul Bellow, *Ravelstein* (New York: Penguin, 2000), 105–06, 124–28.

Bibliography

Manuscript Collections

American Catholic Historical Research Center and University Archives, The
Catholic University of America, Washington, D.C.
National Catholic Welfare Conference Papers
Records of President/Rector

American University Archives, Washington, D.C.
Charles Tansill Personnel File

Bryn Mawr College Archives, Bryn Mawr, Pa.
Marion Edwards Park Papers

Columbia University Archives – Columbiana Library, Low Library, New York,
N.Y.
Central Files

Columbia University Rare Book and Manuscript Library, Butler Library, New
York, N.Y.
Lienhard Bergel Papers
H. R. Knickerbocker Papers
Non-Sectarian Anti-Nazi League Papers
Peter M. Riccio Papers

Columbia University Rare Book and Manuscript Library, Herbert Lehman Suite,
New York, N.Y.
James G. McDonald Papers

Fordham University Archives, New York, N.Y.
Robert I. Gannon Papers

Harvard University Archives, Pusey Library, Cambridge, Mass.
James B. Conant Presidential Papers
Sidney B. Fay Papers

Johns Hopkins University, Special Collections, Milton S. Eisenhower Library, Baltimore, Md.
Records of the Office of the President: Isaiah Bowman Papers

Library of Congress, Washington, D.C.
Franz Boas Papers (microfilm edition)
William E. Dodd Papers
Felix Frankfurter Papers (microfilm edition)
Roscoe Pound Papers (microfilm edition)

Mount Holyoke College Archives, South Hadley, Mass.
Mount Holyoke College Faculty Papers
Mount Holyoke College German Language and Literature Department Papers

National Archives, College Park, Md.
Foreign Counterintelligence, Federal Bureau of Investigation Records, Record Group 65
Security-Segregated General Records, 1953–1955, Records of Foreign Service Posts of the Department of State, Records of Department of State, Record Group 466

New York Public Library, Manuscripts and Archives Division, New York, N.Y.
Emergency Committee in Aid of Displaced Foreign Scholars Papers

New York University Archives, Bobst Library, New York, N.Y.
Harry Woodburn Chase Papers

Queens College Archives, New York, N.Y.
Papers concerning Ernst Toller affair

Radcliffe College, Schlesinger Library, Cambridge, Mass.
Office of the President, Correspondence and Papers: Ada Louisa Comstock

Rutgers University, Special Collections and University Archives, Alexander Library, New Brunswick, N.J.
Trustees Personal Papers, J. Edward Ashmead
Robert C. Clothier Papers
Richard P. McCormick Papers

Smith College, Special Collections, Northampton, Mass.
William Allan Neilson Papers

University of Chicago, Special Collections Research Center, Regenstein Library, Chicago, Ill.
Mircea Eliade Papers
Robert Maynard Hutchins Papers

University of Delaware Archives, Special Collections, Walter Hullihen Library, Newark, Del.
Walter Hullihen Papers
Records of the Foreign Study Plan

University of Maryland, Archives and Manuscripts Department, Hornbake Library, College Park, Md.
Millard E. Tydings Papers

University of Virginia, Manuscript Department, Alderman Library, Charlottesville, Va.
Institute of Public Affairs, Office Administrative Files
President's Office Papers: John Lloyd Newcomb

Vassar College Library, Vassar College Archives, Poughkeepsie, N.Y.
Henry Noble MacCracken Papers

Yale University, Special Collections, Sterling Library, New Haven, Conn.
President's Office: James Rowland Angell Records
Kingman Brewster Jr. Records

Newspapers

Arizona Daily Star (Tucson), 1934
Baltimore *Sun*, 1933, 1934
Barnard Bulletin, 1933, 1937, 1938
Boston *Evening Globe*, 1934, 1937
Boston *Evening Transcript*, 1934, 1936, 1937
Boston *Globe*, 1933, 1934, 1936, 1937, 1938, 1939, 1944
Boston *Herald*, 1933, 1934
Boston *Post*, 1933, 1934, 1935
Bryn Mawr College News, 1930, 1933, 1934, 1936, 1937, 1938, 1939
Campus News (New Jersey College for Women), 1933, 1934, 1935
Capital Times (Madison, Wis.), 1935
Chicago *Tribune*, 1934, 1935, 1936, 1937, 1938, 1940, 1941, 1946, 1954, 1957, 1962, 1968
Christian Science Monitor, 1933, 1934, 1938
College Topics (University of Virginia), 1936
Columbia Spectator, 1919, 1933, 1934, 1935, 1936, 1937, 1938
Cornell Daily Sun, 1936
The Crown (Queens College), 1938

Daily Californian (University of California at Berkeley), 1935
Daily Cardinal (University of Wisconsin), 1935
Daily Maroon (University of Chicago), 1936
Daily Princetonian, 1935, 1938
Daily Progress (Charlottesville, Va.), 1936
Daily Texan (University of Texas), 1935
Dallas *Morning News*, 1934, 1937
The Dartmouth, 1934
The Day (Der Tog), 1934, 1937
Fordham *Ram*, 1934, 1937, 1938
Hartford *Courant*, 1934, 1936
Harvard Crimson, 1926, 1933, 1934, 1935, 1936, 1937, 1938, 1939, 1940,
      1951, 1954, 1961, 1978, 2003
The Heights (Boston College), 1934, 1935, 1938
The Hoya (Georgetown University), 1934, 1936, 1937
Jewish Advocate (Boston), 1933, 1934
Jewish Chronicle (London), 1933, 1936
Jewish Criterion (Pittsburgh), 1935, 1936
Jewish Press (Brooklyn, N.Y.), 2008
London *Times*, 1933, 1934, 1957, 1966
Los Angeles *Times*, 1934, 1937, 1938, 1940, 1954, 1955
Manchester *Guardian*, 1933, 1936
Michigan Daily (University of Michigan), 1936
Minneapolis *Journal*, 1935
Minnesota Daily (University of Minnesota), 1935
Mount Holyoke College News, 1933, 1938, 1939
Newark *Star-Eagle*, 1935
New Haven *Evening Register*, 1934
New Leader, 1935
New York *Evening Post*, 1933
New York *Herald Tribune*, 1933, 1938
New York *Post*, 1936, 1938
New York Times, 1919, 1921, 1922, 1926, 1927, 1930, 1931, 1933, 1934, 1935,
      1936, 1937, 1938, 1939, 1940, 1941, 1943, 1944, 1945, 1946, 1947, 1949,
      1952, 1953, 1954, 1955, 1956, 1957, 1960, 1961, 1981, 1983, 1986, 2004
New York *World-Telegram*, 1934, 1936
Notre Dame Scholastic, 1933, 1934, 1936, 1937
Philadelphia *Inquirer*, 1933
Philadelphia *Jewish Exponent*, 1935, 1936
Philadelphia *Public Ledger*, 1934
Radcliffe News, 1933, 1934, 1938
The Review (University of Delaware), 1935
Richmond *Times-Dispatch*, 1936
St. Louis *Post-Dispatch*, 1937, 1939
San Francisco *Chronicle*, 1933, 1936
Smith College Weekly, 1934, 1935, 1936
The Targum (Rutgers College), 1930, 1933, 1935

The Tech (Massachusetts Institute of Technology), 1933, 1934, 1936, 1937
UCLA Daily Bruin (University of California at Los Angeles), 1939
Vassar Miscellany News, 1933, 1934, 1935, 1936, 1937, 1938, 1939
Washington *Post*, 1933, 1934, 1935, 1936, 1937, 1938, 1939, 1940, 1943, 1945, 1947, 1949, 1955, 1961, 1985, 1988
Washington Square College Bulletin (New York University downtown campus), 1936
Wellesley College News, 1933, 1934, 1938
Williams Record (Williams College), 1938
Wilmington (Del.) *Evening Journal*, 1934
Yale Daily News, 1934, 1936, 1937, 1938

Books

Abzug, Robert H. *America Views the Holocaust, 1933–1945: A Brief Documentary History*. Boston: Bedford/St. Martin's, 1999.
Arad, Gulie Ne'eman. *America, Its Jews, and the Rise of Nazism*. Bloomington: Indiana University Press, 2000.
Baker, Liva. *I'm Radcliffe! Fly Me! The Seven Sisters and the Failure of Women's Education*. New York: Macmillan, 1976.
Baldwin, Neil. *Henry Ford and the Jews: The Mass Production of Hate*. New York: Public Affairs, 2001.
Baltzell, E. Digby. *The Protestant Establishment: Aristocracy and Caste in America*. New York: Vintage, 1964.
Bellow, Saul. *Ravelstein*. New York: Penguin, 2000.
Beyerchen, Alan D. *Scientists Under Hitler: Politics and the Physics Community in the Third Reich*. New Haven, Conn.: Yale University Press, 1977.
Bracher, Karl Dietrich. *The German Dictatorship*. New York: Praeger, 1970.
Breitman, Richard, Barbara McDonald Stewart, and Severin Hochberg, eds., *Advocate for the Doomed: The Diaries and Papers of James G. McDonald, 1932–1935*. Bloomington: Indiana University Press, 2007.
Cohen, Robert. *When the Old Left Was Young*. New York: Oxford University Press, 1993.
Cole, Arthur C. *A Hundred Years of Mount Holyoke: The Evolution of an Educational Ideal*. New Haven, Conn.: Yale University Press, 1940.
Conant, James Bryant. *Germany and Freedom*. Cambridge, Mass.: Harvard University Press, 1958.
My Several Lives: Memoirs of a Social Inventor. New York: Harper and Row, 1970.
Conradi, Peter. *Hitler's Piano Player: The Rise and Fall of Ernst Hanfstaengl, Confidant of Hitler, Ally of FDR*. New York: Carroll & Graf, 2004.
Cornwell, John. *Hitler's Scientists: Science, War, and the Devil's Pact*. New York: Penguin Books, 2003.
Dawidowicz, Lucy S. *The War Against the Jews, 1933–1945*. New York: Bantam, 1975.
Dell, Robert. *Germany Unmasked*. London: Martin Hopkinson, 1934.

Diggins, John P. *Mussolini and Fascism: The View from America.* Princeton, N.J.: Princeton University Press, 1972.

Dinnerstein, Leonard. *Anti-Semitism in America.* New York: Oxford University Press, 1994.

Dodd, Martha. *Through Embassy Eyes.* New York: Harcourt, Brace, 1939.

Dodd, William E., Jr., and Martha Dodd. *Ambassador Dodd's Diary, 1933–1938.* New York: Harcourt, Brace, 1941.

Dorian, Emil. *The Quality of Witness: A Romanian Diary, 1937–1944.* Philadelphia: Jewish Publication Society of America, 1982.

Elbogen, Ismar. *A Century of Jewish Life.* Philadelphia: Jewish Publication Society of America, 1944.

Eliade, Mircea. *Autobiography, vol. II: 1937–1960, Exile's Odyssey,* 2 vols. Chicago: University of Chicago Press, 1988.

Fragments d'un Journal II, 1970–1978. Paris: Gallimard, 1981.

Evans, Richard J. *The Coming of the Third Reich.* New York: Penguin, 2003.

The Third Reich in Power. New York: Penguin, 2005.

Frei, Norbert. *Adenauer's Germany and the Nazi Past: The Politics of Amnesty and Integration.* New York: Columbia University Press, 2002 [1997].

Friedländer, Saul. *Nazi Germany and the Jews, vol. 1: The Years of Persecution, 1933–1939,* 2 vols. New York: HarperCollins, 1997.

Friedman, Saul S. *The Oberammergau Passion Play: A Lance Against Civilization.* Carbondale and Edwardsville: Southern Illinois University Press, 1984.

Gannon, Robert I. *Up to the Present: The Story of Fordham.* Garden City, N.Y.: Doubleday, 1967.

Gay, Peter. *My German Question: Growing Up in Nazi Berlin.* New Haven, Conn.: Yale University Press, 1998.

Gilbert, Martin. *Kristallnacht: Prelude to Destruction.* New York: HarperCollins, 2006.

Gildersleeve, Virginia C. *Many a Good Crusade.* New York: Macmillan, 1954.

Goldhagen, Daniel Jonah. *Hitler's Willing Executioners: Ordinary Germans and the Holocaust.* New York: Alfred A. Knopf, 1996.

A Moral Reckoning: The Role of the Catholic Church in the Holocaust and Its Unfulfilled Duty of Repair. New York: Alfred A. Knopf, 2002.

Heidelberg and the Universities of America. New York: Viking Press, 1936.

Hershberg, James G. *James B. Conant: Harvard to Hiroshima and the Making of the Nuclear Age.* New York: Alfred A. Knopf, 1993.

Herzstein, Robert Edwin. *Roosevelt and Hitler: Prelude to War.* New York: Paragon House, 1989.

Hicks, John D. *My Life with History: An Autobiography.* Lincoln: University of Nebraska Press, 1968.

Hughes, H. Stuart. *The Sea Change: The Migration of Social Thought, 1930–1965.* New York: McGraw-Hill, 1975.

Karabel, Jerome. *The Chosen: The Hidden History of Admission and Exclusion at Harvard, Yale, and Princeton.* Boston: Houghton Mifflin, 2005.

Keene, Frances, ed., *Neither Liberty Nor Bread: The Making and Tragedy of Italian Fascism.* New York: Harper & Brothers, 1940.

Keller, Morton, and Phyllis Keller. *Making Harvard Modern: The Rise of America's University.* New York: Oxford University Press, 2001.

Kendall, Elaine. *"Peculiar Institutions": An Informal History of the Seven Sisters Colleges.* New York: G. P. Putnam's Sons, 1976.

Kertzer, David I. *The Popes Against the Jews: The Vatican's Role in the Rise of Modern Anti-Semitism.* New York: Alfred A. Knopf, 2001.

Krohn, Claus-Dieter. *Intellectuals in Exile: Refugee Scholars and the New School for Social Research.* Amherst: University of Massachusetts Press, 1993.

Lipstadt, Deborah. *Beyond Belief: The American Press and the Coming of the Holocaust, 1933–1945.* New York: Free Press, 1986.

McCaughey, Robert A. *Stand, Columbia: A History of Columbia University in the City of New York, 1754–2004.* New York: Columbia University Press, 2003.

McCormick, Richard P. *Rutgers: A Bicentennial History.* New Brunswick, N.J.: Rutgers University Press, 1966.

MacCracken, Henry Noble. *The Hickory Limb.* New York: Charles Scribner's Sons, 1950.

Malino, Frances, and Phyllis Cohen Albert, eds. *Essays in Modern Jewish History.* Rutherford, N.J.: Fairleigh Dickinson University Press, 1982.

Mandell, Richard D. *The Nazi Olympics.* Urbana: University of Illinois Press, 1987 [1971].

Mann, Erika. *School for Barbarians: Education Under the Nazis.* New York: Modern Age Books, 1938.

Mann, Erika, and Klaus Mann. *Escape to Life.* Boston: Houghton Mifflin, 1939.

Marraro, Howard R. *Nationalism in Italian Education.* New York: Italian Digest & News Service, 1927.

Miller Alice Duer, and Susan Myers. *Barnard College: The First Fifty Years.* New York: Columbia University Press, 1939.

Mowrer, Edgar Ansel. *Triumph and Turmoil: A Personal History of Our Time.* New York: Weybright and Talley, 1968.

Norwood, Stephen H., and Eunice G. Pollack, eds. *Encyclopedia of American Jewish History,* 2 vols. Santa Barbara, Calif.: ABC-CLIO, 2008.

Oren, Dan A. *Joining the Club: A History of Jews and Yale.* New Haven, Conn.: Yale University Press, 1985.

Oshinsky, Daniel M., Richard P. McCormick, and Daniel Horn. *The Case of the Nazi Professor.* New Brunswick, N.J.: Rutgers University Press, 1989.

Petreu, Marta. *An Infamous Past: E. M. Ciordan and the Rise of Fascism in Romania.* Chicago: Ivan Dee, 2005.

Remy, Steven P. *The Heidelberg Myth: The Nazification and Denazification of a German University.* Cambridge, Mass.: Harvard University Press, 2002.

Rogger, Hans, and Eugen Weber, eds., *The European Right: A Historical Profile.* Berkeley and Los Angeles: University of California Press, 1966.

Rosenbaum, Ron. *Explaining Hitler.* New York: HarperCollins, 1998.

Rosenberg, Rosalind. *Changing the Subject: How the Women of Columbia Shaped the Way We Think About Sex and Politics.* New York: Columbia University Press, 2004.

Rosenthal, Michael. *Nicholas Miraculous: The Amazing Career of the Redoubtable Dr. Nicholas Murray Butler*. New York: Farrar, Straus and Giroux, 2006.

Rutkoff, Peter M., and William B. Scott, *New School: A History of the New School for Social Research*. New York: Free Press, 1986.

Sarfatti, Michele. *The Jews in Mussolini's Italy: From Equality to Persecution*. Madison: University of Wisconsin Press, 2006.

Sayen, Jamie. *Einstein in America: The Scientist's Conscience in the Age of Hitler and Hiroshima*. New York: Crown Publishers, 1985.

Schmidt, George. *Douglass College: A History*. New Brunswick, N.J.: Rutgers University Press, 1968.

Sender, Toni. *The Autobiography of a German Rebel*. New York: Vanguard Press, 1939.

Shapiro, James S. *Oberammergau: The Troubling Story of the World's Most Famous Passion Play*. New York: Pantheon, 2000.

Shirer, William L. *Berlin Diary: The Journal of a Foreign Correspondent*. New York: Alfred A. Knopf, 1941.

The Rise and Fall of the Third Reich. New York: Simon & Schuster, 1960.

Sinclair, Upton. *The Goose-Step*. Pasadena, Calif.: privately published, 1923.

Sklar, Robert. *City Boys: Cagney, Bogart, Garfield*. Princeton, N.J.: Princeton University Press, 1992.

Steinberg, Michael Stephen. *Sabers and Brown Shirts: The German Students' Path to National Socialism, 1918–1935*. Chicago: University of Chicago Press, 1977.

Stern, Fritz. *Einstein's German World*. Princeton, N.J.: Princeton University Press, 1999.

Five Germanys I Have Known. New York: Farrar, Straus and Giroux, 2006.

Synnott, Marcia Graham. *The Half-Opened Door: Discrimination and Admissions at Harvard, Yale, and Princeton, 1900–1970*. Westport, Conn.: Greenwood Press, 1979.

Tetens, T. H. *The New Germany and the Old Nazis*. London: Secker & Warburg, 1962.

Thorp, Margaret Farrand. *Neilson of Smith*. New York: Oxford University Press, 1956.

Van Paassen, Pierre, and James Waterman Wise, eds., *Nazism: An Assault on Civilization*. New York: Harrison Smith & Robert Haas, 1934.

Volovici, Leon. *Nationalist Ideology and Antisemitism: The Case of Romanian Intellectuals in the 1930s*. Oxford: Pergamon Press, 1991.

Webster, Richard A. *The Cross and the Fasces: Christian Democracy and Fascism in Italy*. Stanford, Calif.: Stanford University Press, 1960.

Wechsler, James A. *The Age of Suspicion*. New York: Random House, 1953.

Revolt on Campus. Seattle: University of Washington Press, 1973 [1935].

Weinberg, Gerhard L. *The Foreign Policy of Hitler's Germany: Diplomatic Revolution in Europe, 1933–1936*. Chicago: University of Chicago Press, 1970.

Weinreich, Max. *Hitler's Professors: The Part of Scholarship in Germany's Crimes Against the Jewish People*. New Haven, Conn.: Yale University Press, 1999 [1946].

White, Marian Churchill. *A History of Barnard College*. New York: Columbia University Press, 1954.

Wise, James Waterman. *Swastika: The Nazi Terror*. New York: Harrison Smith and Robert Haas, 1933.

Zarnowitz, Victor. *Fleeing the Nazis, Surviving the Gulag, and Arriving in the Free World: My Life and Times*. Westport, Conn.: Praeger, 2008.

Zuckerman, Harriet. *Scientific Elite: Nobel Laureates in the United States*. New York: Free Press, 1977.

Zuckerman, Larry. *The Rape of Belgium: The Untold Story of World War I*. New York: New York University Press, 2004.

Journal Articles

Ascoli, Max. "The Press and the Universities in Italy." *Annals of the American Academy of Political and Social Science* 200 (November 1938): 235–53.

Berger, Adriana. "Fascism and Religion in Romania." *Annals of Scholarship* 6 (1989): 455–65.

Cain, Seymour. "Mircea Eliade, the Iron Guard, and Romanian Anti-Semitism." *Midstream* 35 (November 1989): 27–31.

"Centenary of the University of Göttingen." *Nature* 139 (April 24, 1937): 701–03.

Crosby, Donald F. "Boston's Catholics and the Spanish Civil War, 1936–1939." *New England Quarterly* 44 (March 1971): 82–100.

Feuer, Lewis S. "The Stages in the Social History of Jewish Professors in American Colleges and Universities." *American Jewish History* 71 (June 1982): 432–65.

Greenberg, Michael, and Seymour Zenchelsky. "The Confrontation with Nazism at Rutgers: Academic Bureaucracy and Moral Failure." *History of Education Quarterly* 30 (Fall 1990): 325–49.

"Letter to the Editor." *History of Education Quarterly* 31 (Summer 1991): 318.

"Private Bias and Public Responsibility: Anti-Semitism at Rutgers in the 1920s and 1930s." *History of Education Quarterly* 33 (Fall 1993): 295–319.

Hawkins, Richard A. "Hitler's Bitterest Foe: Samuel Untermyer and the Boycott of Nazi Germany, 1933–1938." *American Jewish History* 93 (March 2007): 21–50.

Lamberti, Marjorie. "The Reception of Refugee Scholars from Nazi Germany in America: Philanthropy and Social Change in Higher Education." *Jewish Social Studies* 12 (Spring/Summer 2006): 157–92.

Norwood, Stephen H. "Complicity and Conflict: Columbia University's Response to Fascism, 1933–1937." *Modern Judaism* 27 (October 2007): 253–83.

"Legitimating Nazism: Harvard University and the Hitler Regime, 1933–1937." *American Jewish History* 92 (June 2004): 189–223.

Tuttle, William M., Jr., "American Higher Education and the Nazis: The Case of James B. Conant and Harvard University's 'Diplomatic Relations' with Germany." *American Studies* 20 (Spring 1979): 49–70.

Valaik, J. David. "In the Days Before Ecumenicism: American Catholicism, Anti-Semitism, and the Spanish Civil War." *Journal of Church and State* 13 (1971): 465–77.

Magazine Articles (Signed)

Adams, Frances. "Junior Year in Munich." *Mount Holyoke Alumnae Quarterly*, May 1938.

Bergel, Lienhard. "Nazi Activities in American Colleges." *Jewish Criterion*, April 3, 1936.

Bliven, Bruce. "For 'Nordics' Only." *New Republic*, December 8, 1947.

Brauer, Jerald C. "Mircea Eliade and the Divinity School." *Criterion*, Autumn 1985.

Chase, Roger. "Academic Napoleons No. III: Nicholas Murray Butler." *Student Advocate*, April 1936.

Farrell, James T. "An 'International Showcase.'" *Student Advocate*, December 1936.

Fisher, Barbara E. Scott. "Notes of a Cosmopolitan." *North American Review*, March 1934.

Hamilton, Alice. "Woman's Place in Nazi Germany." *Advance*, February 1934.

Leonard, William. "Italy's Second Embassy." *Student Review*, December 1934.

Manea, Norman. "Happy Guilt: Mircea Eliade, Fascism, and the Unhappy Fate of Romania." *New Republic*, August 5, 1991.

Marden, Laura. "The First Junior Year in Italy." *Smith Alumnae Quarterly*, November 1932.

Neilson, William Allan. "The Juniors Abroad." *Smith Alumnae Quarterly*, May 1937.

Patterson, Laurence K. "Salazar, the Inspirer of Portugal's New State." *America*, December 18, 1937.

Reynolds, Agnes, Florence J. Cole, Ruth Robinson, and Catherine Elliott, "We Went to Germany." *Vassar Review*, Freshman 1935.

Rubin, Ruth. "I Heckled Luther." *Student Review*, January 1934.

Sonnert, Gerhard, and Gerald Holton. "'The Grand Wake for Harvard Indifference': How Harvard and Radcliffe Students Aided Young Refugees from the Nazis." *Harvard Magazine*, September–October 2006.

Special Investigator. "Fascism at Columbia University." *Nation*, November 7, 1934.

Stoke, Stuart M. "Germany in the Summer of 1934." *Mount Holyoke Alumnae Quarterly*, November 1934.

Thompson, Dorothy. "Germany Is a Prison." *Opinion*, March 1934.

Van Paassen, Pierre. "Silence Is Criminal." *Opinion*, November 1933.

Wechsler, James A. "The Education of Bob Burke." *Student Advocate*, October–November 1936.

Zukerman, William. "Jews and the Fate of Poland." *Nation*, April 2, 1938.

Zylberman, Michael. "Concern from Afar: The Participation of 'Yeshiva' Students and Faculty in World War II Service and Holocaust Relief and Rescue Efforts, 1936–1947." *Chronos*, 2000.

Magazine Articles (Unsigned)

"American Hebrew Medal to Toscanini." *American Hebrew*, February 4, 1938.
"American Scholars and Göttingen." *New Republic*, April 28, 1937.
"Arizona Plagued by Nazi Apologist." *American Hebrew*, March 29, 1935.
"Chicago Bars Film Showing Hitler Terror." *Jewish Criterion*, April 27, 1934.
"Correspondence: Salvemini and the Casa." *Nation*, January 30, 1935.
"Germany: The Goettingen Celebration." *American Hebrew*, July 2, 1937.
"Hail Toscanini!" *American Hebrew*, August 7, 1936.
"Items of Interest." *Jewish Veteran*, May 1933.
"The Juniors Abroad." *Smith Alumnae Quarterly*, May 1931.
"Library of Banned Books Inaugurated Here." *American Hebrew*, December 28, 1934.
Nation, February 27, 1935.
New Republic, March 18, 1936.
"President Butler and Fascism." *Nation*, November 14, 1934.
"Toscanini's Artistic Integrity Calls Attention to Nazi 'Gleischschaltung.'" *American Hebrew*, January 8, 1937.
"They're Not All Cowpunchers." *Jewish Criterion*, February 1, 1935.
"Unity Against Fascism." *Student Outlook*, October 1934.

Unpublished Manuscript

Ioanid, Radu. "Mircea Eliade and Fascism – Myth and Reality," n.d.

Class Report

Entry for Ernst Hanfstaengl, Harvard College, 25th Anniversary Report, Class of 1909, Harvard University Archives, Pusey Library, Cambridge, Mass.

Pamphlet

Prago, Albert. "Jews in the International Brigades in Spain." A *Jewish Currents* reprint, 1979.

Reports

"Academic Freedom and Tenure: St. Louis University" in *Bulletin of the American Association of University Professors*, vol. XXV, no. 5, December 1939.
"Report of the President of Columbia University for the Year Ending June 30, 1936" in *Annual Report of the President and Treasurer to the Trustees with Accompanying Documents for the Year Ending June 30, 1936*. Columbia University Archives and Columbiana Library, Low Library, New York, N.Y.

"Report of the President of Columbia University for the Year Ending June 30, 1937" in *Annual Report of the President and Treasurer to the Trustees with Accompanying Documents for the Year Ending June 30, 1937.* Columbia University Archives and Columbiana Library, Low Library, New York, N.Y.

Index